Fire and Light
in the Western Triduum

Their Use at Tenebrae and at the Paschal Vigil

Alcuin Club Collection Number 71

A. J. MacGregor

The Alcuin Club

 THE LITURGICAL PRESS
Collegeville, Minnesota

Cover design by David Manahan, O.S.B.

Copyright © 1992 The Alcuin Club, Runcorn, Chesire, United Kingdom. Published by The Liturgical Press, Collegeville, Minnesota 56321. Printed in the United States of America.

1	2	3	4	5	6	7	8	9

Library of Congress Cataloging-in-Publication Data

MacGregor, A. J. (Alistair J.)
    Fire and light in the western triduum : their use at Tenebrae and at the Paschal vigil / A.J. MacGregor.
        p.   cm. — (Alcuin Club collections; no. 71)
    Includes bibliographical references and index.
    ISBN 0-8146-2066-3
    1. Paschal triduum—Liturgy.   2. Catholic Church—Liturgy-
-History.   3. Candles and lights.   I. Title.   II. Series.
BX5141.A1A6   no. 71
[BX2045.H7]
200 s—dc20
[264.'.02]   92-9600
                                              CIP

CONTENTS

PREFACE

The 1951 liturgical experiments within the Roman Catholic Church and the 1955 Decree of *Maxima Redemptionis,* which gave official sanction to those experiments, were designed to restore to their former prominence and importance the ceremonies of Holy Week, and especially those of the Triduum. In spite of the abundance of literature treating of the restoration of the paschal rites which has appeared in the wake of these liturgical changes, no monograph has yet been written which is devoted specifically to a study of the use of light in the services of the Triduum. The fullest treatment of this subject is the chapter entitled *The Ceremonies of Holy Week* in D.R. Dendy's *The Use of Lights in Christian Worship.* Being a single chapter in a larger work, the subject is perhaps inevitably treated rather cursorily; and the material is presented somewhat indiscriminately.

The present work, which in its original form was submitted as a doctoral thesis to the University of Durham, is written primarily from an historical point of view. It identifies the cultural and liturgical milieux from which the ceremonies of Tenebrae, the new fire, and the Easter candle emerged; and in describing these three light-featuring rituals of the Triduum, it traces their historical development, incorporating the theological significance and pastoral aspects of each and relating them to the liturgical changes of the 1950s and the reasons for those changes. This study also shows the close connection that existed between the triple performance of Tenebrae and the threefold production of the new fire and examines the reasons for the adoption of the new fire ceremony into the liturgy of the Church and its incorporation into the paschal vigil.

The area covered by the research embraces the whole territorial extent of the medieval Latin West. Documentary evidence is plentiful for England, Germany, and especially France, where the existence of a large number of neo-Gallican missals reveals the survival into relatively modern times of variant Vigil-ceremonials from the Middle Ages. In other parts of Europe, the domination of the Roman rite, as in Spain; or the imposition of a single rite, as in Norway; or the competitive influence of the Orthodox Church inevitably limited the growth of local rites.

The term *Gallican* has been used in two different senses. In the period up to *c.*1000, it refers to the non-Roman rites of France and Western Germany. It also refers to the movement in France in the eighteenth and nineteenth centuries for liturgical independence from Rome and to the diocesan rites associated with that movement. Throughout the present work, 'Vigil' indicates the paschal vigil of Holy Saturday and 'Candle' signifies the Easter candle.

The author wishes to express his gratitude to the following persons who assisted him in a number of different ways during the writing of this book : Aidan Bellenger OSB, Paul Chavasse, Richard Conrad OP, Anthony Gelston, Pierre Grey, Alan Griffiths, John Moakler OCSO, Nicholas Paxton, Jan Rhodes, James Schellman, Michael Sharratt, Aelred Sillem OSB, Andrew Smith O Praem, Kenneth Stevenson, E.M.Stewart, Henry Taylor, Johanne Wiersum, and Timothy Wiersum. He also acknowledges the much-valued support of all the members of his family throughout the years.

Northwich,
Cheshire.
July 1991

ABBREVIATIONS

(a) General Abbreviations

AC	Augustinian Canons
AV	Authorised Version
C	Century
Cerem.	Ceremonial
ET	English translation
GF	Good Friday
HS	Holy Saturday
HW	Holy Week
M.	Missal
MR	*Missale Romanum*
MT	Maundy Thursday
nd	no date
np	no pagination
NT	New Testament
OB	*Ordo Breviarii*
OM	*Ordo Missalis*
OR	*Ordo Romanus*
OT	Old Testament
PG	Migne's *Patrologia Graeca*
PL	Migne's *Patrologia Latina*
Pont.	Pontifical
PV	*Pars Verna*
Rep.	*Repertorium*
Sme. Ste.	*Semaine Sainte*
t.e.	typical edition
tpm	title page missing

(b) Other abbreviations

Alcuin	*Liber de divinis officiis,* formerly attributed to Alcuin
Bindo F.	*Das Zeremonienbuch des Bindo Fesulani*
CA 1706	*Die Sammlung des Codex Avignon 1706*
Caer. Episc.	*Caeremoniale Episcoporum*
CMG	*Consuetudines Monasteriorum Germaniae*
DACSR	*Decreta Authentica Congregationis Sacrorum Rituum*
DAER	*De Antiquis Ecclesiae Ritibus,* (E. Martène) Volume 3
DAMR	*De Antiquis Monachorum Ritibus,* being Volume 4 of *De Antiquis Ecclesiae Ritibus*
Decrees	Lanfranc's *Decreta Pro Ordine Sancti Benedicti*
De Div. Off.	*De Divinis Officiis*
DHCR	*Dictionnaire historique des cultes religieux*
DMC	*Deus mundi Conditor*
Eph. Lit.	*Ephemerides Liturgicae*
Gav/Mer.	Gavanti/Merati, being the *Thesaurus Sacorum Rituum* of B.Gavanti revised by C.M.Merati
GeAng	Gelasian Sacramentary of Angoulême
GeGe	Gelasian Sacramentary of Gellone
GePh	Gelasian Sacramentary of Autun (formerly Phillipps' Gelasian Sacramentary)
GePr	Gelasian Sacramentary of Prague
GeV	The Gelasian Sacramentary *(Gelasianum Vetus)*
HBS	Henry Bradshaw Society
ICEL	International Commission on English in the Liturgy
ILEM	*Institutions Liturgiques de l'Eglise de Marseille*
JTS	*Journal of Theological Studies*
Lib. Cens.	*Liber Censuum*
Lib. de Div. Off.	*Liber de Divinis Officiis*
Lib. de Off. Eccl.	*Liber de Officiis Ecclesiae*
Lib. Off.	*Liber Officialis*
LDOA	*Liber de Ordine Antiphonarii*
LOP	*Liturgies of the Past*
LPB	*Le Liber Politicus de Benoit*
LPS	*Liturgies of the Primatial Sees*
LRC	*Liturgy of the Roman Church*

LRO	*Liturgies of the Religious Orders*
M	Followed by a figure, it refers to a document, cited by E. Martène and classified by A.-G. Martimort in *La Documentation Liturgique de Dom Edmond Martène*
Miss. Gall. Vet.	*Missale Gallicanum Vetus*
MVLA	*Monumenta Veteris Liturgiae Ambrosianae*
Nom. Cist.	*Nomasticon Cisterciense*
OED	Oxford English Dictionary
OEL	*Ordo Officiorum Ecclesiae Lateranensis*
OHS	*Ordo Hebdomadae Sanctae*
OLD	Oxford Latin Dictionary
ONE	*Ordo Nidrosiensis Ecclesiae*
OPA	Ordo of Pierre Amiel
OSS	*Office de la Semaine Sainte*
PGD	*Le Pontifical de Guillaume Durand*
PJSM	*Pope John Sunday Missal*
Poitiers	The ninth-century Pontifical of Poitiers
PR XII	*Le Pontifical Romaine du XIIIᵉ siècle*
PRC	*Le Pontifical de la Curie Romaine au XIIᵉ siècle*
PRG	*Pontificale Romano-Germanicum*
PRMA	*Le Pontifical Romain au Moyen-Age*
PTHW	Passion Time and Holy Week
Reg. Conc.	*Regularis Concordia*
RELR	*Ritus Ecclesiae Laudunensis Redivivi*
SMRL	*Sources of the Modern Roman Liturgy* (Van Dijk)
Statutes	*Statutes of Lincoln Cathedral*
ZRKM	*Die Zeremonienbücher de Römischen*

A NOTE ON THE SOURCES

The principal sources for the period *c.*700–900 are the *ordines Romani,* edited by M.Andrieu. The writer has generally accepted his dating of them. Throughout the present work, each of these has been referred to simply as 'Ordo' followed by an arabic numeral. They are to be distinguished from the later *ordines romani,* first published by Mabillon and subsequently by Migne in Volume 78 of *Patrologia Latina.* The latter group of documents are each indicated by 'Ordo' followed by a Roman numeral. The writer accepts the view that the ninth-century Pontifical of Poitiers relates to the Church in Poitiers, in spite of the doubts of A.-G.Martimort and A.Martini. Neither Mabillon nor Martène question the provenance of the pontifical. Both may have had access to corroborating information which has since been lost. Information relating to Gembloux is contained in the Customary of Sigibert (Albers Vol.2).

Apart from the primary sources themselves, perhaps the most important quarry of information for the student of liturgiology is Dom Edmond Martène's monumental *De Antiquis Ecclesiae Ritibus,* originally published between 1700 and 1702. This work contains extracts from a very large number of liturgical texts which he consulted in the monastic libraries of France. Some of the manuscripts have subsequently disappeared. A.-G.Martimort's *La Documentation Liturgique de Dom*

Edmond Martène provides both a guide to and an invaluable commentary on a work which ranks on a par with other primary documentary evidence.

In 1984 the writer carried out a survey of the paschal vigil as held in the cathedrals of France at the present time. Information gained from the replies received is indicated by '1984 Survey of France'.

INTRODUCTION

There is no firm evidence before the fourth century for the use of either liturgical or functional light at the paschal vigil. However, in view of the close association of Baptism with the Vigil and the equating of Christian initiation with illumination, the centrality in Christianity of Christ the Light of the World, as well as the importance of the concept of light in the mystery religions, which may well have influenced both Christian theology and liturgical practice, it was almost inevitable that the ceremonies marking the climax of the Church's year and the annual commemoration of Christ's victory over the darkness of this world should be held in an ambience of abundant light. The fourth-century evidence from Constantinople, Jerusalem, and Spain would suggest that the holding of the paschal vigil in a milieu of light was by then widespread throughout the Christian world.[1]

However, by the end of the tenth century in the West and by the beginning of the twelfth century in Jerusalem, an alternative tradition of holding the Vigil in semi-darkness emerged from a monastic milieu.[2]

[1]'At Easter . . . Constantine changed the holy all-night vigil into the light of day by arranging for wax candles of very great length to be lit throughout the whole of the city [Constantinople].' Eusebius, *Vita Constantini* 4.22 (PG 20.1169). For the evidence for Jerusalem and Spain, see Wilkinson p.138.

[2]As attested in *Hagios Stauros* 43. See Stevenson p.182.

1

The blessing of the Easter candle, the kindling of the new fire, and the gradual extinguishing of the lights at the three night offices of the Triduum, later to be known as Tenebrae, were ceremonies peculiar to and confined to the West. The first of these rituals formed the central feature of a transformed *Lucernarium,* the ancient office of the lighting of the evening lamp, which itself was incorporated into the paschal liturgy. The production of paschal fire was not unknown in the East. By the ninth century, the ceremony in Jerusalem was accompanied by scenes of frenzied enthusiasm, which have characterised the occasion ever since. By contrast, the corresponding ceremonies of the western rites have entailed the production of newly-kindled fire in circumstances less shrouded in secrecy and mystery than those which obtain at Jerusalem. However, the taking home of the new fire would have been no less meaningful to the faithful of France, for example, than to the pilgrims in Jerusalem. The antecedents of the Easter fire ceremonies of Jerusalem and Northern Europe were different. For whilst the ritual at Jerusalem was intimately linked with the office of the *Lucernarium,* the new fire ceremonies of Northern Europe existed as pre-Christian religious rites, which were taken over and incorporated into the liturgy of the Church in the same way that the Easter egg and the Christmas tree have been accommodated within the traditions of Christianity.

The office of Matins/Lauds, known as Tenebrae, emerged from a monastic liturgical milieu and, as we have argued in Part I, developed as a dramatic and liturgical representation of an historical event recorded in the Gospels.

Unlike the ritual surrounding the Easter candle, which we maintain had its provenance in Northern Italy, the new fire ceremony and the service of Tenebrae emerged from the liturgically-active region of Northern France and Western Germany, according to the earliest surviving documentary evidence. In spite of the known influence of Milan in the regions north of the Alps, the absence of these two ceremonies from the earlier Ambrosian rite, and indeed from the Roman rite, would suggest that both rituals were indigenous Gallican liturgical developments.

The holding of the Vigil in anticipation was already established by the eighth century, probably as a result of changing pastoral needs and circumstances. For in earlier centuries, the sacrament of Baptism, which followed the blessing of the Easter candle and the reading of the prophecies, was administered primarily to adults. By the eighth century, in regions in which Christianity had been established for several centuries, the perhaps-inevitable fall in the number of adults who sought Baptism; the incipient practice of administering this sacrament at other times during the year; and the fact that what had become the traditional time for administering Baptism, namely, a late hour on Holy Saturday or an early hour on Easter Day, was hardly the most suitable for unweaned infants resulted in the bringing forward of the time at which the paschal vigil was held. The anticipation of Tenebrae, though unaffected by these considerations, came to pass, it is believed, through a desire within those churches and cathedrals which were served by non-monastic clergy, to sing the night office at a more convenient time.

By the end of the fifteenth century, it had become the practice in some parts of Western Europe to kindle the new fire at about 9.00 A.M. on Holy Saturday and to hold the paschal vigil on the morning of that day. The abolition by Pope Urban VIII of Holy Saturday as a public holiday in Catholic countries so contributed to the further decay of the Triduum that, until the middle of the present century, it was widespread practice throughout Western Europe to hold the Vigil in the morning light of Holy Saturday.

In 1955, the efforts of the Liturgical Movement over a period of fifty years bore fruit when, following the Decree of *Maxima Redemptionis,* it was officially permitted to hold the paschal vigil at an hour which was liturgically and commemoratively more meaningful and which approximated to the time at which the Vigil had been held in the early Middle Ages. Previously having burned in the daylight hours of Holy

Saturday, the Easter candle reacquired its former importance and significance not only for the members of the clergy, but for the laity also, who in previous centuries had not attended the Vigil either through ignorance or apathy or the demands of work but who were now once more able to participate in the preparation for the mass of Easter and to share meaningfully in the Light of Christ.

Part One

TENEBRAE

Chapter One

MATINS

The origins of the daily offices are obscure. The hymns of the hours by Prudentius suggest that the cycle of offices existed in some parts of the West by the end of the fourth century. Paul Bradshaw has shown that there was a morning and evening service in Augustine's church and in Ambrose's time in Milan.[1] Evidence for the offices at Jerusalem comes from Egeria : by 380 the office of Matins was said daily in the church of the Anastasis in that city.[2] In the absence of any reference by Egeria to illumination at this service, we must assume that in addition to the functional lights in that church, which would have been essential in the early hours of the morning, any liturgical illumination that there may have been was not so unusual.

Matins, known in the West as *vigiliae,* had developed within Christian liturgical practice as a daily re-enactment of the vigil *par excellence,* namely, that held on Holy Saturday. There undoubtedly was functional lighting within the cathedral tradition. However, there is no firm evidence for the use of liturgical light at the night office either in the cathedral or monastic tradition until the eighth century, unless the testimony from Poitiers in the sixth century for the service being

[1]*Daily Prayer* pp.112–13.
[2]Wilkinson pp.66–69.

conducted in total darkness can be classed paradoxically as an instance of the negative use of light.

In the very early church, the real significance of the Easter mystery involved the work of redemption in the death and resurrection of Jesus Christ. When the commemoration of the institution of the Eucharist on the day before Good Friday became attached to the paschal liturgical drama, there emerged the notion of the Triduum, which came to be regarded as a three-day liturgical unit. The incorporation of Maundy Thursday inevitably resulted in the commencement of the Triduum with the celebration of the night office in the early hours of Thursday morning. By 400, the development of the Triduum was complete, in the West at any rate; for the liturgical idea of the sacred Triduum is found as early as the time of Augustine and Ambrose.[3] From their writings it is evident that Maundy Thursday, Good Friday, and Holy Saturday were regarded as a three-day liturgical unity. We may be confident that the night offices of each of these three days were similar in content in that the psalms and readings were characterised by a penitential and funereal but 'hope-touched solemnity'. In structure, the night offices of Maundy Thursday and Good Friday were similar to those of the other nights of the year, but we shall see presently that Matins/Lauds of Holy Saturday was generally quite different throughout the West.

Pierre Batiffol, treating of Matins in the West in the early Middle Ages, was almost certainly correct to claim that 'the office of these days . . . was undoubtedly a purely Roman creation'.[4] As early as the time of John Cassian (*c*.415–435), Matins was divided by the monks into three nocturns.[5] That St Benedict, whose rule was based on Roman liturgical practice and was drawn up between 525 and 550, provided no offices of his own for the Triduum suggests that Matins and Lauds at least existed in Rome in the sixth century in much

---

[3]Ep. 55.24 (PL 33.215) and Ep. 23.12–13 (PL 16.1030), respectively.
[4]*History* p.92.
[5]*De inst. Coen.* 3.8–9 (PL 49.83A and .144A).

the same form as now. It seems unlikely that Augustine's *Tracts on the Psalms,* which came to be read during the second nocturn of each of the days of the Triduum, would have been incorporated into the night office during Augustine's lifetime. Its more-or-less final form, therefore, would have become fixed sometime between 430 and *c.*525; and this would have been in Rome since after the Vandal conquest of North Africa in 429, liturgical ideas between Rome and North Africa probably entailed difficulties of interchange.[6] It is tempting to attribute the fixing of the form of Matins to Pope Gelasius (492–496), who, though it has been shown that the Gelasian Sacramentary was wrongly named after him, has been traditionally associated with liturgical reform. If such is the case, it could well account for the inclusion of Augustine's *Tracts* into Matins by Gelasius, who himself was an African.[7]

The earliest mention of the night office of Matins in the West occurs in the *Life of St Ambrose* by his biographer Paulinus. It can be dated to 385 or 386 :

> At this time Matins with antiphons and hymns began to be celebrated in the Church in Milan. Support for this service survives to this day not only in that church but throughout every province in the West.[8]

The *vigiliae* mentioned in this extract could hardly be the paschal vigil, which in Ambrose's day was an observance of long standing. It must refer rather to the introduction of the daily performance of the night office by Ambrose himself in

---

[6]It is known that in the time of Leo the Great (*c.*450) monks performed the choral office of Lauds in the Roman basilicas. Under their influence Lauds became closely associated with Matins. It was at this time that Matins with its division into three nocturns, was introduced into Rome, according to the evidence of John Cassian *(op.cit.).*

[7]*Liber Pontificalis* I p.255.

[8]Hoc in tempore primum antiphonae, hymni, ac vigiliae in ecclesia Mediolanensi celebrari coeperunt. Cuius celebratis devotio usque in hodernum diem non solum in eadem ecclesia, verum per omnes pene Occidentis provincias manet. *Vita sancti Ambrosii* (PL 14–15.31D).

the basilicas of Milan. This is further borne out by the additional mention of the content, namely, antiphons and psalms
(hymni). Furthermore, Paulinus is witness to the establishment
of the night office in almost all the provinces of the West (that
is, the western Roman empire) at the end of the fourth century. However, it is not clear from his Latin whether the
Church of Milan introduced daily Matins before or after it
was established in the other provinces.

Evidence for the content and ceremonial of the night office for the three days of the Triduum in the fourth and fifth
centuries in the West is lacking. Although we know that the
night office of Holy Saturday was an all-night vigil (Bradshaw
p.132), there is no good reason to suppose that the night offices
of Maundy Thursday and Good Friday differed much in structure from those performed on the other nights of the year.
It is not until *c.*569 in Gaul, and possibly a century and a
half later in Rome, that we have evidence regarding illumination at this service, either functional or liturgical, or the
lack of it; and it would be unwise to read back into an earlier
age the practice of a later century.

*   *   *   *   *

Sixth-century Gaul. The first indication we have for the liturgical use of light at the night office, or rather in this instance
the negative use of it, comes in an incident, described by
Gregory of Tours, which occurred in the Abbey of the Holy
Cross at Poitiers in Gaul and which can be dated with some
confidence to *c.*569. The miracle of light, which took place
in the monastery, was seen to have been caused by the presence of a fragment of the True Cross, which Queen
Radegonde, consort of Clotaire I, had brought back from
Jerusalem in the above-mentioned year.

> When the all-night vigil was being observed without light on
> Good Friday before Holy Easter, a small glint of light like
> a spark appeared before the altar about the third hour of the
> night.[9]

[9]Sexta feria ante sanctum Pascha, cum in vigiliis sine lumine pernoc-

Gregory supplies us with three items of information which are of especial interest and relevance to our investigation :

(i) The incident took place on Good Friday.
(ii) The vigil lasted throughout the night.
(iii) The service took place in darkness.

All-night vigils belong to the older tradition of monasticism, which derived from the East.[10] It would appear, therefore, that Benedict's Rule, which prescribed a shorter night office, had not yet been introduced into the monastery at Poitiers. The apparently-unassailable statement that the night office of Good Friday was conducted in total darkness raises a number of questions and merits further examination. (i) Was Matins in the monastery at Poitiers in the sixth century conducted in the dark on every night of the year? We cannot be absolutely certain; but it does seem likely that some form of illumination was used, if not for liturgical, then for utilitarian reasons, especially for reading. Moreover, the very mention of *sine lumine,* 'without light', would imply that a service held in total darkness was not normal.[11] (ii) Assuming that it was the usual practice to have illumination at the night office, was Matins/Lauds held *sine lumine* on either of the other two nights of the Triduum? The earliest documentary evidence for the night office of Good Friday according to early Gallican practice is Ordo 17. Though written some two hundred years later than the incident in question, it probably reflects some of the usages of a much earlier age. This *ordo* does imply the use of lights at Matins of Good Friday, which conflicts with evidence from the monastery, but, in view of its lateness and unknown provenance, should not be taken as corroborative

tarent, circa horam tertiam noctis apparuit ante altare lumen parvulum in modum scintillae. *Miraculorum Liber de Gloria Martyrum* 1.5 (PL 71.709B).

[10]Aurelian, *Regula ad Monachos* (PL 68.396).

[11]This phrase must indicate total darkness; otherwise, the effect and significance of the pin-point of light would have been considerably weakened.

of Gregory's information. (iii) Is the night office the author has in mind that held in the early hours of Friday morning or that which *followed* Good Friday early on Saturday morning? According to Gregory's account, the *vigiliae* took place *sexta feria ante sanctum Pascha,* 'on the sixth week-day before holy Easter'. The usual interpretation of this phrase requires us to understand that the author is referring to the office held in the early hours of Good Friday. However, if we study the account of the miraculous occurrence more closely, it is possible to arrive at the conclusion that the office which Gregory is referring to is actually that of Holy Saturday morning.

Gregory continues with his narration to relate how this tiny spark of light began to increase in size, and as it did so, scattered rays of brilliance *(comas fulgoris)* in all directions. Then gradually it began to rise into the air, lighting up the sky and bathing the air in luminescence. Little by little it began to fade, and eventually it disappeared from view.

It is clear that the light represents Christ; and its emanation from the fragment of the Cross, kept in a casket under the altar, its upward movement, and the illumination of the entire universe by its brilliance symbolise respectively the Resurrection, the Ascension, and the universality of Christ. We may leave to one side the question of the incident's historicity and rather concentrate on the significance and time of its occurrence within the context of the Triduum and consider the possibility of the miracle having taken place at the night office of Saturday rather than of Friday. It is, of course, not possible to comment upon or rationalise about the timing of a miracle or strange occurrence to the extent that one can say with authority that an incident *should* have occurred at a specific time to suit the circumstances. Nevertheless, if we reflect upon the timing of the miracle in relation to the predicament or situation in which the Pictavian monks found themselves, it may seem that the luminous phenomenon, which was inseparably linked to the fragment of the Cross, can be more readily understood and explained within the context of Friday night's devotions rather than Thursday night's.

Assuming that the Triduum in Poitiers in the sixth century bore the same funereal aspect that was prominently characteristic of it in later centuries, then the significance of the inbursting of light can be interpreted in two different ways, according to whether the miracle occurred at the *vigiliae* of Friday or Saturday. At the night office of Friday, it would be seen as an indication that the darkness of the Passion, which was about to be commemorated, was not permanent, and as an anticipation of the return of the divine light in the early hours of Easter morning. However, this interpretation is strained and detracts from the sequence of events in the Passion narrative since a foretaste, as it were, of the Resurrection at this juncture in the Triduum is both awkward and out of place. On the other hand, the appearance of the light at the night office of Holy Saturday is easier to explain both liturgically and symbolically : (i) This office follows the Veneration of the Cross, upon which the attention of the monks had been fixed some hours before. (ii) Good Friday night/Holy Saturday morning is the time when the Church is in deepest mourning. The appearance of the light, literally as a ray of hope, would have been much more meaningful at that time. (iii) The light is intrinsically associated with the fragment of the True Cross, which may well have figured in the ceremony of Good Friday afternoon.

There are three additional considerations which support the view that the service in question was the night office of Holy Saturday. (i) The first centres around the phrase *sine lumine*. We have already referred to the probability that the night office was usually held with some form of illumination and that total darkness was exceptional at this service. Since the office consisted of psalms, antiphons, and readings from Scripture, the presence of light must be presupposed. It is true that in view of the frequency of repetition by the monks, the whole of the psalter was generally known by heart so that reference to the written word could be dispensed with. At an all-night vigil conducted in darkness, it seems unlikely that lessons were read. The importance, if not necessity, of light for the purpose of reading lessons is clear from a rubric in Ordo 30B.[12]

A clue to the content of Matins/Lauds at Poitiers in the sixth century may be found in the former service of the night office for Holy Saturday according to the Ambrosian rite. This office can be traced back to the tenth century;[13] but the primitive form of the service, especially its structure, suggests a ceremony of considerable antiquity. The combined office of Matins/Lauds comprised twenty-three psalms and one canticle. Like the corresponding office in the Gallican and Roman rites, it featured the *Omissions;*[14] and the entire service took place in darkness. Moreover, Holy Saturday at Milan, even in the reformed rite, is the only day when the night office is said without light. Admittedly, in trying to envisage or reconstruct the form of the night office at Poitiers in the sixth century, one must use the Milanese evidence with caution since it attests the practice of another church and, in spite of its likely antiquity, is valid strictly only as far back as the tenth century; but as we shall see in the next chapter, the Milanese form of Matins, in spite of its relatively late date, in all likelihood preserves the primitive form of the night office for Holy Saturday that was once widespread throughout the West.

(ii) We have already suggested that although the Gallican Ordo 17 is to be dated to the latter part of the eighth century, it may well describe the ceremonial and practice of a hundred or even two hundred years prior to the period in which the ritual was committed to writing. Since this *ordo* attests the absence of light in church on the night of Good Friday (§98), it is reasonable to believe that no lights were lit that night at the monastery at Poitiers.

(iii) Reference has already been made to the all-night monastic vigils, which were held during the night of Good Friday and the early hours of Saturday morning. In view of

---

[12]See *Stage 3* in the next chapter. This is in spite of the notion of a lesson being read 'by heart', which figures in St Benedict's Rule (Bradshaw p.145).

[13]Borella p.107.

[14]See Appendix 1 : *The Omissions.*

this, it is almost certain that it is this vigil to which Gregory of Tours is referring, and not the one held on the previous day.

Chapter Two
THE DEVELOPMENT
OF TENEBRAE

We suggested in the previous chapter that the tenth-century
Matins/Lauds of the Milanese rite may well have preserved
the primitive form of this office in the West, especially in view
of the sixth-century evidence from Poitiers. Fortunately, there
are sufficient references to and descriptions of the night offices
of the Triduum in the *ordines Romani* and elsewhere to trace
the likely and logical development of Matins/Lauds from the
vigiliae of Holy Saturday to the twice-repeated office of
Tenebrae and to confirm our conclusions regarding the night
office of Holy Saturday at Milan and Poitiers. We propose
to reconstruct the stages, showing how the night offices of
Maundy Thursday, Good Friday, and Holy Saturday may
have developed into the service of Tenebrae in the period from
the sixth to the eighth century.[1] However, throughout this
tentative reconstruction, the following preliminary observations should be borne in mind. (i) Although each stage of the
development is to be found in the sections of one or more of
the *ordines* which relate to the night offices, it does not neces-

[1]The practice of extinguishing gradually the lights at Matins/Lauds
emerged within the Gallican Church. It was unknown in the Mozarabic
rite, and in the Ambrosian tradition up to Vatican II corresponded to the
saying of Matins on Holy Saturday without lights.

sarily follow that a particular stage of development occurred
for the first time in that church with which the *ordo* is associated. In view of the fluidity of liturgical practice during this
period, some features of ceremonial may have been borrowed
from elsewhere. (ii) In the likelihood of the interchange of liturgical ideas and customs, it is very doubtful that every church
experienced each of the six stages of development. (iii) This
development was not chronologically parallel throughout the
churches of Gaul. For instance, since Ordo 26, which attests
the fully-developed service of Tenebrae on all three nights (that
is, *Stage 6*), can be dated with some confidence to the period
750–775, that stage antedates *Stage 3* and *Stage 4* by several
years and *Stage 2* by as much as sixty years.

It should also be borne in mind that the evidence from both
Rome and Gaul should be studied closely in conjunction since
the rites of the Roman and Gallican churches were mutually
influential.[2] Moreover, the evidence of the *ordines* is at times
frustratingly fragmentary, the descriptions of the services being
by no means complete. Therefore, the silence of an *ordo* does
not necessarily signify the absence of a particular feature
wherein it might have been expected to appear, and some
omissions of rubrical details may be fortuitous. At times the
latter can be inferred from the complementary evidence of
other *ordines*.

Stage 1. The funereal aspect of the entire Triduum is apparent from the *Omissions* in the Roman Ordo 23 and in the Gallican Ordo 17.[3] Although the former refers only to the
Omissions at Matins/Lauds on Maundy Thursday and the latter
to those on Good Friday, it is reasonable to assume that they
formed a feature of the night office for those two days both
at Rome and in Gaul; and although there is no written evidence for the *Omissions* on Holy Saturday, it is almost certain
that they were also observed on the third day. For not only

[2]See Appendix 2 : *Roman and Gallican Traditions*.

[3]OR 23.1 and OR 17.93. The former, though written in the period
775–790, almost certainly reflects earlier liturgical practice.

would they have contributed to the imposition of liturgical unity on the three night offices of the Triduum; it would be especially at the night office of Holy Saturday that one would most have expected the *Omissions*.

Of greater importance, however, for our study are the statements in both the Romano-Gallican Ordo 16 and in Ordo 17 that on Good Friday night no light was lit in church but that it was hidden away from the sight of all until Holy Saturday.[4] It follows that in the churches to which the two *ordines* relate, the night office of Holy Saturday was held in total darkness. Although direct evidence from the eighth century is wanting concerning the presence or absence of illumination at this particular office in Rome, the absence of light at this service can be inferred with confidence from the testimony of Pope Zachary (741–752). In a letter to Boniface of Mainz, he describes how fire was reserved on Maundy Thursday at the Lateran Cathedral in three large lamps for consecration and use at the Vigil on Holy Saturday.[5] The concealment of the newly-kindled fire or, more likely, an already-living flame in a remote part of the church and the consignment of this element to a state of limbo, as it were, emphasized the unsuitability of the flame for liturgical use. It is true that the two honorific lights, which accompanied the Pope when he walked from the Lateran Palace to the Church of S.Croce in Gerusalemme on Good Friday, were kindled from one of the three reserved lamps.[6] However, these torches or thick candles, which had been adopted by the papal court in the fourth century in imitation of those borne before the Emperor,[7] were civic lights and remained outside the above-mentioned church

---

[4]OR 16.36 and OR 17.93.

[5]For the text of this letter, see the chapter *The New Fire at Rome* in Part Two.

[6]OR 23.10. The writer accepts Andrieu's suggestion that the phrase *ex unguario* refers to one of the three reserved lamps (*Les* Ordines Romani III pp.318–19).

[7]Jungmann pp.132–33; Fulgentius Ferrandus (PL 67.884C).

on Good Friday because their flames were unconsecrated.[8] In view of this, it is hardly likely that lights for the night office of Holy Saturday would have been kindled with a flame taken from one of the three lamps. In Part Four we will suggest that the Lateran Cathedral, in which the night office in question was held, remained unilluminated throughout the whole of Good Friday and for most of Holy Saturday for both liturgical and symbolic reasons. There can be little doubt, therefore, in view of the evidence from Poitiers, Milan, and Rome and the attestation of the two *ordines,* that the primitive night office of Holy Saturday throughout a large part of the Western Church was conducted in darkness. It is also likely that the content of the service was similar to that of the Ambrosian night office, consisting primarily of psalms with accompanying antiphons, and as at Milan, lacked scriptural readings because of the absence of light.

There is no evidence to suggest that the provision of light at the night offices of Maundy Thursday and Good Friday differed from that at the other night offices of the year. According to the *ordines Romani,* illumination on those two days was of two kinds. The church lamps provided the functional light, whilst the seven lamps that were placed before the altar supplied liturgical luminosity. Throughout the centuries in the Ambrosian rite, the lighting arrangements for the night offices of Maundy Thursday and Good Friday remained unchanged.

Summary of evidence : *Stage 1*

MT Matins and Lauds : normal lighting
GF Matins and Lauds : normal lighting
HS *Vigiliae :* psalms sung in total darkness

---

[8]Theodore, the Archdeacon of Rome, is quite explicit about the absence of illumination in S.Croce during the Solemn Prayers and the Veneration of the Cross : nullum lumen habetur lampadum sive cereorum in ecclesia in Hierusalem (Amalarius, *Lib.de Ord.Ant.* XLIV.2). The year was 832.

Stage 2. Evidence for the development of *Stage 1* into *Stage 2* comes from Rome and is recorded by Amalarius of Metz on the occasion of a visit by him to the Italian city in 832. He had asked Theodore, Archdeacon of Rome, about the use of light at the night offices in Rome during the Triduum. The reply came :

> I am accustomed to be with the Pope in the Lateran Cathedral when the service of the Lord's Supper is being held. That night in the cathedral there is no ceremony involving the extinction of lights. On Good Friday there is no light from any lamp or wax candle in the Church of S.Croce in Gerusalemme, when the Pope recites the Solemn Prayers there or during the Veneration of the Cross. However, new fire is kindled on that day, and this is reserved for use at the night office.[9]

At first sight, Theodore appears to have ignored Amalarius' question concerning the extinction of lights at the night office. This has led scholars like H.A.P.Schmidt to believe that Amalarius and Theodore have a different problem in mind. Schmidt goes on to say that Amalarius is concerned with the extinction and production of fire and light at the time of the Holy Triduum, Theodore with the use of light on Good Friday.[10] It is true that in Chapter XLIV, Amalarius is indeed concerned with the extinction and production of fire and light; but Schmidt has overlooked the fact that Theodore has not

---

[9]Soleo esse cum apostolico in Lateranis, quando officium celebratur de caena Domini. Nihil autem ibi in eadem nocte observatur de extinctione luminum. In feria sexta nullum lumen habetur lampadum sive cereorum in ecclesia in Hierusalem, quamdiu domnus apostolicus ibi orationes solemnes facit, aut quamdiu crux salutatur, sed tamen in ipsa die novus ignis accenditur, de quo reservatur usque nocturnale officium (Amalarius, *Lib.de Ord.Ant.* XLIV.2). The first instance of *officium* in this passage must mean 'service' in view of the phrase *de caena Domini,* which here refers to the institution of the Eucharist, and not to Maundy Thursday in general. Otherwise, Amalarius is almost certain to have referred to that day as *quinta feria.*

[10]*Hebdomada Sancta* II p.811.

only mentioned the extinction of lights, he has informed Amalarius about the production of new fire. Dendy, assuming that Amalarius' question is primarily about the extinction of lights at the night office, writes that 'Theodore does not give a complete direct answer';[11] and a superficial reading of the question and answer would suggest that this was so. However, let us examine in greater depth exactly what the question was which Amalarius asked and especially the information from which the question arose. Amalarius wrote :

> During the last three nights of Holy Week, that is, on Maundy Thursday, Good Friday, and Holy Saturday, it is the custom of our Church that the lights of the church building should be extinguished. Concerning the custom of our holy mother Church of Rome, I asked the Archdeacon Theodore, of the said Roman Church. He replied . . .[12]

Two facts concerning the custom of Amalarius' church emerge as being important for our study. (i) The lights of the church were extinguished at night. (ii) This happened on three successive nights. We have already noted that in this chapter, Amalarius is concerned with the extinction and production of fire and light; and in recording these two facts, he wishes it to be known that in his church an extinction of light takes place and that it occurs on three separate occasions. It could be argued that his mention of its having taken place at the night office is almost incidental. We can only surmise as to the actual form of words which Amalarius used when he asked Theodore about the custom of the Roman Church; but in view of his concern about illumination and from Theodore's reply, it is clear that he was interested primarily in the

[11]*The Use of Lights* p.135.

[12]Mos ecclesiae nostrae obtinet per tres noctes, id est per feriam quintam, quae vocatur caena Domini, et per sextam, quae vocatur parascheve, et per septimam, quae vocatur sabbatum sanctum, ut extinguantur luminaria ecclesiae in nocte. De more sanctae matris nostrae Romanae ecclesiae interrogavi archidiaconum Theodorum memoratae ecclesiae, scilicet Romanae, qui respondit. . . .

extinction or rather in the possibility of the extinction of lights at Rome, and not in the night office or even in the fact that the loss of light took place at night. This makes Theodore's reply both intelligible and satisfactory. Theodore had been asked about the extinction of light; he had answered on that subject.

It is clear from the statement of Amalarius and from the reply of Theodore that the development into Tenebrae of the three night offices of the Triduum was almost complete within the church with which Amalarius was familiar, but only at an embryonic stage in Rome.[13] In view of the reply of Theodore, it must be assumed that in Rome in the first third of the ninth century, there was nothing unusual about the provision of light at the night offices of Maundy Thursday and Good Friday. We saw that for the night office of Holy Saturday, according to Theodore's testimony, fire was kindled on Good Friday and then reserved for use at that service. How many lights were kindled at this office we are not told; but a glance ahead at Ordo 30B, which we have adduced as evidence for *Stage 3,* may provide us with the answer. According to that document, a *lamp* was lit at the night office of Holy Saturday for the purpose of reading (§36). This, we suggest, was the result of the inclusion of lessons in the night office for that day. Prior to that time, the service was held in darkness, as Ordo 23 attests *(Stage 1).* It was, therefore, sometime between the first half of the eighth century, when Ordo 23 was compiled, and the archidiaconate of Theodore that illu-

---

[13]Liturgiologists have often commented upon the conservative nature of the Church of Rome; and it is true that in the Middle Ages, liturgical development took place much more quickly in the regions to the north of the Alps. However, to refer to the 'purity' of the Roman rite and to speak of the somewhat colourful developments of transalpine liturgy as 'Gallican corruptions', as Dendy does (*The Use of Lights* p.137), betrays an approach to scholarship which is marred by lack of impartiality. His prejudice is further borne out by a typically vague assertion that Rome was 'for a *considerable* period *largely* successful' in repelling such corruptions. (The writer's italics.)

mination was introduced into the office in question. During the reign of Pope Leo III (795–816), Gallican influence resulted in the appearance in Rome of the Minor Rogation Days. His reign may well have witnessed other importations from Gaul. Andrieu's dating of Ordo 30B to the end of the eighth century is entirely consistent with a Leonine introduction of illumination into the night office of Holy Saturday.

The testimony of Ordo 30B and the even earlier evidence of Ordo 26 conclusively demonstrate that the use of light at this service of Matins/Lauds on Holy Saturday appeared first in Gaul and not in Rome. We suggest that in Theodore's time only one lamp was used at the office.

Summary of evidence : *Stage 2*

MT Matins and Lauds : normal lighting
GF Matins and Lauds : normal lighting
HS Matins and Lauds : one lamp (or candle) for reading

Stage 3. In the evidence of Ordo 30B, which constitutes *Stage 3* in the development of Tenebrae, we encounter for the first time the phenomenon of the gradual extinction of lights. Formerly known as *St-Amand* from its provenance at the Monastery of St-Amand-en-Puelle, this *ordo* has a marked Roman appearance; but its provenance, date, and the distinctive Gallicisms it contains indicate that it was used by a church in Gaul which had adopted the Roman liturgy, possibly as a result of the influence of Charlemagne, but which was still retentive of traditional ceremonies and receptive to indigenous influences. There are three reasons for believing that Gallican influence is present in the night offices of Good Friday and Holy Saturday as recorded in Ordo 30B. (i) There was during this period, that is, the eighth and ninth centuries, a tendency for the austere Roman ceremonial to yield to the more vigorous Gallican ritual, especially if the former had been divorced from its native Italian milieu. (ii) The ceremonial of the night office of Ordo 30B features a development in the use of light at Good Friday's service which was unknown in

Rome in 832. (iii) The evidence of Ordo 26, attesting in Gaul
the gradual loss of light during each of the night offices of
the Triduum, antedates Theodore's testimony by at least fifty
years. It is therefore difficult to believe that the ceremonial
in Ordo 30B, which relates to the use of light in the night
offices of Good Friday and Holy Saturday—soon to be
described—could have had its provenance in any other liturgical tradition but the Gallican.

The silence of Ordo 30B regarding nocturnal illumination
at the office of Matins/Lauds on Maundy Thursday suggests
that the service was held with a display of lights normal for
the night office, and there is no reason to believe that it differed
in this respect from the night office of Maundy Thursday of
Stage 2. Matins/Lauds of Holy Saturday is likely to have been
similar to the corresponding office of *Stage 2* in respect of lights;
for we are told that for the service only one lamp was to be
lit, and that for the purpose of reading.[14] As we suggested
for *Stage 2*, it was almost certainly the addition of lessons from
Scripture to the night office of Holy Saturday that necessitated the introduction of a light into a service previously held
in the dark; and it is reasonable to suppose that this was placed
on or next to the lectern.

However, it is in the use of lights at the night office of Good
Friday that we find a significant development from and contrast with the practice known to Theodore of Rome. Matins
would appear to have been conducted with the usual illumination; it is at Lauds that we encounter for the first time the
gradual extinguishing of lights :

> But as soon as the antiphon for the first psalm at Lauds
> begins, a light is extinguished on the right-hand side and at
> the antiphon of the second psalm one on the left. Similarly
> they are extinguished from right to left before all of the psalms,
> that is, until the sixth or seventh psalm or at the end of the

---

[14]tantum una lampada accendatur propter legendum (§36).

Benedictus. Let the last lamp be concealed and reserved for Holy Saturday.[15]

There can be little doubt that the lamps, extinguished gradually as the office progressed, were the seven sanctuary lamps attested in other *ordines*. The lamp hidden at the *Benedictus* and reserved until Holy Saturday is to be identified with the 'light which was concealed on Good Friday'.[16] From this flame were lit the archdeacon's two honorific candles, which remained burning during the reading of St John's Passion on Good Friday (§30); the lamp for the night office of Holy Saturday (§36); and the two Vigil-candles for the Blessing of the Font.[17] It must be assumed that the seven lamps were alight during Matins also; but the *ordo* makes no mention of any other form of illumination, functional or liturgical, at either of these combined offices. It is likely that at this stage in the development of Tenebrae, church lights were present at Matins and were extinguished before the start of Lauds. In view of the absence of evidence to corroborate this, however, this suggestion must remain suppositional.

It is a matter for speculation whether the lamp removed at the conclusion of Lauds on Good Friday was subsequently brought back into church—its flame having been transferred to another lamp—and replaced in its original position in readiness for the Vigil of Holy Saturday or whether it remained in the place of reservation until the following day. It is unlikely, however, that this lamp provided the light for reading at the night office of Holy Saturday. For the physical removal

[15]Sed tantum inchoat ad matutinum antiphona in primo psalmo, tuta lampada de parte dextra, in secundo psalmo de parte sinistra; similiter per omnes psalmos usque VI aut VII, aut in finem evangelii, reservetur absconsa usque in Sabbato sancto. OR 30B.28. Note the solecisms in the Latin text.

[16]Lumen, quod feria sexta absconsum est. This formula is to be found in Ordines 17, 23, and 30A, and in four Gelasian sacramentaries.

[17]Unlike the flame from the three lamps mentioned by Zachary, this reserved light was obtained from already-consecrated fire and could therefore be used for liturgical purposes.

of the sole source of fire would have exposed the flame of the lamp to the possibility of wick-failure or some other mishap, to the dismay and discomfiture of all.

Summary of evidence : *Stage 3*

MT Matins and Lauds : normal lighting
GF Matins : normal lighting
      Lauds : gradual extinguishing of seven lamps—last light removed
HS Matins and Lauds : one lamp (or candle) for reading —extinguished at conclusion of service

Stage 4. Evidence for *Stage 4* is provided by Ordo 30A, a document from Northern France more or less contemporaneous with Ordo 30B. Section 1 of this *ordo,* which refers to the nine psalms, lessons, and responsories of Matins on Maundy Thursday, makes no mention of illumination at this service. However, at the same office on Good Friday, the rubric states (§5) :

> Then follows Lauds. The lights are extinguished.[18]

Although, unlike Ordo 30B, the points at which the lights were extinguished are not given, it is almost certain that a gradual loss of light is to be understood here; for the presence of light at Matins and its loss at Lauds correspond with the arrangement described in Ordo 30B. It is in the description of the night office for Holy Saturday that a divergence from the practice attested in Ordo 30B occurs. For we read :

> Let the arrangements for the kindling and extinguishing of the lamps be the same as we have described above [that is, for Good Friday].[19]

This duplication of Good Friday's ritual on Holy Saturday is perhaps the most significant stage in the development

---

[18]Deinde sequitur matutinum. Lucerne extinguuntur.
[19]In lucernis accendendis vel extinguendis, sicut superius diximus ita fiat (§12).

of Tenebrae. It is likely that the repetition occurred both to signify the continuing period of mourning within the Church and at the same time to commemorate the three hours of darkness on Good Friday, a suggestion advanced by Rupert of Deutz.[20] Although the number of lamps to be extinguished is not stated, there is no reason to believe that it was other than seven. These were lit on Friday night and extinguished one by one at Lauds which followed.

Elsewhere in this *ordo,* we learn that the fire was hidden away on Good Friday for use at the paschal vigil on Holy Saturday night. There can be little doubt that this fire was obtained from the lamp reserved at the conclusion of Lauds on Good Friday. Since there was no need of a second reserved flame at the end of Lauds on Holy Saturday, the last of the seven lamps would have been extinguished at the conclusion of that office.

Summary of evidence : *Stage 4*

MT Matins and Lauds : normal lighting
GF Matins : normal lighting
     Lauds : gradual extinguishing of seven lamps
HS Matins : normal lighting
     Lauds : gradual extinguishing of seven lamps

Stage 5. It was perhaps inevitable that the light-feature, which now distinguished the night offices of Good Friday and Holy Saturday, should be extended to include Matins/Lauds of Maundy Thursday in view of their common funereal character; and it might have been expected that uniformity would be achieved according to the following scheme :

MT ⎫
GF ⎬ Matins : normal lighting
HS ⎭ Lauds : gradual extinguishing of seven lamps

[20]*De Div. Off.* V (PL 170.148B). He adds that the extinguishing of the candles also signifies the darkness of the Jewish nation which killed the prophets.

However, no evidence has survived to show that development ever took place along these lines. Before any changes occurred in the lighting arrangements for Maundy Thursday's night office, further development took place at Matins/Lauds of both Good Friday and Holy Saturday, in which the gradual loss of light became a feature of Matins as well as Lauds and, in view of the tripartite division of Matins into nocturns, the complement of lights at this office was required to be divisible by three. Gallican Ordo 28 is our sole witness for the employment of this light-feature at Matins of Good Friday and Holy Saturday (§49). According to this same *ordo*, the night office of Maundy Thursday began shortly after midnight; and for its celebration, it was prescribed that the church should be fully illuminated.[21] The silence of this *ordo* in respect of the loss of lights on this day, in contrast with the clear directions to extinguish them on Good Friday and Holy Saturday, again indicates that normal illumination obtained for the duration of this service. The use of the phrase *omne lumen* suggests that the illumination of the church was to be brighter than usual. In two *ordines,* the phrase appears in the rubric prior to the start of Matins, during which the gradual loss of light occured.[22] For those participating in such a service, the experience of passing from a world of light into a darkness that symbolised death must have been quite dramatic.

Although the offices of Matins and Lauds were sung consecutively, the extinguishing of the lights, spread over the two services, had the unifying effect of combining even further the two originally-separate parts and imposing upon them the single name of Tenebrae.

Summary of evidence : *Stage 5*

MT Matins and Lauds : normal lighting
GF Matins : gradual extinguishing of all church lights
      Lauds : gradual extinguishing of the seven lamps

---

[21]At vero ecclesia omni lumine decoretur, 'then let the church be filled with light' (§7).
[22]OR 26.10 and OR 29.11.

HS   Matins and Lauds : as for Good Friday

Stage 6. The final stage in the evolution of Tenebrae is attested in Ordo 26 and Ordo 29.[23] The practice of extinguishing
the church lights at Matins and the seven altar lamps at Lauds
on all *three* days of the Triduum was now established, and the
shape of the service was fundamentally the same as that which
survived into the twentieth century. The attestation of the
twice-repeated service in the early Ordo 26 need not cause
surprise. For in the eighth and ninth centuries, liturgical disorder reigned throughout Gaul; and the development of ritual was sporadic and lacked uniformity, as is apparent from
a comparison of the rubrics of Ordo 26 with those of later
ordines.

In view of the symbolism subsequently attached to the extinguishing of the candles and of the possible origins of that
feature and of the significance of the *Omissions,* the performance of Tenebrae in the early hours of Maundy Thursday
could be said to have been anachronistic. This was a direct
result of imposing liturgical uniformity on each of the services of Matins/Lauds during the Triduum. On the other
hand, the funereal tone of Tenebrae on Maundy Thursday
both foreshadowed the subsequent events of that day and anticipated the period of mourning on Good Friday and Holy
Saturday.

This extraordinary service, known since the twelfth century, and possibly much earlier, as *Tenebrae,* continued to be
performed officially on the last three days of Holy Week until
the liturgical reforms following the Second Vatican Council.[24]
Although the service underwent some modifications in the use
of light, its basic structure remained the same; and in its
eighth-century form, it is clearly and recognisably the same
service as that held in the twentieth century.

[23]OR 26.10 and OR 29.11.
[24]It is still performed in some monastic houses, e.g., at Solesmes, in the
London and Birmingham Oratories, and by the Society of St Pius X.

Ordo 26 contains the following directions for extinguishing the lights (§13) : An unspecified number of lamps or
candles is lit before the start of Matins, as are also the seven
sanctuary lamps. The former set of lights is gradually extinguished throughout the course of Matins, the first at the very
beginning of the office. At the end of the first nocturn, a third
of the lights have been put out, and at the end of the second
nocturn, another third. By the conclusion of the last nocturn,
which is the end of Matins, the remaining third have been
extinguished, and only the seven altar lights remain burning
in the church. These are extinguished one by one during the
course of Lauds. The central light is put out last at the
Benedictus.

Summary of evidence : *Stage 6*

M T   Matins : gradual extinguishing of all church lights
        Lauds : gradual extinguishing of the seven lamps
GF   Matins and Lauds : as for Maundy Thursday
HS   Matins and Lauds : as for Maundy Thursday

Chapter Three
THE TIME OF TENEBRAE

By the end of the eighth century, the two traditions relating to the time at which Tenebrae began were of long standing. Our sources at this time attest the start of this service both at midnight and at the eighth hour. In the cathedral churches, the first office of the day was sung at the former time, which significantly was the beginning of the old Roman civil day. Within the monasteries and those churches which followed monastic practice, the later time was observed. In the sixth century, St Benedict had changed the time of rising for the monks under his discipline so that instead of rising at midnight, 'the brethren shall rise at whatever time shall be calculated to be the eighth hour of the night'.[1] The change was made so as to allow more time for sleep.

Ordo 26 is our oldest authority attesting the start of Matins at the eighth hour of the night and Tenebrae on all three nights of the Triduum, and we find that Ordo 29 in the ninth century and *Poitiers* and the *Pontificale Romano-Germanicum* in the tenth century also prescribe this monastic practice.[2] However, from about 1200, the trend began in Benedictine houses to commence the night office at the earlier time; and it is tempting to discern in this practice the beginnings of that proc-

[1]*Life of St Benedict of Aniane* (PL 103.872A); Bradshaw p.143.
[2]OR 26.11 and .13; OR 29.28; *Poitiers* p.137; *PRG* II p.56 §212.

ess whereby Tenebrae became an anticipated office, generally performed in the late afternoon of the previous day. The
Caeremoniale Episcoporum explains that according to the ancient
Italian method of counting hours, the service should begin
at the twenty-first hour, that is, at 4.00 P.M. in March and
at 5.00 P.M. in April.[3] The former time is attested at Limoges
in the fifteenth century.[4] The change was brought about, it
is generally believed, partly through a wish to make the service more accessible to both secular clergy and laity and partly
by the persistence of the tradition inherited from Judaism,
in which a day is reckoned from sunset to sunset; and this
arrangement obtained generally until the liturgical reforms
following the Decree of *Maxima Redemptionis,* which is dated
16 November 1955. However, in France, certain cathedrals,
such as Rouen and Langres, and the Collegiate Churches of
St-Victor and of the Virgins in Paris continued to observe
the original time of singing Tenebrae as late as the eighteenth
century,[5] whilst at the Abbey of St-Germain at Auxerre and
in several Cluniac hospices, the office was held very early in
the morning up to the same period.[6]

   In the monasteries and houses of some of the religious orders, which were not affected to any appreciable extent by
the presence of the laity at the offices, the primitive tradition
of holding Tenebrae in the early hours of the morning was
perpetuated. In the seventeenth century, some monasteries,
such as St-Maur and St-Vanne in France, reverted to holding the service at the former time of 2.00 A.M.[7] The Cistercians sang the office at about 3.00 A.M. until the time of the
Second Vatican Council. On the other hand, among the
Dominicans, the Franciscans, and in some Benedictine houses,
such as Quarr Abbey, Tenebrae was always an anticipated

[3]II.22 p.264.
[4]Martène, *DAER* 4.22.1 p.81 (M 160).
[5]Martène, *DAER* 4.22.1 p.81; Grancolas p.296.
[6]Grancolas *op.cit.*
[7]Schmitz Vol. 6 pp.166–67.

office, as in the Roman rite. Following the liturgical changes of 1955, Matins and Lauds were no longer to be anticipated on the previous evening but were to be 'said in the morning [of the day itself] at the appropriate hour'.[8] This has allowed a certain flexibility among the religious orders and in those churches where the office of Tenebrae still survives.

[8]Fortescue and O'Connell (11th edition) p.281.

Chapter Four

THE PROVISION OF LIGHT
AT TENEBRAE

In the history of this rite, three main schemes for the provision of light prior to the commencement of the office are
known to have existed. In the period up to *c.*1000, all but one
of our sources mention the extinguishing of a certain number of (church) lights at Matins and also the putting out of
the seven sanctuary lamps, which stood before the altar.[1] In
most places, from the eleventh century onwards, the seven
lamps no longer featured in the ceremony; and the extinguishing of the other lights was spread over Matins *and* Lauds. In
the third phase of the development, which occurred probably in the fifteenth century, the extinguishing of the six altar
candles was incorporated into the ceremonial during the
Benedictus.

(i) The Lighting of the Lamps and Candles

The time for lighting the lamps and candles could vary,
depending upon which of the three days of the Triduum was
involved and upon whether the new fire was kindled on
Maundy Thursday and subsequently reserved or on all three
days or on Saturday only. According to the Customary of Frut-

[1]Ordines 26, 27, 28, 29, 31; *PRG; Poitiers;* and *CMG.*

tuaria, the lights for Tenebrae on Maundy Thursday were lit after Compline on Wednesday;[2] and it is very likely that this was the practice of other monasteries. However, since there was no obvious liturgical or ceremonial reason why they should have been lit at this time, it is reasonable to suppose that in other places, the lights were kindled only shortly before the start of Matins. If the seven lamps before the altar were perpetually alight, it would have been necessary to kindle only the church lights prior to the commencement of Maundy Thursday's office.

The rekindling of the church lights and the seven lamps during the daytime of Maundy Thursday is clearly described in most of our sources for the period up to *c*.1000.[3] They all agree that illumination returned to the church after the new fire had been brought in procession into the building, at times ranging from 11.00 A.M. (the *Pontificale Romano-Germanicum* [*PRG*]) to 3.00 P.M. (OR 26); and it is assumed that until the arrival of the new fire, the lights had remained extinguished since Tenebrae. For between the conclusion of Matins/Lauds and the commencement of Mass in the late afternoon or evening of Maundy Thursday, no liturgical light would have been required in church.[4] Once lit, the lights remained burning throughout the remainder of Maundy Thursday until they were once again extinguished at Tenebrae of Good Friday.[5] This pattern was repeated after the liturgy of Good Friday afternoon, in readiness for the final extinguishing of the lights

[2]Albers IV p.39.

[3]Ordines 26.4; 28.25; 29.17; 31.29; *PRG* II p.58; *CMG* (Albers V p.32).

[4]In churches where either of the primitive Masses of Maundy Thursday were still celebrated, liturgical light would have been obtained from the lamp reserved for that purpose at the conclusion of Tenebrae. The statement in *Poitiers* (p.138) that the clergy enter church 'for all the Masses' after the new fire ceremonies relates to the one Mass of Maundy Thursday celebrated in the several churches of Poitiers, and not to the celebration of more than one Eucharist on that day.

[5]Usque ad vigilias, 'until Matins'. Thus, OR 26.10; OR 27.11; OR 31.31; *Poitiers* p.138; *PRG* II p.58 §221.

at Tenebrae of Holy Saturday. Long after the seven sanctuary lamps ceased to be used at Tenebrae, this arrangement for the triple provision of fire obtained in those churches and monasteries where the new fire was brought into church on three successive days.[6]

In churches in which the kindling of the new fire was confined to Holy Saturday, the lighting of the candles for the ceremonies of Maundy Thursday and Good Friday would have been effected by means of a flame already burning within the precincts of the church : either a brazier or some device for providing heat or the fire of a kitchen near a monastic church or very likely, one suspects, the perpetual flame that burned before the reserved Sacrament.

Our sources provide few details regarding the lighting of the lamps and candles for Tenebrae. At Poitiers in the tenth century the thirty lamps were lit by the sacristan using a candle. This done, he took up a position in the doorway of the church, where he extinguished the candle as a signal to mark the start of Matins.[7] The Ordinal of Barking records that the candles for Matins on Maundy Thursday were lit by an official called the *secretaria,* but for the corresponding office on Good Friday, it was the duty of the sacristan.[8] The Ordinal of Exeter merely states that the candles were lit (just) before Matins.[9]

(ii) The Disposition of Lights

SCHEME 1   *Nave and choir lights extinguished during Matins; the seven lamps before the altar extinguished during Lauds.*

(A) SEVEN LAMPS. The arrangement and disposition of these sanctuary lights is discussed at the end of this chapter in the section entitled *The Origin of the Seven Lamps.*

[6]For example, at Barking (HBS 65 pp.91 ff.) and Canterbury (HBS 23 pp.379 ff.).
[7]*Poitiers* p.193, but recorded only for Good Friday.
[8]HBS 65 p.91 and p.97.
[9]HBS 37 p.132.

(B) NAVE AND CHOIR LIGHTS. It is not clear whether the twenty-four lights mentioned by Amalarius, by *PRG,* and by *Alcuin;* the twenty-seven of Ordo 32; and the thirty-nine of Ordo 29 were originally different from the functional illuminations of the churches in question; but the relatively large number of lamps involved and the positioning of them both in the choir and in the nave would suggest that these were the normal church lights, even though in some churches they may have been realigned in a more symmetrical arrangement to suit the liturgical requirements of Tenebrae. However, the very act of extinguishing them one by one during the course of divine service and the fact that from at least the time of Amalarius, the number of lights featuring in the ritual was given a symbolic interpretation, endowed the lamps, perhaps inevitably, with a liturgical significance.

The display and arrangement of the lights in the five above-mentioned sources is unknown. However, a careful study of the description of Tenebrae in the Pontifical of Poitiers makes it possible for us to reconstruct with some confidence the actual disposition of lights not only at Poitiers but in other Gallican churches where the office of Tenebrae was held. On page 139 of this pontifical is the following instruction :

> On these three nights at the night office let thirty lamps be lit. These must be arranged *in three rows of equal spacing.*[10]

The silence of the source in respect of the direction in which the rows of lamps ran presents us with the possibility that they may have run parallel to the main axis of the church in an east-to-west direction. Alternatively, the lamps may have been placed in rows which ran from one side of the church to the other. Arguments may be advanced in favour of either orientation.

1. *East-West Orientation.* The possibility that the rows of lamps ran in this direction raises a number of points. (i) If

[10]The Latin of the words italicised by the writer reads : Aequo spacio trino ordine. The phrase *aequo spacio* must refer to the distances or intervals between each of the rows and not to those between the individual lamps.

the length of the church was greater than its width, as was usual, rows of lamps running in an east-to-west direction would have been more in keeping with the design and general appearance of the building. (ii) In such an arrangement, the intervals between the lamps would have provided a more satisfactory form of illumination than would a north-south orientation. Three rows of lamps extending across the church and parallel to the altar would have necessitated smaller intervals between each lamp which could have resulted in an unnecessary concentration of light over the areas immediately beneath these rows and darkness in the rest of the church. (iii) If the rows of lamps ran from north to south, were all three located in the nave, or was one row positioned in the choir? The former possibility should not be dismissed on the grounds that there would have been insufficient light in the choir for the lectors since a certain amount of light for reading is likely to have emanated from the seven sanctuary lamps during the whole of Matins.[11] It is not clear whether the thirty lamps extinguished during Tenebrae at Poitiers were also used as normal church lights; nor is it known if any other functional lights, not lit on this occasion, existed elsewhere in the church. However, the gerundive in the rubric in question, *aptandae*, 'fitted out' or 'arranged', may well indicate that these thirty lights were set out in this order, especially for the night offices of the Triduum. This in turn raises the interesting question of whether the lights were pendant lamps or candles in free-standing candlesticks. It is almost certain that the lamps in question would have been oil-lamps and not candles, though the use of candles for functional illumination should not be completely ruled out. However, the difficulty of suspending a single candle from a beam and the even greater problem of placing a candle upon a lofty roof beam seem to preclude the use of this genre of light at Poitiers. The objection might

[11]There is no reason to believe that these lamps were of the hooded variety similar to those which hang before St Peter's tomb in Rome and which provide little illumination.

also be raised that the limited and restricted use of the lamps hung in abnormal positions within the church would hardly have justified the possibly lengthy preparation involved in the fixing and suspending of thirty lamp-chains. The objection, however, largely disappears if one supposes that in the beams were hooks for the chains, which remained permanently in position from year to year.

In support of the view that the lights for Tenebrae comprised three rows of candles in their holders, which extended from the west end of the church to the sanctuary, it may be said that the portability of the candelabra would have permitted a rapid disposition of the lights and have allowed the lamps in the same row to be spaced with whatever intervals were required in a church unencumbered in those days by lines of chairs or pews. The objection that the use of candleholders was impracticable amid the jostling of the congregation cannot really be sustained; for the night office was probably never attended anywhere by hordes of the faithful. A much more serious objection arises over the height the candleholders would need to have been. Both from the point of view of safety and to ensure that the lights provided maximum illumination, it would have been necessary for the candlesticks to stand at least six feet from the ground. Although it is not entirely beyond belief, it does seem very unlikely that a church, such as that at Poitiers, should have possessed a set of thirty very large candelabra for use only at three relatively-short services each year. Moreover, it is most unlikely that such candleholders would have been used for the church's functional illuminations. Oil-lamps almost certainly were used. It is, therefore, difficult to escape the conclusion that the functional oil-lamps of the church at Poitiers were used liturgically at Tenebrae, either *in situ* or temporarily repositioned during the latter part of Holy Week.

2. *North-South Orientation.* The possibility of an arrangement of lights in rows running parallel to the north-south axis of the church invites two comments. (i) Rows of lights arranged

according to this orientation are actually attested in *Scheme 2,* but they were confined to one part of the church. The position occupied by the sacristan before the start of the service shows that at least some of the lights were burning in the nave. An arrangement of one line of lights in the choir and two in the nave seems unlikely; three rows in the nave would have provided illumination in that part of the church but would have left the choir in gloom. (ii) A later rubric from the same description of Tenebrae in *Poitiers* would, on first reading, appear to favour a north-to-south orientation :

> The lamps which begin to be put out on the western side of the church.[12]

It would also, at first, appear to indicate that the sacristan proceeded to move along the western row of lamps until all ten were extinguished and then to put out next those in the middle row. However, the evidence of this rubric is inconclusive since the instruction is qualified by the words *begin to be extinguished* and gives no indication either of the direction in which the sacristan then proceeded or of the direction in which the rows of lamps ran.

The arrangement of the church lights in three rows for the service of Tenebrae, as attested by *Poitiers,* was probably typical of many Gallican churches in the period prior to 1000, regardless of the number of lamps lit before the start of Matins. However, an interesting but intriguingly concise statement by Martène reveals that the display of lights in some churches was perhaps not as orderly as that at Poitiers. For he records that at Corbie and at Monte Cassino in the ninth and tenth centuries, the lamps to be extinguished at the night office were dispersedly arranged throughout the church.[13] This does not imply a random disposition of lights. It suggests that the normal church illuminations were used rather than specially-arranged rows of lamps.

[12]Lucernarum quae ab occidentali parte ecclesiae incipiantur extingui (p.137).
[13]*DAMR* 3.13 p.122.

SCHEME 2   *Lights lit only in the choir and extinguished during Matins and Lauds.*

Writing in the first half of the eighteenth century, Jean Grancolas records that in some churches candles were placed upon or lamps were suspended from beams which spanned the entire width of the choir.[14] It is unfortunate for our enquiry that Grancolas does not specify any churches where this arrangement obtained or mention the period when these beams were used, nor does he mention the number of candles or lamps or even the number of beams that were involved. His vagueness about these beams with their lights is perhaps indicative of his own ignorance in this matter and may suggest that he is recording only the half-remembered facts of an informant about former practice. However, the use at Tenebrae of candles placed upon or lamps hung from beams in the choir does represent a significant transitional stage in the development of the ceremonial between the earliest recorded arrangement, whereby the lights of the whole church were extinguished *(Scheme 1)*, and the practice of extinguishing gradually only those candles which were placed on a candelabrum or hearse near to the altar *(Scheme 5)*. It is significant that Grancolas employs the term *hirpices* when he refers to the wooden beams with their iron spikes for impaling wax candles or for hanging lamps therefrom. The same word in the singular, *hirpex,* is also used to describe the hearse of candles which stood in the sanctuary during Tenebrae.

Three factors may have contributed to the abandonment of the practice of extinguishing lights in the nave during Tenebrae and to the restriction of their use in the choir. (i) In those cathedrals and monastic churches where those attending the night office could comfortably be accommodated within the choir, the extinguishing of lights in an unused part of the building may have seemed superfluous and may even have gone unnoticed, especially if a large choir-screen effectively

---

[14]*Commentarius* p.296.

isolated the choir from the nave. One of two developments may then have occurred. Either the lights in the nave ceased to be lit so that most of the church remained in darkness; or in churches, such as Salisbury, where the nave lights continued to burn in the background, their presence was disregarded until almost the end of Lauds when it was necessary to have the whole of the building in total darkness. (ii) When Tenebrae became an anticipated service held in the late afternoon, the illumination of the nave would in some places have perhaps been unnecessary and may have gone unnoticed, especially if the building was flooded with strong vernal sunshine towards the close of the day.[15] (iii) The lighting of the lamps in the choir only and the concentration of light in one particular area heightened the effect of the proceedings both for those in the choir itself, who were aware of the darkness in the rest of the building, which was symbolic of the darkness of the world, and especially for those in the darkness of the nave, who observed the lights and their extinction at a distance. The drama in the presentation of the passion and death of Jesus was, after all, an important element in the funereal content of Tenebrae.

Unless the supports for the lamps were the permanent tie-beams of the roof itself,[16] one can only speculate about the number and position of temporary horizontal bars, if such devices were used. It seems reasonable to conjecture that they were placed at the sanctuary end of the choir so as to allow the whole of the beam to be used, thereby permitting greater intervals between each light, especially if twenty-four or

[15]Augustus Hare quotes the vivid description from Anderson's *Improvisatore* of Tenebrae on Wednesday afternoon in the Sistine Chapel. The service, it seems, was timed to end when 'the descending sun . . . threw his last beams in through the uppermost window' and strongly illuminated Christ and the Apostles. The sun set just as the last psalm was ended. (*Walks in Rome* Vol.2 p.297).

[16]It should be borne in mind that lofty ceilings and stone vaultings belong to later medieval churches. Earlier cathedrals and monastic churches were buildings of considerably more modest dimensions.

twenty-five were placed on each beam. A location for the beams in this place would also have given the sacristan ready access to the lights.

SCHEME 3   *Candles lit on a stand near the altar and extinguished during Matins and Lauds.*

The next stage in the development of the use of light would find the choir lamps of *Scheme 2* replaced by a row or cluster of lights, usually candles, placed and extinguished in the vicinity of the altar. The display of lights in this position represents the final stage in the transition from the use of functional lamps with symbolic associations to the use of liturgical lights with a minimal functional purpose. It was perhaps inevitable that functional lights, once put to liturgical use and interpreted symbolically, should subsequently be placed in close proximity to the altar and mounted on a stand or candelabrum to underline their importance and to give them visual prominence. In a later chapter, we will show how the desirability of concentrating the lights in one place so as to enable those participating in Tenebrae to observe better the decrease in the loss of light was the principal factor in contributing to the location of these cultic lights within the sanctuary.

Scheme 2 and *Scheme 3* represent two successive increases in the concentration of light, progressively in the direction of the altar : first in the choir, then in the sanctuary. The area where the light ultimately became concentrated, namely, the vicinity of the altar, was also partly determined by the need to have close by illumination for reading. It was also perhaps inevitable that the last light to be extinguished should be placed within the sanctuary; for this was usually identified with Christ. Within this scheme should be included most of the documents which attest the use at Tenebrae of twenty-four or twenty-five lights; scant information concerning the use of other numbers, apart from fifteen, prevents our inclusion of them also, with confidence, within this scheme. Most of our sources do not mention the use or even the presence of lights in the choir or nave *vis-à-vis* those extinguished on the stand by the altar. However, the evidence from Norwich, Rouen, Salisbury, and a number of other churches, which we shall examine later, suggests that background illumination existed within the cathedral tradition at least.

SCHEME 4   *Hearse-lights and lights* in front of *the altar.*

(i) At the monastery of Farfa in the eleventh century, we encounter the somewhat puzzling statements that thirty candles were lit before the high altar and that fifteen candles were extinguished at Tenebrae.[17] In a later chapter, we shall examine this information in greater detail and offer our own solution as to the manner in which the lights at Farfa and other monasteries were displayed.

(ii) In the former cathedral church at Laon *c.*1090, eighteen lights were placed on either side of the sanctuary.[18] We are not told at what stage these additional lights were extinguished or what the purpose was in placing them in these positions. The number, too, is strange; thirty-six (or eighteen plus eighteen) seems to have no special liturgical or symbolic significance. Moreover, unlike the fifteen hearse-candles, which burned before the altar and were liturgically integrated into the office of Tenebrae, these additional lights were presumably at some distance from the altar. Their purpose may have been to provide light for the readers, but it is not at all clear at what stage in the ceremony they were extinguished. There may have been a similar disposition of lights at Coutances, where forty-four candles were lit for Tenebrae.[19] If a hearse of twenty-four candles was used, the number mentioned by John of Avranches,[20] the remaining twenty lights may have been placed in two groups of ten on either side of

[17]Albers I p.46 (= PL 150.1197B).

[18]Martène, *DAER* 4.22.2 p.81 (M 156).

[19]Heuser p.228. Unfortunately, he gives no other details.

[20]*Lib. de Off. Eccl.* 52 (PL 147.48C). The dioceses of Avranches and Coutances were coterminous.

the altar or sanctuary. At Chartres-en-Vallée in the twelfth century, it is possible that twenty-four of the thirty-four lights kindled at the night office burned on the hearse while the remaining ten were perhaps disposed as at Coutances.[21] On the other hand, it is possible that the additional lights both at Coutances and Chartres-en-Vallée may have been placed in the choir to provide functional illumination. Alternatively, the possibility of candelabra holding forty-four or thirty-four candles should not be completely ruled out. However, the frequency of twenty-four-candle and fifteen-candle hearses, the silence of Sicardus and Durandus, and the lack of attestation from any other source make the existence of candelabra designed to hold large numbers of lights seem very doubtful. Mention should here be made of the continued use of the seven sanctuary lamps at the Monastery of Monte Cassino and at Chartres Cathedral.[22]

SCHEME 5(A) *Hearse-lights and lights* upon *the altar.*

The disposition of lights according to this scheme differs from that of *Scheme 5(b)* only in the number of candles used. At Soissons in the late twelfth century, twenty-four candles burned on a candelabrum in front of the altar, and an unspecified number stood on the altar itself.[23] This is the first recorded instance of the use of altar-candles in connection with Tenebrae and, incidentally, one of the earliest references to candles placed upon the altar. Martène's silence concerning the number of these candles would suggest that the original ritual did not specify a figure. The six candles attested at Tongres in the fifteenth century are almost certain to have been placed on the altar; there, only seven other candles were lit on the hearse.[24]

---

[21]Martène, *DAER* 4.22.2 p.81 (M 76). This relates to the Church of St-Jean.

[22]Martène, *DAMR* 3.13.11 p.123 (M 1139); and Ordinary p.108.

[23]Martène, *DAER* 4.23 p.137 (M 305).

[24]Ordinary p.150.

SCHEME 5(B)   *Hearse-lights and lights* upon *the altar.*

This is the disposition of lights officially prescribed by the Church of Rome for those parts of the Western Church which owed allegiance to her and which were required to adopt the new Roman service-books in the sixteenth century.

(A) 1568–1955. As at Soissons, the Roman rite involved a tripartite use of light, namely, altar-candles, hearse-lights, and the functional lamps of the church; but it appears to have been unique in its use of the six altar-candles in that they were extinguished during the singing of the *Benedictus* at Lauds and not at intervals during the course of the whole office, as the seven sanctuary lamps had been. The origin of this feature is obscure. The use of six candles in this way did not form part of the old Dominican rite, which was based on the Roman rite of the late twelfth century.[25] In the liturgical revisions of 1255–1256, Dominican Tenebrae remained unaffected and survived unchanged until the twentieth century.[26] Neither do the Franciscan *ordines* of 1243–1244, which were closely based on the Roman practice of the papal court, mention the six candles within this context;[27] and Durandus, writing *c.* 1280, does not refer to them.[28] There are two likely periods when the practice of extinguishing the six altar-candles during the *Benedictus* may have been introduced into the Roman liturgy. (i) During the residence of the Popes at Avignon from 1309 to 1377, the papal liturgy was in direct contact with the influences of the Gallican Church. We have noted elsewhere that the Gallican ceremonial was somewhat less restrained than the austere and sombre Roman ritual. If the use of the six candles was introduced into Tenebrae during this period, it was very likely via the papal court at Avignon, though it must be added that there is no contemporary direct evidence from

[25]*Office of Holy Week* p.82.
[26]King, *LRO* p.337.
[27]HBS 85 p.76; Van Dijk II p.84.
[28]*Rationale* VI.72 fol.331.

the liturgy of that church to corroborate this theory. In the chaotic state of the city of Rome at this time, liturgical innovations there appear most unlikely. (ii) The second period to be considered is the reign of Pope Martin V (1417–1431). This pontiff inaugurated the restoration of the Roman Church after the Great Schism and was responsible for the refurbishment of many of Rome's churches and for the improvement of liturgical worship within the city.

According to Roman practice up to 1955, the six altar-candles were lit for Tenebrae on each day of the Triduum. Under the former dispensation, each of these days was a Double Feast of the First Class; and though it was not usual to have six altar-candles lit at Matins/Lauds, the funereal character of Tenebrae placed this office on a par with a Requiem. Since it was customary to light the six candles at this latter service, they were therefore kindled for Tenebrae.

(b) 1955 TO DATE. As a result of the reforms of 1955, which affected many of the services of the Triduum, whilst the six altar-candles remained in use at Tenebrae on Maundy Thursday, alterations to the ceremonial of Maundy Thursday itself and of Good Friday involved changes which affected Tenebrae on both of those days. After the stripping of the altar on Maundy Thursday, the altar remained bare until the Veneration of the Cross on the following day. As a result, there were no candles on the altar during Tenebrae of Good Friday. During the Veneration of the Cross, the cross to be venerated was brought into church, along with two candles; and after the Veneration, these candles were placed upon the altar. Then the Sacrament was brought in, accompanied by two more candles, and these were also placed upon the altar. Thus, at Tenebrae of Holy Saturday, four candles were alight and then extinguished during the *Benedictus*. [29]

Interestingly and somewhat paradoxically, the Dominican Order, which before 1955 had not used the six candles at

---

[29]Wuest p.263.

Tenebrae, adopted from the Roman rite the practice of lighting the six candles at about the same time that the hearse
ceased to be used in the Roman rite. These candles continue
to feature at Dominican Matins/Lauds in those houses which
still observe Tenebrae on all three days of the Triduum.

(iii) The Origin of the Seven Lamps

The presence of seven lamps or candles which stood or were
suspended from the ceiling in front of the high altar is more
widely attested in the Gallican than in the Roman tradition.[30]
They are mentioned in five *ordines* of Gallican origin as featuring either at Lauds, where they were extinguished gradually,
or at the illumination of the church on the evenings of Maundy
Thursday or Good Friday.[31] They are also attested in three
other early documents.[32] Ordo 30B, which purports to describe papal ceremonial, mentions them within the context
of the extinction of light at Tenebrae (§28). But Tenebrae
as such was unknown at Rome at the end of the eighth century, the date assigned to that *ordo;* therefore, the description
of that service in the *ordo* relates to a non-Roman church.
Nevertheless, there is no reason to believe that seven lamps
did not burn before the high altar of St John Lateran in Rome.

The seven lamps, however, must not be confused with the
seven candles, borne in procession by acolytes, which were
always present at any Stational Mass which the Pope celebrated.[33] These lights were carried by six acolytes and one
subdeacon or head acolyte and were placed before the altar

[30]It has yet to be shown that the seven-branched *menorah*, which stood
in the sanctuary of a number of larger churches, was ever substituted for
the seven altar lamps. At Durham, for instance, the central holder of the
menorah held the Easter candle. (Raine p.9).

[31]OR 26.9; OR 28.30; OR 29.17; OR 31.13; OR 32.5.

[32]*Poitiers* p.138; *PRG* II p.57 §213; *Alcuin, Lib.de Div.Off.* (PL 101.1205D).

[33]Ordo I records the ceremonial for the Mass of Easter Day. This description of the liturgy is applicable to any of the eighty-nine Stational Masses.

immediately after the Peace. They are to be distinguished from the two honorific (civic) candles which preceded the Pope on every occasion and which at Mass were placed *behind* the altar.[34]

The function of these seven candles and what they represented or symbolised are matters for some debate. The city of Rome had been divided by Pope Fabian (236–250) into seven ecclesiastical districts, in all likelihood using as a basis the fourteen civil regions which the Emperor Augustus had constituted. Ordo I records that whenever the Pope celebrated Mass, six acolytes and one subdeacon for the district 'on duty' for the day would act as candle-bearers.[35] The candle of each of these seven ministers may well have represented one of the seven districts of Rome. That all seven ministers on any one occasion should come from the same district and that six of them were severally representing the other six districts does seem somewhat strange. It seems much more likely that if we are dealing with a situation which involved district-representation, there would have been one acolyte from each of the districts. But since we are told that the seven acolytes were all from the same region on any one occasion, it casts some doubt on whether each candle stood for one district.

The writer believes that a much more profound symbolism was attached to the seven papal candles. The celebration of a Stational Mass by the Pope was a time of great importance and solemnity. He was accompanied by all the dignitaries of the Church since the occasion represented both the unity and the totality of the Roman Church at its most solemn function. To a point, the presence of all the Roman clergy symbolised the fact that the Mass was being celebrated on behalf of the whole city of Rome. In a more visible and dramatic way, the presence of the seven processional candles also symbolised the major constituent elements of the Church, on

[34]OR 4.7 and OR 30B.37.

[35]Atchley, *Ordo Romanus* p.39. For the concept of the division of duties among the Jewish priesthood, see, *inter alia,* Luke 1:8.

whose behalf the whole congregation had gathered, in the following way.

We read in the Book of Revelation (1:12, 20) that the seven golden lamp stands symbolised the Seven Churches of Asia and, by extension, the whole of the Church in the Roman province of Asia. The writer believes that the symbolism was borrowed by the Roman Church in view of the existence of the seven so-called Constantinian basilicas within the city of Rome,[36] and that each of the seven processional candles in question represented one of those seven major basilicas. At what period this feature of seven lights first appeared in Rome, we can but hazard a guess. We have already observed that the concept of seven patriarchal basilicas arose after the time of Sixtus III. It is possible that the use of the seven candles is much older and that they previously represented some other ecclesiastical heptad, either in the world-wide Church or in that of Rome. We might consider, for instance, the seven seasons of the Christian year;[37] the seven suburbicarian dioceses; the seven Stational Masses at the Cathedral of St John Lateran;[38] or the seven martyrs, venerated at Rome, who are mentioned in the *communicantes* prayer in the canon of the Tridentine Mass.

When we turn to consider the origin of the seven stationary lamps which stood or hung before the high altar and which were extinguished at Tenebrae, it is not difficult to believe that these lights were scripturally-inspired, like the seven

[36]It is now known that the Basilica of S.Maria Maggiore, unlike the other six, is not of Constantinian foundation, but dates from the pontificate of Sixtus III (432–440). It seems unlikely, therefore, that the notion of the *seven* major churches of Rome arose before the second third of the fifth century.

[37]Advent, Christmas, Epiphany, Lent, Easter, Pentecost, Common Time.

[38]It is interesting to note that of the 89 Stational Masses at Rome, 49 (that is, 7x7) were celebrated in the major basilicas : St Peter's 13, S.Maria Maggiore 12, St John Lateran 7, St Paul's 6, S.Lorenzo 4, S.Sebastiano 4, S.Croce in Gerusalemme 3.

processional candles of the Roman rite, also from the last book
of the New Testament. According to Revelation 4:5, 'before
the throne burn seven torches of fire, which are the seven
spirits of God'. Within the context of the liturgy, the throne
of God was represented by the altar; and the seven 'torches
of fire', which burn perpetually and have an essential relationship with God, were quite clearly portrayed by the seven
liturgical lamps which burned in front of the altar.[39] For they
were permanent lights whose use was not restricted to one
service. On the other hand, the seven candles which formed
part of the Pope's procession were placed temporarily in front
of the altar, and their use was confined to papal High Mass.
The objection cannot be sustained that two sets of seven lights
would be unlikely; for there is still a simultaneous use of seven
acolytes' torches and seven altar candles at High Mass in the
papal liturgy today.

In the same way that the flame of each lamp in Revelation
4:5 was perpetually burning, it is possible that the seven lamps
of the earthly liturgy were never allowed to be extinguished,
except once a year. The evidence of Ordo 30B would suggest
that this is likely to have occurred at the conclusion of Mat-
ins/Lauds of Good Friday, the last of the lamps being removed
rather than extinguished at the end of the service.[40] Possible
support for this view is to be found in the rubrics of a number of documents which relate to the entry into church on
Maundy Thursday of the procession bearing the new fire. All
attest the concern that the seven lamps should be rekindled
speedily and efficiently.[41]

---

[39]Another, though less likely, explanation is given by John the Deacon.
He explains that seven is a sacred number since it is the sum of four, the
number of Gospels which attest the Trinity, and three, the Trinity itself
(PL59.403B). On the face of the tribunal above the apse in the Church
of S.Prassede in Rome is a mosaic portraying the Lamb, who is flanked
on either side by three and four candlesticks. These are said to be 'allegorical of the seven mysteries' (Forbes p.257).

[40]OR 30B.28.

[41]OR 26.9; OR 29.17; *PRG* II p.58 §220; *Alcuin* (PL101.1205D).

Chapter Five

THE NUMBER OF LIGHTS AT TENEBRAE

(i) The Early Period

In view of the evidence of *Poitiers* and *Alcuin,* it is our contention that in the period up to *c.*1000, the lamps and candles extinguished during the course of Matins comprised the functional lights of the church. There were two factors which determined the number of lights to be used. As early as the time of Amalarius, symbolic interpretations were given to some numbers, especially if they suggested a biblical precedent. It was more important, however, that the number of lights to be extinguished should be divisible by three in order to maintain liturgical symmetry within each of the three nocturns of Matins. Thus, we encounter in this period thirty-nine, thirty, twenty-seven, and twenty-four lights lit at the start of the night office.[1] The silence of Ordo 26 may suggest that any suitable number could be used.

According to the ceremonial of the church with which Amalarius was familiar, twenty-four candles or lamps were lit on each day of the Triduum. His mention of seventy-two lights represents the total for the three days; and though he

---

[1]OR 29.12 *(39); Poitiers* p.137 *(30);* OR 32.5 *(27);* Amalarius, *Lib.Off.* 4.22.1 *(24); PRG* II p.56 §213 *(24); Alcuin* (PL 101.120B) *(24).*

dwells on the significance of seventy-two rather than twenty-four, twice he states that only twenty-four lights were lit for each of the three celebrations of Tenebrae.[2] Amalarius' commentary on the various features of the service is reminiscent of the symbolic and allegorical interpretations of ceremonial and vestments recorded by later medieval writers, such as Rupert of Deutz, John Beleth, and Sicardus. His twofold and sometimes threefold interpretations of the symbolism which he finds in the ceremonial is not always consistent, but it does highlight the belief of that age that the ceremonial of the Church reflected the teaching and theology of the Bible and was therefore of both divine inspiration and divine approbation.

For Amalarius, each of the twenty-four lights represents an hour, or more precisely an hour of daylight; and collectively they symbolise Christ, 'who illuminates his Church by day and by night, and who, as *verus sol,* "the true Sun", rests in the tomb during the Triduum, mourned by his Church and hidden from view in the same way that the sun is not visible during an eclipse. For that reason and as a sign of sorrow the lights are extinguished.'[3] Over the three-day period, the seventy-two lights signify the seventy-two hours which Jesus lay in the tomb.[4] In addition to the temporal aspect of the symbolism, the extinguishing of the seventy-two lights over the three-day period is interpreted somewhat freely as the desertion of the seventy-two disciples.[5] Similar comparisons and analogies are to be found in *Alcuin.*[6]

[2]Accenduntur per singulas noctes XXIIII *and again in the same chapter* per singulas noctes memoratarum feriarum viginti quattuor lumina accenduntur . . . hoc enim fit ter. 'Twenty-four lights are lit each night' *and* 'on each night of the said days twenty-four lights are lit . . . for this happens three times.'

[3]*Lib. Off.* 4.22.1.

[4]The phrases *on the third day* and *after three days* in reference to Jesus' resurrection were frequently thought of as embracing three whole days. This was a result of the inclusive system of reckoning time.

[5]Luke 10:1, alternative reading.

[6]*Lib. de Div. Off.* (PL 101.1203B).

Evidence from the *Pontificale Romanum-Germanicum (PRG)* shows that even by the tenth century Tenebrae was not universally observed throughout Northern Gaul and Northern Germany in spite of its attestation two hundred years earlier :

> During this night twenty-four lights are lit in some places.[7]

The alternative interpretation that *in some places* numbers of lights other than twenty-four were lit is unlikely.

The importance of the symbolism attached to numbers may have been responsible for the disappearance of or at least the lack of evidence for the use of twenty-seven, thirty, and thirty-nine lights at Tenebrae in subsequent centuries; the evidence for the use of twenty-four lights is plentiful and persists well into the twentieth century *(Table 1)*. For none of the three former figures have obvious associations with biblical numbers or situations.

(ii) The Later Diversity of Numbers

(A) 72 LIGHTS. Both John Beleth and Sicardus, but not Durandus, attest the practice of lighting seventy-two candles at Tenebrae. Beleth, who, like Sicardus, states that the service of Tenebrae represents the darkness of Christ's three hours on the cross, repeats Amalarius' analogy with the seventy-two disciples.[8] Sicardus also refers to their desertion.[9] Beleth, echoing Amalarius, also likens the number of candles to the hours Christ lay in the tomb, to the number of nations, and by extension, to the number of languages. Since both commentators record that Tenebrae took place on each day of the Triduum and that it was possible to light different numbers of candles at this service, of which one was twenty-four, it seems almost certain that they are both attesting the use of

---

[7]Accenduntur in quibusdam locis in hac nocte viginti quattuor lumina (*PRG* II p.56 §213).

[8]*Rationale* (PL 202.105A).

[9]*Mitrale* (PL 213.298D).

seventy-two candles on each of the three nights of the Triduum and not referring to the total number for the three services, as Amalarius did. The arrangement in which they were disposed is unknown; the very large number would suggest a fairly concentrated display in the region of the altar, rather than a sporadic disposition throughout the whole of the church. Moreover, one can only conjecture that these lights were extinguished in groups of three at the same points in the service at which twenty-four candles were put out. Durand's silence at the end of the thirteenth century may suggest that the practice of lighting seventy-two candles at Tenebrae had everywhere fallen into desuetude.

(B) 44 LIGHTS. We referred earlier to the forty-four candles at Coutances and suggested a possible disposition for these lights. The 1499 Breviary of Coutances does not record the number of lights that were lit for Tenebrae. Its silence on this score may indicate that a not unusual number of candles were placed on the hearse. John of Avranches, whose own diocese was adjacent to that of Coutances, clearly states that twenty-four lights were to be lit for the night office.[10] The occurrence of four as the second digit both at Coutances and at Chartres-en-Vallée, where thirty-four lights were lit, may suggest the presence of a twenty-four-candle hearse within the total number of lights.

(C) 39 LIGHTS. Dom Edmond Martène records that an *ordo Romanus*, which he examined, stated the monks at Monte Cassino lit thirty-nine lights for Tenebrae, which they extinguished in more-or-less the same way as that described in Ordo 26 or *PRG*.[11] Elsewhere, he mentions that the lights were dispersedly arranged throughout the church.[12] To a point, Dendy

---

[10]*Lib. de Off. Eccl.* 52 (PL 147.48C).

[11]*DAMR* 3.12.13 p.123. The *ordo Romanus*, to which Martène is here referring, was one similar to either OR 28 or OR 31. See Appendix 10 : *Monte Cassino A*.

[12]*DAMR* 3.12.2 p.122.

is correct in stating that 'the lights appear to be those of the whole church'; but he is wrong to assert that Martène has 'misunderstood a MS. in giving the number thirty-nine'. Dendy, one suspects, has noticed that when Martène refers to the position of the lamps, he states that at Monte Cassino there were fifteen; and perhaps understandably, Dendy has come to the conclusion that Martène is in error in respect of the thirty-nine lights.[13] However, on reflection, it would appear from what Martène informs us that it is not that he has misread or misunderstood his sources but that he has been puzzled by seemingly-contradictory evidence from the same monastery and possibly also by some confusion in his original notes. This would account for a further statement that the number of candles used at Monte Cassino is not clear.[14]

A plausible explanation for the conflicting information emerges from a closer examination of the sources which Martène consulted. Two documents, separated by several centuries and attesting the practice of two different periods, were examined by Martène. (i) We suggested above that the *ordo Romanus,* which Martène inspected for information relating to Monte Cassino, had its provenance within the same liturgical tradition as Ordo 28 and Ordo 31. It also had elements in common with Ordo 29. For instance, it attested the use of thirty-nine lights at Tenebrae. Moreover, at Monte Cassino seven small lamps hung in front of the apse;[15] and unlike other early *ordines* and pontificals, Ordo 29 was compiled primarily for use in a monastery.[16] (ii) The second document relating to Monte Cassino, which Martène consulted, was an ordinary of *c.*1100 (M 1139). This probably did not specify the number of lights to be lit for Tenebrae—hence Martène's

---

[13] *The Use of Lights* p.146.

[14] *DAMR* 3.12.3 p.123.

[15] *Ordo Casinensis* p.101. These lamps are almost certainly a survival of the seven primitive sanctuary lamps.

[16] OR 29.29 and 29.45. Compare OR 26.19 and 26.20; OR 28.26; OR 30B.37; OR 31.65; *PRG* II p.59 §221; and *Poitiers* p.139.

statement about the number not being clear. Moreover, Martène did not know how many candles were lit for Tenebrae at Rome during this period. Therefore, since he knew that the monks at Monte Cassino observed the Roman rite at Tenebrae, he contented himself by giving elsewhere the number which he knew the Roman Church subsequently used and which was correct at the time he was writing : fifteen.

Amongst the liturgical features shared by the monasteries of Corbie and Monte Cassino, was the 'scattering' of lights for Tenebrae throughout the church building.[17] The linking of the two monasteries in this way and the affinity between Martène's *ordo Romanus* and Ordines 28, 29, and 31 increase the likelihood that thirty-nine lights were also used at Corbie, especially in view of Grancolas' testimony. Admittedly, he records that thirty-eight lights were lit at this monastery in Northern France;[18] however, this figure is otherwise unknown within the context of Tenebrae; it has no relevant biblical significance; and it cannot be divided by three into equal parts. A likely explanation for the occurrence of this number is that Grancolas or the copyist whose manuscript Grancolas read mistook XXXVIIII for XXXVIII. If, however, this figure is correct, it would suggest that at Corbie, for a reason lost to us, only twelve lights were extinguished during one of the nocturns.

(D) 34 LIGHTS. We have already suggested how the thirty-four candles at Chartres-en-Vallée may have been displayed. No other instance is known of the use of thirty-four lights at Tenebrae.

(E) 30 LIGHTS. *Poitiers* attests the use of thirty lights at the night office. Their arrangement is discussed in a later chapter, as is the disposition of the thirty candles at Farfa.

(F) 27 LIGHTS. Our only evidence for the presence of twenty-seven lights at Tenebrae comes from Ordo 32 (§5). Although

[17]Martène, *DAMR* 3.12.3 p.123.
[18]*Commentarius* p.296.

the information relating to the night office and to the Easter candle is assembled from two different manuscripts, there is nothing to suggest that both do not belong to the same *ordo*. The Cambridge manuscript records the number of lights, whilst the seven sanctuary lamps are mentioned by the Paris manuscript. It is the opinion of Andrieu that the *ordo* originated in Northern France and possibly at Corbie. If, however, thirty-nine lights were used at this monastery, as we have suggested, the Cambridge manuscript may well have had its provenance in a neighbouring church, in view of the discrepancy in the numbers.

The fact that the numbers twenty-seven, thirty, and thirty-nine have no obvious biblical associations may be only one of the reasons why they did not survive in use at Tenebrae in the succeeding centuries. Perhaps a more weighty factor was the influence of the Gallican liturgical commentator Amalarius, the author of *Alcuin,* and later, John of Avranches, for all of whom twenty-four lights was the norm; and this number is known to have been used in the influential churches of Mainz, Rouen, and York in the tenth and eleventh centuries *(Tables 1* and *2).*

(G) 26 LIGHTS. It is not known why twenty-six lights were lit at Amiens, Fontanelles, and possibly Exeter at one time.[19] Since this figure was not suggested by a precedent from Scripture, its existence may be accounted for in one of three ways. (i) In Paris and Reims, there were instances of the use of thirteen candles. If it could be shown that at the three former churches, two candles were extinguished at a time, as at Tongres, then there may possibly have been a connection with the ceremonial of these two churches. On the other hand, two

[19] Heuser p.228; Spicilegium Fontanellense, MS. 394 cited by Dendy (p.146). Feasey (1897) does not give the source for his reference to the twenty-six hearse-candles mentioned at the Synod of Exeter in 1289 (p.394). No figure is given in the Statutes of Exeter, edited by Bradshaw and Wordsworth; but we know from the Ordinal of Exeter that in 1337 twenty-four lights were used in that cathedral (HBS 37 p.132).

separate hearses may once have been used, as we shall show in the next chapter. This number may have resulted from the combination of two hearses into one. (ii) The twenty-sixth candle may originally have been the sacristan's light, which provided illumination for those entering a darkened church and which was subsequently placed on or near a hearse designed to hold twenty-five candles. (iii) It is just possible that the lamp which burned in front of the Sacrament was included in the twenty-six.

Church/Commentator	Date	Source
Amalarius	832	*Lib. Off. 4.22*
PRG	*c.*950	*PRG* II p.56
Rouen	*c.*1050	PL 147.168D
Alcuin	*c.*1000	PL 101.1203B
Lanfranc	*c.*1070	PL 150.458A
John of Avranches	*c.*1070	PL 147.48C
Honorius of Autun	*c.*1140	PL 172.665
Gilbertines	1150 +	HBS 59 p.30
Beleth	*c.*1180	PL 202.105D
Soissons	1180–1190	*DAER* 4.23 p.137
Sicardus	*c.*1200	PL 213.298D
Salisbury	*c.*1210	Ordinal p.66
Nidaros	13 C	*ONE* p.222
Durandus	*c.*1280	*Rationale* VI.72 fol.331
Canterbury	13 C	HBS 28 p.274
Trier	*c.*1300	Ordinary p.486
Exeter	1337	HBS 37 p.132
Senlis	*c.*1390	*DAER* 4.22 p.81
Barking	1404	HBS 65 p.91
Salisbury	1531	Breviary Fasc.1
Rouen	18 C	De Moléon p.206
Orléans	18 C	De Moléon p.206
Premonstratensians	1930	Breviary p.386

Table 1. The Use of Twenty-four Lights at Tenebrae

Church/Commentator	Date	Source
Fruttuaria	*c.*1000	Albers IV p.39
York	*c.*1050	Breviary I p.375
Lanfranc	*c.*1070	PL 150.458A
Gembloux	*c.*1080	Albers II p.90
Norwich	*c.*1265	HBS 82 p.79
Hereford	13 C	HBS 26 p.308
Fleury	13 C	*DAMR* 3.12 p.123
Bec	*c.*1200	*DAMR* 3.12 p.123
Lincoln	*c.*1440	*Statutes* II p.303

Table 2. The Use of Twenty-five Lights at Tenebrae

(H) 24 AND 25 LIGHTS. The use of twenty-five lights at
Tenebrae is a variant or development of the twenty-four lights
prescribed by Amalarius and *PRG*. This is clear from the Breviary of York, which states that twenty-four candles are lit
at Tenebrae with an additional one in the middle (of the
hearse) higher than the rest (p.375). Moreover, the use of
twenty-four or twenty-five candles was not confined exclusively to either the cathedral or monastic tradition *(Tables 1
and 2)*. However, though the two numbers are found in both
traditions, the additional candle almost certainly had its origin in monastic practice. For in the later days of medieval
monasticism, it was the practice at the beginning of the day,
as the bell was tolling, summoning the monks to Matins, for
a junior brother to carry a lantern to show them the way.[20]
Alternatively, the use of twenty-five candles may have been
a survival from the earlier period when the seven lamps were
extinguished during Lauds. The possible substitution of seven
hearse-candles for the seven sanctuary lamps presupposes that
six candles were extinguished during each of the three nocturns of Matins. Although the use of eighteen candles is at-

[20]Crossley p.83.

tested in later practice, there is no evidence for this number in the earlier period.

Another possibility to be considered is that the increase from twenty-four to twenty-five was the result of the symbolic association attached to the latter number. For at Hereford, where the candles were identified with the prophets and the Apostles, the twenty-fifth candle represented Christ, an identification presumably also made at York. This accounted for that candle's elevated position.[21]

At Salisbury and Exeter, the twenty-four candles also symbolised the Old Testament prophets and the Twelve Apostles.[22] The ordinal from Exeter adds that the extinguishing of them signifies the cruelty of the Jews, who persecuted or murdered them. Dendy claims that the number twenty-four was '*generally* taken to stand for the Apostles and the prophets',[23] although only three of our twenty-three sources actually mention this symbolism. However, there is no evidence at all for his assertion that the twenty-four candles could include Christ if Judas was not reckoned in the number. Durandus, regarding the number in a wholly New Testament context, substitutes *apostolic men* for prophets and elaborates the idea by declaring that for twenty-four hours the Apostles and apostolic men serve Christ by day and the Church by night.[24] Durandus also states that the twenty-four candles are extinguished because the Apostles hid for twenty-four hours, and he reiterates the analogy, drawn by Amalarius, that Christ is the Sun who gives light to the world for twenty-four hours. On a different level, Honorius of Autun writes that the candles indicate the number of *Gloria*'s which are omitted during the whole of Tenebrae.[25] This negative kind of symbolism is

[21]HBS 26 p.308.
[22]Ordinal p.146 and HBS 37 p.132.
[23]*The Use of Lights* p.145. (The writer's italics.)
[24]*Rationale* VI.72 fol.331.
[25]*Gemma Animae* (PL 172.665).

echoed by Beleth.[26] He adds that the *Gloria*'s are not said because Christ is lying in the tomb.

(1) 23 LIGHTS. The twenty-three candles lit at Worcester may have been placed on a hearse designed for twenty-four lights.[27] A twenty-fourth candle may have been the light which guided the monks into the cathedral for the night office. If the twenty-three candles did stand for the twelve prophets and the Apostles without Judas, that fact has not been recorded.

Church/Commentator	Date	Source
Corbie	*c.*1100	*DAMR* 3.12 p.122
St-Bénigne, Dijon	11 C	*DAMR* 3.12 p.122
Cluny	11 C	PL 149.657B
Farfa	11 C	PL 150.1197B
St Paul's, Rome	11 C	*DAER* 4.22 p.124
Grandmont	*c.*1100	*DAMR* 3.12 p.122
Beleth	*c.*1180	PL 202.105D
Chalon-sur-Saône	1226 +	*DAER* 4.22 p.81
Durandus	*c.*1280	*Rationale* VI.72 fol.331
Laon	13 C	*DAER* 4.22 p.81
Fleury	13 C	*DAMR* 3.12 p.122
Uzès	14 C	*DAER* 4.22 p.81
St-Vincent, Laon	14 C	*DAMR* 3.12 p.122
St Mary's, York	*c.*1400	HBS 75 p.271
Rome	1568	Breviary I p.445
Camaldoli	1634	Ceremonial p.56
Besançon	1682	Ceremonial p.263
Braga	1724	Breviary p.295
Alès	1758	Breviary p.272
Paris	1778	Breviary *(PV)* p.280
Coutances	1825	Ceremonial p.311
Verdun	1832	Ceremonial p.293

Table 3. The Use of Fifteen Lights at Tenebrae

[26]*Rationale* (PL 202.105D).

(J) 15 LIGHTS. The use of the fifteen-candle hearse mainly in religious houses strongly suggests that this number emerged from a monastic milieu. The earliest evidence for a candelabrum of fifteen lights comes in the eleventh century from the Monastery of St-Bénigne at Dijon, but the use of fifteen candles at Tenebrae is probably much older. The number is attested in the Customary of Cluny, which was compiled by Ulric, who died in 1086. The great emphasis which Cluny placed on the choir office and on elaborate and well-executed liturgical observance created an ambience conducive to changes in ritual. From such a milieu, the fifteen-candle hearse may first have emerged.

The success and rapid spread of Cluny's liturgical influence, as well as her political power, were in part the result of her reforming zeal and in part the result of the number of monasteries which owed allegiance to the mother house.[28] The Monastery at Farfa was influenced by Cluniac ideals during the time of Abbot Hugh (997–1038); and the long-established Benedictine houses, Corbie and Chezal-Benoit in France, Monte Cassino, and St Paul's in Rome, were all affected by Cluniac practice. All adopted the use of fifteen candles at Tenebrae.[29] The Grammontines, with their sixty houses in France, also seem to have been influenced by Cluny in this respect. It would therefore appear that the three French cathedrals of Chalon-sur-Saône, Laon, and Uzès had adopted monastic usage in the Middle Ages *(Table 3)*.

There is some uncertainty as to when the use of fifteen candles first entered the Roman rite. Cluniac influence in this respect during the pontificate of Pope Gregory VII at the end of the eleventh century may be discounted; for we know that in the cathedral of St John Lateran in the middle of the twelfth

[27]Antiphonary p.62.

[28]At the zenith of Cluny's influence in the mid-twelfth century there were 314 dependent houses.

[29]Cluniac reforms were also introduced at Subiaco and at S.Maria on the Aventine.

century only twelve candles were extinguished at Tenebrae.[30]
Medieval Roman breviaries do not specify the number of
candles to be used, possibly because ritual variants existed
within the Roman Church before a semblance of uniformity
was achieved, largely through the labours of the Franciscan
friars. They popularised the ceremonial of the papal court,
which they both admired and adopted as their own rite. Since
Haymo's *Ordo Breviarii* of the mid-thirteenth century does not
prescribe a specific number of candles, it is likely that none
was mentioned in the breviary of Pope Innocent III (1198–
1216), upon which Haymo's service-book was based.[31] The
earliest documentary evidence for the use of fifteen candles
at Rome comes from the definitive *Breviarium Romanum* of
1568, although the practice of lighting that number of candles
at Tenebrae was probably by then well-established.

(κ) 14 LIGHTS. Martène merely mentions that this number was
used, but he gives no details of period or place.[32]

(ʟ) 13 LIGHTS. Evidence for this number comes from Tongres,
Paris, Angers, Seville, and Reims.[33] De Moléon also mentions the use of thirteen candles, but does not identify any
churches.[34] This number almost certainly would have suggested Christ and the Apostles or Mary and the Apostles, as
at Seville. At Tongres, the six altar-candles were included in
the thirteen, no distinction being made, apparently, between
them and the remaining seven within the context of Tenebrae.

(ᴍ) 12 LIGHTS. The testimony of Beleth, Sicardus, and Durandus would suggest that the use of twelve candles at Tenebrae
was more widespread than the three known instances would
lead us to believe. These were at Rome; at Le Mans; and

[30]*OEL* pp.45–46.
[31]Van Dijk II p.41.
[32]*DAER* 4.22.2 p.81.
[33]Ordinary pp.150–51; 1662 Cerem. p.337; 1731 Cerem. p.223; Doblado p.284; Heuser p.228.
[34]*Voyages* p.298.

at St Vedast's Abbey, Arras.[35] How they were arranged is unknown. At Rome in the twelfth century, they burned before the *Image (maior imago)*. The possibility that at Arras there were originally twenty-four candles on two hearses, as at Farfa, and that the one referred to in the ordinal is the survivor that continued to be used at Tenebrae are interesting and likely suggestions, but ones which in our present state of knowledge cannot be substantiated. Beleth states simply that the twelve candles symbolise the Twelve Apostles,[36] whilst Sicardus likens the extinguishing of the twelve candles to the scattering of the Apostles,[37] as opposed to Durandus, who refers to the Apostles' loss of faith.[38] St Bruno of Segni's mention of the Twelve Apostles, 'by whose teaching the darkness has been dispelled' and of the twelve candles which represent them may be a reference to Tenebrae in the eleventh century.[39] The context is certainly in favour of this.

(N) 11 LIGHTS. The only known instance of this number occurs at St James' Monastery in Liège.[40] Here, the extinguishing of the candles would seem to have symbolised the desertion of the Apostles after the arrest of Jesus in Gethsemane.

(O) 9 LIGHTS. The lighting of nine candles for Tenebrae is attested only at Nevers,[41] although its mention by Beleth may well suggest that this number was used in other churches as well.[42] According to him, the number nine symbolised the human race cut off by sin from the nine orders of angels and excluded from the true light. One candle may have been put out at the conclusion of each nocturn and six during Lauds.

---

[35]*OEL* p.48; Heuser p.228; HBS 86 p.156.
[36]*Rationale* (PL 202.106A).
[37]*Mitrale* (PL 213.298D).
[38]*Rationale* VI.72 fol.331.
[39]Quorum doctrina fugatae sunt tenebrae (PL 165.1100B).
[40]Ordinary p.20.
[41]Heuser p.228.
[42]*Rationale* (PL 202.106A).

(P) 7 LIGHTS. The use of seven lights at Tenebrae is attested by Beleth, who compares the putting out of the lights to the gifts of the Spirit, which were almost extinguished in the hearts of the disciples, and by Martène.[43] Both writers may well be referring to churches which had either used seven sanctuary lamps at Tenebrae in addition to other lights or continued to do so. Presumably all seven lights were extinguished during Lauds, as in the Carmelite rite.

(Q) 5 LIGHTS. In the Carmelite rite until 1955, five candles were lit at the beginning of the night office. This practice had remained unchanged since the fourteenth century.[44] In some churches the number of candles to be lit was not specified.[45] Rupert of Deutz, writing *c.*1111, refers to '*numerosa luminaria*' at the start of the night office. These, he declares, are the saints who foretold the coming of Christ and who were murdered.[46] Beleth and Durandus both mention that in some places there was no fixed number.[47] This, says Beleth, allows any man or woman to make an offering of a candle to be lit at Tenebrae. These candles are the prophets and the saints.

It would seem that from the establishment of their order, the Cistercians neither used a hearse at Tenebrae nor extinguished the lights one by one. Instead, a single lighted candle was placed on the first step of the choir. This was in keeping with their strict form of monasticism and the austere character of their liturgy. The lighting of the single candle recalls the period when only one lamp was lit for reading at the night office of Holy Saturday.

[43]*Rationale* (PL 202.106A); *DAER* 4.22.2 p.81.
[44]Ordinary p.162.
[45]The 1492 Ordinary of Liège refers to *plures* (np).
[46]*De Div.Off.* V (PL 170.148C).
[47]*Rationale* (PL 202.106D) and *Rationale* VI.72 fol.331.

Chapter Six
THE TENEBRAE HEARSE

(i) The Origin of the Hearse

The evidence for the earliest form of hearse is monastic. In the eleventh century at Fruttuaria and Gembloux, we find that twenty-five candles were placed on a wooden stand *(lignum)* behind the altar,[1] whilst at Cluniac Farfa and St Paul's Monastery in Rome fifteen candles were lit *in instrumento lignorum* and placed in front of the altar.[2] It is not incorrect to translate both *lignum* and *instrumentum lignorum* as 'wooden stand', as Dendy does (p.146); but it is unwise to overlook the possibility that the two terms refer to stands of differing construction. The singularity of *lignum* and the plurality of *lignorum* do suggest that a difference existed. Moreover, it is wrong to suppose that continental monastic practice was everywhere uniform and to ignore variations in three important aspects of the hearse, namely, the type or shape of the device, its position, and the number of candles it held. Let us consider whether any differences can be detected in the two above-mentioned terms.

(A) *LIGNUM.* The singular form of the word may provide some clue about the design of the device. The Customary of Sigibert

---

[1] Albers IV p.49 and II p.90.
[2] Albers I p.46 and Martène, *DAER* 4.22.8 p.124.

informs us that the *lignum* was especially made for use at Tenebrae.[3] Whilst more than one piece of timber may have been used as supporting members in its construction, the section that held the candles was probably one length of wood and almost certainly horizontal. Contemporary evidence from York seems to confirm this supposition.[4] For we read that the middle candle of the twenty-five lit for Tenebrae stood higher than the others. This suggests that the bases of all the candles, including the central one, rested on the same level. If we accept that the candles were displayed in a line along a length of wood, it would give further credence to our theory that the *lignum* was a development of the choir beam (or beams) on which the lights had once been placed (Chapter 4, *Scheme 2*). At Fruttuaria and Gembloux, the *lignum* was placed behind the altar. If the altar stood next to the east wall, the device must have rested on a retable and of necessity must have been elongated *(Fig. 1).*[5]

(B) *INSTRUMENTUM LIGNORUM.* It must be admitted that this phrase could equally refer to the wooden device for holding twenty-four or twenty-five candles, which we discussed in the previous section, if the use of the plural noun *lignorum* denotes both the supporting timbers and the horizontal length of wood that held the candles. If, however, the meaning of *lignum* is restricted to the one plank or length of timber on which the candles rested, it would follow that the occurrence of the noun in the plural number denoted two or more such lengths of wood. The twenty-four candles may have been mounted on three, or even four, separate and parallel lengths of wood on

[3]Albers II p.90.
[4]Breviary I p.375.
[5]Altars began to be placed against the east wall of the church from the sixth century onwards (Klauser p.100). Even if the altar had stood forward of the east wall at Fruttuaria and Gembloux, the candelabrum used at Tenebrae would almost certainly have comprised a single length of timber *(Fig. 1).* Twenty-four candles behind the altar, arranged in three parallel rows, seems less likely *(Fig. 2).*

the same plane *(Fig. 2)* or constructed in tiers *(Fig. 3)*, as in contemporary frames for votive lights, with a twenty-fifth candle somehow incorporated into the arrangement.[6] The device's three-dimensional shape, as it were, would have required it to be placed in front of or to one side of the altar. Regrettably for our enquiry, the existence of these twenty-four-light candelabra, though likely, must remain suppositional since the two recorded instances of *instrumentum lignorum* attest the use of fifteen candles.

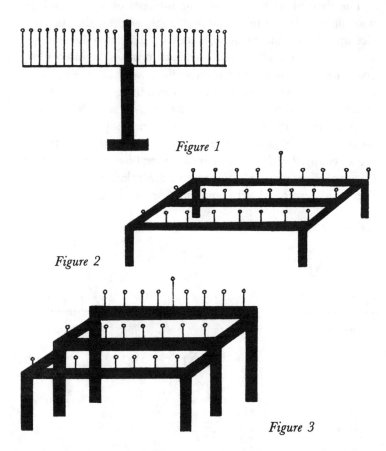

Figure 1

Figure 2

Figure 3

[6]If a quarter of the lights were extinguished during Lauds, a fourth bar for holding these candles may have been used.

(ii) The Development of the Hearse

It is fortunate that there has survived from the lost Customary of St-Bénigne, Dijon, which was compiled in the eleventh century, a reference not only to a fifteen-light Tenebrae candelabrum but also to its shape and appearance :

> Fifteen candles are lit before the sacred altar, arranged in the manner of a pyramid.[7]

The date of its attestation, the number of lights, and its position in relation to the altar strongly suggest that the device upon which these candles were placed merited the description of *instrumentum lignorum*. This in turn raises the interesting possibility that the candelabra at Farfa and at St Paul's in Rome, which we discussed in the previous section, were also triangular in shape. Exactly what is meant by *in modum Pyramidis* is not immediately clear; Martène does not elaborate the phrase from the passage he has quoted. Given that the frame was of triangular shape, the candles must have been displayed in one of three ways in order to give the onlooker the impression of a pyramidal arrangement *(Figs. 4, 5,* and *6)*.

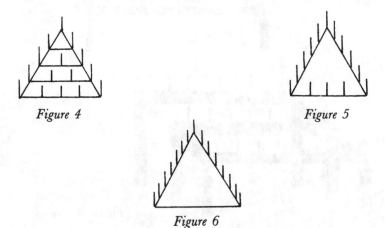

Figure 4   Figure 5

Figure 6

[7]XV candelae in modum Pyramidis ante sanctum altare accenduntur. Martène, *DAMR* 3.12.2 p.122 (M 1150).

Though the candles in all three figures could be said to be disposed in the form of a pyramid, one could claim with confidence that the successive decrease in the number of candles in an upward direction, as exemplified in *Figure 4,* corresponds more closely to the usual interpretation of the phrase *in modum Pyramidis,* if one were to observe the candles by standing immediately in front of the candelabrum. However, practical problems arise in the use of a two-dimensional candelabrum of triangular construction. In the arrangement depicted in *Figure 4,* where six internal candles are mounted on the three lower cross-bars, there is a danger that the flames of these candles will set alight the cross-bars immediately above them unless the frame is large enough to provide sufficient clearance between the flame and the underside of the cross-bar or unless the horizontal sections are made of metal. The practicability of the latter, however, is doubtful; cross-bars made of metal make unsuitable supports for candles if they are subjected to the heat from the naked flame below. We have no indication of the size of these candelabra in the eleventh century, but we have noted that the frames were made of wood. However, if the candles were mounted on a three-dimensional frame *(Fig. 7)* or on a triangular-shaped device studded with nails to hold the candles and sloping in a backward direction *(Fig. 8),* then not only does the problem of frame-damage by the candles disappear, but the very structure of the candelabrum takes on more the shape and appearance of a pyramid.

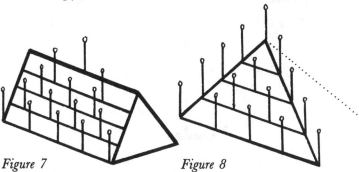

Figure 7   *Figure 8*

The arrangement of lights, as shown in *Figure 6,* is illustrated on page 265 of the first edition, in 1600, of the *Caeremoniale Episcoporum,* which contains the official instructions for the procedure at Tenebrae according to the Roman rite. We believe that this disposition of lights represents both a development and a simplification of the hearse which was used at Dijon in the eleventh century, so modified that the device of three dimensions has been reduced to two and the candles have been placed on the two angled sides because a display, as shown in the hypothetical *Figure 5,* would almost certainly have caused damage to both frame and candles, as we have already suggested. The mounting of the candles on the outside edges of the frame *(Fig. 6)* was obviously done for reasons of safety and for ease in arranging the candles. For if iron spikes, rather than cups or candle-sockets, were used to affix the candles to the frame, a straight vertical nail on the outside edge of the hearse would provide a simpler candle-spike than a nail protruding horizontally from the face of the hearse to clear the frame and then bending upwards like a right-angled cup-hook to hold the candle.

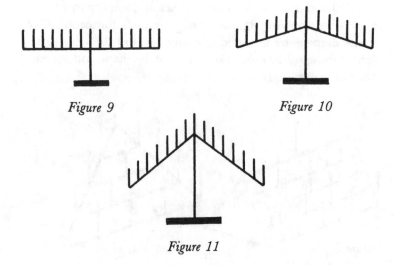

Figure 9   Figure 10

Figure 11

It is not known when the triangular hearse was first used in the Roman rite. We stated earlier that there was some uncertainty about the introduction of the fifteen-candle hearse into Rome. Little can be added to that statement other than that its use may have entered the papal ceremonial either through the influence or because of the proximity of St Paul's Monastery in Rome.

We have so far argued in favour of the development of the triangular hearse from the pyramidal device as typified by that used at Dijon. Two other possibilities, however, remain to be considered, though it must be added that the lack of corroborative evidence prevents us from drawing firm conclusions about either. (i) In view of the limited nature of the evidence upon which we have based our theory, the converse of our supposition may equally be true, namely, that the pyramid-shaped candelabrum, such as that at Dijon, is an elaboration of the two-dimensional triangle; and, therefore, it could be argued that the pyramidal device did not survive partly because its construction required additional effort and workmanship and partly because the sombre aspect of Tenebrae discouraged liturgical extravagance. Alternatively, both types of hearse may have evolved in semi-isolated liturgical milieux from a common ancestor. *Figures 9* to *11* illustrate how the development of the triangular or pyramidal candelabrum from the horizontal hearse may have been induced by the superior elevation of the central candle. (ii) It is just possible that the great seven-branched candlesticks which were popular in the cathedrals of Europe during the Middle Ages[8] may have provided inspiration for the shape of the much smaller Tenebrae hearse on account of their quasi-triangular display of lights.

(iii) The Hearse of Twenty-four Lights

The use of the twenty-four-light hearse at Tenebrae derives from the liturgical tradition known to and recorded by

[8]Zarnecki p.134.

Amalarius. We have already noted that the hearse of twenty-five candles was a simple variation of the other candelabrum with an additional candle included for practical or symbolic reasons. We have already suggested that they were displayed in linear formation and stood on one frame; but in some churches, they may have stood in individual candlesticks or have been set upon a circular candelabrum of the kind similar to the two candelabra in Great Budworth Church in Cheshire. Grancolas refers to the great candlestick with many branches, which stood near the altar in some churches, and associates its use with the extinguishing of lights at Tenebrae.[9] Artistically-wrought metal candelabra were to be found in the cathedrals and more prosperous monasteries; and the evidence suggests that they were usually seven-branched, like the *menorah*.[10] However, there is no reason to believe that these ornate artefacts were designed to hold as many as twenty-four candles, though their position to the right of the altar (as you face it) may have influenced the siting of the twenty-four-light hearse; and at Tongres, the wooden hearse was even superimposed upon a bronze candelabrum.[11] The possibility should also be considered that twenty-five candles were mounted upon a triangular candelabrum in the same way as fifteen : one at the apex and twelve down either side. Such a frame would have been considerably larger than its fifteen-light counterpart. With twenty-four lights, however, there would have been problems of presentation. Either there would have been two candles at the apex, or there would have been an asymmetrical display. Neither arrangement would have been visually satisfactory. Nevertheless, according to the Gilbertine Ordinal the last of the twenty-four candles, which was to be no larger than the rest, was placed 'at the top'.[12]

However, there are two reasons for believing that the twenty-four candles may not always have been displayed in

[9]*Commentarius* p.296.
[10]Zarnecki pp.134–35.
[11]Ordinary p.151.
[12]HBS 59 p.31.

this way. (i) We previously saw that at an earlier period, it was important for the number of lights to be extinguished to be divisible by three; and we also observed that at Poitiers these lights were arranged in three rows. The suggestion is worthy of consideration that when the Tenebrae lights became confined to the sanctuary, the triple line of lamps that formerly hung in the nave was retained in the form of a frame, similar to those depicted in *Figures 1* and *2*, which stood in front of or to one side of the altar. If such a frame was used, it is more likely to have been of the type shown in *Figure 3* since this device provides a better view of all the candles, especially if it stands on the dais for the altar. The variation from church to church in the number of candles used meant that the three rows might each contain eight, nine, thirteen, or as many as twenty-four lights. In churches where the full complement of lights was extinguished during Lauds as well as Matins, the division of candles into three groups ceased to have relevance.

(ii) According to the thirteenth-century Customary of Fleury, the candles were arranged *super pronas*. The phrase is otherwise unknown. One possible interpretation involves regarding *pronas* as the accusative case of the otherwise-unrecorded noun *pronae,* formed from the adjective *pronus -a -um,* 'inclined' or 'leaning forwards', and used as the technical term for the banks or tiers of candles on a frame such as that illustrated in *Figure 3*. For in a way, the candles do incline and lean forward away from the altar. The existence of a stepped frame of this type could easily have suggested the idea for the pyramid at Dijon; and if so, a frame of this construction would antedate the pyramidal device. For the use of twenty-four lights at Tenebrae is anterior to that of fifteen by a century and a half.[13] It would, therefore, be not unreasonable to conclude that the *pronae* at Fleury was similar in shape and appearance to the pyramid used at Dijon.

[13]Amalarius (832) : 24; Farfa (*c.*1000) and Cluny (11th C) : 15.

(iv) The Origin of the Fifteen-candle Hearse

There is no clear evidence that allows us to explain why the fifteen-candle hearse emerged in the tenth century from a monastic milieu at a time when the use of twenty-four lights was recommended by the influential *Liber Officialis* of Amalarius and prescribed by the *Pontificale Romano-Germanicum*, a pontifical used widely in Gaul and Germany. A clue to its possible origin is to be found in the eleventh-century Customary of Farfa, which gives these directives :

> On Maundy Thursday before Matins let thirty candles be lit in front of the high altar, one for each of the psalms to be said—fifteen on a wooden frame. There being thirty psalms to say, let fifteen be said in silence after the three prayers and before the start of Matins. Let the sacristan make an audible signal in the usual way after each psalm is said. When all fifteen have been said, let the priest who is on duty for the week begin the antiphon *The zeal for your house*. Let a candle be immediately extinguished on one side, and a second (at the beginning of the next antiphon) on the other side, and so on alternately at the beginning of all the psalms.[14]

At the beginning of Psalm 148 all the candles have been extinguished except one. When the antiphon of the *Benedictus*, the *Traditor autem*, begins, the last candle is put out.

These rubrics from the above-mentioned customary may be summarised as follows :

1. Thirty candles are lit, and fifteen are placed on a wooden stand in front of the altar.

---

[14]Coena domini quinta feria, ante Nocturnos quindecim in instrumento lignorum, ante maius altare XXX sint accensae candelae quot psalmi sund *(sic)* imponendi. Et remanentibus triginta psalmis, ante nocturnas dicatur quindecim sub silentio post ternas orationes facta. Signa sonet secretarius sicut solitus est. Quibus dictis sonantibus signis, postquam dismissis fuerint aebdomadarius incipiat antiphonam Zelus domus tuae. Et statim extinguatur una candela huic, alia inde, sicque fit omnibus psalmis incipientibus. (Albers I p.46.)

2. Thirty psalms are said, fifteen silently, fifteen aloud.

3. A candle is extinguished before each of the psalms of Matins.

4. At the beginning of the twenty-ninth psalm, twenty-nine candles have been put out.

5. After the *Traditor autem* has been sung for the first time, there is darkness in the church.

The rubrics also tell us that the sacristan, who presumably calculated the length of time sufficient for the silent repetition of each psalm, informed the monks, by means of a noise at the conclusion of each period, that they should commence the next psalm.[15] The sacristan, however, did not indicate which that psalm was. The fifteen psalms said silently after the triple prayer were the *gradual* psalms, which formed an introductory period of meditation between the entry of the monks into church and the start of Matins.[16] The above-quoted extract from the Customary of Farfa leaves us with the impression that the candles began to be extinguished only when the second group of fifteen psalms, that is, the nine set for Matins and the six, including the Old Testament canticle, set for Lauds, began to be sung. Yet at the *Benedictus*, all thirty lights had been extinguished; and as only one candle was put

[15]*Quibus dictis sonantibus signis.* The somewhat ambiguous Latin indicates that a single noise was made at the end of each psalm, rather than several repeated sounds at the conclusion of all fifteen psalms. The nature of the noise is not specified. Martène records an alternative method of regulating the silent repetition of the gradual psalms. According to the lost Customary of St-Bénigne, Dijon, after the saying of the triple prayer, the fifteen gradual psalms were said in silence; and as each monk finished his psalm, he leaned forward across his stall. When all the monks had assumed this position, it was time to proceed with the next psalm. (*DAMR* 3.12.2 p.122.)

[16]*Graduales psalmi* or *cantica graduum* (Psalms 119–133 [120–134]). They are mentioned in Lanfranc's *Decrees;* an *ordo* of Corbie; the Use of Bec; the Customaries of Cluny, St-Bénigne, Fleury, St-Denis, Laon, St-Germain-des-Prés, Lyre; and the *Compendienses* (Martène, *DAMR* 3.12.2 p.122); and also in the *Ordinal of St Mary's, York* (HBS 75 p.271).

out at the beginning of each psalm, the other fifteen in the
first group must have been extinguished at some point between the beginning and the end of the gradual psalms. However, there is no indication from the text as to when this
occurred.

Writing nearly a hundred years ago, Hartmann Grisar, followed by other commentators, suggested that the extinguishing
of the lights at Tenebrae was a way of keeping track of the
number of psalms which had been sung.[17] Ludwig Eisenhöfer
drew attention to the practice in the Circus Maximus of indicating to the spectators the number of laps which had been
completed by the chariots.[18] Later research has shown that
the method of counting the number of laps in that stadium
approximated more closely than Eisenhöfer realised to the way
the progression of psalms was noted at Farfa and almost certainly in other monasteries.[19] Whilst this method of counting
at Farfa was obviously not borrowed directly from the Circus Maximus, the notion of using a decreasing number of markers for reckoning seems to have survived from the ancient
world into the Middle Ages. We therefore believe that the
gradual extinguishing of lights as a way of counting psalms
was used, not at Matins and Lauds, as Grisar and others believed, but during the silent repetition of the gradual psalms.
For, whereas at Matins the antiphons, lections, and divisions
into nocturns marked the progress of the night office and the
various stages which had been reached, in the period of silence before the service there was nothing to indicate which
psalm was intended to be repeated during a given period of
silence, in the event of a lapse in concentration on the part
of a monk through tiredness or inattentiveness; for the sound

[17]Bugnini and Braga p.123.

[18]'Wie man bei den Zirkusrennen, um dem Volke die Zahl der Um-
läufe der Wagen anzuzeigen, grosse hölzerne Eier an der Spitze der Spina
nach jedem Umlauf aufstellte.' (Handbuch I p.514.)

[19]At one end of the central spine or barrier were seven marble eggs, at
the other a line of dolphins. At the end of each lap or half-lap an egg or
a dolphin was removed. (Mannix p.12.)

produced by the sacristan merely marked the conclusion of such a period. The number of candles that remained burning, therefore, would indicate at a glance the correct psalm to be said at that time. The gradual loss of light during this period of preparation adequately accounts for the extinguishing of the first group of candles prior to the start of Matins.

Additional support for our argument can be gleaned from a closer examination of that part of the text which states that fifteen candles were placed 'upon a wooden stand' *(in instrumento lignorum),* and that thirty were lit before the high altar. A superficial reading gives us the impression that the candles on the wooden stand were intended for Tenebrae and that the rest were placed somehow in front of the altar, possibly in separate candleholders. On the other hand, if our theory, that the first group of candles were extinguished one by one as each of the gradual psalms was said, is correct, it would have been necessary for the candles to have been arranged in such a way as to indicate to the monks at a glance which psalm they should have been repeating. It is obvious that the candles would not have been scattered at random in front of the altar, and one might reasonably suppose that the *instrumentum lignorum* was used for this purpose. However, we have the impression that this device held the Tenebrae-candles. If, on the other hand, the wooden stand was used during the saying of the gradual psalms, we must ask how the candles extinguished at Tenebrae were then arranged. Crucial to the solution of this difficulty is the correct interpretation of *in instrumento lignorum.* If the phrase is translated 'on *the* wooden stand', it follows that only one stand was used and that the other candles were arranged in an unknown way on freestanding candlesticks. However, if the phrase means 'on *a* wooden stand', the entire sentence becomes capable of quite a different interpretation. For, bearing in mind the fact that the Latin of the whole passage is at times both grammatically and orthographically incorrect, it is possible that 'fifteen candles are lit on a wooden stand' should be interpreted 'a wooden stand is used for lighting groups of fifteen candles' or, expressing it another way, 'fifteen candles are lit on each wooden stand'. It would then be reasonable to assume, in view of the uncertainty regarding the exact function of the wooden stand, that two wooden stands were used, one for the gradual psalms and one for the psalms of the night office.[20]

It is our belief that at the beginning of the monastic day at Farfa, two candelabra, each of fifteen lights, stood in front of the altar. That to the right of the altar may have held the candles extinguished during Matins and Lauds.[21] The desirability of positioning the lights in a convenient and visible place for the purpose of keeping a tally of the number of psalms said silently must have been an important factor in locating the candelabrum near to the altar. For not all of the church lights may have been in full view of those in the choir-stalls if those lights had been used for that purpose; and the necessity of an upward glance, in the event of the use of lights displayed on choir-beams, was likely to have caused inconvenient distraction. In the interest of a symmetrical display of light, both candelabra are likely to have been identical. Since one of these served to indicate what stage the silent repetition of the gradual psalms had reached, an arrowhead or pyramidal-shaped stand had obvious advantages over a frame on which the lights were arranged horizontally in a row.

* * * * *

In the following chapter we will show that in the period before 1000, the candles were extinguished at Matins in con-

[20]It is not for us to suggest how the compiler of the customary should have expressed with greater clarity the existence and use of two stands. For the passage contains a number of linguistic errors, so that a careless turn of phrase should not come as a surprise to us. Nor can we be sure that the writer would have used either the phrase *in utroque instrumento* or *in quoque instrumento,* either of which we maintain in what the context demands. *XXX candelae in duobus instrumentis* could imply uneven distribution; *XXX candelae in instrumentis lignorum* might suggest more than two stands.

[21]This may partly explain why in subsequent centuries the Tenebrae-hearse was often located on the Epistle side of the altar.

sonance with the singing of the psalms and the reading of the lessons. The greater the number of lights extinguished, the greater was the scope for elaboration of ceremonial. It is, therefore, somewhat surprising to find that in the ritual of Cluny, with its emphasis on ceremonial splendour, there was a certain austerity in the number and use of lights at Tenebrae. If, however, we accept that at Cluny, where we believe the fifteen-candle hearse originated, thirty lights were formerly used at Matins, as indeed they were at Farfa and Poitiers, it is not difficult to see how, in view of the recognised centrality of the psalms at the night office and also the importance of the gradual psalms, one light may have come to symbolise and be assigned to each psalm. With the convenient coincidence of fifteen gradual and fifteen Tenebrae psalms, it is likely that the thirty lights were divided into two equal groups and placed on two separate candelabra. These would almost certainly be identical since liturgy generally favours a symmetrical arrangement.

A number of reasons may be advanced to explain why the arrangement we have suggested is not attested either in other rites or in subsequent centuries. (i) Not all monasteries employed this method of counting the gradual psalms, and perhaps some that did found it distracting. (ii) The extinguishing of the two groups of candles in close succession would tend to make some attribute the same importance to the gradual psalms as that which the office psalms held. Within the liturgical context in question, both groups of lights served different functions and clearly were of unequal status. (iii) The repetition of the ritual act of extinguishing fifteen lights would inevitably detract from the significance of that act during Tenebrae. (iv) There is no evidence to show that the gradual psalms were said prior to the start of Matins in the cathedral tradition or in a number of other religious rites in which Tenebrae was observed as an anticipated office. In these circumstances, the use of two hearses would have fallen into desuetude once the gradual psalms ceased to be said, the candelabrum used at Tenebrae alone surviving.

(v) The Significance of Fifteen Candles

In more recent times, the fifteen candles have been understood to represent the wisdom of the centuries, which was lost
progressively from the time of Moses onwards.[22] In the Middle
Ages, they symbolised the Twelve Apostles and the three
Mary's.[23] Durandus adds that the extinguishing of the lights
symbolises the flight of the Apostles and the fear of the
Mary's.[24] The same writer gives an alternative explanation
according to which fourteen of the candles signify the fourteen articles of faith, which were extinguished by the flight
of the Apostles, and the fifteenth stands for the death of Christ.
The *Ordinal of St Mary's, York,* whilst identifying twelve of the
candles with the Apostles, equates the remaining three with
the Law, the Prophets, and Christ.[25]

It is somewhat strange that Sicardus, on whom Durandus
draws for much of his information and who records the use
of seventy-two, twenty-four, and twelve lights at Tenebrae,
does not mention the use of fifteen when, at the time at which
he is writing (*c.*1200), this number is well established. Beleth,
writing some years before, knows of it. Discounting the unlikely possibility that Sicardus omits any reference to it because of personal disapproval, one can only guess either that
he is interested in Tenebrae primarily according to the cathedral tradition (fifteen at this time being mainly a monastic number), or that the omission is an error on the part of
a copyist.

[22]Heuser p.227.
[23]Beleth, *Rationale* (PL 202.106A). It could be argued that this forced
symbolism is further evidence of the late and almost fortuitous origin of
the fifteen-candle hearse.
[24]*Rationale* VI.72 fol.331.
[25]HBS 75 p.271.

(vi) The Position of the Hearse

(A) TO THE RIGHT OF THE ALTAR.[26] According to the Roman rite, the hearse was supposed to stand to the south of the altar, on the Epistle side. This is the position prescribed by the *Caeremoniale Episcoporum* of 1600;[27] and the various editions of Fortescue and O'Connell contain this regulation.[28] It is claimed that the hearse stood to the south of the altar in imitation of the *menorah* in the Temple at Jerusalem.[29] However, the analogy was not strictly accurate in that the *menorah* stood in the south-west corner of the *hekal,* rather than to the south of the altar. Surprisingly, there is no firm evidence before the end of the sixteenth century for the placing of the hearse in this position; but it is difficult to believe that on the publication of the *Breviarium Romanum* in 1568, the south position was a recent innovation. It may have been placed there for centuries in some churches. However, with the doubtful exception of St Vedast's Abbey at Arras and the ambiguous testimony from St Mary's, York, all the surviving evidence refers to the position of the hearse behind, on top of, or in front of the altar; and all three positions occur in France up to the eve of the Revolution.

The *Ordinal of St Vedast's Abbey* gives the following directions :

> After Compline the veil which is (hung) between the two altars is raised, and a hearse with twelve candles is put in position.[30]

[26]From the point of view of the congregation.

[27]Page 264. However, the line-drawing on the opposite page of this book shows the hearse on top of the altar apparently in a central position. It is just possible that because of the perspective the hearse only appears to be perfectly central, but is actually to the right of the centre.

[28]For example, 4th edition (1932) p.303, and 11th edition (1960) p.281. The 1682 Ceremonial of Besançon places it at the Epistle side (p.263).

[29]Heuser p.229. He does not enlarge upon the analogy.

[30]Post completorium velum tollitur quod est inter duo altaria et hercia ponitur cum duodecim candelis. (HBS 86 p.156.)

It is not clear whether this veil served the same purpose as that at St. Mary's, York; or whether it separated the altars from the rest of the building, as was the custom in medieval churches in Lent. Since both altars were exposed to view for the performance of the office, it seems reasonable to suppose from the limited information available to us that the rubric prescribes that the hearse should stand either close to one altar or between the two altars.

The *Ordinal of St Mary's, York,* states that the hearse is placed *coram altari.*[31] It is true that the English translation 'in the presence of' could be understood to mean *in the vicinity of,* and therefore it would be possible to argue in favour of a position to the right of the altar. On the other hand, this interpretation is perhaps forced; and a more likely rendering of *coram* would be 'in front of', which conveys the usual meaning of the phrase 'face to face'.

(B) TO THE REAR OF THE ALTAR. The wooden stand *(lignum)* for the twenty-five candles at Fruttuaria and Gembloux was placed behind the altar. Credence is given to our theory that the hearse at these two monasteries was a wooden bar with one row of candles when it is realised that from about the year 1000 it became the general rule for the altar to be placed against the east wall of the church so that the priest, with his back to the congregation, could celebrate Mass facing the east.[32] Any device placed on the gradine or retable would of necessity have been elongated in design because of the restricted space. The placing of the candles behind the altar is first firmly attested by John of Avranches;[33] and the placing of them in this position survived in parts of France until the Revolution, as is evidenced by the 1778 Breviary of Paris, which allows the choice of placing the hearse in front of or to the rear of the altar.[34] The presence of candles on a gra-

[31]HBS 75 p.271.
[32]Klauser pp.100-01.
[33]*Lib.de Off.Eccl.* 52 (PL 147.48C).
[34]*Pars Verna* p.280.

dine behind the altar or on the altar itself virtually precludes the use or even the presence of the six altar-candles. Even when the hearse stood before the altar, the six altar-candles, if indeed set out, were not lit. For in the two Parisian breviaries of 1763 and 1778 and in the Romanised manual for the Royal Chapel in Paris, the altar-candles are not mentioned.

(c) UPON THE ALTAR. Evidence for the placing of the hearse upon the altar is slender and vague. The above-mentioned illustration on page 265 of the *Caeremoniale Episcoporum* would suggest that in spite of the directive on page 264 to place the hearse on the Epistle side, the practice of setting it upon the altar was not unknown. Also, the statement by Grancolas that hearses were still placed *super altaria* in some churches shows that the practice survived into the first half of the eighteenth century.[35]

(d) IN FRONT OF THE ALTAR. The earliest recorded instance of the placing of the Tenebrae-candles in front of the altar occurs in the eleventh-century *Acta* of the Cathedral Church of Rouen.[36] The frontal position also featured in the monasteries at Dijon and Farfa in the eleventh century; in Soissons Cathedral and probably at St Mary's, York, in the twelfth century; and in the Gilbertine rite.[37] Sieur de Moléon, writing at the beginning of the eighteenth century, specifically mentions the hearse at Rouen Cathedral, as though its position in front of the altar was unusual.[38] On the other hand, he may be simply stating a fact about the ritual of the cathedral; for Grancolas, writing several years later, observes that the placing of the triangular candelabrum in front of the altar was contemporary practice.[39] Earlier, De Grassis refers

[35]*Commentarius* p.296.

[36]PL 147.168C.

[37]Martène, *DAMR* 3.12.2 p.122 and Albers I p.46; Martène, *DAER* 4.23 p.137 and HBS 75 p.271; HBS 59 p.30.

[38]*Voyages* p.298.

[39]It stood in this position at Trier (Ordinary p.486), at Auxerre (1736 Breviary p.243), and at Alès (1758 Breviary p.272).

to this central position;[40] but Bisso, writing a hundred years later, states that the hearse should not stand in front of the altar.[41] The choice of positions allowed at Paris suggests that local usage in this respect probably survived in other French dioceses which retained their traditional Gallican ritual.

(vii) The Construction of the Hearse

No Tenebrae hearse in England is known to have survived from the Middle Ages. Most of those used in parish churches would have been constructed of timber to a simple design, as in more recent times.[42] Even without the iconoclasm of the Reformation, the vast majority of these wooden candelabra would not have survived.[43] Those made for the cathedrals and more opulent monastic houses would have been of a more intricate and elaborate design and very likely fashioned of metal. Those in England in more recent times were usually made of wood; and whilst the detail and ornamentation varied, the basic shape remained a triangular frame of timber supported on a tall staff and having fifteen spikes or sockets for the candles, as was officially prescribed.[44] A triangular hearse is also attested at Auxerre and in a Capuchin ceremonial.[45] Commenting on the shape, Colti observes that the hearse symbolised the Trinity and the single foot, upon which it rested, expressed the unity of God.[46] The reference by Dendy to the hearse at Stanford-in-the-Vale, which was sus-

[40]*De Ceremoniis* II fol.123.

[41]*Hierurgia* I p.148.

[42]The writer is indebted to Mr D.Searle of Trowbridge for the description of the wooden hearse with its metal candle-holders and drip-pans, which was made by his father for use in his parish church in the early years of the present century.

[43]For the destruction of church furniture following the Reformation, see Peacock pp.106, 163, 164.

[44]Fortescue and O'Connell, (11th edition) p.281 note 3.

[45]1736 Breviary p.243 and 1775 Ceremonial p.93.

[46]*Dictionarium* II p.97.

pended by means of a rope, is surely inapposite.[47] It is much more likely that it is the funeral hearse (the wooden or iron frame holding the tapers that was placed on a coffin in church) which is here intended and which, like the font covers in some churches, could be raised by means of a rope attached to a pulley in the roof. Moreover, the movement and sway of a Tenebrae-hearse suspended by a rope not only might have proved an unwanted distraction for worshippers at this solemn service but might have made difficult the extinguishing of the candles, an action which required careful synchronisation.

The hearse at the Birmingham Oratory is heavily baroque and ornately carved with emblems of the Oratory. Perhaps the most elegantly-designed hearse in England is that at Downside Abbey. It is fashioned of wrought iron and stands about nine feet on a tripod base. It has a profusion of leafy and grape-like ornamentation around the central shaft to which seven pairs of corresponding candle-holders are linked by curved strips of iron, reminiscent in a way of the threads in a spider's web. From the outstretched arms, the nails of the Crucifixion are suspended by chains on the left and a crown of thorns in iron on the right. 'Its fine and yet sombre design is most appropriate to the occasions on which it is used. It is large and well proportioned to the height of the Abbey Church.'[48] At Seville, a brass candlestick, fifteen to twenty feet high, stood between the altar and the choir. Triangular in shape, it had twelve candle-sockets, six on either arm of the candelabrum, next to each of which was a figurine of an Apostle. The Virgin Mary was represented at its apex, adjoining the holder for the thirteenth candle.[49] The use of ornately-executed candelabra is also attested by Bauldry in the eighteenth century.[50]

In some monasteries in the Middle Ages, the hearse acquired embellishment. It may have been in imitation of the

[47]*Antiquary* XVII (1888) p.119, cited in *The Use of Lights* p.146.
[48]James, *The Story of Downside Abbey Church* p.71.
[49]Doblado p.284.
[50]*Manuale* p.167.

drapery which surrounded the *chapelle ardente,* or candle-bearing funeral hearse, that tapestries or embroidered cloths covered the lower part of the candelabrum at St Mary's, York, and at Worcester;[51] or it may have been done to match the altar-frontal, especially if the hearse stood in front of the altar. Whatever the reason for its presence elsewhere, at St Mary's, York, this cloth was used as a screen to hide from view the acolyte or sacristan, whose duty it was to extinguish the candles.

At Tongres, seven candles were affixed to the top of a spear.[52] This may have been the same device that held the triple candle; for this shaft with its three lights was at times known as a hearse.

(viii) The Name *Hearse*[53]

Further support for our theory that the Tenebrae-candles were at one time arranged on wooden frames similar to those depicted in *Figures 1, 2,* and *3* comes from the traditional name for the candelabrum, *hearse,* a word derived, like the French *herse,* from the late Latin *hercia,* which itself is a corruption of the classical Latin *(h)irpex, (h)irpicis,* meaning 'large rake' or 'harrow'.[54] In addition to the occurrences at Exeter and Canterbury, the word is also found in the *Ordinal of St Vedast's Abbey c.*1300;[55] and it is to be supposed that where the device is not referred to by name, it was usually known by this term.[56] It is generally held that the Tenebrae-hearse received its name because of the similarity of the device in both shape and ap-

[51]HBS 75 p.271; Antiphonary p.62.

[52]Ordinary pp.150–51.

[53]Officially it was known as the *candelabrum triangulare* (*Sacrarum Caeremoniarum* fol.155; Bisso I p.148; Grancolas p.296).

[54]The first recorded use of the word in England occurs in the statutes of the Second Synod of Exeter in 1287 (Powicke and Cheney II pt. 2 p.1008), unless the reference in the thirteenth-century Customary of St Augustine's Abbey is older (HBS 28 p.274).

[55]HBS 86 p.156.

[56]However, in the Statutes of Lincoln Cathedral (Bradshaw and Wordsworth II p.131) it is called *cratis tenebrarum,* 'a harrow for Tenebrae'.

pearance to the instrument of tillage which bears the same name, and we noted earlier that the beams *(hirpices)* referred to by Grancolas received their names from the protruding spikes which caused the spars of wood to resemble harrows.[57] The three-sided candelabrum, familiar from the Roman rite, was also referred to as a hearse since harrows of triangular shape were also used in former times.[58] In Italy, these hearses were known by the clergy and sacristans as *saette,* 'bolts', from the representation of lightning by artists.[59]

In English the word *hearse* formerly had three other applications, all within the context of the provision of light in church. (i) It referred to the wooden or iron frame placed over a corpse or coffin to hold the funeral candles. Within the same context, the word is now applied to the vehicle which bears the deceased person. (ii) In an inventory of Christ Church, Canterbury, dated 1563, mention is made of a hearse of three lights for the carrying of the new fire on Holy Saturday.[60] Here it signifies the triple candle. (iii) The English antiquarian Edward Peacock describes a triangular frame of wood, called a hearse, which was suspended from the roof of a church by a cord or chain. Across the frame ran three bars; and at the points where the bars crossed, there were sockets for holding candles.[61] Its purpose, apart from providing light, is unknown. It is unlikely to have been a Tenebrae-hearse since in such a device the bars intersect each other only at three points.

[57] That is, harrows comprising a single wooden board with protruding spikes.

[58] In heraldry harrows are represented as triangular objects having three transverse bars into which tines are fixed.

[59] Armellini p.354. *Saetta* also signifies 'arrow'.

[60] OED under *hearse*.

[61] Andrews pp.214–15.

Chapter Seven

THE EXTINGUISHING OF LIGHTS

(i) The Order in Which the Lights Were Put Out

(A) BEFORE 1000. Seven of our ten sources for Tenebrae in this earlier period stipulate that regardless of the number used, a third of the lights of the church should be extinguished during the course of each nocturn of Matins—hence, as we have seen, the numbers that have come down to us are all divisible by three. Grisar cites Durandus' statement that in some churches the lights were put out in three stages, and understands 'three stages' to signify *three groups of lights*.[1] He believes that this method of extinguishing the lamps preceded that of quenching them one by one. Durandus gives no instance of a church where the former method obtained; and three early sources, including the earliest, Ordo 26, record that they were extinguished 'gradually' *(paulatim)*,[2] whilst *Poitiers* states that it was done 'one by one' *(singulatim)* (p.137). Amalarius also attests the decrease of light by degrees.[3] We have already observed that *Poitiers* records that the lights began to be extinguished at the western end of the church so that with the lights arranged in three rows in an east-to-west direction, the last re-

---

[1] *Rationale* VI.72, in *Das Missale* pp.110 ff.
[2] OR 26.13; OR 31.13; *PRG* II pp.56–57 §213.
[3] *Lib. Off.* 4.22.1.

maining lamps would be still burning in the choir while the last lessons of Matins were being read. We believe that the lights attested in other *ordines,* and especially in Ordo 29, were arranged in a similar way so as to provide illumination for the lector at the end of Matins.

Poitiers also provides us with the valuable information that at Matins on Good Friday, because of the cessation of bells, which would have been used to signal the start of the night office, the sacristan stood in the doorway of the church holding a lighted candle in his hand. This he extinguished to mark the start of Matins.[4] We do not know for certain whether the compiler of this pontifical envisaged at which door the sacristan would stand. It would almost certainly have been the south or west door; for the pontifical states that 'the lamps . . . begin to be put out on the western side of the church' (p.137). If the practice observed at Poitiers corresponded to that described by *Alcuin,* the sacristan would have stood at the south door. The above-mentioned rubric would appear to allow the possibility of the sacristan moving in either an easterly or a northerly direction along a row of lamps, were it not for the qualification of a subsequent rubric :

Let a lamp from each row be extinguished.[5]

This makes it quite clear that the three lights at the west end of the church were put out first, but we cannot be sure of the order in which the three lights (1, 2, and 3) were extinguished *(Fig. 12).* The evidence of *Alcuin,* however, leaves us in no doubt about the order :

At the start of the first psalm, the sacristan is ready with a reed on the right-hand side of the church; and when he hears the first antiphon, he extinguishes the first light. At the end of the following psalm, a lamp is put out on the left, and then

[4]Ilico antiphona primae nocturnae incipiatur a cantore, stante custode in ostio eclesiae *(sic)* et illuminatam candelam tenente, quam primam extinguere debet (p.193).

[5] Lucerna cuiusque ordinis . . . extinguatur (p.137).

one in the middle is extinguished. This order is repeated for the rest.[6]

Although we are not told where the sacristan initially took up his position, it is safe to assume that this was near the south door.[7] That the practice of extinguishing first the lamp nearest the door of the building also obtained in other churches is clear from the evidence of other documents that the lights began to be extinguished 'at the entrance to the church'.[8] Martène's statement that 'the monks at Monte Cassino used to begin to extinguish the lights at the entrance to the church' shows that the practice was also observed at that monastery in the tenth century.[9]

Figures 12 to *14* represent the amount of illumination in three churches, in each of which a different number of lights were lit for the service of Tenebrae. According to the scheme attested by *Alcuin,* the central light at the eastern end of the lamps (shaded in *Fig. 13*) would have been extinguished last. The sacristan would then have moved to the sanctuary, causing a minimum amount of distraction, in order to attend to the seven lamps. Visually, the display of thirty lamps at Poitiers *(Fig. 12)* and the twenty-four attested by *Alcuin (Fig. 13)* would not have been as satisfying at the end of the first and second nocturns as the twenty-seven lamps of Ordo 32 *(Fig. 14),* assuming that the lights of that *ordo* were arranged in a similar way. On the other hand, the intervals between the nocturns would not have been of such lengthy duration as to permit

[6]In initio primi psalmi, est custos paratus cum canna in loco dexterae partis ecclesiae, et mox ut primam antiphonam audierit, extinguit primam lucernam. In fine vero sequentis psalmi ex parte sinistra, tutat aliam, in medio tertiam. Hoc ordine de aliis prosequitur. *Lib. de Div. Off.* (PL 101.1203C).

[7]Liturgical commentators traditionally referred to the sides of the church, sanctuary, altar and so forth, from the point of view of a priest facing the congregation.

[8]Either the west or the south door. OR 26.13; OR 27.13; OR 28.30; *PRG* II p.56 §213.

[9]*DAMR* 3.12.3 p.123.

protracted periods of asymmetrical presentation. The extinguishing last of those lamps nearest to the altar meant that
there was sufficient light for the lectors, who would be standing in the vicinity of those lamps, even at the end of Matins.

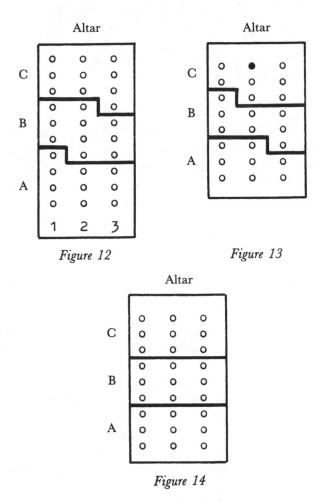

Figure 12

Figure 13

Figure 14

A : section of lights extinguished after first nocturn.
B : section of lights extinguished after second nocturn.
C : section of lights extinguished after third nocturn.

Alcuin records that the seven sanctuary lamps were extinguished at Lauds in the same order as the church lights at Matins.[10] Presumably, the outer lamp on the Gospel side of the altar was the first to be put out, then the furthest on the Epistle side. Since it clearly states, however, that the middle lamp was removed for reservation, it would seem that the third light to be extinguished was another lamp on the Gospel side, almost certainly that next to the lamp which had first been extinguished. This order for extinguishing the altar lights survived in the Roman rite.

(B) AFTER 1000.

1. *The Hearse-Lights.* The only known description of the order in which the hearse-lights were extinguished relates to the Roman rite. The first candle to be extinguished on the triangular candelabrum was the lowest on the Gospel side, then the lowest on the Epistle side, and so forth alternately in an upward direction. After the liturgical changes of 1955, the candle at the apex was not removed but continued to burn.[11]

2. *The Altar Lights.* A distinctive feature of Tenebrae according to the Roman rite was the extinguishing of the six altar-candles during the *Benedictus*. The relationship between their use in this way and the extinguishing of the seven sanctuary lamps at Lauds in the period before 1000 is not clear. It is likely that the use of the latter fell into desuetude in many churches, though their survival as a feature at Tenebrae after 1000 is attested at Monte Cassino in the twelfth century and at Chartres in the thirteenth century.[12] On the other hand, the number of lights known to have been used may have included these seven lamps; for the thirteen candles at Tongres included the six altar lights, which were used without distinction from the rest.[13] Neither the seven lamps nor the hearse-

[10]*Lib. de Div. Off.* (PL 101.1203C).
[11]Wuest p.259 and p.263; Fortescue and O'Connell (11th edition) p.282.
[12]Leuterman p.101; Ordinary p.108.
[13]Ordinary p.150.

candles were used at Rome in the twelfth century,[14] and Righetti is probably correct in concluding that the custom at Rome of extinguishing the altar-candles during the *Benedictus* was 'somewhat recent'.[15]

According to the Roman rite prior to 1955, the six altar-candles were put out during the last six verses of the *Benedictus,* beginning with the outer candle on the Gospel side.[16] Then the furthest on the Epistle side was extinguished, and so on alternately. Customarily, however, in most places, it was usual to extinguish them after every other verse of the Song. The routine was carried out on all three days. As a result of the reforms of 1955, this could be performed only at Lauds of Maundy Thursday. On Good Friday, there were now no candles on the altar during Matins/Lauds, and on Holy Saturday only four.[17]

(ii) The Extinction-points[18]

(A) POITIERS AND ORDO 29. Of all our sources for the period up to 1000, only *Poitiers* and Ordo 29 contain the points at which the lights were extinguished during Matins. *Poitiers* states :

> One by one they are put out stealthily with a reed, by the sacristan, during the lessons, the antiphons, and the responsories, and also the versicles before the lessons of the three nocturns. The sacristan should be particularly alert for the moment when the precentor's voice is raised for the antiphon, the responsory, and the versicle and when the reader begins

[14]*OEL* p.45.

[15]*Manuale* II p.158.

[16]*Caeremoniale Episcoporum* II.xxii.11. In the Camaldolese rite the first candle to be extinguished was the furthest on the Epistle side. Ceremonial p.57.

[17]During the Good Friday liturgy two had accompanied the venerated cross, and two had been brought in with the Blessed Sacrament.

[18]Throughout this section the reader is referred to *Tables 4* and *5*.

a lesson. (The lamps are extinguished) straightaway at the first or second syllable.[19]

The provision of light for the lector was important. Hence, at the beginning of the first lesson of the third nocturn, six lights were still burning. It is important to bear in mind that these were the functional lights of the church. In later Roman practice, the gradual loss of illumination affected the liturgical lights primarily, whilst the church lights provided background illumination.

There might be some uncertainty about the precise moment at which the lamps were extinguished, particularly those put out at the antiphons, were *Poitiers* the only document from this period which specifies the extinction-points. For it is not completely clear whether a light was put out at the first antiphon before the psalm or at its repetition after the psalm, though it must be admitted that the sense of the passage and the absence of reference to the repetition of the antiphon make the latter place seem most unlikely. However, if we examine the slightly earlier Ordo 29, which we believe envisages a similar arrangement of lights and contains similar ceremonial details, we see clearly that the first lamp was extinguished *before* the first psalm. But not only does Ordo 29 inform us of the point at which the first light was extinguished; it is also by far the most important and valuable document for our research since we learn from it the precise moment at which all thirteen lights were extinguished during any nocturn (§12).

Light No.	Point in Nocturn
1	start of the first antiphon
2	end of the first psalm

---

[19]Et singulatim a custode ecclesiae per singulas antiphonas, lectiones et responsoria sed et versus trium nocturnarum, qui ante lectiones proferuntur, cum harundine latenter quasi raptando extinguntur. Qui custos summopere observare debet, quatinus mox ut praecentoris vox elata in antiphona, responsorio, seu versu nec non et lectoris in lectione fuerit, continuo aut in prima aut in secunda syllaba (p.137 §196).

3	start of the second antiphon
4	end of the second psalm
5	start of the third antiphon
6	end of the third psalm
7	'while they pray'
8	after the first reading
9	start of the first responsory
10	during the second reading
11	at the second responsory
12	start of the third reading
13	start of the third responsory

The prayer being said when the seventh lamp was extinguished must have been the *Pater noster*. No other prayers were said during this part of a nocturn. The *ordo* then states that after the thirteenth light had been put out, a third of the lamps of the church had been extinguished. The second nocturn followed the form of the first; therefore, at its end, though the *ordo* does not actually state it, two thirds of the lights had been extinguished. Ordo 29 then informs us, somewhat to our surprise, that during the third nocturn only six lamps were extinguished and the extinction-points were as follows :

Light No.	Point in Nocturn
1	at the first antiphon
2	at the second antiphon
3	at the third antiphon
4	at the first reading
5	at the second reading
6	at the third reading

The *ordo* concludes that all the lights had now been put out except the seven lamps in front of the altar.

The use of only six lights during the third nocturn is puzzling, especially as thirteen were used in each of the other two nocturns; and since two thirds of the church lights had been extinguished by the end of the third nocturn, the *ordo* should mention a third set of thirteen lights in the rubrics for the third nocturn, making a total of thirty-nine lights in all. Instead, only thirty-two seem to have been used.[20] If these figures are correct, we must conclude that to the writer the concept of a third does not signify, in a mathematical sense, a strict numerical division into three equal parts; rather, it would seem to imply any one of three divisions of a group, none of which necessarily contains two identical numbers. However, again somewhat surprisingly, we are informed in Section 11 of the *ordo* :

> Then let the church be fully illuminated, that is, with twenty-eight lights.[21]

If this figure is correct, it follows that nine lights were extinguished during the second nocturn; for we already know from the *ordo* that thirteen and six lights were extinguished during the first and second nocturns respectively. Christian liturgy and ceremonial have always been characterised by balance and symmetry, as the structure of Matins clearly demonstrates. The combination of 13–9–6 seems most unlikely. Clearly, something is wrong.

Since we know that the structure, though not the content, of each nocturn was similar, let us re-examine the nocturns of Ordo 29. The detailed analysis of the first nocturn and the clarity of the information it contains leave us in little doubt that the information is genuine and authentic. Nor is there any justification for doubting that the structure of the second nocturn was identical with that of the first. Therefore, in view of the statement of the *ordo* that the second nocturn was like the first, it follows that thirteen lights were extinguished during the second nocturn. Although we are told that only six

[20]13 + 13 + 6 at the three nocturns respectively.
[21]Et tunc ecclesia omni lumine sit decorata, id est XXVIII luminaribus.

lamps were extinguished during the third nocturn, it is difficult to believe that this information is correct and that there
were not thirteen lights, as in the other two nocturns. We
therefore believe that at the start of the service, thirty-nine
and not twenty-eight lamps were lit, even though to question
the authenticity of the number twenty-eight on the grounds
that it is an embarrassment and a potential stumbling block
to the argument may be viewed as an act of desperation. However, in this instance, we believe that there are very good reasons why this figure should not be accepted as genuine. (i)
The numbers of lights specified in other documents, namely,
twenty-four *(Pontificale Romano-Germanicum [PRG])*, twenty-
seven (Ordo 32), and thirty *(Poitiers)*, are all divisible by three;
twenty-eight is not. (ii) If the figure of twenty-eight is correct
and six lights were extinguished during the third nocturn, we
have to assume that nine lamps were put out during the second nocturn. However, not only does the compiler of Ordo
29 inform us that the lights in the second nocturn were extinguished in the same manner as those in the first nocturn; he
omits any mention of the number of lamps used during the
second nocturn. He assumes that we will take it for granted
that the number of lamps extinguished in both nocturns was
the same. (iii) It is difficult to believe that the compiler regarded the concept of a third so imprecisely and in a way different to our understanding of the notion. If thirteen lights were
extinguished during the first nocturn—the evidence leaves us
in no doubt that this was so—and they comprised one third
of the total number, we can say with some confidence that
a total of thirty-nine lights were extinguished at Matins according to Ordo 29 and that the figures which the *ordo* gives
for the total, namely, twenty-eight, and for the third nocturn,
namely, six, are both incorrect.

From the table below, we can see how the arrangement for
the extinguishing of lights during the third nocturn compares
with that for the first and second nocturns according to the
information given in Ordo 29.

Nocturns 1 and 2		*Nocturn 3*
Light		**Light**
1	start of the first antiphon	1
2		
3	start of the second antiphon	2
4		
5	start of the third antiphon	3
6		
7	at the first reading	4
8		
9	start of second reading	5
10		
11		
12	start of third reading	6
13		

Lights 1, 2, and *3* of Nocturn 3 corresponded to *Lights 1, 2,* and *5* of Nocturns 1 and 2 in that they were extinguished at the first singing of the antiphons. *Lights 4* and *5* came between *Lights 7* and *8* and *Lights 9* and *10* respectively of Nocturns 1 and 2, and *Light 6* of the third nocturn corresponded exactly with *Light 12* of the first two nocturns. The positioning of the extinction-points in Nocturn 3 appears to be part of a deliberate attempt on the part of the compiler of the *ordo,* or a copyist, to harmonise them with the extinction-points in the first and second nocturns in order to rectify a mistake which he wrongly believed to exist. It is our belief that where the order for the extinguishing of the lights in the third nocturn now stands, the text originally stated that the last nocturn was similar to the first and the second. We further believe that a copyist, knowing the ordo stated that thirty-nine lights were lit for Matins (§11), mistakenly assumed this figure related to the whole of the combined office of Matins/Lauds and thought the seven lamps to be extinguished at Lauds were to be included in the thirty-nine and realising the total number of lights extinguished at Tenebrae came to forty-six (13

+ 13 + 13 + 7), deliberately reduced the number of lights
in the third nocturn to six in order to make what he believed
to be the total number of lights for the whole service add up
to thirty-nine. A possible objection has been dealt with above.
For we have already shown that the figure of twenty-eight,
which this *ordo* records for the total number of lights lit at
Matins (§11), is incorrect and that thirty-nine lamps were lit.
It must be admitted that the alteration of thirty-nine into
twenty-eight cannot readily be explained. However, we may
well have here an instance of a copyist's double haplographic
error in which XXVIII has been read for XXXVIIII.

(B) THE EVIDENCE OF OTHER DOCUMENTS. The three remaining documentary sources which specify the number of lights
lit for the night office during this period are the *Liber Officialis* of Amalarius, Ordo 32, and *PRG*. We have already noted
that Ordo 29 is the only document from this period which
explicitly states that the first lamp was extinguished at the antiphon *before* the first psalm. However, there is nothing in any
of the other sources to suggest that this was not the general
practice. Indeed, Ordo 26, our earliest source, and Ordo 27,
both from the eighth century, state that the lights began to
be extinguished *ab initio cantus nocturnae,* 'from the beginning
of the night song', which almost certainly indicates 'at the
first antiphon'.[22] The phrase is also found two centuries later
in *PRG*.[23] There is no reason to believe that in the service
of Tenebrae described by Amalarius and set out in Ordo 32,
practice differed in this respect.

Having established that the antiphon *before* the first psalm
was the starting point for extinguishing the lights in this period, we are now able to reconstruct with some confidence,
using the three above-mentioned sources, the points in the
service at which the rest of the lights were put out.

1. According to Amalarius, twenty-four lights were extinguished at the antiphons and responsories of Matins, eight

---

[22]§13 in both *ordines.*
[23]II p.56 §213.

during each nocturn.[24] If the first light was extinguished at the antiphon which introduced the first psalm, it seems reasonable to place the extinguishing of the second and third lamps at the antiphons which preceded the second and third psalms respectively. The remaining five lights clearly belong to the points in the nocturn where the five responsories were said. The extinguishing of the two lamps at the responsories after the third reading may seem strange, but it need not be questioned. For it is found in *PRG*, at Norwich, and possibly at Tongres. Admittedly, the evidence of these later instances should not be adduced in corroboration of the practice familiar to Amalarius; but it is important to remember that during the reading of the ninth lesson, two lights still burning, as opposed to one, would have provided additional illumination for the reader at the end of Matins.

2. According to *PRG*, the twenty-four lights were to be extinguished 'after each reading and responsory' and began to be put out 'at the beginning of the night song'.[25] Taken literally, the instructions for extinguishing the lamps present us with a very unusual scheme; for one light was put out at the very start of each nocturn, and seven in the latter part of the nocturn, after the psalms had been sung. *PRG* would appear to be alone amongst all the documents in not featuring the loss of light at the antiphons (either before or after) of all of the psalms, and it is strange that a lamp should have been put out before the first psalm but not before the second or third. It is true that Ordo 29 attests the extinguishing of the seven lights at the readings and responsories in the latter part of the nocturn; but this was done of necessity since thirteen lamps were required to be extinguished during each nocturn, and only sixteen points were available for the accommodation of each light.[26] Moreover, since *PRG* also states that the

[24]*Lib. Off.* 4.22.1.

[25]II p.56 p.213.

[26]The psalms alone of the nineteen constituent elements of Matins were never used as extinction-points.

lights should be put out *gradually,* [27] a statement at variance with the literal interpretation of the rubrics, we suspect either that a phrase relating to the antiphons has been accidentally omitted from the text or that the compiler of this pontifical assumed that the reader would understand and take for granted a phrase such as 'at each antiphon'. Nevertheless, the possibility must remain that the prima facie interpretation of the text of *PRG* is correct; and in *Table 4,* we have given a scheme for the loss of light according to the literal evidence of the pontifical, as well as an arrangement suggested by our interpretation of the text in conjunction with other documentary evidence from this period.

3. Ordo 32 gives no indication of the extinction points at which nine lamps were put out during each nocturn. It is tempting to reconstruct the scheme based on the detailed description in Ordo 29, which we examined above, especially as both *ordines* are of Gallican provenance and are more or less contemporaneous. However, the details concerning the Triduum in Ordo 32 generally show little correspondence with those in Ordo 29. Even at Tenebrae, where the structure of the office and the ceremonial were similar, affinity in respect of lights should not be taken for granted. On the other hand, the similarities between Ordo 32 and *PRG* show that the latter document, compiled some fifty or so years later, almost certainly derives from the same liturgical milieu. The suggested scheme for the loss of light, therefore, is based on the information contained in Ordo 29 and in *PRG*.

As in *Poitiers,* it is not immediately clear from *Alcuin* at which of the two antiphons each light was extinguished. [28] In view of the dependence of this document on *PRG,* we have suggested a scheme similar to the latter.

Two of our nine principal sources for Tenebrae in the period before 1000 do not refer to the points at which the seven sanctuary lamps were extinguished during Lauds. They are

[27]Lumen . . . incipiat paulatim tutari *(op. cit.).*
[28]That is, at the first chanting of the sentence or at its repetition.

Amalarius and Ordo 32.[29] Ordo 31 and *PRG* mention only the first two lamps and the last. However, Ordo 29 and *Poitiers* concur that six were extinguished at the antiphons preceding and following the first three psalms of Lauds and that the seventh was put out at the *Traditor autem,* the antiphon before the *Benedictus.* The extinguishing of the sixth lamp at the repeated antiphon of Psalm 66 (67), thus reducing illumination in the church for the chanting of the Canticle and the *Laudate Dominum* to one light, would have made more urgent the plea of the *Deus misereatur,* for God 'to show the light of his countenance,' and have anticipated in a way the total loss of light before the *Benedictus.*

It is almost certain that this arrangement regarding the extinguishing of the seven lamps at Lauds also obtained in *Alcuin,* in spite of the concern this document shows for the order in which the lamps were extinguished, rather than the extinction-points. *Alcuin*'s reference to the use of the last of the seven lamps on Maundy Thursday is not entirely clear. For the document informs us that at the conclusion of Lauds on that day, the central lamp was removed and reserved for the lighting of the Easter candle on Holy Saturday; yet, it also informs us that later the same day the sacristans prepared the seven lamps in front of the altar in readiness of the evening liturgy.[30] The difficulty is by no means insuperable. Either the last lamp was returned, extinguished, to its customary place, once its flame had been used to kindle another lamp in the place of reservation; or it remained in the same place whither it had been taken; or an eighth, spare, sanctuary lamp was subsequently placed with the other six.

(C) EXTINCTION-POINTS AFTER 1000. The fact that in the period after 1000, the seven sanctuary lamps are rarely known to have been extinguished at Lauds strongly suggests that their

---

[29]Although Amalarius does not refer to Lauds, there is no reason to believe that the seven lamps were not extinguished during the course of the service that was familiar to him.

[30]*Lib.de Div.Off.* 16 (PL 101.1203D).

use at this office had generally fallen into desuetude. Their demise at Tenebrae seems to have coincided with the emergence of the fifteen-candle hearse and to have been a consequence of the innovatory practice of extinguishing all the lights, formerly lit for Matins, during Matins *and* Lauds. As a result, the loss of lights from the same set of candles during Matins and Lauds thus imposed a uniformity on the whole of the service in respect of the use of illumination. This is borne out at Tongres, where the candles, which formed two different sets of lights, were regarded without discrimination for the purpose of Tenebrae.[31]

A distinctive characteristic of Tenebrae before 1000 was the practice of extinguishing a light at the antiphon preceding a psalm. In the later period, however, it became customary to extinguish each light at the repetition of the antiphon. The adoption of the latter practice, which was probably linked with the appearance of the hearse at Tenebrae, is first attested at York in the eleventh century,[32] and became a feature of the Roman rite.[33] The extinguishing of a candle at the antiphon preceding the psalm at Cluny and Farfa, where a hearse of fifteen lights was used, represents a transitional stage between the practices of both periods. *Tables 4* and *5* show that a number of different schemes for extinguishing the candles at Tenebrae are known to have existed.

1. *Fifteen Candles Extinguished* before *the Psalms*. At Cluny, and presumably at most of her 314 dependent houses, the fifteen candles were put out at the antiphons before the psalms of Matins and Lauds. Further possible support is added to our theory that at Farfa two hearses stood in front of the altar since at this monastery also the candles were extinguished

---

[31]Ordinary p.150.

[32]Breviary I p.376.

[33]*Caeremoniale Episcoporum* II.22 p.264. It is not known when this change took place. In the Dominican rite, which was modelled on the Roman rite, the candles were extinguished *before* the psalms in actual practice, even though the *Office of Holy Week* prescribed 'at the close of each psalm' (p.82).

before the psalms. For if the candelabrum on the Gospel side
of the altar was used to keep a tally of the fifteen gradual
psalms, the extinguishing of the first light on the other candelabrum may have acted as the signal for the start of Matins and for the singing of the antiphon before the first psalm.
With the first candle extinguished before the first psalm, the
pattern was set; and the remaining lights would also have been
put out before the psalms. At St Mary's, York, the candles
may have been extinguished before the psalms, but the phrase
from the rubric of the ordinal *ad inceptionem uniuscuiusque anti-
phone,* 'at the beginning of each antiphon', is ambiguous and
could equally refer to the antiphon or to its repetition.

   2. *Fifteen Candles Extinguished* after *the psalms.* It is not clear
why the practice arose of extinguishing the lights at the antiphons following the psalms. It might be thought that the uttering of only the opening words of the antiphon which
preceded the psalm was too short a period of time to allow
a candle to be extinguished with decorum and that in consequence of this the candles came to be extinguished after the
psalm, as occurred in the Dominican rite. However, in the
Roman rite, in which the candles were put out at the conclusion of a psalm, the antiphons were doubled since each of the
three days of the Triduum was a Double Feast. Moreover,
as we have observed above, the Dominicans in practice extinguished the candles at the abbreviated antiphon before the
psalm. The evidence from local rites, such as, Besançon, Coutances, and Verdun, would suggest that by the eighteenth century Roman practice had become the norm.[34]

   3. *Twenty-four Lights Extinguished at the Antiphons and Responsories.* The use of twenty-four lights at Tenebrae was determined not only by the symbolism readily suggested by that
number but also by the very structure of the combined office
of Matins and Lauds. For the three psalms and the three les-

[34]1707 Ceremonial p.235; 1825 Ceremonial p.311; 1832 Ceremonial
p.294.

sons of each nocturn of Matins, together with the four psalms, the Old Testament canticle, and the *Benedictus* of Lauds provided twenty-four convenient points at which to extinguish the candles; and though variations are found at Norwich and Trier, these points are specified by the majority of service-books and by the liturgical commentators.

From a number of our sources, however, it is not clear whether the candles were extinguished at the antiphon preceding or following the psalm. The Ordinals of Barking, Exeter, and the Gilbertines refer only to the antiphons and responsories, as does Lanfranc;[35] and John of Avranches mentions only that the lights were put out 'at the psalms and readings'.[36] However, Rupert of Deutz and Honorius of Autun both state that the lights were extinguished after the psalm,[37] and this is borne out by evidence from York.[38] In instances where the antiphon is not specified, it would seem reasonable to assume that the light was extinguished at its repetition; for this accords well with the firm evidence for the practice.

It is desirable to record a few observations about several churches.

Salisbury. The rubrics of the various Sarum breviaries state that a candle was to be extinguished 'at the beginning of each antiphon'.[39] It is almost certain that the repetition of the antiphon is here intended. Immediately following Psalm 148 is the rubric : 'While this psalm is being sung, let a light be hidden where it cannot be seen.'[40] This relates to the twenty-third candle, which was reproduced at the end of the service. The twenty-fourth and last candle continued to burn and was extinguished at the conclusion of the *Benedictus*.

[35]HBS 65 p.91; HBS 37 p.132; HBS 59 p.30; *Decrees* (PL 137.458A).
[36]*Lib.de Off.Eccl.* (PL 147.48C).
[37]*De Div.Off.* (PL 170.148C); *Gemma Animae* (PL 172.665D).
[38]Breviary I p.376.
[39]Procter and Wordsworth col.dcclxxiii.
[40]Dum iste Psalmus canitur, lumen ubi videri nequeat abscondatur *(op.cit.).*

Nidaros. The Ordo of Nidaros prescribes twenty-four candles and informs us that, as the service is about to start, the sacristan is ready on the right-hand side of the church. It continues :

> At the first antiphon he puts out the first candle; then (the others) *at the other antiphons or at the end of the psalm itself.* At Lauds they are extinguished in a similar way, one on one side, one on the other, until the start of the *Benedictus.* [41]

A superficial reading of the above rubric leaves us with the impression that a choice existed of extinguishing the candles before or after each psalm and that the first antiphon and the antiphons mentioned are those which preceded the psalms, in view of the alternative point seemingly offered : at the end of the psalm. A more careful reading of the rubric, however, reveals that another interpretation exists regarding the choice of point. For if, as the present writer believes, the antiphons mentioned in the rubric are those which followed the psalms, the choice lay in extinguishing the candle either at the conclusion of the psalm itself or during the antiphon which followed the psalm. Either point accords with the above-mentioned testimony of Rupert of Deutz and Honorius of Autun.

Norwich. From the Benedictine Customary of Norwich we learn that six candles were extinguished during each nocturn in the following way : [42]

> three at the antiphons *(almost certainly after the psalms),*
> one at the versicle,
> one at the third responsory,
> one at the repetition of the third responsory.

We also learn that the seven candles still burning at the start of Lauds were extinguished in the following way :

---

[41]*ONE* p.223. The rubrics have much in common with the directions for conducting Tenebrae, as prescribed by *Alcuin. ONE* adds the words italicised by the writer.

[42]HBS 82 p.79.

five at the antiphons of each psalm,
one at the *Deus misereatur* (Psalm 66 [67]),
one at the *Laudate Dominum* (Psalm 150).

On the first reading, it might appear that the antiphons
at which the candles were extinguished were those sung after
the five psalms of Lauds (including the Old Testament
canticle). However, the extinguishing of the sixth candle 'at
the *Deus misereatur*' rules out this interpretation and indicates
that the first five lights were put out before the start of Psalm
62 (63). In other words, one candle was extinguished at each
antiphon and at its repetition as far as Psalm 62 (63). Since
the extinguishing of the sixth candle would not have taken
place during the singing of Psalm 66 (67), it must be placed
at the antiphon following that psalm. The arrangement so far
corresponds exactly with that found in *Poitiers*.

The information that 'one is put out at Psalm 150' (that
is, the seventh and last candle is put out at the repetition of
the antiphon) is followed by a further statement that when
the sacristan has taken a light in a lantern outside the choir,
'there will now be no light in the choir'. The description then
ceases to be lucid when we are subsequently informed that
the last of the twenty-five candles is put out at the *Traditor
autem,* the antiphon of the *Benedictus;*[43] for we were previously
told that the last light was extinguished at Psalm 150. Since
the last candle could have been extinguished at only one point,
perhaps the most satisfactory explanation is to assume that
this seventh light was extinguished at the very end of the repeated antiphon of Psalm 150 and that a later hand added
the statement that it was put out at the *Traditor autem,* in view
of the fact that this antiphon immediately followed the quenching of the flame. Alternatively, the mention of the two points

---

[43]The *Traditor autem* was the antiphon of the *Benedictus* only on Maundy
Thursday. However, as the structure of Lauds was the same for each day,
the words *Traditor autem* have been used to indicate this antiphon on the
other two days of the Triduum.

may be viewed as evidence of a choice, even though such a choice is not specified.

Trier. The imprecise rubrics of the cathedral's thirteenth-century ordinal allow two possible interpretations.[44] Of the twenty-four candles to be extinguished, the first was put out at the first antiphon, the second after the first psalm, and the rest after the subsequent psalms of Matins and Lauds. All were extinguished by the *Traditor autem* preceding the *Benedictus*. These directions, however, taken literally, account for only sixteen candles. One solution is to assume that *two* lights were extinguished after each psalm of Lauds (see *Tongres* below); but this would still leave two candles to be accounted for. Alternatively, we must assume that a light was also extinguished at each of the antiphons which preceded the psalms, as we have suggested in the tables.

Tongres. The scheme at Tongres was unusual in two respects. The lights were extinguished two at a time; and apart from two at the end of Matins, they were all extinguished during the course of Lauds. This latter feature was reminiscent of Carmelite practice. Moreover, the thirteen candles comprised the six altar-candles and seven atop a spear.[45]

Seville. At Seville, where a thirteen-light hearse was used, during Lauds the candles were extinguished only after the first three psalms. This matched the scheme for extinguishing the candles in each of the three nocturns of Matins.

* * * * *

It is clear from the earlier evidence that the person responsible for extinguishing the lights was the sacristan.[46] In more recent times, the duty fell to a server or to the master of

[44]Ordinal p.486.

[45]The spear for bearing the new fire in the Gilbertine rite had five candles. HBS 59 p.39.

[46]*Poitiers* p.137; OR 29.12; *Alcuin* (PL 101.1203B); *PRG* II p.57 §214; Breviary of York I p.376.

ceremonies.[47] At St Mary's, York, a server was concealed for this purpose behind the veil or curtain which was suspended from the base of the hearse.[48]

In addition to a snuffer, three different implements are known to have been used for extinguishing the lights. (i) According to *Poitiers, PRG,* and *Alcuin,* the sacristan used a reed.[49] How it was used is clear from the first of these documents, which states that a lamp from each row 'should be blown out with one puff of breath, if possible'.[50] The exhortation to emit only one puff of air from the reed was no doubt intended to avoid embarrassment. The use of a reed would suggest that the lamps were positioned above the height of a person. (ii) Writing about the churches of Italy, John England records that in some places, a moist sponge was used to extinguish the candles.[51] (iii) Possibly of greater antiquity than the preceding extinguisher was the use of a wax hand, known as a 'Judas hand'. It is first attested by Beleth, who comments that it may have represented the hand described in Daniel 5:5; but he does not elaborate.[52] Presumably the Judas hand at Tenebrae was associated with the loss of light in the same way that the hand that wrote upon the wall heralded the loss of Belshazzar's life. However, Beleth admits that the wax hand was more likely to recall Jesus' prediction in Matthew 26:23, an opinion shared by Durandus, who adds that the hand was made of wax because it 'bends towards evil'.[53]

(iii) The Candles

The practice of using yellow or unbleached candles for both the hearse-lights and those on the altar is probably of a vener-

[47]Fortescue and O'Connell (4th edition) p.304.
[48]HBS 75 p.271.
[49]For references, see above.
[50]Uno, si potest fieri, extinguatur flatu.
[51]*Ceremonies of Holy Week* p.50.
[52]*Rationale* (PL 202.106B).
[53]Ad malum flexibilis. *Rationale* VI.72 fol.331.

able antiquity. The use of sombre-coloured wax signified the
funereal aspect of Tenebrae.[54] In many places the custom arose
of placing a white candle at the apex of the hearse to indicate
that the light symbolised Christ.[55] Thurston would appear to
regard this practice as the norm.[56] However, Fortescue and
O'Connell state, 'There is no authority for using a white
candle in the centre';[57] and in the Sistine Chapel all fifteen
candles were yellow.[58] It was recommended that each candle
should consist of one pound of wax,[59] a weight attested at Lincoln in the late Middle Ages.[60] At Canterbury, each of the
twenty-four candles weighed three quarters of a pound.[61]

(iv) The Light before the Blessed Sacrament

Although an altar-lamp is attested in Bergamo Cathedral
as early as 922[62] and although the presence of a light before
the Blessed Sacrament was common in parish churches by
the thirteenth century,[63] there is little reference to this perpetual lamp at Tenebrae before 1600, largely, one suspects,
because it remained unlit on Good Friday and Holy Saturday with the removal of the *Sanctissimum* on Maundy Thursday to a place of reservation. With regards to most churches,
it must remain a matter of speculation as to whether or not
the sanctuary-lamps were extinguished at any point during
Tenebrae of Maundy Thursday. However, it is recorded at
Canterbury in the thirteenth century that the lamp *(bacinus)*

---

[54]Candles of unbleached wax are recommended for funerals.
[55]England p.50; Heuser p.229. If the highest candle was identified with
Judas, presumably it remained unbleached.
[56]*Lent and Holy Week* pp.243 ff.
[57]*The Ceremonies of the Roman Rite* (4th edition) p.303.
[58]England p.50.
[59]*Caeremoniale Episcoporum* II.22 p.264; Le Vavasseur p.363.
[60]Bradshaw and Wordsworth II p.303.
[61]HBS 23 p.380.
[62]Ughelli IV pp.616-21.
[63]King, *Eucharistic Reservation* p.129.

before the high altar and those lights *(bacini)* which honoured the bodies of the saints should be extinguished at Lauds during the singing of the last psalm.[64]

According to the *Caeremoniale Episcoporum,* the sanctuary-light was not to be extinguished at Tenebrae.[65] This directive is also enjoined by Le Vavasseur, and Fortescue and O'Connell.[66] The Camaldolese Ceremonial states that the *Sanctissimum* should be transferred to another tabernacle, whose light was presumably unobtrusive.[67] However, Grancolas mentions that the last hearse-candle was hidden rather than extinguished and that the sanctuary-light was kindled from it as soon as possible *(tam cito).*[68]

There is no need to see at Tenebrae of Maundy Thursday a paradox in the concealing or extinguishing of the last candle, which represented Christ, whilst the sanctuary-light continued to burn in the darkness, which commemorated His passion and death. The celebration of Tenebrae on Maundy Thursday was an anticipation or foreshadowing of the events of the following day, so that the use of light during that office was in a sense detached from and did not relate to the events of Maundy Thursday. Seen from a different perspective, the removal of the last candle symbolised the presence and specifically the death of Christ within an historical context; and the continuing flame of the sanctuary lamp represented his universality. At a higher theological level, the two lights virtually portrayed, within the liturgy, respectively His human and His divine natures.

[64]HBS 23 p.380.
[65]Typical edition (1886) I.xii.17.
[66]*Cérémonial* p.365; *The Ceremonies of the Roman Rite* (4th edition) p.304.
[67]1634 Ceremonial p.56.
[68]*Commentarius* p.296.

Table 4. *Extinction-points at each nocturn of Matins.* [69]

	1	2	3	4	5	6	7	8	9	10	11	12	13	14	15	16	17	18	19	20	21	22	23	24
	Ordo	Ordo	Amalarius	Ordo	Ordo	Ordo	Poitiers	PRG	Alcuin	Cluny	Farfa	Gembloux	Trier	Nidaros	Salisbury	Norwich	Tongres	Rome	Besançon	Angers	Auxerre	Seville	Coutances	Verdun
	26	28		29	31	32																		
No. of lights *per Nocturn*	?	?	8	13	?	9	10	8	8	3	3	8	6	6	6	6	2*	3	3	3	3	3	3	3
1 Antiphon				x				(x)	x			x	x	x	x	x		x	x			x	x	x
2 Psalm (i)																								
3 Antiphon			x	x		x						x	x	x	x	x		x	x			x	x	x
4 Antiphon				x		x		(x)	x	x														
5 Psalm (ii)																								
6 Antiphon			x	x		x						x	x	x	x	x		x	x			x	x	x
7 Antiphon				x		x		(x)	x	x														
8 Psalm (iii)																								
9 Antiphon			x	x		x		x	x			x	x	x	x	x		x	x			x	x	x
10 Versicle			x			x	x	x	x							x								
11 Responsory				x								x	x											
12 *Pater noster*																								
13 Reading 1			x	x		x	x	x				x		x	x	x					x			
14 Responsory				x		x	x	■						x						x				
15 Reading 2			x	x		x	x	x				x			x	x					x			
16 Responsory				x		x	x	■						x		x	x			x				
17 Reading 3			x	x			x	x				x‡				x	xx				x			
18 Responsory			x	x		x	x	x	x			(x)		x	x	x	x			x				
19 Responsory			x	x		x	x	x	x								xx							

† York is identical.
* 3rd Nocturn only.
‡ Choice with Point 19.
■ Disputed point.

[69]*References:* (1) OR 26.13. (2) OR 28.30. (3) *Lib. Off.* 4.22.1. (4) OR 29.12. (5) OR 31.13. (6) OR 32.5. (7) Page 137. (8) II p.56 §213. (9) PL 101.1203C. (10) Albers II p.56 §213. (11) Albers I p.46. (12) Albers II p.91. (13) Ordinary p.486. (14) *ONE* p.223. (15) Breviary col. dcclxxxii; (York Breviary I p.376). (16) HBS 82 pp.79-80. (17) Ordinary pp.150-51. (18) Breviary I p.445. (19) Ceremonial p.253. (20) 1731 Ceremonial p.224. (21) Breviary p.243. (22) Doblado p.284. (23) Ceremonial p.311. (24) Ceremonial p.294.

Table 5. Extinction-points at Lauds.[70]

	1	2	3	4	5	6	7	8	9	10	11	12	13	14	15	16	17	18	19	20	21	22	23	24
	Ordo 26	Ordo 28a	Ordo 28b	Ordo 29	Ordo 31	Poiers	PRG	Alcuin	Cluny	Farfa	Carmelite	Trier	Nidaros	Sarum†	Norwich	Tongres	Rome	Besançon	Angers	Angers	Auxerre	Seville	Coutances	Verdun
No. of lights at Lauds	7	7	7	7	7	7	7	7	6	6	5	6	6	6	6	11	6	6	13	4	6	4	6	6
1 Antiphon	1	1	1	1	1	1	1	1	1	1	1	1	1	1	1	1	1	1	1		1	1	1	1
2 1st Psalm																								
3 Antiphon	1	1	1	1	1	1	1	1		1	1	1	1	1	1	2	1	1			1	1	1	1
4 Antiphon	1	1	1	1	1	1	1	1		1		1	1	1	1		1	1				1	1	
5 2nd Psalm															1									
6 Antiphon	1	1	1	1	1	1	1	1		1	1	1	1	1	1	2	1	1			1	1	1	1
7 Antiphon	1	1	1	1	1	1	1	1		1					1									
8 Psalm 62			1																					
9 Psalm 66																								
10 Antiphon	1	1	1	1	1	1	1	1	1		1	1	1	1		2	1	1			1	1	1	1
11 Antiphon																								
12 OT Canticle									1		1													
13 Antiphon	1	1		1	1	1	1	1		1	1	1	1	1		2	1	1			1	1	1	1
14 Antiphon														1										
15 *Laudate*									1	1			1		1									
16 Antiphon	1	1	1	1	1	1	1	1	1	1	1	1	1		1	2	1	1			1	1	1	1
17 *Tradior*	1	1	1	1	1	1	1	1		1	1	1	1	1		1								
18 *Benedictus*	x	x	x	x	x	x	x	x	x	x	x	x	x	x	x	x	1	1	12		1	1	1	1
19 *Tradior*								1	1	1	1	1	1	1	x	1	1	1	1	4	1	1	1	1

x *Benedictus* sung in darkness.

† York is identical.

⁷⁰*References.* (1) OR 26.13. (2) OR 28.7. (3) OR 28.30. (4) OR 29.12. (5) OR 31.13. (6) Page 137. (7) II p.57 §214. (8) PL 101.1203C. (9) Albers I p.16. (10) Albers II p.47. (11) Ordinary p.162. (12) Ordinary p.486. (13) *ONE* p.223. (14) Breviary col. dccxxxii; (York Breviary I p.376 and 382). (15) HBS 82 pp.79-80. (16) Ordinary pp.150-51. (17) Breviary I p.445; *Car. Episc.* II.xxii p.265. (18) Ceremonial Ordinary p.253. (19) 1734 Ceremonial p.260. (20) 1731 Ceremonial p.284. (21)Breviary pp.224-26. (22)Breviary p.243. (23) Ceremonial p.311. (24) Ceremonial p.294.

Chapter Eight
THE CONCLUSION OF TENEBRAE

(i) The Tradition of the *Benedictus* without Light

The practice of singing the *Benedictus* in darkness is well attested in the period before 1000. According to most of the documents, the seventh sanctuary lamp was extinguished at the *Traditor autem* before the *Benedictus*.[1] However, according to the *Pontificale Romano-Germanicum*, the choice was allowed of either extinguishing the light at this point or withdrawing and reserving it for use on Holy Saturday, a practice we have already encountered in *Alcuin*.[2] The custom of singing the *Benedictus* without light was perpetuated in both the cathedral and monastic traditions. At Exeter, it was hidden during the chanting of the last psalm and extinguished, as at Cluny and presumably at most Cluniac houses, at the repeated antiphon.[3] At Worcester, it was extinguished;[4] but at Rouen and Salisbury, it was only hidden at Psalm 148.[5] According to the thirteenth-century Franciscan *ordo*, the penultimate candle was

---

[1]OR 26.13; OR 28.30; OR 29.12; OR 31.13; *Poitiers* p.137. OR 30B.28, which attests Tenebrae only on Good Friday, offers the choice of extinguishing the last lamp either at the last psalm or at the *Benedictus*.

[2]Tutatur media lampada, vel subtrahitur et servatur (II p.57 §214).

[3]HBS 37 p.132; Albers II p.16.

[4]Antiphonary p.62.

[5]1480 Breviary np; Breviary col.dcclxxxii.

hidden at either the last psalm or its antiphon, and the last candle was extinguished at the *Traditor autem*.[6] The *Regularis Concordia* merely states 'at the *Benedictus*',[7] whilst at Nidaros and at Trier, it is recorded that the *Benedictus* was sung in the dark.[8] Elsewhere, the final candle was put out at the first rendering of the *Traditor autem*.[9]

It is not difficult to see why the practice of singing the *Benedictus* in darkness had developed. The Hymn of Thanksgiving related primarily to the events that occurred prior to the birth of Jesus. In the same way that the ministry of John the Baptist was preparatory to the advent of the Light of the World, so the three days of the Triduum recalled the temporary absence of that Light. As early as the ninth century, Amalarius saw in the extinguishing of the candles a commemoration of Jesus' resting in the Tomb :

> The extinguishing of the church lights during these nights seems to me to relate to the very Sun of Justice, whose light was extinguished and buried for three days.[10]

The reference in the final verse of the Song to 'those that sit in darkness and in the shadow of death' was therefore particularly appropriate to those who were chanting these verses from the Gospel in total darkness.

[6]HBS 85 p.76; Van Dijk II p.84. The Carmelites extinguished the last candle at the antiphon of the last psalm. Ordinary p.163.

[7]PL 137.490A.

[8]Breviary fol.lviii; Ordinary p.486.

[9]At Farfa (PL 150.1197D); Gembloux, Fruttuaria, Chester (Albers II p.91, IV p.49, IV p.245); St Mary's, York (HBS 75 p.273); St Paul's, Rome (Martène, *DAMR* 4.22.8 p.124); Norwich (HBS 82 p.79); Canterbury (HBS 23 p.380); among the Gilbertines (HBS 59 p.31). It is mentioned by John of Avranches (PL 147.48C).

[10]Quod lumen ecclesiae extinguitur in his noctibus, videtur nobis aptari ipsi soli iustitiae, qui exstictus est et sepultus tribus diebus et tribus noctibus. *Lib. Off.* 4.22.

(ii) The Tradition of the *Benedictus* with Light

(A) A SINGLE CANDLE. In view of the above-quoted reference
from the *Benedictus* to the gift of light to those who exist in
darkness, it is perhaps not surprising that the practice arose
of allowing the final lamp or candle to remain lit until the
conclusion of the *Benedictus* so as to portray that light emphat-
ically in a symbolic way. The practice is first attested at York
in the eleventh century[11] and was subsequently incorporated
into the Roman rite.[12] The practice is also found at Seville
and in a number of French dioceses, such as Besançon, Coutances, Paris, and Verdun, and in the Premonstratensian and
Camaldolese rites.[13]

(B) ALTAR LIGHTS. The extinguishing of the six altar-candles
during the *Benedictus* in the Roman rite has already been discussed. The six candles were also put out in like manner at
Paris, Besançon, and Seville.[14] Somewhat surprisingly, two
manuals from Angers, separated by only a three-year interval, record different schemes for extinguishing the hearse-
candles, not the altar-lights, during the *Benedictus*. According
to the earlier one, nine of the candles were extinguished during Matins, the remaining lights during the last four verses
of the *Benedictus*.[15] The other manual, however, prescribes that
one candle was to be extinguished at each of the twelve verses
of the *Benedictus*, the last one being removed at the repeated
Traditor autem.[16] In the late fifteenth century, the six lights

[11]Breviary I p.382. The document is assigned to this century by
J.M.Neale *(Christian Remembrancer XX* (Oct.1850) p.285, cited in Breviary
ibidem).

[12]*Caeremoniale Episcoporum* II.22 p.266.

[13]Doblado p.284; 1682 Ceremonial p.265; 1825 Ceremonial p.318; 1778
Breviary, *Pars Verna* p.289; 1832 Ceremonial p.294; 1930 Breviary p.402;
1634 Ceremonial pp.56–58.

[14]1662 Ceremonial of Paris p.340. Other references as above.

[15]1731 Ceremonial p.223.

[16]1734 *Diurnale* p.260.

above the chancel in the Sistine Chapel were also extinguished simultaneously with the six altar-candles.[17]

(iii) The Last Candle

Writing in the later part of the thirteenth century, Durandus states that the last candle at Tenebrae was extinguished at the *Benedictus;* but he gives no indication of whether this was done at the antiphon before or after the Gospel canticle.[18] Since he makes no reference to the *Benedictus* having been sung in darkness, it is possible that his statement is deliberately imprecise so as to allow a choice of points for extinguishing the final candle. It is perhaps surprising that he makes no overt reference to the practice, which had existed since the eighth century,[19] and which was widespread in his day, of removing rather than extinguishing the last candle and subsequently restoring it before the end of the service.[20]

Regardless of whether the last candle had been removed before or after the *Benedictus,* the service always ended in darkness. The general practice, then, appears to have been to reproduce a light at the conclusion of the office, which was originally intended to provide illumination for those leaving a church in complete darkness. Thus, in those places where the last candle had actually been extinguished, another light was produced.[21] At Gembloux, the last candle was relit.[22] In the Dominican rite, the sacristan's lamp, hidden during the fifth psalm, was reproduced.[23] Where the last candle had only

[17]Dykmans II p.366.

[18]*Rationale* VI.72 fol.322.

[19] Ordo 30B.28.

[20]The possibility should be considered that Durandus, who wrote *'extinguitur'* of the last candle, was using the verb in the sense of 'remove from view' in addition to 'extinguish'.

[21]St Mary's, York (HBS 75 p.273); Haymo's *Ordo Breviarii* (Van Dijk II p.84); Worcester (Antiphonary p.63); York (Breviary I p.382).

[22]Albers II p.91.

[23]The writer is grateful to R.Conrad OP for this information.

been hidden, it was customary to bring it forth at the end of the service.[24] At St-Agnan, Orléans, where Lauds, even in the eighteenth century, appears to have been held in darkness, several candles were relit at the very end of the office.[25]

According to the Roman rite, official practice until 1955 was to remove the last candle at the repetition of the *Traditor autem,* to place it momentarily on the altar, and then to hide it under the altar at the Epistle corner, thence to bring it forth once more at the very end of the service, before extinguishing it after the departure of the congregation.[26] An alternative, but unofficial, practice was to leave the candle burning until the conclusion of the service and then to hide it.[27] After the reforms of 1955, this alternative practice was officially adopted,[28] except that the candle was not hidden but simply extinguished when the church was empty.

The custom of bringing back the last candle arose for practical reasons and had its origin, in the days when Tenebrae ended before dawn, in those churches where the *Benedictus* was sung by the light of the candle which was subsequently hidden but not extinguished. Before a symbolic interpretation became attached to this candle, its function was similar to the sacristan's lamp before the start of the service : to provide illumination for the faithful as they left the church.[29] At Norwich, Farfa, and St Paul's, Rome, a candle was lit in a lantern before the last light had been extinguished; and at Norwich, it was removed from the choir.[30] At Worcester, it had already been lit outside the church before the start of the service.[31] After a signal from the under-sacristan, it was

[24]Rouen Breviary np; Premonstratensian Breviary p.402; Beleth, *Rationale* (PL 202.106D).

[25]De Moléon p.206.

[26]Roman Breviary p.445; Fortescue and O'Connell (4th edition) p.305.

[27]Thurston, *Lent and Holy Week* p.243.

[28]Fortescue and O'Connell (11th edition) p.282; Wuest p.263.

[29]Crossley p.83.

[30]HBS 82 p.79; Albers I p.46; Martène, *DAER* 4.22.8 p.124.

[31]Antiphonary p.62.

brought into the building to guide the monks back to their dormitory. At St Mary's, York, where the last candle was put out at the *Benedictus,* the sacristan, on hearing the knocks made by the abbot at the end of the service, produced a candle, lit from the *copiosum lumen,* which he had kept hidden away in a lantern *(sconsa).* This was then placed on the chancel step.[32] In the Cistercian rite a candle was lit in a lantern *(sconsa)* before the last light was extinguished, and brought into the choir when the abbot began the *Pater noster.*[33]

(iv) The Last Candle : Symbolism and Size

In the same way that the medieval mind attached a symbolic interpretation to other liturgical features of Tenebrae, the last candle came to be regarded especially with great importance and to be understood in a number of different ways. This was to a large extent due to the darkness which was to follow the extinction of its flame. According to Hugh of St-Victor, the last candle stood for Christ, who was the last prophet to be killed. However, since he was regarded as a prophet while he was proclaiming the Gospel during his ministry, the candle was to be of the same size as the rest.[34] Hugh obviously understands this light to represent only the human nature of Jesus. The same rationale probably lies behind the stipulation in the Gilbertine Ordinal that the candle at the top of the hearse was to be no larger than the rest.[35] On the other hand, the central candle of the twenty-five at York Minster appears to have been larger than the rest, an opinion shared by Dom André Mocquereau.[36] The identification of Christ with the last candle is also found in the *Ordinal of St Mary's, York,* where Christ is compared to the *candela preemi-*

[32]HBS 75 p.273.
[33]*Nomasticon Cisterciense* p.99.
[34]*Miscellanea* (PL 177.889C).
[35]HBS 59 p.31.
[36]Breviary I p.375; Worcester Antiphonary p.63.

nens on the hearse.[37] Durandus, aware of the two traditions regarding the size of the last candle, comments that 'according to some men it is larger than the others, because Christ was greater than men. According to others, it is the same size—Christ was one of the prophets.'[38]

John Beleth also compares the concealment of the last candle to the physical death of Christ and regards its reappearance at the conclusion of the office for the kindling of the church lights as an anticipation of the Resurrection.[39] Pope Benedict XIV also likens the concealing of the last candle behind the altar to the burial of Jesus. For him the fact that the candle remained lit, whilst hidden, signified the activity of the Lord in the Underworld; and the restoration of the candle to its original place on the hearse symbolised the coming Resurrection.[40] At Angers, the significance and symbolism attached to the reappearance of the light at the conclusion of Tenebrae was dramatically enacted by the senior choir boy. He produced a lighted torch, which had been hidden behind the choir stalls prior to the start of the service, and chanted *'Lumen Christi'*.[41]

It is Durandus who records the wide range of symbolic interpretations which the last candle had acquired by the end of the thirteenth century.[42] For it could represent :

1. The Blessed Virgin Mary in whom alone the faith remained.

2. Christ who was dead according to the flesh.

3. The faith which was hidden in the Apostles.

4. The Apostles' faith after their infidelity.

5. The fire of the Holy Spirit which seemed extinct.

[37]HBS 75 p.271.
[38]*Rationale* VI.72 fol.331.
[39]*Rationale* (PL202.106D).
[40]*De Festis Domini Nostri Jesu Christi* Pt 1 §126, cited by Eisenhöfer, *Handbuch* 1 p.514.
[41]1731 Ceremonial pp.226-27.
[42]*Rationale* VI.72 fol.331.

6. The renewal of Christ's light.

7. The commemoration of the Resurrection after the deaths of the prophets.

It is not difficult to see why the light of the last candle came to be identified with Christ, or some aspect of the Godhead, for those who sang the last verse of the *Benedictus* in almost total darkness.

Christopher Wordsworth records a different symbolism, which in England became attached to the last candle on the hearse. This light was sometimes known as the 'Judas candle' because the antiphon at which that light was extinguished or hidden, began, 'He that betrayed him . . . ' *(Traditor autem).*[43]

[43]*Medieval Services* p.168. The name is found in medieval documents. (a) 'In j Judas de novo facto adserviendum in choro per iij dies, videlicet diebus mercurii, Jovis et Parasceven' (1402-3). *Memorials of Ripon* III p.212 (Surtees Society Publications 81). (b) 'In uno Judas de novo fact' p' candel tenebrar' deferend' festin' Pasch xxd.' R. Dymond, 'History of St Petrock's', *Transactions of the Devonshire Association,* Vol.XIV (1882), p.410.

Chapter Nine
THE NAME AND ORIGIN
OF TENEBRAE

(i) The Name *Tenebrae*

The name by which the combined office of Matins and
Lauds was popularly known is first recorded by Peter Abelard
in the first half of the twelfth century.[1] Beleth also uses the
term a little later,[2] but the name is almost certainly much older.
In the eighth-century Ordo 28, we read, 'septima . . .
tenebratur candela', 'the seventh lamp is extinguished' (§30);
and the *Regularis Concordia* of *c.*970 states that the service is
a commemoration of Jesus' three hours on the Cross and of
the *'tenebrarum terror'* which prevailed because of the Crucifixion.[3] However, in addition to the content of the service, the
time at which the office was sung and its conclusion in darkness almost certainly contributed towards the name.

(ii) The Origin of Tenebrae

(A) THE TRADITIONAL THEORIES. It was formerly believed that
Tenebrae recalled the time when services were held in the

---

[1]*Letter 10* (PL 178.340A) : Atque hinc vulgo horum dierum Vigiliae nun-
cupantur Tenebrae, 'And so for this reason the night office of these days
is called Tenebrae'.

[2]*Rationale* (PL 202.105B).

[3]PL 137.490B.

catacombs or in the darkness of a church building because of the fear of persecution;[4] or even that it commemorated the Apostles' hiding in the Upper Room.[5]

(B) THE UTILITARIAN THEORY. According to this theory, which was first propounded by Claude de Vert at the beginning of the eighteenth century, the practice of extinguishing the lights gradually at Tenebrae emerged in the period when Matins and Lauds were sung in the very early hours of the morning. With the gradual increase of light at dawn, the church lights were put out one by one until, by the time that the last lamp was extinguished, there was sufficient natural light for the needs of those at worship. The theory seems to have been accepted by the reformers of the Holy Week Liturgy in the 1950s; for commenting on the Decree of *Maxima Redemptionis* of 16 November 1955, which authorised the liturgical changes, P. Jounel observes that Tenebrae had now been restored to the correct time of day, so that the gradual extinguishing of the lights coincided with the rising of the sun.[6]

The theory, which is based largely on assumptions unsupported by documentary evidence, must be challenged and exposed to further scrutiny. Dendy doubts the genuineness of the explanation; but apart from drawing attention to the phrase *media nocte surgendum est*, 'they must rise at midnight', which occurs in four of the earlier *ordines*,[7] he offers no explanation of his own.[8] Any vindication of this theory depends on two major factors : (i) the time or times at which the office is known to have commenced and (ii) the duration of the combined office of Matins and Lauds. We propose to consider the length of the service first and then to look at the time at which it began, so as to calculate the hour at which the office ended.

[4]Amalarius, *Lib. Off.* 4.22.
[5]Houssaye p.460.
[6]*Le nouvel ordo* p.25.
[7]OR 28.29; OR 30A.1; OR 30B.1; OR 31.11.
[8]*The Use of Lights* p.147.

1. *The Duration of Tenebrae.* Possibly the only reference in medieval literature to the duration of Matins/Lauds is to be found in the *Gemma Animae* of Honorius of Autun.[9] According to that writer, Tenebrae lasted three hours, the time that Jesus was on the Cross. A glance at the contents of Matins and Lauds shows that the whole of the combined service, with its fifteen psalms, nine lessons, *Benedictus, Miserere,* as well as its antiphons, responsories, versicles, *kyrie's*, and prayers, can be performed in much less time than three hours. It is true that during the last century in the Sistine Chapel in Rome, Tenebrae, with its renowned singing of the *Miserere* and the musical accompaniment, was known to last upwards of two hours;[10] but in a medieval monastery without the same protracted musical accompaniment and contrived effects, which made use of the late afternoon sun and the frescos of Michelangelo, the entire office must have been performed in rather less time. C.Butler is of the opinion that the average length of time for Matins in the winter was an hour and a half and for Lauds between a half and three quarters of an hour.[11] Honorius' three hours should be reckoned inclusively, in much the same way as Jesus' three days in the Tomb, so that the service probably began at the end of one hour and ended shortly after the start of the third hour. Ninety minutes seems to be a more realistic figure for the duration of Tenebrae and at the same time does not contradict Honorius' statement. At Seville Cathedral in the last century, the service lasted one hour.[12] When we come to examine the time at which Tenebrae ended, we shall allow an upper limit of about two and a quarter hours duration for the purposes of our calculations.

[9]PL 172.665.

[10] Hare II p.297; Newman p.14.

[11]*Benedictine Monachism* pp.278–79. The present writer has in his possession a 1927 Dominican *Office of Holy Week,* in which a previous owner of the book has inscribed in 1971 next to the rubric for Tenebrae on Maundy Thursday, 'Tenebrae 9.30 A.M. Finish 10.15 A.M.'

[12]Doblado p.284.

2. *The Time at which Tenebrae Began.* We have already observed that in the earlier period, when Tenebrae was sung at the start of the monastic day, the office began either at midnight or at the eighth hour of the night. The practice of gradually extinguishing the lights at Tenebrae emerged from a monastic milieu, long after St Benedict had changed the hour of rising for the monks from midnight to the eighth hour of the night. Although there is evidence that the earlier time continued to be observed in some monasteries, we may discount it for our purposes with some justification. For it is inconceivable that Tenebrae could have been such a protracted and prolonged service that it lasted from midnight until dawn. Services in the West have never been noted for their seemingly interminable duration. We must therefore concern ourselves with the later time of the eighth hour.

The Benedictine injunction relating to the time of rising was observed from the first day of November until Easter, regardless of the date when that festival occurred.[13] Lauds, originally a separate office, used to be sung at dawn *(incipiente luce);* but long before 700, it had become customary to sing Lauds immediately after Matins, in the early hours of the morning.[14] We hope to show that by the eighth century, when the service of Tenebrae is first attested, the office of Matins/Lauds ended in darkness before sunrise and that the utilitarian theory for the gradual extinguishing of lights at that service cannot be upheld.

St Benedict adopted the traditional ecclesiastical system of dividing the day and the night each into twelve hours of equal length, in so far as this was possible, given the chronometri-

[13]PL 103.872A.
[14]By the time of the compilation of Ordo 26 *c.*750, the union of Matins and Lauds had already taken place. The *Regularis Concordia,* which mentions that Lauds finished before dawn and that Prime took place 'after daybreak' *(mane facto),* is too late a document (*c.*970) to be of much relevance for practices of the eighth century, when the custom of extinguishing gradually the lights at Tenebrae first became established. After Vatican II, Matins and Lauds became separated once again.

cal devices available at the time—hence the qualification 'at whatever shall be calculated to be the eighth hour'. *Table 6* shows the earliest date (18 March) upon which Maundy Thursday can fall and also the latest (22 April). The fifth day of April represents the mid-point between the two extremes. It is quite clear that at the earliest date for Maundy Thursday, one twelfth of the period of darkness (that is, from sunset to sunrise) is, depending on the latitude, either one hour or almost sixty minutes according to the modern system of measuring time, so that everywhere between Rome and York on 18 March, an hour of darkness is of virtually the same duration according to the former method of reckoning time. After the vernal equinox, the time differential begins to increase in accordance with the degrees of latitude. The amount of daylight increases in the northern hemisphere with a corresponding decrease in darkness so that the further north one travels the more noticeably smaller the length of each hour of darkness grows.

Table 6 also shows the modern corresponding time for the eighth hour. This is arrived at by dividing the total period of darkness by twelve and then calculating to what period during the night the eighth division would correspond by modern reckoning. C.Butler is right to point out that *at the eighth hour* referred to the completion of the hour and not to its inception; but when instancing the city of Rome, where on 25 March the sun rises and sets at six o'clock and there are exactly twelve hours of darkness, he is incorrect in stating that the eighth hour of the night lasted from 2.00 A.M. to 3.00 A.M. and that *at the eighth hour* indicated 3.00 A.M.[15] For the first hour extended from 6.00 P.M. to 7.00 P.M., the second from 7.00 P.M. to 8.00 P.M., and so forth. The eighth hour would therefore have lasted from 1.00 A.M. to 2.00 A.M., and this latter time would be the modern equivalent of *at the eighth hour.*[16]

[15]*Benedictine Monachism* p.275.
[16]It is known that the length of hours was adjusted in N.Germany

Date	Latitude	Sunset	Sunrise	Minutes in one hour	8th hour +
18 March	40°	18.10	06.08	59.8	01.01–02.09
18 March	50°	18.09	06.08	59.9	01.09–02.09
18 March	60°	18.08	06.09	60.0	01.09–02.09
5 April	40°	18.28	05.38	55.8	00.59–01.55
5 April	50°	18.38	05.29	53.4	00.59–01.54
5 April	60°	18.52	05.14	51.8	00.57–01.49
22 April	40°	18.45	05.13	52.3	00.51–01.43
22 April	50°	19.04	04.54	49.1	00.47–01.36
22 April	60°	19.35	04.24	44.0	00.43–01.27

+ The times given in this column are *ante meridiem* and correspond approximately to the hours calculated in the early Middle Ages.

* * * * *

Latitudes of various liturgical centres

Palermo	38°*	Rouen	49° 30'*
Rome	42°*	Mainz	50°
Poitiers	46° 30'*	Salisbury	51°*
Paris	49°*	York	54°*

*Approximate.

Table 6. The 8th hour of the night by modern reckoning

We are now in a position to calculate the varying times at which Tenebrae finished, both geographical and seasonal differences being taken into consideration. We have already indicated that we shall use the longer time of two and a quarter hours for the duration of Tenebrae.

(a) *18 March*   All three latitudes can be grouped together in view of the almost-identical times of sunrise.

throughout the year. The variation and adjustment is referred to in the rubrics for the new fire ceremony in *PRG* II p.57.

Tenebrae, starting at 2.09 A.M. or thereabouts and lasting for two and a quarter hours, would finish at 4.24 A.M. This is over one and a half hours before sunrise.

(b) *5 April*   Tenebrae would end :
at 40° one and a half hours before sunrise.
at 50° one hour twenty minutes before sunrise.
at 60° one hour ten minutes before sunrise.

(c) *22 April*   Tenebrae would end :
at 40° an hour and a quarter before sunrise.
at 50° just over an hour before sunrise.
at 60° about forty minutes before sunrise.

Both the time allowed for Tenebrae and the figures given for 40° and 60° represent extremes. For the times relating to places on or near the 50° line of latitude are of more relevance to our study in view of the fact that this service, with its gradual extinguishing of lights, had its origins in Northern Gaul or Western Germany, through both of which passes the fiftieth parallel.

We have shown that on 18 March, the earliest possible date on which Tenebrae could be held, the entire office of Matins/Lauds terminated, at places in Central Germany and Northern France, over an hour and a half before dawn and that even at the latest date of 22 April, there was still over an hour to pass before sunrise. The theory, therefore, that the lights of Tenebrae were put out gradually as the amount of daylight increased and the need for artificial illumination decreased cannot be upheld. Moreover, it should be borne in mind that even on a cloudless spring morning in March or April, the interiors of some churches in the period under discussion would have continued to remain badly illuminated in view of their architectural design and system of fenestration.

An explanation to account for the loss of light at the night office must be sought elsewhere. Herbert Thurston wrongly thought that it grew lighter more quickly in southern latitudes in late March and April and supposes that northern monks found it hard to get through the office of Matins without better light.[17] For more serious consideration is the possibility that because of the funereal aspect of Tenebrae, the practice of extinguishing lights was inherited from a corresponding pagan custom, according to which a gradual decrease in the number of lights was regarded as a mark of respect or honour for a deceased person. In view of the absence of corroborative evidence, however, such a theory must remain conjectural. Moreover, universal practice throughout Europe and the Near East involved the lighting of a lamp or candle in honour of the dead, rather than the extinguishing of it. We suggested previously that the Tenebrae-hearse may have been used for counting the number of gradual psalms, silently recited before Matins; but its use for this purpose was a much later development. For whilst the extinguishing of the candles may subsequently have been used for monitoring the progress of these psalms, there is no reason why this practice should have been originally adopted at Lauds any more than at the other offices of the day when the psalms were sung aloud.

The most likely explanation for the emergence of this liturgical feature at the night office is, in the opinion of the present writer, to be found in the Maundy Thursday rites in Jerusalem, which were held in and around the Garden of Gethsemane. Since ceremonies held in the original and historic locations could hardly be transferred out of their Jerusalem milieu, it seems likely that in the gradual loss of light at the night office, an attempt was made to commemorate the events of that late Thursday evening within the context of a service in church. Ferdinand Cabrol is the first to hint at the derivation of Tenebrae from the Jerusalem rites, but he does not attempt to elaborate the connection between the Western night office and the historical events in Gethsemane.[18] He merely notes that the offices of Tenebrae on Maundy Thursday and

[17]*Lent and Holy Week* p.262.
[18]*Les Origines* p.181.

Good Friday may have been influenced by the localised Jerusalem rite of Maundy Thursday evening. Cabrol was possibly closer to the truth than he realised. For it is significant that in searching for the origin of Tenebrae's gradual loss of light, we find that the first recorded instance of this liturgical phenomenon occurred during Lauds on Good Friday, which was sung at the corresponding time or not long after the time at which Jesus was arrested in Gethsemane. Since the lights, first extinguished at Lauds and subsequently at Matins and Lauds, were unlikely to have represented the torches which, we are told, the chief priests' soldiers carried (John 18:3), it would seem that they symbolised a non-luminary element in the story. Later medieval commentators may have been preserving an ancient tradition when they compared the extinguishing of the lights with the flight and desertion of the Apostles. Alternatively, the quenching of the lamps may have symbolised the heaviness of the eyes of the disciples, who were unable to stay awake and keep watch with Jesus.[19]

[19]The commemoration of the three hours of darkness on Good Friday is much more likely to be associated with Tenebrae of Holy Saturday, which follows the Crucifixion.

Part Two

THE NEW FIRE CEREMONY

Chapter Ten
THE DEVELOPMENT
OF THE CEREMONY

In order to observe the changes which occurred within the new fire ceremony and to trace more easily the influences which contributed to these changes, we have classified the different known forms of the ceremony as stages of development and have entitled these stages *modes*.

(i) The Older Roman Tradition

MODE A1

In Chapter One, we discussed the provision of new fire in mid-eighth-century Rome, attested in the letter of Pope Zachary to Boniface. We suggested that the three large lamps were reserved during the consecration of the Host at Mass on Maundy Thursday. These remained in the Cathedral of St John Lateran and continued to burn *in loco secretiore* until the fire was hallowed for use on Holy Saturday and used to light the two Vigil-candles and kindle the other lamps of St John's.

MODE A2

In the eighty or so years which separate the pontificate of Zachary from the visit of Amalarius to Rome in 832, a development in the procedure for the provision of new fire dur-

ing the Triduum occurred within the Roman Church. It had
been the practice at Rome in the time of Zachary to obtain
new fire on Holy Saturday from the flame of one of the three
lamps which had been hidden from view on Maundy Thursday. However, according to the subsequent testimony of Archdeacon Theodore, new fire was kindled on Good Friday for
use at the night office of Holy Saturday.[1] The clarity of this
statement is matched by the resulting uncertainty which we
experience regarding the provision of fire at other times during the Triduum. For it raises two important and closely-
connected questions : (a) Did the new fire for the ceremonies
of Holy Saturday continue to be taken from one of the three
lamps reserved on Maundy Thursday? (b) Was the new fire
kindled on Good Friday destined for use only on Good Friday night and subsequently extinguished at the conclusion
of the night office of Holy Saturday? Since Theodore is silent
on this matter, there are two possibilities to be considered.
(i) If the practice of reserving the three large lamps on Maundy
Thursday had been discontinued, it would follow that the new
fire kindled on Good Friday was reserved not only for the night
office at the end of that day but also for the Vigil during the
evening of Holy Saturday. (ii) On the other hand, the continuing reservation of Maundy Thursday's fire would have
restricted the use of Friday's newly-kindled fire to the night
office of Holy Saturday since a second reserved source of fire
would have been superfluous. Theodore's silence, however,
regarding the three lamps is not decisive; for the conversation between the Archdeacon and Amalarius had revolved
around the loss of illumination at the night office, not the provision of light for the Vigil of Holy Saturday.

The external evidence, which it is possible to adduce in
favour of both the above views, is necessarily inconclusive.

---

[1]In ipsa die novus ignis accenditur, de quo reservetur usque ad nocturnale officium. 'On that day [Good Friday] new fire is kindled, and from
it a flame is reserved for the night office.' Amalarius, *Lib.de Off.Ant.*
XLIV.2.

For the practice of reserving fire was well-established in the Gallican Church *(Mode B2)* and featured in the *Pontificale Romano-Germanicum (PRG),* the service-book which the Roman Church adopted in the tenth century. On the other hand, the Pontifical of Poitiers, which bears the marks of Roman influence, records that the Easter candle was lit with a flame *kindled anew* on Good Friday (p.215), whilst the reservation of fire on Good Friday is attested in three *ordines* and four sacramentaries.[2]

It is safe to assume from the evidence of Amalarius that at Rome, the new fire was kindled shortly after the conclusion of the liturgy of Good Friday afternoon :

> In the Roman Church all fire is extinguished and (subsequently) rekindled on Good Friday. By this action fire, which is fuelled and maintained by stocks of firewood, imitates the principal source of fire, that is, the sun in the sky, which hid itself from human eyes from the sixth to the ninth hour at the time of our Lord's passion so that those who wickedly rejoiced at the shame of their Lord and Creator might not enjoy its light. For this reason that fire, which is obtained for our use, may be extinguished on Good Friday at about the sixth hour and renewed at about the ninth hour of the day.[3]

However, we can only surmise that it took place somewhere in the vicinity of St John Lateran, wherein the night office of Holy Saturday would be held. Similarly, we can but guess at the means employed in the production of that fire.

[2]For the references, see *Mode B1.*

[3]In Romana ecclesia extinguitur totus ignis in sexta feria et reaccenditur. In hoc facto imitatur ignis, fotus et conservatus per congesta lignorum, principalem ignem, id est solem corporeum, qui ab humanis obtutibus se abscondit tempore passionis Domini a sexta ora usque ad oram nonam, ne suo lumine fruerentur qui male gaudebant de ignominia domini sui et creatoris. Hac ratione ignis iste, qui nostris usibus procuratur, potest extingui in sexta feria circa sextam oram diei et renovari circa nonam horam diei. *Lib. Off.* 4.22.2.

(ii) The Gallican Traditions

MODE B1

The use of fire reserved on Good Friday to light the Easter candle is attested in three *ordines* and four sacramentaries.[4] According to Ordo 23, it was used to light the two Vigil-candles, which were a feature of the old Roman tradition (§24). This light is to be identified with that, described in Ordo 30B, which was reserved at the conclusion of Lauds on Good Friday and which was also used for the provision of illumination at the night office of Holy Saturday. The practice of reserving Good Friday's fire must have been of considerable antiquity and suggests a period when the liturgical milieu was characterised by a complete absence of light between the end of the night office of Good Friday and the Vigil of Holy Saturday. It also dated from a time anterior to that in which Tenebrae had reached its final stage of development, since the loss of light at Maundy Thursday's night office caused the need for a fresh supply of fire the same day. The reservation of *old* fire was possibly a Gallican development of the Roman practice attested by Zachary *(Mode A1)* and took place at the conclusion of the night office of Good Friday because of the necessity of illumination at that service; whereas, in the circumstances familiar to Zachary, the singing of Matins/Lauds of Good Friday in the Church of S.Croce in Gerusalemme, followed by the celebration of that day's liturgy in the same church, enabled the fire to be reserved at St John Lateran in circumstances undisturbed by any liturgical activity.

MODE B2

According to an alternative Gallican tradition, the flame for lighting the Easter candle was obtained from newly-kindled fire, and not from an already-existing source of hallowed fire

---

[4] OR 17.103; OR 30A.15; OR 30B.28; *GeV* p.68; *GePr* p.55; *GeAng* p.52; *GeG* pp.92-93.

which had been reserved for that purpose *(Mode B1)*. The earliest evidence for the kindling of new fire, as opposed to the reservation of *old* fire, is to be found in Ordo 26 (§3). The ceremony took place on Maundy Thursday, and it is not difficult to see why it occurred on that day. For within this Gallican tradition, the production of new fire was closely linked to the performance of Tenebrae on all three days of the Triduum—a situation attested by this *ordo*. In churches in which the development had reached *Stage 3, Stage 4,* or *Stage 5,* the supply of fire for the night office and Vigil of Holy Saturday was obtained from the lamp hidden and reserved at the conclusion of Lauds on Good Friday. With the loss of fire at the end of the night office of Maundy Thursday, however, it was now necessary to ensure that a supply of fire was available not only for the night office of Good Friday but also for kindling the liturgical lights for the Mass or Masses of Maundy Thursday. There is one recorded instance of the reservation of *old* fire on Maundy Thursday,[5] but according to the majority of our sources the fire was kindled anew on that day.

Four of the early *ordines* and *Alcuin* state that the fire was then reserved for lighting the Easter candle on Holy Saturday,[6] but they omit any reference to the blessing of the fire on Maundy Thursday. However, according to *PRG,* which attests the same ceremonial, the fire was first blessed before

[5]According to the Gradual of Gregory, cited by Macri, *Hierolexicon* pp.141-42 : Deinde venit Archidiaconus ante altare accipiens lumen, quod *quinta* feria absconditum fuit, faciensque crucem super cereum et illuminans eum, ac benedicens, dicente ipso Lumen Christi, respondent omnes Deo Gratias. (The writer's italics.) 'Then the Archdeacon comes in front of the altar. He takes the light which was hidden away on Maundy Thursday, and making the sign of the cross over the candle, he lights the candle and blesses it. Then he acclaims, ''The Light of Christ'', and all reply, ''Thanks be to God''.' The form of words used recalls the corresponding rubrics in the *ordines* and sacramentaries referred to above. However, the occurrence of *quinta* and the reference to *Lumen Christi* suggest that the gradual is a later document.

[6]OR 26.3; OR 27.6; OR 28.25; OR 31.29; PL 101.1205C.

being reserved.[7] Although the difficulty arising from the subsequent hallowing of the fire on Holy Saturday precludes this
document from being regarded with complete confidence as
corroborative evidence,[8] nevertheless, it is very likely, in view
of other similarities of ritual between *PRG* and the above-
mentioned *ordines,* that a blessing of the new fire prior to its
reservation should be understood. According to this arrangement, fire required for any of the subsequent services during
the remainder of the Triduum could be taken from the reserved flame without the requirement of a preliminary act of
benediction.

However, according to *PRG,* the Mass of the Chrism was
celebrated at the third hour of the day.[9] Since the new fire
was kindled no earlier than the fifth hour, according to the
same pontifical, the flame for the lights at this Mass clearly
could not have been taken from the new fire. The rubric for
the conclusion of Lauds on Maundy Thursday, however,
states that before the *Benedictus* was sung, the last lamp was
either extinguished or withdrawn and reserved (p.58 §220).
The writer believes that the purpose in reserving the lamp
at this service was to provide light for the above-mentioned
Mass in those churches where it was still celebrated. For by
the tenth century, the Mass of the Chrism was no longer
celebrated in many churches, so that it was no longer necessary to reserve a flame at the conclusion of the night office
of Maundy Thursday. The kindling of the new fire later that
same day took place *before* the late-afternoon Mass, which commemorated the institution of the Lord's Supper.

Mode B3

The new fire ceremonial attested in *PRG* bears a close
similarity to that described in the *ordines* of *Mode B2.* The pontifical differs from these documents, however, in that in the

[7]II p.57 §216.
[8]See *Mode B3* below.
[9]II p.57 §216.

ritual of Holy Saturday, there is a seemingly-superfluous hallowing of the new fire, which had previously been blessed on Maundy Thursday. It must be admitted that a second act of benediction is not unknown in the ceremonies relating to the new fire,[10] but it is certainly unusual. This second blessing contained in *PRG* may be a survival of an older Gallican tradition in which the new fire was kindled and hallowed on Holy Saturday. Its presence in the tenth-century *PRG* reveals the composite character of that document and is in all likelihood the result of a synthesis of different traditions relating to the new fire. This is particularly borne out by the benediction-formulas used on Holy Saturday and especially in the use of the *Deus mundi Conditor*. This prayer constitutes the formula for the blessing of the Easter candle attested in the Gelasian sacramentaries and is not strictly a blessing for the new fire. *PRG* also includes *Formula H* for the blessing of Holy Saturday's fire. This prayer differs from the other formulas in that both the fire and the candle, which is lit from the fire, are included in the words of sanctification.

The twofold blessing of the new fire is also found at Salzburg.[11] There the new fire was blessed on Maundy Thursday with *Formulas A, B,* and *C* and on Holy Saturday with the *Deus mundi Conditor* and *Formula H,* as in *PRG* on both days.[12] From other rubrical similarities there can be little doubt that the Missal of Salzburg derives directly from the pontifical.[13] For even after the lapse of five and a half centuries, the new fire ceremonial of Salzburg is still recognisably the ritual prescribed by *PRG.* (*Mode B3* is alluded to in the twelfth-century *Pontificale Romanum.*[14])

[10]For instance, the so-called double blessing of the lamp and candle in the Mozarabic rite.

[11]1507 Missal fol.lxxxv (MT) and fol.xciii (HS).

[12]These two latter formulas for the blessing of the fire on Holy Saturday were also used at Mainz, Ratisbon, and Abo *(Table 20).*

[13]For instance, the choice of times for kindling the new fire on Maundy Thursday (*PRG* II p.56 §215 and 1507 Missal fol.lxxxv).

[14]*PRMA* I.xxxii.1.

There is no evidence to suggest that the new fire, once kindled, was reserved in an unhallowed state for the duration of the Triduum and that only fire taken from this source was blessed on each of these last three days of Holy Week.

Mode B4

In *Mode B2,* we observed that the loss of fire occasioned by the extinguishing of the lights at each of the three performances of Tenebrae was made good by the kindling of the new fire on Maundy Thursday and by its subsequent reservation for use during the remainder of the Triduum. Within the same liturgical milieu, in what could be argued was an obvious and logical development in the ritual for the provision of the new fire, there emerged the practice of kindling fire on each of the days of the Triduum. It is first attested in Ordo 29,[15] and it became widespread throughout the Western Church through its adoption by a very large number of monasteries.[16]

It might have been expected that with a fresh supply of new fire available on each of the three days, the need to reserve Maundy Thursday's fire would disappear. However, according to Ordo 29, there was not only a production of new fire on each day of the Triduum; Maundy Thursday's fire was also reserved for lighting the Easter candle on Holy Saturday. Since the Candle could have been lit with the fire kindled on Holy Saturday, the reservation of Maundy Thursday's fire would appear to be a superfluous survival of a former practice. Ordo 29 is in fact a composite document. The ceremonial

[15]OR 29.14, .28, and .45. H.A.P.Schmidt wrongly supposed that *PRG* records the kindling of new fire on each of the three days (*Hebdomada Sancta* II pp.820–21). The pontifical actually states that on Good Friday : *lumen deportatur,* 'a light is brought' (II p.86 §304); and on Holy Saturday : *deportatur lumen quod quinta feria fuerat excussum,* 'fire is brought which had been kindled on Maundy Thursday' (II p.94 §342). There is no mention of a *production* of new fire on either of the last two days of Holy Week.

[16]Lanfranc, *Decrees* (PL 150.467B); John of Avranches, *Lib.de Off.Eccl.* 53 (PL 147.49A). See *Tables 8a* and *8b.*

of Holy Saturday is unique; for it combines the Roman practice of lighting the two Vigil-candles, prior to the reading of the prophecies, with the Gallican ritual of kindling the Easter candle so that the Vigil-candles were lit with the fire struck on Holy Saturday, whilst the Easter candle was lit with fire reserved from Maundy Thursday. In the Holy Saturday liturgy of Ordo 29, we have a synthesis of both Roman and Gallican elements.

MODE B5

As in Ordo 29, we find in the Pontifical of Poitiers elements derived from both the Roman and the Gallican traditions. There is a triple kindling of fire during the Triduum, and the two Vigil-candles are a feature of the liturgy of Holy Saturday.[17] It differs from Ordo 29 in that the fire for lighting both the Easter candle and the Vigil-candles is that kindled and reserved on Good Friday. It is possible that this practice was derived from the Gallican tradition, attested in *Mode B1,* of lighting the Easter candle with fire reserved on Good Friday. However, in view of the presence of Roman elements in other aspects of *Poitiers'* Holy Saturday liturgy,[18] it is more likely that the fire was kindled on Good Friday and subsequently reserved, in imitation of the Roman practice described by Archdeacon Theodore *(Mode A2).*

(iii) The Spanish and Italian Traditions

MODE C1   THE MOZARABIC, AMBROSIAN, AND BENEVENTAN
                        RITES

In the three above-named traditions, the absence of light during Good Friday or the loss of light at the Passion on that day necessitated the provision of newly-kindled fire on Holy Saturday for the lighting of the Easter candle,[19] since in none

---

[17]*Poitiers* p.138 and p.215.

[18]For instance, the use and significance of the Vigil-candles (p.215) and the reference to the wax Agnus Dei's.

[19]Antiphonary of Léon p.276; Beroldus p.106.

of these three traditions was a flame reserved from either Maundy Thursday or Good Friday.[20] The single production of new fire on Holy Saturday at Ripoll and at Vich was almost certainly due to Mozarabic influence, and there is evidence for this tradition within the Gallican Church. For one of *PRG*'s two principal manuscripts records a blessing of the new fire on Holy Saturday, thus duplicating the hallowing of fire on Maundy Thursday.[21] It strongly suggests that formerly in one tradition the fire had been kindled on Holy Saturday. This may have been the primitive Gallican practice. On the other hand, it may be argued that this was the result of Milanese influence; for that rite is known to have been used in Southern Germany as late as the eleventh century.[22] The single kindling of fire on Holy Saturday is also attested by Lanfranc and may have featured in the pre-Conquest English Church. *Table 10a* lists the early evidence for this mode.

Mode C2   The later Roman tradition

When the Roman Church adopted the Romano-Germanic Pontifical in the tenth century, the arrangements for the production of the new fire, as prescribed by that document, were not adopted into the Roman rite in their entirety. For at Rome, the new fire had previously been kindled on Holy Saturday; and although *PRG* directed that the new fire should be produced on Maundy Thursday, the former day remained unchanged after Rome's adoption of that pontifical. This is clear from the rubric of the twelfth-century *Pontificale Romanum* :

> Now on this day [Holy Saturday] at the fifth or sixth hour, let the new fire be produced from a lens outside the church—or it may be done in any other way—if it has not already been

---

[20]It is very likely that Beneventum's Good Friday liturgy closely followed that of Milan. Borella p.109.

[21]Manuscript C (II p.96 §344).

[22]Borella p.105.

kindled on Maundy Thursday, according to the custom of some churches.[23]

The churches in which it was customary to kindle the new fire on Maundy Thursday were those whose rites were regulated by *PRG* and other early *ordines*. One of them was the Church of Salzburg, whose new fire ceremonial, even in the sixteenth century, was still fundamentally the same as that described in *PRG*.

It is not immediately clear why the practice of kindling the new fire on Maundy Thursday and reserving it until Holy Saturday was not adopted by the Roman Church, especially as it had been the custom at Rome to reserve Maundy Thursday's fire. It may have been felt more convenient not to kindle anew and reserve the fire on that day, especially as the use of two churches for the ceremonies of the Triduum may have caused difficulties in the reservation or the transportation of the new fire.[24] On the other hand, there may have been some reluctance to change what had become a well-established practice, which was also observed in the contemporary rites of Beneventum and Milan.

[23]Hora autem quinta vel sexta, novus ignis, si non fuerit excussus in caena domini, iuxta morem quarumdam ecclesiarum, excutiatur hoc die extra ecclesiam de crystallo, vel etiam alio modo fiat. *PRMA* xxxii.1 p.238.

[24]St John Lateran and S.Croce in Gerusalemme.

Chapter Eleven

THE TRIPLE AND THE SINGLE PRODUCTION OF FIRE

(i) The Triple Production of Fire

There were two main procedures for the provision of fire on each of the days of the Triduum, both of which have been described in the previous chapter. According to the arrangement outlined in *Mode B2,* the new fire was kindled on Maundy Thursday and reserved for use on the following two days. *Table 7* presents the evidence for this mode. This, the earlier of the two traditions involving a threefold production of fire, was almost everywhere replaced by the alternative procedure outlined in *Mode B4.* This arrangement involved a separate act of kindling fire on each of the days of the Triduum to replace that lost at the conclusion of each of the three night offices.

In addition to the implicit evidence of the early *ordines* and other documents, the loss of fire on each day of the Triduum may be inferred with confidence from Lanfranc's *Decrees;*[1] but it is clearly attested by Rupert of Deutz, who remarks, 'Having lost the fire *(amisso igne)* which was extinguished at Matins, for those three days we resort to a stone'.[2] Durandus also re-

---

[1] PL 150.467B.
[2] *De Div. Off.* V (PL 170.149A).

Church/Document	Date	Source
Ordo 26	750–755	OR 26.3
Ordo 27	750–800	OR 27.6
Ordo 28	c.800	OR 28.29
Ordo 31	880–900	OR 31.29
PRG	c.950	Vol.II p.57 §215
Ordo of Corbie	950–1000	*DAMR* 3.13.34 p.126
Alcuin	c.1000	PL 101.1205C
Avellana	11 C	PL 151.881B
Monte Cassino	c.1100	*DAMR* 3.15.34 p.141
Salzburg	1507	Missal fol.lxxxv

(Feasey, *The Paschal Candle*, p.355, stated that the practice was attested in a missal of Auch, in a sacramentary of Albi, and at Toulouse in 1555.)

Table 7. Evidence for the single kindling of the new fire and for its reservation on Maundy Thursday

cords that fires were extinguished on the three days.[3] Centuries earlier, Amalarius had explained that the fire was rekindled during the Triduum, rather than having been allowed to remain extinguished for the whole of that period, because of human weakness : services could not be held in church without light,[4] and it enabled food to be cooked.[5]

Table 8a presents the unequivocal evidence for a triple production of fire by three separate acts of ignition. The rubrics of a number of customaries and service-books are too imprecise to allow us to state with complete confidence that there was a threefold kindling of new fire during the Triduum. Some of these documents refer to a blessing of the fire on each of the three days, whilst others prescribe a repetition on Good Friday and on Holy Saturday of Maundy Thursday's new

[3] *Rationale* VI.80 fol.350.
[4] *Lib. Off.* 4.22.
[5] *Lib. de Ord. Ant.* XLIV.6.

148 *The New Fire Ceremony*

Church/Commentator	Date	Source
Ordo 29	870–890	OR 29.15, .29, .45
Rupert of Deutz	c.1111	PL 170.149A
John of Avranches	c.1070	PL 147.49A
St Mary's, York	c.1400	HBS 75 p.275
Rouen	c.1700	De Moléon p.299

(Grancolas states that there was still a threefold kindling of fire at Reims and Cluny—*Commentarius* p.316.)

Table 8a. Firm evidence for a kindling of fire on each day of the Triduum

Church/Monastery	Date	Source
Regularis Concordia	c.970	PL 137.491B, .494C
Fruttuaria	c.1000	Albers IV p.54
Cluny	c.1000	Albers II p.18
German Monasteries	c.1000	Albers V pp.32, 38
Fleury	c.1000	Albers V p.143
Farfa	c.1000	Albers I pp.48, 52, 54
St-Bénigne, Dijon	11 C	*DAMR* 3.13.34 p.126
Lanfranc	c.1070	PL 150.467B
St Paul's, Rome	11 C	*DAER* 4.22 p.124
Nidaros	13 C	*ONE* p.232
Worcester	c.1250	Antiphonary p.69
Evesham	c.1250	HBS 6 cols.80, 88, 90
Canterbury	13 C	HBS 28 p.274
Norwich	c.1265	HBS 82 pp.81, 88, 91
Reims	14 C	*DAER* 4.22.5 p.97
Cluny	1510	Missal fol.xlix
Braga	1531	Missal np
St-Martin d'Ainay	1543	*DAER* 4.22 p.125
Bayonne	1568	Missal pp.42, 46
Valladolid	1674	King, *LPS* p.214
Tibaes	1674	King, *LPS* p.268

Table 8b. Additional evidence for the triple production of new fire

fire procession. All the sources which do not specifically refer
to the kindling of fire on each of the three days have been
assigned to *Table 8b*. However, in each instance, it is safe to
infer that there was a triple kindling of fire and that the newly-
kindled fire of Maundy Thursday was not reserved on that
day.

Regardless of whether the new fire was kindled and reserved
on Maundy Thursday or kindled afresh on each of the three
days, the schedule of events relating to the provision of new
fire during the Triduum would have assumed the following
pattern :

Maundy Thursday 1. Loss of fire at the night office.
2. Production of fire during the day for :
(a) Mass of the Lord's Supper
(b) *Lotio*
(c) Matins/Lauds of Good Friday.

Good Friday 1. Loss of fire at the night office.
2. Production of fire during the day for :
(a) Mass of the Pre-sanctified
(b) Matins/Lauds of Holy Saturday.

Holy Saturday 1. Loss of fire at the night office.
2. Production of fire for the Vigil.

In some of the earlier documents which record a threefold
procession of fire, we find that there was a gradation in the
seniority of the personages who bore the fire on the second
and third days. The assignation of the function to the bishop
or abbot on Holy Saturday indicates that the fire which lit
the Easter candle was considered to be of greater importance
than the fire of the previous two days. *Table 9* illustrates the
gradation in rank of those who bore the new fire.

Dendy's statement that the evidence for the threefold blessing of the new fire is primarily monastic is correct.[6] Liturgical development and the evolution of new forms of ceremonial

---

[6] *The Use of Lights* p.142.

		Thursday	Friday	Saturday
Ordo 26 *PRG*	S	Sacristan	Archdeacon	Junior Bishop
Poitiers *Alcuin*	M	Sacristan	Prior	Abbot
Ordo 29	M	Sacristan	Prior	Abbot
Regularis *Concordia*	M	Sacristan	Deacon	Prior
Cluny Farfa Fleury Corbie Dijon Lanfranc Reims	M	Sacristan	Prior	Abbot (or Bishop)
St Mary's, York	M	Sacristan	Prior	Abbot's principal chaplain
Salzburg	S	Sacristan	?	Archdeacon

S = *secular*   M = *monastic*

(For references, see *Tables 7, 8a,* and *8b.*)

Table 9. The bearers of the new fire

are more likely to occur in the conducive surroundings of a monastic institution. Nevertheless, according to the eighth-century Ordo 26, the triple production of fire was well-established in both the cathedral and monastic traditions by the middle of that century *(Table 9);* and in the absence of further evidence, the judgement should be withheld that the practice arose out of a monastic milieu. The appearance in Ordo 26 of the cathedral officials (§19) prior to their monastic counterparts (§20) would indicate that the *ordo* was compiled for use in a cathedral church in the first instance.

(ii) The Single Production of Fire

It is generally agreed that the ceremonial surrounding the production of the new fire on Holy Saturday according to the Mozarabic rite has much in common with the ritual attested by documents illustrating the former Jerusalem liturgy of Holy Saturday, and it is also possible to detect in the Milanese rite the influence of Jerusalem. In our discussion of the provision of new fire in the previous chapter *(Modes C1* and *C2)*, we suggested that the production of fire on Holy Saturday at Rome may have been the result of both liturgical changes within her own rite and the utilisation of two church buildings for the services of the Triduum. Also worthy of consideration is the possible influence of the ritual surrounding the 'miraculous fire' at the Holy Sepulchre, which may have resulted following the renewal of contact between Rome and the Holy Land and the establishment of the Latin Patriarchate of Jerusalem in 1099.

As we observed in our discussion of *Mode C2,* the *Pontificale Romanum (PR XII)* recognised that the production of fire took place on Maundy Thursday 'in some churches'. Subsequent documents relating to the Roman rite confine the ceremony to Holy Saturday; and the influence of the Franciscans, who were instrumental in the popularisation of the Roman rite, ultimately ensured that the Gallican-derived Benedictine practice of kindling new fire on three days yielded to the Roman observance of a single production of a new fire on Holy Saturday *(Tables 10a* and *10b).*

1. Léon	10 C	18. Apamea	1214
2. Beneventum	10–11 C	19. Nidaros	1200–1220
3. Ripoll	1038	20. Haymo	1243–1244
4. Vich	1038	21. St-Pierre-sur-Dive	1273
5. Lanfranc	*c.*1070	22. Lesnes	13 C
6. Leofric	10–11 C	23. Salisbury	13 C
7. Wulfstan	11 C	24. Hereford	13 C
8. Chester	11 C	25. St-Vedast, Arras	*c.*1300
9. Milan	12 C	26. Fontanelles	*c.*1310
10. Cistercians	1119	27. Exeter	1337
11. Ordo XI	*c.*1140	28. Strasbourg	1364
12. Rome	*c.*1150	29. Westminster	1362–1368
13. Gilbertines	*c.*1150	30. Durham	14 C
14. Ireland	*c.*1150	31. Laon	14 C
15. Beleth	*c.*1180	32. Lyre	14 C
16. York	12 C	33. Toul, St-Epvre	14 C
17. Sicardus	*c.*1200		

Table 10a. Early evidence for the single production of fire[7]

[7]*References.* (1) Antiphonary p.280. (2) Hesbert p.188. (3) Sacramentary p.92. (4) Sacramentary pp.4–5. (5) PL 150.466–7. (6) M.p.223. (7) HBS 56 p.536. (8) Albers IV p.209. (9) Beroldus P.109. (10) *Nom. Cist.* p.104. (11) PL 78.1041C. (12) *OEL* p.61. (13) HBS 59 p.39. (14) M.p.126. (15) PL 202.110B. (16) M.p.109. (17) PL 213.322D. (18) *DAER* 4.24 p.160. (19) *ONE* p.232. (20) Van Dijk II p.245. (21) *DAMR* 3.13.35 p.127. (22) HBS 95 p.47. (23) HBS 91 p.19. (24) M.p.105. (25) HBS 86 p.160. (26) *DAMR* 3.15.5 p.141. (27) HBS 37 p.322. (28) *DAER* 4.22 p.162. (29) HBS 5 col.574. (30) M.p.185. (31) *DAMR* 3.13.35 p.127. (32) and (33) *DAMR* 3.15.5 p.141.

1. Abo (1522)	26. Lund (1514)
2. Amiens (1555)	27. Mainz (1507)
3. Angers (1498)	28. Melk (1495)
4. Aquileia (1519)	29. Minden (1513)
5. Arbuthnot	30. Narbonne (1528)
6. Arras (1508)	31. Noyon (1541)
7. Barking (1404)	32. Osma (1561)
8. Basel (1488)	33. Palencia (1568)
9. Bremen (1511)	34. Passau (1503)
10. Breslau (1483)	35. Poitiers (1524)
11. Burgos (1546)	36. Ratisbon (1570)
12. Bursfeld (1498)	37. Rennes (1523)
13. Carmelites (1504)	38. Rouen (1497)
14. Monte Cassino (1507)	39. St-Malo (1503)
15. Chezal-Benoit (1541)	40. Saragossa (1552)
16. Cologne (1494)	41. Sens (1520)
17. Cordoba (1561)	42. Seville (1507)
18. Cosenza (1549)	43. Spires (1512)
19. Dominicans (1482)	44. Tongres (15 C)
20. Esztergom (1501)	45. Tournai (1540)
21. Freising (1487)	46. Trier (1487)
22. Hamburg (1509)	47. Uzès (1495)
23. Hildesheim (1499)	48. Valence (1504)
24. Langres (1492)	49. Verdun (1481)
25. Liège (1492)	50. Würzburg (1477)

Table 10b. Evidence for the single production of fire : 1400–1570[8]

[8]*References.* (1) Manual p.238. (2) Pont. p.18. (3) M.np. (4) M.fol.91. (5) M.p.150. (6) M.fol.lxiv. (7) HBS 65 p.101. (8) M.fol.xci. (9) M.fol.lxxxv. (10) M.np. (11) M.fol.ciii. (12) M.fol.lxxxviii. (13) M.fol.xcv. (14) M.fol.91. (15) *DAMR* 3.15 p.141. (16) M.fol.cxxii. (17) M.fol.ciiii. (18) M.fol.115. (19) M.fol.69. (20) M.fol.lxxiii. (21) M.fol.ciii. (22) M.fol.xc. (23) M.fol.xcvi. (24) M.fol.lxv. (25) Ordinary np. (26) M.fol.xc. (27) M.fol.xcii. (28) M.fol.lxvii. (29) M.fol.ciii. (30) M.fol.lxxxiv. (31) M.fol.lix. (32) M.fol.lxxxix. (33) M.fol.c. (34) M.fol.lxxxiv. (35) M.fol.lxix. (36) Cerem.np. (37) M.fol.lxxii. (38) M.np. (39) M.np. (40) M.fol.lxxii. (41) M.fol.c. (42) M.fol.lxxv. (43) M.fol.xciii. (44) Ordinary p.164. (45) M.fol.lxix. (46) M.fol.cii. (47) M.fol.lxiii. (48) M.fol.liiii. (49) M.fol.lxiii. (50) Ordinary np.

Chapter Twelve
THE BLESSING OF THE NEW FIRE

(i) Preliminary Procession : Psalms, Litany, and Reading

In many of our sources, mention is made of a procession of clergy and people˙to the place where the new fire was to be kindled;[1] and the negative characteristic of movement in silence is found in a number of the early *ordines*. Included amongst these are three *ordines Romani*, the *Pontificale Romano-Germanicum (PRG)*, the *ordo* at Corbie mentioned by Martène, and the Customary of the German Monasteries *(CMG)*, all of which are of northern Gallican provenance and were compiled before 1000.[2]

At a relatively early date and almost certainly originating from a monastic milieu, where liturgical experimentation and elaboration of ceremonial were more likely to have occurred, a preliminary procession took place, either to the accompaniment of or followed by the chanting of the first or all the penitential psalms. The earliest recorded use of Psalm 50 (51) on this occasion comes from Farfa at the beginning of the elev-

---

[1]There was no procession in the Cistercian rite (*Nom. Cist.* p.104) or in churches such as Lyon Cathedral, where the new fire was kindled at the altar.

[2]OR 26.9; OR 29.17; OR 31.63; *PRG* II p.58 §220; *DAMR* 3.13.34 p.126 (M 1145); Albers V p.32.

enth century, but the practice may have originated at Cluny in the tenth century. *Table 11* shows that it featured prominently within the monastic tradition and survived in places into the sixteenth century. On the other hand, the chanting of all seven psalms, either during the procession to the new fire or at the place where the fire had been kindled, was a feature of the rites of a number of central European churches, even though it is first attested in the French monastery of Corbie *(Tables 13* and *14)*. At Breslau and Würzburg, the procession moved around the fire as the psalms were being chanted, nine circumambulations being accomplished at the latter

Church/Commentator	Date	Source
Cluny	10 C	Albers II p.47
Farfa	11 C	Albers I p.48
Fruttuaria*	11 C	Albers II p.93
Gembloux*	11 C	Albers IV p.53
St-Bénigne, Dijon	11 C	*DAMR* 3.13.34 p.126
John of Avranches	c.1070	PL 147.49A
Lanfranc	c.1070	PL 150.446D
Magdelen College Pont.†	12 C	HBS 39 p.169
Avranches	12 C	*DAER* 4.24.3 p.145
Evesham‡	c.1250	HBS 6 col.80
Norwich*	c.1265	HBS 82 p.81
St-Vedast, Arras	c.1300	HBS 86 p.160
Durham	14 C	Missal p.185
Reims	14 C	*DAER* 4.22.5 p.97
Camaldolese	1503	Missal fol.89
Vallombrosa	1503	Missal fol.xci
Carmelites	1504	Missal fol.xcv

*Psalm 42 (43) was also sung.
†The point at which it was sung is not stated.
‡Psalm 24 (25) was also sung.

Table 11. Psalm 50 (51) sung in procession

Church	Date	Procession
Salisbury	c.1486	Missal fol.lxxxiii
Burgos	1546	Missal fol.ciii
Palencia	1568	Missal fol.c

Table 12. Psalm 26 (27) sung in procession

Church	Date	Source
Meissen	1502	Breviary np
Halberstadt	c.1505	Missal fol.lxx
Mainz	1507	Missal fol.xcii
Salzburg	1507	Missal fol.xciii
Spires	1512	*Agenda* fol.xciii
Abo	1522	Manual p.130

Table 13. Seven penitential psalms sung in procession to the new fire

Church	Date	Source
Corbie	10 C	PL 78.336D
Cologne	12 C	*DAER* 4.24.3 p.145 (Gg 15)
Strasbourg	1364	*DAER* 4.24 p.162
Würzburg	1477	Ordinary np
Freising	1487	Missal fol.ciii
Trier	c.1487	Missal fol.cii
Prague	1498	Missal fol.xci
Passau	1503	Missal fol.lxxxiv
Breslau	1519	Missal fol.lxxix
Ratisbon	1570	Ritual cii

Table 14. Seven penitential psalms sung at the new fire

church,[3] whilst at Breslau and Ratisbon, banners were borne in the procession.[4] Both features seem to be survivals of pre-Christian ritual.

In a number of French diocesan rites, a litany was sung during the blessing of the fire.[5] Although all of the evidence is comparatively late, the fact that this feature is attested over a wide area of France would suggest that it belongs to Gallican practice dating from the Middle Ages.[6] At St-Bertrand and Mende, it was sung by six choristers who remained in the choir. Whilst the fire was being consecrated at Cahors, a senior cleric chanted the reading from the first chapter of the Second Book of Maccabees, which commemorates the discovery by Nehemiah of the sacred fire.[7]

(ii) The Formulas

The forty or so surviving prayers or benediction-formulas for the blessing of the newly-kindled fire (see Appendix 4) belong to two main categories : those which were specifically composed as benediction-formulas for the hallowing of the new fire, and those, already in existence within related liturgical situations, which were adapted or reapplied to the circumstances appertaining to the new fire ceremony. The prayers belonging to the former group were composed in response to the adoption by the Church of the pagan practice of kindling new fire. Others, inherited from well-established ceremonies, such as the *Lucernarium,* contain no overt reference to the production of the new fire; but their references to light and illumination rendered them suitable for adoption as blessings of the new fire.

[3] 1519 Missal fol.lxxix; 1477 Ordinary.

[4] 1519 Missal fol.lxxix; *Obsequiale* fol.cii.

[5] At Breslau, a litany was sung at the end of the blessing *(op.cit.).*

[6] Paris (1666 Missal p.238); Sées (1742 Missal p.185); Carcassonne (1749 Missal p.194); St-Bertrand (1773 Missal p.209); Mende (1766 Missal p.186); Luçon (1828 Missal p.213); La Rochelle (1835 Missal p.186); Autun (1845 Missal p.239).

[7] 1760 Missal p.172.

(A) THE USE OF ONE FORMULA. It subsequently became common practice to hallow the new fire using two or more prayers. Earlier practice, however, was to pronounce only one bless-

Beneventum	*c.*1000	A	Cluny	1510	B2a
Vallombrosa	11 C	A	Poitiers	1524	B2a
Besançon	11 C	A	St-Martin, d'Ainay	1531	B2a
Rupert of Deutz	*c.*1111	A	Milan	11 C	B2b
Benedictines	1481	A	Ripoll	1038	B2b
Uzès	1495	A	Braga	1512	B2e
Bursfeld	1498	A	Rouen	1497	B5a
Valence	1504	A	Coutances	1557	B5a
Seville	1507	A	Auch	1838	B5c
Narbonne	1528	A	Milan	1902	B6
Bayonne	1543	A	Leofric Collectar	11 C	B7a
Besançon	1766	A	Toul, St-Epvre	14 C	B7a
Reims	1770	A	Rheinau	1114	B9
Meaux	1845	A	Milan	1981	B11
Rome	1955	A	Bec	13 C	?C
Rome	1970	A	Lyre	*c.*1400	C
Mozarabic	10 C	B	Tongres	15 C	?C
Wulfstan	11 C	B1	Dominicans	1482	D
Palermo	*c.*1130	B1	Vich	1038	E
Lateran Missal	13 C	B1	St-Malo	1503	F
Tours	13 C	B1	Sens	1520	F
St-Denys	*c.*1273	B1	Troyes	1736	F
Cistercians	1487	B1	Beneventum	*c.*1100	H
Hildesheim†	1499	B1	*Sacramentarium Vetus*	11 C	J
Rennes	1523	B1	Cluny	11 C	L
Fontevrault	1534	B1	St-Florian	12 C	L
Amiens	1555	B1	Boulogne	1780	N
Prague			Toulouse	1490	P
Sacramentary	8 C	B2a	Burgos	1546	P
Egbert Pontifical	10 C	B2a	Strasbourg	1742	R
St-Bénigne, Dijon	11 C	B2a	Beauvais	1783	R
Barking	1404	B2a	Cambrai	1507	T
Angers	1489	B2a			

†Excluding the *Veniat quaesumus.*

Table 15. One prayer for the blessing of the new fire

Avellana†	11 C	A	*B*1	Norbertines	1578	B1	C
Nantes	1503	A	B1	Cologne	1514	B2a	E
Minden	1513	A	B1	Hereford	1502	B2d	G
Cahors	1760	A	B1	Fulda	10 C	B2e	K
Poitiers	1767	A	B1	Cologne	1626	B3	E1
Périgueux	1782	A	B1	Milan	1560	B6	O
Le Puy	1783	A	B1	Tournai	1540	B10	E
Odense†	1483	A	B^9	Nidaros	13 C	C	B1
Viborg†	1500	A	B^{10}	Carmelites	c.1312	C	B1
York	12 C	A	C	Bayeux	1780	F	C
Camaldolese	1503	A	C	Trier	1488	H	B1
Passau	1503	?C	A	Arras	1508	H	B2e
Lisieux	1752	A	C	Roskilde	1513	H	B9[11]
Chartres	1782	A	C	Saragossa	1552	H	A
Ireland	c.1200	A	D	Cordoba	1561	P	I
Lyon	1510	A	D	Carmelites	1664	S	B1
Uzès	1495	A	I				

†Excluding the *Veniat quaesumus.*

Table 16. Two prayers for the blessing of the new fire

ing, a feature which survived in a number of non-Roman rites *(Table 15)* and which since 1955 has been part of the Roman rite itself. The use of a single prayer is found in the Mozarabic rite, the older Ambrosian rite, the Beneventan rite, and the earlier English rite. Likewise, one formula is attested in the eighth-century Sacramentary of Prague and in *PRG*.[8]

[8]In the sacramentary, the prayer for the blessing of the fire (§96) follows the *Exultet* (§95). Its position here suggests that it was a later insertion which made provision for the kindling of the fire. *GePr* is the only Gelasian sacramentary to record such a formula. Had it been intended for the blessing of Good Friday's reserved fire (§94), it would surely have been placed in close proximity to the relevant rubric.

[9]Stromberg gives only the opening invocation *Dominus sancte pater, omnipotens aeterne deus, exaudi nos lumen indeficiens* (p.34).

[10]This is the same as the second prayer at Odense, but it contains an additional reference to the three who were saved from the fiery furnace.

[11]Stromberg gives only the opening clauses of this prayer (p.36).

(B) THE USE OF TWO OR MORE FORMULAS. The earliest evidence
for the existence of more than one prayer for the blessing of
the new fire is to be found in *PRG*. Although this pontifical
contains three benediction-formulas, it is almost certain that
only one was uttered when the new fire was blessed. The three
prayers of *PRG*[12] are separated from each other by the rubrical word *alia*, 'another', which indicates that a choice of formula was available for the officiating priest. This choice is
also found in the twelfth-century *Pontificale Romanum (PR XII)*
and in the Pontifical of the Roman Curia;[13] in the thirteenth-
century Ritual of Evesham, *alia* appears between the two
prayers in that book. In subsequent Roman documents and
other service-books which contain two or more benediction-
formulas *(Tables 16–18)*, there is no indication that a choice
existed. In some rites, this may suggest that all the prescribed
prayers were said. However, in other rites, such as the Roman,
in which the new fire could be kindled with either a flint or
a lens, presumably benediction-formulas such as *A* and *S*
would have been omitted when the latter means of kindling
fire was used, in view of the explicit reference in those prayers
to *silex*.

The influence of *PRG* will be noticed, either directly or
through its adoption by the Roman Church, in the use of
benediction-formulas *A, B1,* and *C* in churches where three
or more prayers were said at the blessing of the new fire. The
adoption of Roman practice is well illustrated in the Cistercian rite, in which the single prayer of the 1487 Missal was
replaced in 1669 by the three formulas from the Roman Missal, and in the rite of Braga, where in the 1558 Missal those
same three Roman prayers took the place of *Formula B3* of
the 1512 Missal.

Within the Ambrosian rite, an interesting development occurred. According to the eleventh-century *Manuale Ambrosia-*

[12]*Viz. A, B1, and* C.
[13]*PRMA* I.xxxii p.238 and II.xliv p.470. Only Manuscripts C and E
of *PGD* record *alia* (*PRMA* III p.587).

num[14], a single prayer was used for the blessing of the fire. However, Manuscript M of the *manual* records a tradition in which a triple blessing was used,[15] and these three prayers were incorporated into the Ambrosian Missal of 1475. The number was reduced to two in the 1560 Missal, increased to three in 1594 and 1669, and reduced to a single formula in 1902.

It is possible to explain the presence in a rite of two or more prayers for the blessing of the fire in a number of ways. (i) We have already noted that the benediction-formula for the new fire produced by friction could not necessarily be pronounced over fire kindled by means of a lens. An alternative prayer would be required. (ii) With the incorporation of the new fire ceremony into the liturgy of the Vigil, it was perhaps inevitable that the prayer with which the lamp was blessed at the commencement of the *Lucernarium,* having been displaced as a benediction of the light by the *Exultet* and Preface, should be reapplied to the new fire. (iii) Similarly, as a result of the universal adoption of the *Exultet*/Preface formula for the blessing of the Easter candle and the consequent displacement of the older blessing, *Deus mundi Conditor,* this latter prayer and in particular its concluding pericope, which, as the *Veniat quaesumus,* became a prayer in its own right, was reassigned to a different function and, in the isolated instances where it survived, became associated with the consecration of the new fire, and not of the Easter candle as formerly. (iv) The acquisition of additional formulas for the blessing of the new fire may in some instances have been the result of borrowing from different liturgical traditions. (v) At St Augustine's Abbey, Canterbury, in the thirteenth century and at Reims during the following century, it was the practice to use a different prayer for the blessing of the fire on each day of the Triduum. It is possible that this arrangement obtained in other churches whose service-books prescribed three prayers.

[14]*MVLA* II p.199.
[15]*MVLA* II p.198.

Rome	12 C	A	B1	C
St-Germain-des-Prés	12 C	A	B1	C
Basel	1488	A	B1	C
Austin Friars	1491	A	B1	C
Melk	1495	A	B1	C
Vallombrosa	1503	A	B1	C
Monte Cassino	1507	A	B1	C
Bremen	1511	A	B1	C
Braga	1558	A	B1	C
Osma	1561	A	B1	C
Rouen	1640	A	B1	C
Paris	1666	A	B1	C
Cistercians	1669	A	B1	C
Evreux	1740	A	B1	C
Maison du Roy, Paris	1741	A	B1	C
Sées	1742	A	B1	C
Carcassonne	1749	A	B1	C
Paris	1762	A	B1	C
Mende	1766	A	B1	C
St-Bertrand	1773	A	B1	C
Vienna	1782	A	B1	C
Tours	1784	A	B1	C
Luçon	1828	A	B1	C
Metz	1829	A	B1	C
Limoges	1830	A	B1	C
Toulouse	1832	A	B1	C
La Rochelle	1835	A	B1	C
Auch	1836	A	B1	C
Nantes	1837	A	B1	C
Autun	1845	A	B1	C
Freising	1487	A	B1	D
Slesvig	1512	A	B2	C
Durham	14 C	A	B4	D
Lyon	1771	A	B1	D
Westminster	*c.*1370	B1	D	F
Evesham	*c.*1250	B1	D	G
Cosenza	1557	B2a	A	C
Fruttuaria	11 C	B2a	C	G
Reims	14 C	B2a	B7b	F
Camaldolese	1503	B3	A	C
Salisbury	13 C	B4	D	G

Langres	1492	B5a	D	G
Milan†	11 C	B6	O	E
Milan	1475	B6	O	E
Milan	1768	B6	O	C1
Notmark	15 C	B7b	D	G
St Augustine's Abbey, Canterbury	13 C	F	W	B5d
Leofric	c.1000	H	B8	Q
Spires	1512	H	B2a	A
Auch	c.1000	L	B2a	D

†Manuscript M of the Manual.

Table 17. Three prayers for the blessing of the new fire

(C) THE FORMULAS AND THEIR CONTENTS.

1. *Benediction-formulas* A, S, J, P. These four prayers appertain specifically to the act of kindling fire. The first two relate to a situation in which the fire is produced by means of a flint, and in *J* we have a blessing of the fire kindled by the refraction of the sun's rays through a lens. The reference to *lapis* in *Formula P* would suggest fire by friction, in view of the use of the verb *prosilire,* 'to leap out', to describe the manner in which the fire appeared. This, the sole prayer for the blessing of the fire in the Missal of Burgos, is inapposite for the kindling of fire by refraction. However, the difficulty largely disappears if *lapis* can also be interpreted 'gem' or 'precious stone.' The word would then refer to a beryl or some other translucent stone capable of producing fire by the refraction of the sun's rays.

2. *B-category Benediction-formulas. Formulas B1 to B10* are all variants of a common original; and it is claimed that their Western archetype is the prayer for the first blessing of the

PRC	13 C	A	B1	C	H*		
Esztergom	1501	H	U	A	I	C	
Mainz	1507	H	DMC	B2a	A		
Hamburg	1509	A	B1	C	H	D	B5a
Bystorp	c.1505	A	B5b	D	H	V	
Copenhagen	1510	A	B5b	D	H		
Lund	1514	A	B5b	D	H		
Breslau	1519	A	V	D	C		
Abo	c.1522	DMC	H	A	B1	C	V
Braga	1558	A	B1	C	I†		
Palencia	1568	D	A	B1	C		

*Found only in MS Vat.Lat. 1154.
†Follows the blessing of the incense.

Table 18. Four or more prayers for the blessing of the new fire

lamp in the Mozarabic rite, *Formula B*.[16] All share a similar structure and have common themes and close linguistic affinities. God is addressed as both the 'unfailing light' *(lumen indeficiens)* and the creator and source of all light. The petition for the blessing of the light is followed by a request for a share in that light and for inward illumination. The reference in the Spanish prayer *(B)* to 'the light. . . .which we bear in our hands' and the emphasis of the prayer on light as opposed to fire strongly suggest that this benediction-formula, and by extension the variants within this same group, was the prayer, or the development of the prayer, formerly used in the daily (or weekly) office of the *Lucernarium* for the blessing of the lamp; and there is no reason to disagree with Kenneth Stevenson's view that in view of the similarity in structure and theme with the blessing of the light in the Byzantine tradition, this prayer and its variant forms in other Western rites derives from a common Jerusalem original. However,

[16]Bernal pp.1034 ff.; Stevenson, *The Ceremonies* pp.181–82.

the claim that *Formula B* of the Mozarabic rite is the Western archetype of the rest of the *B*-category benediction-formulas must be challenged, since it has yet to be shown that Spanish influence was a major factor in the development of the other Western rites. Elsewhere,[17] we have argued that the Mozarabic liturgy of Holy Saturday assumed its final form as a result of Gallican influence. In view of the widespread incidence of *B*-category prayers and of their presence in the Milanese rite and the early Gallican rite, as attested in the Prague Sacramentary,[18] it is more likely that they all derive from an archetype, which was the prayer from the *Lucernarium* for the blessing of the lamp inherited from the Jerusalem rite and that the differences of language and theme are the result of their use in a number of different liturgical traditions over several centuries.

We noted above that the theme of light is prominent in the Mozarabic benediction-formula *B*. This accords well with the suggestion that the prayer originated in the office of the *Lucernarium*. Moreover, it is significant that the prayer was used, not for the hallowing of the new fire, as in other Western traditions, but for the blessing of the light of the lamp lit with the new fire. Further support for the *Lucernarium* origin of the variant *B*-category benediction-formulas is provided by the fact that the petition in *Formulas B1, B2, B3, B8, B9,* and *B10* is also for the blessing of the light, rather than the new fire. The blessing of the latter is sought in *Formulas B4, B5,* and *B6,* whilst *Formulas B7a* and *B7b* both refer to the 'light of the new fire'. In view of the likely origin of these prayers, they must rank amongst the earliest surviving benediction-formulas for the blessing of the new fire.

3. *The Mosaic Motif.* Unlike the Mozarabic benediction-formula *B,* whose pre-eminent theme is the permeation of God's light throughout creation, the remaining *B*-category

[17]Appendix 12, *The Mozarabic and Milanese Rites.*
[18]*GePr* p.57.

prayers (with the exception of *B5*) include a reference to the pillar of fire, which preceded Moses and the Israelites as they departed from Egypt, and in this way closely link the provision and the blessing of the new fire with the Passover, the dominant theme of the Holy Saturday Vigil in the Romano-Gallican tradition.[19] The column of fire in the Book of Exodus not only foreshadowed the flame of the Easter candle at the Christian Passover; it was seen as a fiery manifestation of the Lord's presence, as was His appearance to Moses in the Burning Bush. In the same way, therefore, that a reference to God's use of this element was inserted into the above-mentioned *B*-category prayers, thus forging a thematic link between the new fire ceremony and the Vigil itself, His appearance to Moses in the Burning Bush is also commemorated in a group of benediction-formulas, *F, Y, B8,* and *B9*. For the Mosaic motif, which ran through the paschal vigil, included incidents from the life of the Old Testament lawgiver other than his passing through the Red Sea. *Formula B9* also makes reference to Moses' mission to Pharaoh and to his ascent of Mt Sinai. Moreover, it is significant that in the shorter Vigil-tradition,[20] there are a number of instances where two of the four prophecies were Mosaic readings, namely, Exodus 14:24–15:1 and Deuteronomy 31:22-30.[21]

4. *Fire-concepts Inherited from Paganism.* (i) According to the purificatory theory for the origin of fire-festivals, first propounded by E. Westermarck and favoured by J.G. Frazer,[22]

[19]In the prayer following the second blessing of the lamp in the Mozarabic rite, there are references to the departure from Egypt and to the pillar of fire. Pinell, *La Benediccio* p.116.

[20]With four or five prophecies, as opposed to twelve.

[21]For example, in *PRG*, OR 28, and in the Missals of Salisbury, Mainz, Verdun, Passau, Bressanone, Eichstadt, and Palencia amongst others. These two prophecies were retained in the Roman rite when the number was reduced in 1955 from twelve to four; and in the revised Missal of 1970, of the nine prescribed for the Vigil, the Exodus passage was the only reading to be made obligatory.

[22]*Golden Bough* Vol.10 pp.342 ff.

the new fire acted as a cleansing agent and a disinfectant; and the purpose of its being kindled was to destroy all harmful influences, such as witches and disease, which threatened the survival of a community. This pagan belief is echoed in *Formula J*. Closely linked to and almost certainly deriving from this belief is the petition, expressed in *Formulas O, T,* and *B*-category prayers, for the eradication of sin within ourselves and spiritual purification. (ii) The pre-Christian belief that the harnessing and control of fire gave power to the possessor, is discussed in a later chapter. *Formula C* would appear to express this notion and to warn that power deriving from the possession of fire is important, since that element is also used by the Devil.

5. *The* Deus mundi Conditor. This prayer was originally a prayer for the blessing of the Easter candle, but as such was replaced universally by the *Exultet*/Preface formula. It survived, however, as a prayer for the consecration of the new fire, the flame of the newly-hallowed candle forming a dominant theme. In each of the instances in which it is recorded as a benediction-formula for the new fire *(Table 19)*, it is difficult to know whether it had formerly served as a prayer for the blessing of the Easter candle or whether it was borrowed from another rite. In the rite of Salzburg, it is clearly derived from *PRG*. In all six instances listed in *Table 19*, the *Exultet*/Preface was used to bless the Easter candle.

Church/Document	Date	Source
PRG	*c.*950	Vol.II p.95 §343
Salzburg	1507	Missal fol.xciii
Mainz	1507	Missal fol.xcii
Aquileia	1519	Missal p.91
Abo	*c.*1522	Manual p.238
Ratisbon	1570	Ritual fol.cii

Table 19. The use of DMC *as a new fire blessing*

6. *The* Veniat quaesumus. This prayer, which subsequently became the formula for the blessing of the five grains of incense in a large number of rites, including the Roman,[23] formed the final pericope of the *Deus mundi Conditor (DMC)*, being a concluding petition for God's blessing on the Easter candle, which had been kindled shortly before. As such, it is found in the Gelasian Sacramentary[24] and contains the phrase *super hunc incensum,* 'on this lighted candle'.[25] A subsequent request in the prayer invites God to 'intensify the splendour of this night' *(hunc nocturnum splendorem intende).* Detached from the *DMC* and made an independent prayer for the blessing of the new fire, it is first encountered in *PRG* and then in subsequent documents, listed in *Table 20.* In the former pontifical, it follows the benediction-formulas *A, B1,* and *C* and forms a fourth prayer for the blessing of the new fire. The rubric which immediately precedes it, *oratio postquam incenditur,*[26] indicates that the prayer was uttered after the small candle used for bearing the new fire had been lit. It was now the small candle, and no longer the Easter candle, over which the *Veniat quaesumus* was said; and the emphasis of the blessing is on the fire and not the candle. This is clear from the phrase in the prayer *super hoc incensum,* 'on this fire', which has replaced *super hunc incensum* of the Gelasian Sacramentary.[27]

---

[23]As such it is found in *PR XII (PRMA* I.xxxii.5 p.239) and subsequent Roman documents. The prayer is also found as a blessing of (i) the incense in the thurible, as at Barking (HBS 65 p.101) and Liège (1540 Missal fol.lxxvii); (ii) the *cereus minor,* as at Amiens (1752 Missal p.182); (iii) and the Easter candle itself, as at Bourges (1741 Missal p.225).

[24]*GeV* p.69.

[25]*Incensum* may be treated in two ways. Either it is the masculine form of the perfect participle of the verb *incendere,* used as a noun to mean 'a lighted candle'—compare the adjective *cereus,* which regularly had the force of the noun 'candle'—or it is the perfect participle, used as an adjective with the noun *cereus* understood.

[26]Also found in the Pontifical of St-Germain-des-Prés (M 230).

[27]A later modification of the prayer centred around the above-mentioned imperative *intende,* 'intensify', found in *GeV.* In *PRG,* the Pontifical of St-Germain-des-Prés, and other documents, this command has become *at-*

The possibility of confusion arising over the use of *incensum*, which had widely displaced the earlier term for incense *thus*, was recognised, at least at Verdun. In the *Veniat quaesumus* of that church's 1481 Missal, *ignem* has replaced *incensum* in the above-mentioned phrase.

Church/ Document	Date		Formulas				Source
PRG	c.950	A	B1	C	V		II p.57 §219
Avellana	11 C	A	B1		V		PL 151.881A/B
St-Germain- des Prés	12 C	A	B1	C	V		*DAER* 4.24 p.158
Verdun	1481	A			V		Missal fol.lxiii
Hildesheim	1499		B1		V		Missal fol.xcvi
Odense	1483	A	V	*B*			Stromberg p.34
Viborg	1500	A	V	*B*			Stromberg p.34
Bystorp	c.1505	A	B5b	D	H	V	Stromberg pp.80–82
Breslau	1519	A	V	D	C		Missal fol.lxxix
Abo	c.1522	*DMC*	H	A B1 C V			Manual p.238
Ratisbon	1570	*DMC*	H	C	V		Ritual fol.cii

Table 20. The use of Veniat quaesumus *as a new fire blessing in conjunction with other benediction-formulas*

7. *General Prayers and Further Observations.* A number of prayers are simple petitions for God's hallowing of the new fire. To this group belong *Formulas D, E, G, I, K, M,* and *O.* The first of these asks that the new fire may benefit humankind. *Formula L,* which is attested at Cluny and St-Florian

---

tende, 'pay heed to', 'observe' *(the splendour of this night).* When the prayer subsequently became a blessing of the incense, the verb in question underwent a further change and became *accende,* 'kindle'. In 1955, when the *veniat quaesumus* reverted to its original function as a preliminary blessing of the Easter candle (at Bourges it had continued to serve this purpose), the former request, *intende,* was restored to the text.

for the blessing of the new fire, is strictly a prayer to be used at Candlemas. *Formula Q,* found as a blessing of the fire only in the Leofric Missal, is excerpted from the Preface for the blessing of the Easter candle. At Fruttuaria, the *Pater noster* preceded the blessing of the fire; and at Seville, *Formula A* was followed by the *Deus qui divitias,* a prayer which was said in other rites prior to the reading of the prophecies. At Würzburg, a short threefold litany was sung : V. *Ut ignem istum benedicere digneris;* R. *Te rogamus audi nos.*[28] In the romanised Sacramentary of Vich, the use of *Formula B1* for the blessing of the light and *Formula E* for the new fire derived from Mozarabic practice. *Formula R,* attested at Beauvais and Strasbourg in the eighteenth century, was introduced into the respective rituals of those churches as a blessing of the Easter candle on a day other than Holy Saturday. It was prescribed for use in the event the flame of the Easter candle failing during the period it was supposed to burn continuously.

In some service-books, such as those of Würzburg and Aquileia, the benediction-formulas are mentioned but not given. In the Missal of the latter church, they are said to be contained 'in the Pontifical'.[29] There are a number of instances where none but the opening words of the prayer are given. However, only at Tongres is there some doubt about how the first three words were meant to be continued.

8. *The* Pontificale Romano-Germanicum. We have already mentioned the seemingly-double blessing of the new fire in this document and have suggested that this twofold hallowing represents a synthesis of two separate liturgical traditions. The *DMC,* pronounced on Holy Saturday, was strictly an offering of the lighted candle, a blessing of the *berakah*-type, rather than an invocatory benediction. The use on Holy Saturday of *Formula H,* which follows the *DMC,* presents a greater problem since the blessing of the fire is quite clearly stated :

[28]1477 Ordinary np.
[29]1519 Missal p.91.

benedicimus hunc ignem, 'we bless this fire'. The formula, however, continues, 'and we sanctify it [the fire] together with the wax and all its component elements . . . '.[30] The presence and use of this prayer presents less of a difficulty if, in view of the second clause, we regard the formula as a blessing of the small candle, soon to be lit, which supplements the oblatory expressions of the *DMC*.

(iii) Aspersion and Incensation

Although documentary evidence for the sprinkling with holy water and the censing of the new fire exists only from the eleventh century,[31] it is likely that this twofold ritual at the new fire ceremony goes back much further in time. The earlier evidence for these two acts is presented in *Table 21*. There is no reference to them in *PR XII,* though their omission from this pontifical should not necessarily be regarded as conclusive evidence for their absence from the Roman rite at that time. A number of later missals do not contain rubrics relating to the two rituals, but one suspects that in most instances they formed features of the rites since the evidence for the twofold act is plentiful after 1500. Attestation of their occurrence at Milan dates only from 1560.[32] According to Lanfranc's *Decrees,* the new fire was only aspersed; and it is significant that an act of incensation is prescribed in the same work during the blessing of the Easter candle. A similar arrangement is also found in the older Cistercian rite and in the fourteenth-century Westminster Missal.[33] It is unlikely, however, that there is any direct connection between the omission of incensation at the new fire ceremony and the censing of the Easter candle during the singing of the Preface, since

---

[30]Et cum cera et omnibus eius alimoniis sanctificamus . . .

[31]Customary of St-Bénigne, Dijon, cited by Martène, *DAMR* 3.13.34 (M 1150).

[32]Martène, *DAER* 4.24 p.169.

[33]Guignard pp.116–17; HBS 5 col.576.

at Durham, Evesham, and Norwich, the new fire and the Easter candle were honoured with incense.

Church/Commentator	Date	Source
St-Bénigne, Dijon	11 C	*DAMR* 3.13.34 p.126
John of Avranches	c. 1070	PL 147.49A
Evesham	c. 1250	HBS 6 col.81
Norwich	c. 1265	HBS 82 p.81
Salisbury	13 C	Missal pp.265–66
Rome	13 C	*PRMA* III p.588
Durham	14 C	Missal p.186
Reims	14 C	*DAER* 4.22.5 p.97
Rome	1474	HBS 17 p.175

Table 21. Aspersion and incensation of the new fire

The *Missale Romanum* of 1474 does not state the number of times the fire was to be aspersed and censed. Later Roman and other diocesan missals, as well as liturgical manuals, specify three times.[34] At Lesnes, the fire was aspersed and censed after it had been brought into church.[35] Throughout the history of the new fire ceremony, the order has been invariably aspersion followed by incensation.

(iv) *The Officiant*

The preparation and kindling of the new fire were preliminary and functional duties comparable with the lighting of the lamps and candles before the start of Tenebrae and could therefore have been performed by a lay person; and though we shall shortly consider instances in which it was either obligatory or considered desirable that a person possessing sacer-

[34]For example, *MR* 1570; 1762 Missal of Paris p.237; Colti, *Dictionarium* II p.56.
[35]HBS 95 p.47.

dotal authority should kindle the new fire, it seems very likely that in many churches the production of fire was included amongst the duties of the sacristan. The greater importance attached to the blessing of the fire, as opposed to the kindling of the fire, may well account for the fact that the official responsible for the latter act is rarely mentioned in our sources. At Nidaros, Spires, Auch, Besançon, and Le Puy, it was the responsibility of the sacristan,[36] and of the sacristan's assistant at St-Bénigne, Dijon.[37] Amongst the Cistercians, a servitor lit the new fire.[38] At Milan Cathedral in the eleventh century, it was the duty of the *cicendelarius,* the official responsible for church illuminations, to prepare the new fire.[39]

In the Mozarabic rite, it was probably the unusual circumstances in which the new fire was kindled that made it obligatory for a priest to perform this ritual act. Indeed, in the cathedral churches, it was the bishop himself who kindled the fire.[40] The importance of the beryl in the production of fire at St-Bénigne, Dijon, perhaps made it inevitable that one of the monastery's dignitaries should hold the lens.[41] At Soissons in the late twelfth century, the task of providing the new fire devolved upon a deacon.[42] This may have been the result of a desire to make the kindling of the new fire parallel and complementary to the archdeacon's blessing of the Easter candle. At Liège, the fire was lit by the Treasurer and at Palencia, by the priest on duty for the week.[43]

Within the Roman Church, the *Caeremoniale Episcoporum* of 1600 recommends that the new fire should be kindled by a

---

[36]*ONE* p.32; 1512 *Agenda* fol.xciii; 1836 Missal p.191; 1707 Ceremonial p.315; 1836 Ceremonial p.373.

[37]This person officiated only if the new fire was kindled from a stone. Martène, *DAMR* 3.13.34 p.126 (M 1150).

[38]1689 Ritual p.245.

[39]*MVLA* II p.198.

[40]Antiphonary of Léon p.280; Férotin §86 for the older Mozarabic rite; PL 85.437A for the *Missale Mixtum* of the reformed rite.

[41]Martène, *DAMR* 3.13.34 p.126 (M 1150).

[42]Martène, *DAER* 4.24 p.161 (M 305).

[43]1492 Ordinary np; 1568 Missal fol.c.

bishop wherever possible (p.296). However, the rubrics of
Roman service-books from *PRG* to the Missal of 1970 have
always expressed the action of kindling the fire in the passive
voice of the verb and have never specified an agent.[44] Thus,
the performance of this duty by a sacristan is not precluded.
Both before and after the Second Vatican Council, the custom has been for a priest to kindle the new fire. French missals of the eighteenth and nineteenth centuries are as non-
committal as the Roman in this respect; but it seems likely
that in those cathedrals in which the new fire is still kindled
by the bishop or by a priest, the ancient custom is perpetuated. In twenty-seven of thirty-eight French cathedrals for
which information is available, a bishop or priest strikes the
new fire; and in four cathedrals in which this act is performed
by the sacristan, the kindling may have been one of that official's traditional duties. In some places, following the reforms
of 1955, which were intended to increase lay participation in
the liturgy, the task of kindling the fire has been given to lay
persons. This has happened at Agen, Bayeux, Belley, Digne,
and Vannes. At Reims, it is always a young lay person; and
in the Cathedral of Troyes, the duty of kindling the new fire
is performed by a nun.

Whilst the kindling of the new fire could be performed by
a cleric or lay person alike, its commissioning for use in Christian worship required a sacerdotal blessing. *Table 22* lists instances where the new fire is known to have been blessed by
the bishop or abbot in a cathedral or monastic church. At
Rome, where in the later Middle Ages the Pope was not always present at the ceremony, two other dignitaries presided :
a minor cardinal priest or a minor cardinal deacon.[45] At Salisbury, the duty was performed by a priest, known as the *ex-
ecutor,*[46] whilst at Naples, the blessing was pronounced by the
cimiliarcha, the cathedral treasurer.[47] In the Milanese rite, the

[44]See *Table 38.*
[45]*PRMA* I.xxxii.1 p.238; *Ordo Albini* p.130.
[46]*Missal of c.1486* fol.lxxxiii.
[47]Constitutions of J.Orsini (Mallardo p.33).

officiating priest was formerly a cardinal;[48] but in more recent times, this official is not specified.[49] Martène informs us
that at Arles and Soissons, the duty was formerly carried out
by a deacon.[50]

By Abbot	By Bishop
Regularis Concordia (PL 137.491B)	*PRG* (II p.95 §342)
Cistercians (*Nom. Cist.* p.104)	Corbie (PL 78.336B)
Lesnes (HBS 95 p.47)	Tolédo (Férotin §86)
Evesham (HBS 6 col.80)	Rouen (PL 147.176A)
St-Vedast, Arras (HBS 86 p.160)	Nidaros (*ONE* p.232)
Cluny (1510 Missal fol.xlix)*	Rome (*PRMA* III.iv.2 p.587)**
	Vienne (De Moléon p.23)
*Or the celebrant.	**Or another priest.

Table 22. The blessing of the new fire

[48]MS M in *MVLA* II p.98; 1475 Missal fol.lxxx.
[49]1902 Missal, Rep. p.34; 1986 Missal (t.e.) p.242.
[50]*DAER* 4.24.3 p.145 (M 31/32), and 4.24 p.161 (M 305).

Chapter Thirteen

THE PRODUCTION OF NEW FIRE : TIME, LOCATION, AND MEANS

A. TIME

(i) Within the Tradition of the Threefold Kindling

(A) MAUNDY THURSDAY. According to Ordo 26, which is the earliest document to record a time for this ceremony, the new fire was kindled at the ninth hour of the day.[1] This time became traditional for most churches which observed the rite on Maundy Thursday. It is found in other early *ordines* and in the Ordo of Corbie, in the *Regularis Concordia* and in Lanfranc's *Decrees,* and in several of the eleventh-century monastic customaries *(Tables 23* and *24).* The Ritual of Evesham also records the same time. Since the Office of None was sung at this hour, the phrase *post nonam* should not be interpreted in a strictly temporal sense with the meaning of 'at the end of the ninth hour', that is, at the start of the tenth; it indicates simply that the ceremony should take place at the con-

---

[1] OR 26.3. On 18 March, the earliest day on which Maundy Thursday can fall, the ninth hour would have lasted from approximately 2.10 P.M. to 3.10 P.M. On 22 April, the latest date for Maundy Thursday, the same period would last from approximately 2.22 P.M. to 3.33 P.M. by modern reckoning. The times relate to the fiftieth parallel.

clusion of that office. At St Mary's, York, the fire was kindled during the singing of None. When in the later Middle Ages the services of the Triduum came to be anticipated, the new fire ceremony and the Office of None continued to take place in conjunction with one another. However, by the sixteenth century, when the new fire came to be kindled during the morning of Holy Saturday, the link between the two ceremonies was generally no longer maintained. At Bayonne in that century, the new fire was struck at 9.00 A.M. The rubric in the missal of that church shows that *hora nona* was now understood to refer to the modern system of reckoning time.

In the period before the ceremony began to be held by anticipation on Holy Saturday morning, two documents record exceptions to the time of the ninth hour, namely, *Poitiers* and the *Pontificale Romano-Germanicum (PRG)*.[2] We propose to discuss *Poitiers* presently. The latter pontifical, together with *Alcuin,* is unique in recognising that the amount of daylight on Maundy Thursday depends on when that day falls and makes allowance for the variation in the lengths of the days.

Document	Hour of the New Fire			Source
	MT	*GF*	*HS*	
Ordo 26 (8 C)	9	—	—	OR 26.3
Ordo 28 (*c.*800)	9	—	—	OR 28.25, .58
Ordo 29 (9 C)	—	8	7	OR 29.29, .45
Ordo 31 (9 C)	9	—	8	OR 31.29, .62
Poitiers (9 C)	6	6	9	Pont. p.138
PRG (*c.*950)	9/5	5	7	II §§215, 304, 342
Reg.Conc. (*c.* 970)	9	9	9	PL 137.491B/494C
Ordo of Corbie (10 C)	9	—	—	*DAMR* 3.13.34 p.126 (M 1145)

Table 23. The earlier evidence for times within the tradition of the threefold production of fire

[2]Strictly there are three. *Alcuin* (PL 101.1205C) derives from *PRG* and contains identical information to that found in the pontifical concerning this point. It cannot be regarded here as an independent source.

Church/Document	Hour of the New Fire			Source
	MT	GF	HS	
Cluny (11 C)	9	9	9	PL 149.658D, .661C, .663A
Farfa (11 C)	9	9	9	PL 150.1198D, .1201C, .1203C
Avellana (11 C)	9	—	9	PL 151.880D, .883A
St-Bénigne, Dijon (11 C)	9	9	9	*DAMR* 3.13.34 p.126 (M 1150)
Gembloux (11 C)	—	9	9	Albers II p.96, p.99
CMG (11 C)	9	—	—	Albers V p.32
Lanfranc (*c*.1070)	9*	9*	9	PL 150.446D
St-Germain-des-Prés (12 C)	5	5	7	*DAER* 4.23–24 p.135, p.158
Evesham (*c*.1250)	9	9	9	HBS 6 col.88
Norwich (*c*.1265)	—	—	9	HBS 82 p.91
St Mary's, York (*c*.1400)	DN	DN	DN	HBS 75 p.275
Salzburg (1507)	9/5	—	9	Missal fol.lxxxv
Cluny (1510)	AN	AN	AN	Missal fol.lxix
Braga (1512)	AN	AN	AN	Missal np
Bayonne (1543)	9.00 A.M.	9.00 A.M.	9.00 A.M.	Missal p.41

AN = After None.
DN = During None.
*Implied in PL 150.467B.

*Table 24. The later evidence for times
within the tradition of the three fold production of fire*

At the ninth hour when the days are longer or at the fifth hour
when they are shorter. . . .[3]

Any interpretation of this statement seems fraught with
difficulties. On first examination, the rubric appears to recog-

[3]*PRG* II p.57 §215 = *Alcuin* (PL 101.1205C).

nise that on the longer days, that is from 5 to 22 April, the
new fire was to be struck at the ninth hour (between approximately 2.22 P.M. and 3.33 P.M.) and that on the shorter days,
that is from 18 March to 4 April, the ceremony was to take
place some time between approximately 10.00 A.M. and 11.00
A.M., which period is by former reckoning the fifth hour. Unfortunately, the pontifical does not define shorter and longer
days, so that the division we have suggested, though a reasonable one, must remain tentative. On the other hand, it might
be argued that the fifth hour and the ninth hour respectively
represent the times for the new fire on the earliest and latest
dates when Maundy Thursday can fall. This presupposes that
an adjustable scale of times was in operation for the kindling
of the new fire, to accommodate the varying dates when
Maundy Thursday can fall. Thus, for example, on 5 April,
which lies midway between the two extremes, the new fire
would have been struck at the seventh hour, or by modern
reckoning, between approximately 12.11 P.M. and 1.18 P.M.
The medieval churchmen of Mainz may not have used such
a scale that featured the exactitude of modern chronometry,
but that they adjusted the time for the ceremony between the
two extremes of the fifth and the ninth hours is not an unreasonable assumption. To the modern mind, however, a
difference of four hours between the two extremes of times
at which the new fire ceremony took place seems excessive
since the length of daylight on 18 March at the one extreme
is approximately twelve hours by modern reckoning, but on
22 April a little over fourteen hours. The view cannot be sustained that the variation in time was prescribed so as to facilitate the kindling of fire by the refraction of the sun's rays.
A lens may be used for this purpose at a time of day both
earlier and later than the two prescribed by the pontifical.

Two suggestions may be advanced to explain the occurrence of this variation in times, not attested independently
elsewhere. (i) It may be argued that since *PRG* is a composite document, amongst the diverse elements in its composition is a choice of times for the new fire, which come from

differing liturgical traditions,[4] and that in order to accommodate or to justify the retention of both times, the fifth hour was assigned to those days when Maundy Thursday fell before 5 April, and the ninth hour to those that followed that date. For in spite of the strong evidence of the earlier *ordines* for the kindling of the new fire at the ninth hour, the evidence of *Poitiers,* which prescribes the sixth hour on Maundy Thursday, shows that an earlier time was not unknown at this period. Moreover, it is significant that a twelfth-century pontifical from St-Germain-des-Prés records the time of the fifth hour for the new fire. However, we cannot be sure whether this represents a survival of the earlier and alternative tradition we suggest may have existed or whether that church originally observed the times enjoined by *PRG,*[5] and subsequently opted for the fifth hour as the customary time for the ceremony, regardless of the date upon which Maundy Thursday fell. (ii) The striking of the new fire at the earlier time may have been the result of a concern about the weather. The compilers of the pontifical were obviously not unaware of the possibility of having inclement weather at the time the new fire was kindled. It could be argued that in mid to late March, the temperature is higher at the fifth hour than at the ninth hour, or at least that the weather is more likely to appear favourable in the late morning to a congregation assembled in the open air for a ceremony which ideally should take place out of doors.

   Although John of Avranches and Rupert of Deutz both refer

---

[4]Support for a time inherited from an alternative tradition might come, it could be argued, from the fact that in the rubrics of *PRG* for Good Friday, the new fire is brought at the fifth hour, if it could be proved that within this tradition, Good Friday was the original day on which the new fire was produced and that when the ceremony was extended to the other two days of the Triduum, the need for liturgical symmetry demanded the same hour on those days also. The kindling of the new fire at the seventh hour on Holy Saturday in *PRG,* however, makes it difficult to theorise with confidence concerning this alternative tradition.

[5]Martimort suggests that the pontifical may have originated at Trier.

to the blessing of the new fire on Maundy Thursday,[6] neither writer specifies the time at which the ceremony was to take place. The omission of this information may possibly indicate that in the rites of the two churches with which these writers were familiar, the times for this ceremony were flexible. For it seems most unlikely that they both inadvertently omitted to mention the time on this day, especially as both record the times for the ceremony on Good Friday and Holy Saturday.

(B) GOOD FRIDAY. The evidence for the blessing of the new fire on Good Friday shows that a greater variety of times at which the ceremony was performed existed than did on Maundy Thursday. This is perhaps not surprising in view of the other ceremonies held during the afternoon of Good Friday and the difficulty experienced by some churches in accommodating this ceremony at the usual time of the ninth hour. *PRG* and the pontifical from St-Germain-des-Prés enjoin the fifth hour of the day, and *Poitiers* the sixth; the new fire ceremony would thus have taken place before the Passion. According to Ordo 29, the ritual took place at the eighth hour, possibly between the Veneration of the Cross and the Mass of the Presanctified. However, of the sources which record a time for Good Friday, the majority prescribe the ninth hour, the time observed in most churches on Maundy Thursday. It will be noticed that the evidence for the ninth hour on Good Friday before 1500 is drawn entirely from the monastic tradition. Although a number of monastic documents contain omissions of time, in view of the influence of the tenth-century Benedictine *Regularis Concordia*, which attests the times on all three days, the ninth hour may be inferred with confidence in all such instances and on all three days.

(C) HOLY SATURDAY. Some of the earlier sources severally record a variety of times. Ordo 29, *PRG,* and the pontifical from St-Germain-des-Prés prescribe the seventh hour, Ordo 31 the

---

[6]*Lib. de Off. Eccl.* (PL 147.49A); *De Div. Off.* V (PL 170.149A).

eighth, and Ordo 28 and *Poitiers* the ninth. This last-mentioned time is specified in the *Regularis Concordia* and by Lanfranc in the following century. John of Avranches also refers to the same time.[7] The kindling of the fire at St Mary's, York during None may suggest that None was no longer held at the ninth hour and that the new fire ceremony took place earlier in the day.

Church/Order	Date	Time	Source
Lanfranc	*c.*1070	after None	PL 150.466D
Nidaros	*c.*1210	,,	*ONE* p.232
Salisbury	13 C	,,	Missal p.265
Marseille	13 C	,,	*ILEM* p.84
Westminster	1362–1388	,,	HBS 5 col. 574
Strasbourg	1364	,,	*DAER* 4.24 p.162
Durham	14 C	,,	Missal p.185
Barking	1404	,,	HBS 65 p.101
Cistercians	1487	,,	Missal np
Basel	1488	,,	Missal fol.xci
Langres	1492	,,	Missal fol.lxv
Rouen	1497	,,	Missal np
Camaldolese	1503	before None	Missal fol.89
Vallombrosa	1503	after None	Missal fol.xci
Carmelites	1504	,,	Missal fol.xcv
Seville	1507	,,	Missal fol.lxxv
Braga	1558	,,	Missal fol.xcvi
Freising	1579	,,	Missal fol.85
Evreux	1740	,,	Missal p.186
Besançon	1766	,,	Missal p.206
Poitiers	1767	,,	Missal p.244
Chartres	1782	,,	Missal p.171
Metz	1829	,,	Missal p.158
Toulouse	1832	,,	Missal p.205
Auch	1836	,,	Missal p.191

Table 25. Time of kindling in relation to None

[7] *Lib. de Off. Eccl.* (PL 147.52B).

(ii) Within the Tradition of the Single Kindling

The problem of interpreting the phrase *post horam nonam* has been mentioned above. The Office of None was formerly sung at the ninth hour of the day, so that the new fire ceremony, which followed that office, took place more or less in the middle of the afternoon. Subsequently, when None came to be sung at midday and the new fire ceremony was also transferred to the earlier hour in a number of monastic and cathedral rites, the phrase *hora nona* lost its former temporal significance in those instances. Moreover, at times, None was sung together with the other Little Hours *before* the principal Mass of the day, so that the phrase *post nonam*, 'after None', in the later Middle Ages and beyond was capable of three different interpretations, depending on when that office was sung : 1. during the morning; 2. at midday; and 3. in monastic churches, where the traditional times for the offices were still strictly adhered to, during the middle of the afternoon. There is little doubt that in most of the rites dating from the late fifteenth century and beyond listed in *Table 25,* where the time of the new fire ceremony is given in relation to the singing of None, one of the two former times obtained. The Missals of Vallombrosa and Poitiers also add *hora competenti*, 'at a convenient hour'. In the Ambrosian rite, the new fire was formerly kindled also after None.[8] According to the revised Missal of 1902, the ritual took place during None.[9]

The interpretation of *post nonam* is further complicated by the fact that in the fifteenth and sixteenth centuries two systems of calculating the time of day were in use in different parts of the Western Church,[10] so that it is possible that in some of the instances listed in *Table 25,* the phrase should be interpreted 'after 9.00 A.M.', especially since in some places the new fire ceremony had been performed during the morn-

[8]1560 Missal fol.110; 1768 Missal p.110.
[9]Repertorium p.34.
[10]The old Roman system of dividing the hours of light and darkness into twelve equal parts and the modern method of reckoning time.

ing of Holy Saturday from at least the close of the fifteenth
century.

Church	Date	Source
Verdun	1481	Missal fol.lxiii
Sens	1520	Missal fol.c
Osma	1561	Missal fol.lxxxix
Soissons*	1856	Ritual p.90

*Before 9.00 A.M.

Table 26. New fire kindled at 9.00 A.M.

Church	Date	Time	Source
Esztergom	1501	sixth hour	Missal fol.lxxiii
Lübeck	1505	about the sixth hour, after None	Missal fol.lxix
Mainz	1507	about midday	Missal fol.xcii
Arras	1508	midday	Missal fol.lxiv

Table 27. New fire kindled at midday

Church	Date	Time	Source
Melk	1495	convenient hour	Missal fol.xcvi
Hildesheim	1499	convenient hour	Missal fol.lxvii
Monte Cassino	1507	after Sext	Missal fol.91
Ratisbon	1518	convenient hour	Missal np
Cordoba	1561	usual hour	Missal fol.ciiii
Bayeux	1780	convenient hour	*Sem.Ste* p.493
Tours	1784	convenient hour	Missal p.191
Meaux	1845	convenient hour	Missal p.169

Table 28. An unspecified time for the new fire

Table 26 lists four instances where we can be confident that the new fire ceremony took place at 9.00 A.M. or earlier. At Verdun and Osma, the modern method of telling the time was used, whereas at Sens, the time was expressed according to the older system.[11] Churches where *noon* was specified as the time for the new fire are given in *Table 27*. These followed earlier Roman practice. A glance at *Table 28* shows that in a number of places no specific time was prescribed for the new fire ceremony. This flexibility was also a feature of the later Roman rite *(MR 1570)*. These churches were therefore at liberty to begin the liturgy at any suitable time during the morning of Holy Saturday. At Cahors, the new fire was kindled at the end of the Little Hours.[12]

An unusual feature of the Roman rite was the interval of time which elapsed between the kindling and the blessing of the fire. There is no evidence to suggest that this development occurred much before the twelfth century. According to *PRG*, the fire was both kindled and blessed at the same ceremony.[13] Since the rubric of the twelfth-century *Pontificale Romanum (PR XII)* states that the new fire should be kindled at the fifth or the sixth hour, it is likely that 'the sixth hour', attested in other twelfth-century Roman documents *(Table 29)*, also signifies 'midday'; but in later documents, the new fire is kindled after the Office of Sext, which may not necessarily have taken place at noon, as it had done previously. Whether the new fire was blessed at the ninth hour during the twelfth century is not clear since the Ordo of the Lateran Church and subsequent documents record that this ceremony took place after the Office of None. However, since in the twelfth century, None on Holy Saturday was sung after the kindling of the fire, which had taken place at midday, there is good reason to believe that the new fire was blessed at some point during the middle of the afternoon. Moreover, it is clear from

[11]At Bayonne *(Table 24)* where the new fire was kindled at 9.00 A.M., the rubric of the Missal states : *hora tertia post ortum solis.*
[12]1760 Missal p.172.
[13]II p.57 §219.

Document	Date	Time		Source
		Kindling of fire	Blessing of fire	
PR XII	12 C	5th/6th hour	*postea*	*PRMA* I p.238
OEL	*c.*1140	—	after None	*OEL* p.60
Ordo XI	*c.*1140	6th hour	—	PL 78.1041C
PRC (= OR X)	12 C	6th hour	(MS y : None)	*PRMA* II p.470.
Ordo Albini	*c.*1190	6th hour	—	*Lib. Cens.* I p.130
Ordo of Apamea	1214	5th/6th hour	—	*DAER* 4.24.3 p.145
PGD	*c.*1295	6th hour, after Sext	after None	*PRMA* III p.587
Haymo's *Ordo Miss.*	1243	after Sext	after None	Van Dijk II p.245
Codex A 1706	*c.*1350	—	at None	*ZRKM* p.213
Bindo F.	1377	—	usual hour	*ZRKM* p.276
Missale Romanum	1474	after Sext	after None	HBS 17 I p.174
Missale Romanum	1950	at a convenient hour	after None	typical edition p.186

Table 29. Times for the new fire at Rome

PR XII that there was an interval of time between the kindling and the blessing of the fire : 'Later, at the hour at which the Pope should enter the cathedral . . . '.[14]

Following the Roman reforms of 1955, which were intended to restore some of the primitive character to the paschal vigil, it became obligatory for the liturgy of Holy Saturday to begin after sunset; and the acts of kindling and consecrating the new fire became complementary aspects of the one ritual.[15] Likewise, in the revised Ambrosian rite, the ceremonies of Holy Saturday do not begin before nightfall.[16]

B. LOCATION

(i) The Early Period

Our earliest sources for the new fire ceremony within the Romano-Gallican tradition relate to the region of Northern France and Western Germany and stipulate in the first instance that the new fire should be struck from a stone and that it should be performed out of doors. The external as opposed to the internal location for the new fire almost certainly derived from earlier pre-Christian practice and was retained after the new fire ritual had been adopted by the Church for liturgical, theological, and cultural reasons. It need hardly be stated that an external location was essential if the new fire was to be obtained by means of a lens.

All of our early sources, except *Alcuin,* record the additional stipulation that the kindling of the new fire should take place in the doorway of an *oratorium,* if one existed.

---

[14]Postea hora qua . . . pontifex intrare debet ecclesiam. *PRMA* I xxxii.1 p.238.

[15]Fortescue and O'Connell (11th edition) p.302.

[16]*Missale Ambrosianum* (1981 t.e.) p.242.

If they have an *oratorium* in the same place, they strike (the fire) there in the doorway.[17]

Because of the variation in meaning of *oratorium,* this sentence is capable of two different interpretations. In the early Middle Ages, *oratorium* could either describe a small chapel built over the tomb of a martyr; or it could refer to a place of worship in a rural area, which facilitated the spiritual life of those living at a distance from their parish church and was the forerunner of the later medieval chapel of ease. Either interpretation is possible in the rubric above. However, if *oratorium* is understood in the latter sense, the meaning of *ibidem* becomes strained. For if *oratorium* indicates a chapel of prayer in a small village or hamlet, it is difficult to see what *ibidem* is referring to. The only likely translation would be 'in the same area', where 'area' refers to the diocese. However, it would follow from this that the new fire rubrics related only to cathedral churches—they in fact applied to monastic churches as well—and would imply that some dioceses had no *oratoria* at all, whilst others had only one. Much more likely is the view that *oratorium* bears the former meaning, and refers to a shrine in close proximity to a cathedral or monastic church. *Ibidem* would then have its usual meaning, 'in the same place', and would indicate the shrine's location within the vicinity of a church.

None of the six documents which refer to the *oratorium* offers any explanation why the new fire should be kindled in the doorway of this chapel. Since the word does not occur elsewhere in connection with the new fire ceremony, we can but make a few observations and advance tentative theories in order to throw light on the use of the building on this occasion. If an external location was an obligatory feature of this ceremony—the rubrical phrase *extra ecclesiam* implies that it

[17]Si ibidem oratorium habuerint, super portam ibi excutiunt. OR 26.3; OR 28.25; OR 29.14; OR 31.29; *PRG* II p.57 §217; Ordo of Corbie (Martène, *DAMR* 3.13.34 p.162 [M 1145]). In the 1764 edition of *DAMR, sub idem oratorium* should read *si ibidem oratorium.*

was—it would perhaps explain why the kindling took place in the doorway of the *oratorium,* rather than in the *oratorium* itself. In this period before 1000, our sources attest that the old fire was extinguished on Maundy Thursday and the new fire kindled the same day. In the older Roman tradition, fire was hidden on Maundy Thursday and continued to burn *in loco ecclesiae secretiore* until it was required for Baptism on Holy Saturday. The reservation of fire was a feature of the Gallican rites also; but whereas three lamps were used in the Roman rite, according to Gallican practice, only one lamp was required. This is borne out by a number of *ordines* which state :

> Let one lamp be lit from the newly-kindled fire, and kept burning in the same church or in the place where it was kindled until Holy Saturday, so that the Easter candle may be lit from it.[18]

The phrase *in eadem ecclesia* implies the existence and use of a *locus secretior,* whilst *loco ubi accenditur* may relate to the use of an *oratorium* for the reservation of the new fire.

We believe that in both the Roman and Gallican traditions, the concealment and reservation of the fire symbolised Jesus' seeming lack of animation in the Tomb and the remote part of the church building in which the fire was reserved recalled the Sepulchre. In larger churches, the reservation of fire would have occasioned little difficulty if a crypt or sacristy could have been readily utilised for that purpose. However, it is conceivable that problems may have arisen if the church building contained no suitable side chapels or convenient niches for concealing the lamp of reservation. It is our contention, therefore, that the desirability of having a conveniently-remote place of safe-keeping was one of the main reasons why the *ordines* recommended that an *oratorium* should be used if one was lo-

---

[18]Et de ipso igne continuo, in eadem ecclesia vel loco ubi accenditur, lampada una servetur usque in sabbato sancto ad illuminandum cereum. OR 26.5; OR 28.27.

cated near to the church. For such a building would have
provided protection both from the weather and from the gaze
of humanity, and the sepulchral nature of the building would
have increased the significance of the reserved fire and heightened the symbolism associated with it. As already mentioned,
this alternative place for the reserved fire is indicated by the
phrase *vel loco ubi accenditur;* and since this is an alternative
location to *eadem ecclesia,* it is almost certain that because of
the necessity of protecting the flame for at least forty-eight
hours, the writer has in mind the *oratorium* in whose doorway
the new fire was kindled.

Evidence from the sixth century shows that it had become
customary by then in parts of Gaul to keep a perpetual flame
burning at the tomb of a saint, above which an *oratorium* had
been built.[19] Since our sources state that the old fire was extinguished on Maundy Thursday and rekindled the same day,
as we have noted, it is our belief that an additional reason
for the reservation of fire in an *oratorium* was the possible feel-
ing of unease caused by leaving the saint's tomb unattended
by a light; for the loss of fire on Maundy Thursday was total. In later centuries, the light which burned before the Sacrament was also extinguished. The placing of the new fire on
or near the saint's tomb, therefore, ensured that his or her
presence continued to be honoured in this way. Alternatively,
it may have been believed that the placing of the fire in an
oratorium diminished the chances of its being extinguished since
it enjoyed the protection of the saint. Then again, the placing of the newly-kindled fire in the presence of such a holy
person may have been regarded as a means of enhancing in
some way the essence or efficacy of the fire. In the absence
of contemporary corroborating evidence, these suggestions
must remain tentative. Nevertheless, it is not completely inapposite to cite evidence from *c.*1400 in possible support of
these suggestions. It comes from St Mary's Abbey in York
and concerns the disposition of the new fire at that monas-

---

[19]Gregory of Tours, *History of the Franks* 4.36 (PL 71.291).

tery. After the kindling of the new fire, the rubric of the abbey's ordinal states :

> Let them place lighted coals from that fire on the tombs of the abbots in the chapter house, while None is being sung.[20]

The ordinal does not comment upon or explain the purpose of this practice, but it is clear from what we are told in this section that the fire placed on these tombs was not reserved for the lighting of the Easter candle on Holy Saturday; burning coals would last only for limited period of time. There are two possible explanations for the use of the coals in this way : (i) The placing of the fire on the tombs meant that the former abbots were the first to be honoured with the new fire. (ii) The fire, which was about to be blessed for immediate liturgical use, would, by being so placed, acquire some of the *virtus* of the former abbots of the monastery.

As previously mentioned, *Alcuin* omits any reference to an *oratorium,* though in other respects it closely follows the wording of the new fire ceremony described in *PRG*. It is generally thought that *Alcuin* was compiled considerably later than *PRG,* although it incorporates many early elements. It therefore seems reasonable to conclude that by the mid-eleventh century, the custom of utilising *oratoria* for the kindling and reservation of the new fire had fallen into desuetude.

Immediately after the injunction in the *ordines* for the kindling of the fire in the doorway of an *oratorium,* where an *oratorium* existed, follows the directive for churches which did not possess this shrine :

> sin vero, in loco quo consideravit prior, ita ut ex eo possit candela accendi.

This concise and grammatically-defective Latin sentence can be interpreted in a number of different ways since it lacks

---

[20]Accensas carbones de illo igne ponent super tumbas Abbatum in capitulo dum cantatur hora Nona. *Ordinal and Customary of St Mary's, York* (HBS 75 p.275).

a main verb and the meaning of *candela* is not immediately clear. As the verb *excutiunt* occurs in the previous clause, one solution would be to supply the same verb to complete the sense of this sentence. However, the dominant idea of the fire's reservation, which this sentence contains, makes equally probable the understanding of a verb denoting protection or concealment. A third possibility would be to supply two main verbs, one of kindling and one of reservation. Accordingly, the sentence would admit of three equally-valid translations :

1. But if there is no *oratorium,* they *strike* the fire, in a place which the Prior [the bishop or abbot] has deemed suitable, in such a way that a *candela* may be lit from it.

2. But if there is no *oratorium,* they *reserve* the fire, in a place which the Prior has deemed suitable, in such a way that a *candela* may be lit from it.

3. But if there is no *oratorium,* they *strike* the fire, in a place which the Prior has deemed suitable, and *reserve* it in such a way that a *candela* may be lit from it.

It is clear that the next stage in correctly interpreting this sentence is to establish the meaning of *candela;* for the word may be translated both 'lamp' and 'candle' and within the present context may refer either to the lamp of reservation or to the candle which was carried into church on each of the three evenings of the Triduum or to the Easter candle. The first of the tentative translations is solely concerned with the action of kindling the fire and with the manner in which it is done, even though the manner is not explicitly stated. Here, *candela* would indicate the small candle or taper which was used to transfer the new fire from the tinder to the lamp of reservation and was carried in procession into church on the evening of Maundy Thursday. However, it is difficult to see what is the significance of *ita,* 'in such a way', and how the striking of the fire in this instance should differ from that on any other occasion. Since the information it conveys appears to be gratuitously irrelevant, we conclude that the first interpretation in incorrect.

The third interpretation is an expanded form of the second. The two may be treated together since the dominant notion of reservation is common to both. Moreover, though the third version only states that the Prior selected the location for the kindling, it may be safely inferred that the decision regarding the location for the reservation of the fire was also his. Of the three possible interpretations of *candela*, that of 'lamp of reservation' may be eliminated since it would have been in that lamp that the fire burned from which the processional candle was lit. There are two reasons why it cannot be the Easter candle. (i) It was kindled on Holy Saturday, not on Maundy Thursday. (ii) *The ordines* use *cereus* to denote the Easter candle, not *candela*. There remains the processional candle, which was lit from the reserved fire on each of the three evenings of the Triduum. This is surely the most obvious interpretation and the one best suited to the context of the reserved fire. That *candela* signifies 'candle' and not 'lamp' is clear from the fact that it was subsequently placed at the end of a reed and carried on high in procession.

(ii) The Later Middle Ages

(A) THE EXTERNAL LOCATION. The evidence for an external setting for the kindling of the new fire beyond the period covered by the earlier *ordines* is set out in *Tables 30, 31,* and *32,* and like that of the *ordines*, relates to churches belonging to both the cathedral and monastic traditions. The practice of kindling the new fire in the open air was adopted by the Roman Church in the eleventh or early twelfth century, probably as a result of Cluniac influence. Later in this chapter we will suggest that it had previously been kindled in church. A number of medieval Roman documents do not specify a location. The *Ordo Albini* prescribes 'before the doors of the

Lateran';[21] and the open-air location, enjoined by Durand's pontifical, was a feature of the Pian Missal of 1570 and survives unchanged to this day.[22] The rubric of the Revised Order for Holy Week of 1955 specifies that the ceremony should take place at the door of the church;[23] and the 1970 *Missale Romanum,* with its emphasis on the participation of all the faithful, enjoins that a large fire, visible to all, should be prepared out of doors, with the proviso that in the event of inclement weather or the difficulty of staging a fire outside the church, the ceremony should be adapted accordingly.[24]

As with other liturgical or ritual acts which had a utilitarian origin, medieval writers explained the external location for the kindling of new fire with reference to Scripture. Rupert of Deutz cites Hebrews 13:11, itself an allusion to Leviticus 16:28, as the reason for the production of fire out of doors. The allusion is to the Jewish practice of burning 'outside the camp' the bodies of animals whose blood had been shed to atone for the transgressions of the people. Since, therefore, the Jews led Jesus outside the city, where his atoning sacrifice took place, our going outside the church to kindle the new fire is obeying dutifully the injunction of the writer to the Hebrews, that we should 'go forth to him outside the camp'.[25] It need hardly be said that this analogy is not apposite in every detail. Durandus is content to record that the new fire is kindled in an external location in commemoration of the Jewish place of crucifixion.[26] Dom Prosper Guéranger's comment is both apt and relevant. He argues that the sparks of the new fire symbolise the Spirit of Jesus and the stone from which

[21]*Liber Censuum* II p.130.

[22]*MR 1474* appears to be the exception. Its rubrics relate primarily to the new fire at the Cathedral of St John Lateran. In any case, the striking of fire in the cloister is a partial external kindling.

[23]Schmidt I p.118.

[24]1970 typical edition p.267.

[25]*De Div.Off.* V (PL 170.149C). This symbolism is also found in the *Mitrale* of Sicardus (PL 213.323B).

[26]*Rationale* VI.80 fol.350.

they are struck represents the Sepulchre. Just as the Resurrection took place in a tomb situated outside the city walls of Jerusalem, so the striking of the fire should be performed outside the walls of the church building.[27]

Church/Document	Date	Comment	Source
Farfa	11 C	blessed in cloister	PL 150.1199A
Gembloux	11 C	or in cloister	Albers II p.93
Rupert of Deutz	*c.*1111		PL 170.149A
PR XII	12 C	blessed *in atrio*	*PRMA* p.238
Ireland	*c.*1200		Missal p.126
Sicardus	*c.*1210		PL 213.323B
Apamea	1214		*DAER* 4.24 p.162
St-Vedast, Arras	*c.*1300	on hospice step	HBS 86 p.160
Strasbourg	1363	on the grass outside church	*DAER* 4.24 p.162
Rome	1570		1950 Missal p.186
Laon	1662	blessed inside	Rite p.813
Austin Friars	1714		Ceremonial p.307
Amiens	1752		Missal p.182
Cahors	1760		Missal p.173
Poitiers	1767		Missal p.244
Auch	1836		Missal p.191

Table 30. An external location for the kindling of the new fire (Churches where a lens was used are not included.)

Table 31 lists the evidence attesting the kindling of the new fire in the doorway or porch of a church. Whether this practice owes its origin to the procedure, found in the earlier *ordines* and in *PRG*, of striking the fire in the doorway of an *oratorium*, is difficult to say. The *Regularis Concordia* and John of Avranches' *Liber de Officiis Ecclesiaticis* were written close enough in time to the aforementioned documents for there

[27]*Liturgical Year* (PTHW) p.555. The strong evidence in favour of an extramural location for the tomb in which Jesus was laid has been forcefully summarised by John Wenham in *Easter Enigma* pp.18–19.

to be some direct link, but the instances in French cathedrals
may well have been the result of local development in neo-
Gallican times. The alternative location to the porch presumably was used if the weather was fine.

With the exception of *MR 1474*, the evidence for the kindling of the fire in the cloister is entirely monastic *(Table 32)*.
For these colonnaded walkways provided a convenient loca-

Church/Document	Date	Comment	Source
Reg. Conc.	*c.*970		PL 137.491B
John of Avranches	*c.*1070		PL 147.49A
Naples	14 C		Mallardo p.33
Tongres	15 C	west door	Ordinary p.164
Uzès	1495	P	Missal fol.lxiii
Mainz	1507	in the atrium	Missal fol.xcii
Rouen	1640	P/outside W.door	Ritual p.305
Desideri	1739	P/before door	*Praxis* p.143
Sées	1742	P	Missal p.186
Carcassonne*	1749	P	Missal p.194
Lisieux	1752	at door of church	Missal p.189
Mende*	1766	P	Missal p.220
St-Bertrand*	1773	P	Missal p.209
Capuchins*	1775	P/outside at door	Ceremonial p.124
Vienna*	1782	P	Missal p.215
Chartres	1782	P	Missal p.171
Périgueux	1782	at door of church	Missal p.158
Bayeux	1790	at main door	Missal p.168
Poland	1819	P/threshold	Manual II p.467
Coutances	1825	P/door of church	Ceremonial p.329
Metz*	1829	P	Missal p.158
Toulouse	1832	P	Missal p.206
La Rochelle*	1835	P	Missal p.186
Le Puy	1836	P/door of church	Ceremonial p.373
Nantes	1837	P/before door	Missal p.198
Autun	1845	P	Missal p.239

P = porch.
*Indicates that another location was allowed—see other tables.

Table 31. The kindling of fire near the church door

tion for the ceremony, in that the striking of the fire could still be regarded as an externally-performed act; and yet, at the same time, the measure of protection afforded by the cloister would have largely overcome the difficulty experienced in lighting a fire in the open air during particularly inclement weather. As we have already observed, the injunction of *MR 1474* must relate specifically to the Cathedral of St John Lateran since non-monastic cathedrals and churches did not normally possess the luxury of cloisters. Those at the Mother of Cathedrals were built sometime between 1222 and 1230,[28] a fact reflected in the *Ordo Missalis* of Haymo of Haversham, whose service-books were modelled on the ceremonial of the papal court. The Gilbertine rite also allowed the new fire to be kindled in an unfrequented part of the church. This wish for a secluded location is also found at Palencia.[29]

Church/Document	Date	Comment	Source
Fleury	11 C	at door of treasury	Albers V p.143
Lanfranc	*c.*1070		PL 150.466D
Gilbertines	12 C	or *in secreto loco*	HBS 59 p.39
Bec	*c.*1200		*DAMR* p.127
Haymo's *Ordo Miss.*	1243	blessed before altar	HBS 85 p.208
Worcester	*c.*1250	near refectory	Antiphonary p.69
St-Denys	*c.*1273	corner of cloister	*DAMR* 3.13.34 p.127
St-Epvre, Toul	14 C		,,
Lyre	*c.*1400		,,
Rome	1474	blessed before altar	HBS 17 p.174
Austin Friars	1491		Missal np
Melk	1495		Missal fol.lxvii
Monte Cassino	1507	in front of chapter house	Missal fol.91
Cistercians	1689		Ritual p.245
Sens	1715	at door of treasury	Missal p.238
Fréjus	1745		De Rubeis p.327

Table 32. New fire kindled in the cloister

[28]Masson p.305.
[29]1568 Missal fol.c.

Desideri's recommendation that in country churches, both the place of kindling and the route leading to the altar should be strewn with flowers is almost certainly a sanctioning of traditional practice.[30] The use of 'sweet-smelling flowers' either on the parvis outside the main door or in the entrance or in the *atrium* is also prescribed in the Capuchin Ceremonial of 1775.[31]

(B) THE INTERNAL LOCATION.[32] Evidence for the kindling of the new fire in the church itself comes from both England and France. The practice is first attested by John of Avranches in the eleventh century. At Lyon, where the custom has survived until the present day, the new fire is kindled behind the altar. This location, which is peculiar to the rite of Lyon, was very likely a feature of the earlier Roman rite; for it is generally agreed that in a number of respects, the ceremonial of Lyon preserves the primitive form of the Roman rite. On the other hand, in the absence of direct evidence for the practice at Rome, it can be argued that the kindling of fire behind the altar was a local development confined to the Church of Lyon. It may have been a survival of a pre-Christian ritual, or there may have been some connection with the concealing of the last candle at Tenebrae. Again, it is tempting to attribute its origin to the Old Testament practice of maintaining a perpetual fire at the altar of sacrifice. This may have come about in the wake of the Judaising movement in the twelfth century, which resulted in, amongst other things, the introduction of the *menorah* into Christian churches. Possible support for this view might come from Narbonne, where, according to former practice, the new fire was kindled *ad cornu altaris*. Here, it is not difficult to see a close connection between the Jewish altar of sacrifice with its four horns and the High Altar of the former cathedral at Narbonne, whose corners are purposely termed *horns*.

[30]*Praxis* p.141.
[31]*Memoriale* p.124.
[32]See *Table 33*.

Church/Rite	Date	Comment	Source
(i) *Near the font*			
York	12 C	between two columns, on S.side	Missal p.109
Salisbury	13 C	between two columns, on S.side	HBS 91 p.20
Exeter	1337	near south column	HBS 37 p.322
(ii) *In the nave*			
John of Avranches	c.1070	in the church	PL 147.49A
Cosenza	1549		Missal fol.115
Braga	1512	east end of nave	King, *LPS* p.223
(iii) *At the altar step(s)*			
Cistercian	1119	only blessed	*Nom.Cist.* p.104
Bursfeld	12 C	only blessed	Mocquereau p.69
Dominican	1504		Missal fol.lxxxv
Norbertine	1578		King, *LRO* p.190
(iv) *At the altar*			
Lyon	1392	behind altar	King, *LPS* p.59
Narbonne	1528	at horn of altar	*DAER* 4.24.3 p.145
Saragossa	1552	at Epistle corner of altar	Missal fol.lxxii
(v) *Near Easter candle*			
Soissons	1745		Missal p.163

Table 33. An internal location for the kindling of the new fire

It is significant that all three non-monastic English churches whose service-books record the new fire ceremony enjoin the same location for its kindling. The Exeter Ordinal stipulates 'near the south column', whilst the books of Salisbury and York agree that it should take place between the two columns on the south side of the church, the Missal of the latter church adding 'near the font'. Although it is generally agreed that the rite of Exeter was greatly influenced by that of Sarum, the relationship between the rites of Salisbury and York in the matter of the new fire is not at all clear. The ceremonies at both churches may both have derived from a common rite. Nor is it known why this particular location was to be found only in England, and only in the secular or cathedral tradition. For according to the surviving evidence for the monastic tradition in England, the new fire was kindled outside the church and at times in the cloister. Since both Exeter and Salisbury Cathedrals possessed a cloister, it is likely that this internal location was a feature of an indigenous new fire tradition. Moreover, the rationale underlying the use of the place is unknown. We know of the close connection between the light of the Easter candle and the blessing of the font at Baptism, but a link between the kindling of the new fire and the font is otherwise unknown.

By the nineteenth century, the striking of the new fire at St John Lateran had been transferred to the sacristy,[33] the place where it had been kindled at Toledo, Léon, and Milan since the early Middle Ages. The reason for the change of location at Rome is unknown. It may have resulted from a desire to have the ceremony held in a more convenient place. Milanese influence may be discounted. The use of the sacristy in the eighteenth-century and nineteenth-century instances, listed in *Table 34,* was probably also the result of ritual convenience, caused by the decay of the ceremonies of the Triduum during those centuries, including the seemingly-futile procession with the new fire in an empty church. However,

[33]Baggs p.98.

in Spain and almost certainly in Milan, the practice of kindling the new fire in the sacristy had its antecedents in the Holy Saturday liturgy of Jerusalem. At Auxerre in the sixteenth century, the fire was kindled in one church and blessed in another;[34] and at Rouen in the eighteenth century, the fire was kindled in the Church of St-Etienne and then carried in procession to the cathedral.[35]

Church	Date	Source
Léon	10 C	Antiphonary p.280
Milan	12 C	Beroldus p.109
St Mary's, York†	*c.*1400	HBS 75 p.292
Besançon‡	1682	Ceremonial p.329
Angers	1731	Ceremonial p.258
Carcassonne*	1749	Missal p.194
Mende	1766	Missal p.200
Reims	1770	Missal p.204
St-Bertrand*	1773	Missal p.209
Vienna*	1782	Missal p.215
Chartres*	1782	Missal p.171
Metz*	1829	Missal p.158
Toulouse*	1832	Missal p.191
Verdun	1832	Ceremonial p.312
La Rochelle*	1835	Missal p.186
Meaux	1845	Missal p.169
Autun*	1845	Missal p.239

†Fire kindled in chapter house.
‡Fire blessed at Gospel corner of altar.
*See *Table 31* for other locations.

Table 34. New fire kindled in the sacristy

[34]Missal of 1537/8 (M 39) cited by Martène, *DAER* 4.24.3 p.145.
[35]De Moléon p.299.

(C) THE TWENTIETH CENTURY. It had formerly been customary in many parts of France and Italy for the lighting and blessing of the new fire to function as both a religious and civic ceremony, especially if one of the doors of the church opened onto the town square. The custom had largely fallen into desuetude, either because of the anticipation of the paschal vigil during the morning of Holy Saturday or in France because of its suppression at the time of the Revolution. It was not until after the liturgical reforms of 1955, which permitted the holding of the Vigil in the evening of Holy Saturday, that the kindling of the new fire in the open air in front of churches and cathedrals took place again on any widespread scale, although at a small number of cathedrals, such as Lyon and Rodez, the ceremony continued to be performed in the traditional place. In a survey carried out in 1961 in thirty-four French dioceses to ascertain to what extent the recently-revived ceremony had been popular and successful, it was discovered the main problem had been climatic.[36] From a number of replies it was found that on an inclement Holy Saturday evening, rain, wind, smoke, the difficulty in lighting the incense, and the unexpected extinction of the flame of the Easter candle as a result of a sudden gust of wind produced lack of concentration and, in places, ridicule. Subsequently, at Arras and at Vannes after 1978, the new fire was kindled inside the cathedral.[37] It is significant that the 1970 Roman Missal makes the alternative provision that if the weather is intemperate, the blessing of the fire is adapted to the circumstances.[38]

C. MEANS

The production of the new fire was achieved universally by one of two time-honoured methods derived from pre-Christian religious milieux : the generation of fire by the fric-

[36]Morlot p.115.
[37]1984 Survey of France.
[38]*PJSM* p.318.

Outside	Square/Parvis	Porch
Bayeux	Carcassonne	Pamiers
Coutances	Angers	Paris
Versailles	Strasbourg	Reims
Le Mans	St-Dié	Angers
Belley	Montpellier	Autun
Arras†	St-Flour	St-Brieuc
Vannes†		Le Mans
Dijon		Tulle
		Mende
		Bayeux
		Troyes

Outside main door	Nave	Cloister
Limoges	Carcassonne* (W.End)	Aix
Amiens‡	Bayonne* (W.End)	Bayonne
Nîmes	Agen	St-Dié*
Orléans	Orléans*	

West Choir	Transept	Behind Altar
Nevers	Nancy	Lyon
	Rodez	

*If wet.
†Now performed indoors.
‡Since 1969 there has been no new fire ceremony in the cathedral.

Table 35. The new fire location in French cathedrals (1984)

tion of iron against stone or wood against wood, and the concentration of the sun's rays onto flammable material by means of a translucent lens. Some churches prescribed the former means, some the latter, and a number permitted both. The means favoured by one church was probably determined by the method employed in producing fire in pre-Christian times in the region in which that church was located. The choice offered in a number of service-books or referred to by medieval writers indicates the validity of either method in the eyes of the Church; and we shall discuss presently the arguments put forward to justify the use of the flint and the lens, as well as the symbolism associated with both the frictional and refractive methods.

(i) Fire by Friction

Evidence for the production of fire by the friction of wood against wood within a Christian liturgical context relates to parts of Central Germany. It is recorded that in Swabia the use of the fire-drill was the only permissible means of kindling the new fire,[39] and there is no good reason for doubting that this was local practice. Unfortunately, the 1555 Missal of Augsburg does not contain the new fire ceremony. Elsewhere throughout the Western Church, the frictional method of producing fire involved the use of a stone.

The earlier *ordines Romani,* our oldest sources for the new fire ceremony, stipulate that the new fire should be kindled by the striking of a stone.[40] There is no mention of an alternative method. Since the object struck was considered more important than the implement used for striking, it is the stone which is referred to in the rubric; and this is true of all subsequent documents which refer to the new fire kindled by friction. Of the medieval writers who refer to the ceremony, only John Beleth mentions that the spark is produced by striking the stone *saxo calibe aut ferro,* 'with iron pyrites (FeS_2) or iron'.[41] The ancients had long known the result of striking either of these minerals against flint. The use of the two-rock method, that is, iron pyrites and flint, when it had long been known that a spark is more easily obtained by using iron and flint,

---

[39]Frazer, *Golden Bough* Vol.7.1 p.145.
[40]OR 26.3; OR 28.25; OR 29.14; OR 31.29.
[41]*Rationale* (PL 202.110B).

may suggest the survival, from a pagan religious ceremony which antedated the discovery of iron, of a very primitive means of producing fire. Its mention by Beleth implies that in some places two stones were struck together to obtain fire, whilst elsewhere the method of striking the flint with iron or steel had been adopted. Since it is almost invariably only the flint or the stone object struck that is referred to, we can have no idea how widespread the more primitive method was.

One of the areas where this primitive method may have been in use was Southern Italy; for according to the Beneventan rite, the principal means of generating a spark was *'ex ignario'*, that is, 'from a fire-stone'.[42] *Ignarium* is probably to be identified with the mineral copper pyrites ($CuFeS_2$).[43] This ore, like iron pyrites, produces a spark when struck with a flint. If this interpretation of *ignarium* is accepted, we may have in the Beneventan ceremonial an instance of the two-rock method of obtaining fire. On the other hand, it is possible to interpret *ignarium* 'flint' since *lapis igniarius* is found with this meaning.[44] The word may be dialectal or a synonym for *silex*. A similar confusion exists in English regarding *fire-stone;* for the word may refer to the flint or to the iron pyrites.

The survival into historical times of this primitive method of obtaining fire should cause no surprise. For it would seem that Christian *homo religiosus* in Europe is just as traditional and conservative as his or her pre-Christian forebears; and in an age when fire can readily be obtained by matches,

---

[42]*Gradual* and *Missale Antiquum.* Text in Hesbert, *L'Antiphonale* p.188.

[43]Thus Du Cange. In classical Latin *igniarium* signified 'a stick for making fire' (OLD), as is clear from Pliny, *Natural History* 16.207. It is most unlikely that *ignarium* retains this meaning in the rubrics of the Beneventan service-books since the Beneventan formula for the blessing of the new fire *(A)* contains a reference to flint *(silex)*. The discrepancy in spelling *(ignarium* and *igniarium)* is not crucial. Both the *Gradual* and the *Missale Antiquum* contain orthographical oddities.

[44]Marcellus Empiricus 33.

cigarette-lighters, or electrical current, in many places the Church perpetuates the tradition of using flint.[45]

In some documents and service-books, which record only the frictional production of fire, the word *lapis* is used to refer to the medium employed in obtaining the fire. It is true that this word may indicate any hard stone capable of causing iron or steel to produce a spark. However, in the majority of instances, including Ordo 26, our earliest authority, the stone is specifically said to be *silex*, 'fire-stone', otherwise 'flint' ($SiO_2.nH_2O$). There are three main reasons for its almost-universal adoption as the means of creating a spark for the new fire. (i) It is easily and cheaply obtained in most parts of Europe and requires little attention to commission it for service. (ii) Whereas a sunny day is a prerequisite for the production of fire by means of a lens, a flint may be used within or without a building and in any type of weather. (iii) In addition to its use in the Milanese and Mozarabic rites and in many parts of Gaul, the adoption of the flint by the Roman Church encouraged its use in those churches in whose rites the new fire was kindled by means of a lens *(Table 36)*.

The principle involved in the use of flint and steel is exactly the same as that which lies behind the use of the tinder-box in more recent times. The flint was struck with the steel, and the sparks thus generated fell into a *patella* or chafing-dish,[46] if the fire was kindled within the church. In this receptacle lay *sarmentum*, 'touchwood' or 'punk', twigs converted into an easily ignitible consistency.[47] At Freising, Vallombrosa, Cologne, and Prague, dried twigs from vines were used,[48]

[45]In the survey of forty French cathedrals, undertaken by the writer in March 1984, a flint continued to be used as the sole means of kindling the new fire in twenty-six churches.

[46]*Nom. Cist.* p.104; Lesnes Missal (HBS 95 p.47); Dominican Missals : 1504 fol.lxxxvi and 1908 p.62. The Lateran Missal (Schmidt II p.110), and *MR 1474* (HBS 17 p.174) use the term *vas*.

[47]Colti II p.156. Also, Sicardus, *Mitrale* (PL213.322D) and MS Gg 15 (Martène, *DAER* 4.24.3 p.145).

[48]1487 Missal fol.ciii; 1503 Missal fol.xci; MS Gg 15 (Martène, *op.cit.*); 1498 Missal fol.xci.

whilst a number of service-books mention simply *ligna*, 'twigs'.[49] Also in the dish or close at hand were pieces of charcoal *(carbones)*, which would catch fire once the touchwood was ablaze.[50] Some of the charcoal would then be transferred to the thurible, in order that the new fire might be censed. The rest would continue to burn in the vessel, if the fire had been kindled in church, until the Easter candle was alight and there was no danger that its flame would fail. This is attested in the Dominican rite.[51] If some form of bonfire had been prepared for the new fire outside the church, the touchwood would have been used to kindle the mound of wood. There is, however, little documentary evidence for the construction of bonfires. The mention of *strues* at Spires leaves open the possibility of a large mound of wood;[52] and at the Monastery of St-Martin d'Ainay near Lyon, the woodpile was sufficiently large for the monks to warm themselves as they returned into church.[53] In parts of Germany until recent times, bonfires were lit at Easter from the new fire.[54] These, however, appear to have been comparable with the Lent and Midsummer fire of Northern Europe and in all probability were kindled at a distance from the church, after the completion of the paschal vigil, by way of celebrating Easter. In more recent times, wood-fires observed by the writer, and by those with whom the writer has communicated, have been of very modest proportions.

[49]1570 Ratisbon Ritual fol.cii; 1664 Carmelite Missal p.156. At Poitiers, tow was also used (1524 Missal fol.lxix). The Carmelites used small palm and olive branches *(op.cit.)*, whilst the Augustinian Friars placed flowers and fragrant herbs on top of the olive twigs which they used (1714 Ceremonial p.307).

[50]Their use is well documented in a number of missals : Lesnes (HBS 95 p.47); Cistercian (1669 p.154); Evreux (1740 p.186); Sées (1742 p.186); Amiens (1752 p.182); St-Bertrand (1773 p.209); Périgueux (1782 p.158); Le Puy (1783 p.159); Dominican (1482 fol.69).

[51]1504 Missal fol.lxxxvi.

[52]1512 *Agenda* fol.xciii.

[53]Martène, *DAER* 4.22 p.125 (M 175).

[54]Van Gennep 1.3 p.1259; Frazer, *Golden Bough* Vol.7.1 p.141.

Early Evidence

1	Ordo 26	750–775
2	Ordo 28	c.800
3	Ordo 29	870–890
4	*PRG*	c.950
5	*Alcuin*	c.1000

Monastic Evidence

6	Austin Friars	1491
7	Camaldolese	1503
8	Capuchins	1775
9	Carmelites	c.1312
10	Cistercians	1689
11	Cluny	1510
12	Dominicans	1504
13	Franciscans	1243
14	Melk	1495
15	Monte Cassino	12 C
16	*Regularis Concordia*	c.970
17	Vallombrosa	1503

Secular Evidence

18	Amiens	1752
19	Anderlecht	14 C
20	Aquileia	1519
21	Autun	1845
22	Basel	1488
23	Bayonne	1543
24	Beneventum	c.1000
25	Besançon	1707
26	Bourges	1741
27	Braga	1558
28	Breslau	1483
29	Cahors	1760
30	Carcassonne	1749
31	Chartres	1782
32	Cosenza	1549
33	Coutances	1825
34	Esztergom	1501
35	Evreux	1740
36	Florence	c.1300
37	Fréjus	1754
38	Halberstadt	c.1505
39	Hildesheim	1499
40	Ireland	c.1200
41	Laon	1662
42	La Rochelle	1835
43	Léon	10 C
44	Le Puy	1783
45	Liège	1492
46	Limoges	1830
47	Lisieux	1752
48	Luçon	1828
49	Lyon	1510
50	Mainz	1507
51	Meaux	1845
52	Mende	1766
53	Metz	1829
54	Milan	1560
55	Nantes	1837
56	Palencia	1568
57	Paris	1662
58	Passau	1503
59	Périgueux	1782
60	Poitiers	1524
61	Reims	1770
62	Rouen	1640
63	St-Bertrand	1773
64	Salisbury	13 C
65	Salzburg	1507
66	Saragossa	1552
67	Sées	1742
68	Seville	1507
69	Soissons	1745
70	Toulouse	1832

71 Tours	1784	74 Valence	1504
72 Trier	1488	75 Vienna	1782
73 Troyes	1736	76 Würzburg	1477

Table 36. Evidence for the use of flint and steel[55]

The anticipation of the ceremonies of Holy Week was only one of the causes which led to the decay of the Triduum. The abolition of the three-day holiday by Pope Urban VIII in the seventeenth century must have further reduced the tiny congregations of the faithful who during the morning of Holy Saturday could hear the deacon chant *'Haec nox est'*.[56] Moreover, one of the results of the increase in solemnity of the liturgy, a sacerdotal domain in which the discharge of ceremonial came to be regarded, increasingly after the Counter-Reformation, as the sole prerogative of the priesthood, was the consequent exclusion and almost irrelevant presence of the laity at any divine service other than the Mass; and whereas in

[55]*References.* (1) OR 26.3. (2) OR 28.25. (3) OR 29.14. (4) II p.57 §215. (5) PL 101.1205C. (6) np. (7) M.fol.89. (8) Cerem.p.125 (9) Ordinary p.171. (10) Ritual p.245. (11) M.fol.xlix. (12) M.fol.lxxxv. (13) Van Dijk II p.245. (14) M.fol.lxvii. (15) *DAMR* 3.15.10 p.142. (16) PL 137.491B. (17) M.fol.xci. (18) M.p.182. (19) Ordinary p.87. (20) M.fol.91. (21) M.p.239. (22) M.fol.xci. (23) M.p.41. (24) Hesbert p.188. (25) Cerem.p.315. (26) M.p.225. (27) M.fol.xcvi. (28) M.np. (29) M.p.172. (30) M.p.194. (31) M.p.171. (32) M.fol.115. (33) Cerem.p.329. (34) M.fol.lxxiii. (35) M.p.186. (36) Frazer, *G.B.* 10 p.126. (37) De Rubeis p.327. (38) M.fol.lxx. (39) M.fol.xcvi. (40) M.p.126. (41) Bellotte p.813. (42) M.p.186. (43) Antiphonary p.280. (44) M.p.159. (45) Ordinary np. (46) M.p.219. (47) M.p.189. (48) M.p.214. (49) M.fol.lxvii. (50) M.fol.xcii. (51) M.p.189. (52) M.p.200. (53) M.p.158. (54) M.fol.109. (55) M.p.198. (56) M.fol.c. (57) Cerem.p.375. (58) M.fol.lxxxiv. (59) M.p.158. (60) M.fol.lxix. (61) M.p.204. (62) Manual p.305. (63) M.p.209. (64) Manual p.20. (65) M.fol.lxxxv. (66) M.fol.lxxii. (67) M.p.186. (68) M.fol.lxxv. (69) M.p.163. (70) M.p.206. (71) M.p.191. (72) M.fol.ci. (73) M.p.227. (74) M.fol.liiii. (75) M.p.215. (76) Ordinary np.

[56]Beauduin p.6.

the Middle Ages the ritual that accompanied the kindling of the new fire provided a liturgical pageantry which was capable of winning the attention of the laity, to say nothing of the excitement there must have been at the prospect of carrying some of the new fire to their homes, the ceremony of the new fire in later centuries lost much of its former significance and importance. The anticipated ritual on Holy Saturday morning was now of little liturgical relevance to the laity, and those who did attend were present out of either habit or curiosity.

The Holy Week reforms of 1955 within the Roman Catholic Church were an attempt not only to restore the ceremonies of the Triduum to their original times of performance but to bring about a much greater lay participation in the paschal liturgy. In the surge of enthusiasm following those reforms, the presence of a large congregation in the parvis of a church or cathedral encouraged the construction of a large bonfire. But the frustration, disappointment, and even ridicule experienced when the rain-sodden wood refused to catch fire, and the wane in interest in the ceremony in recent years have resulted in fires of considerably less magnitude. Other problems encountered in staging the ceremony in the open air include the danger to life and limb, risked by the clergy attempting to read the prayers by the light of a small fire, and the inclemency of the weather, which makes difficult the lighting of the incense, not to mention the new fire itself, and the possibility of having the flame of the Easter candle extinguished by a sudden gust of wind.[57] In some churches, such as the Cathedrals of Annecy and Arras, the charcoals, which used to be brought into church in a small portable stove, have been replaced by a rag soaked in spirits. In 1983 at Tulle Cathedral, a quantity of methylated spirit burned in a small dish until the paschal vigil had ended.[58]

The Roman Catholic Church never officially countenanced

---

[57]For the problems encountered following the revival of the ceremony in the open air in France, see Morlot pp.114–22.

[58]1984 Survey of France.

the use of matches for the kindling of the new fire until 1970. However, in many parishes in England and France and in some cathedrals, matches have been used for many years, mainly because of their reliability and because of the speed with which fire can be obtained—the use of flint and steel requires some skill. It is significant that most matches are ignited by striking their heads against glass-paper, one of the constituents of which is silicon dioxide (SiO_2), the basic compound of flint. The 'matches' referred to in C.M.Merati's *Ceremonies of the Roman Church* were fire-sticks *(ligna sulphurata)*. These are described in a later chapter.

The earliest evidence for the use of flint as the sole means of obtaining fire in the Roman rite is to be found in the Roman Missal of 1474.[59] Although the possibility that a lens may have been used at Rome in the fifteenth century must not be ruled out, the latest documentary evidence for the use of a lens antedates this missal by about a century.[60] The use of a flint, prescribed in the Pian Missal of 1570,[61] was also enjoined in the 1955 Revised Order of Holy Week;[62] but in the 1970 *Missale Romanum,* the historical and symbolic method of kindling the new fire has been abandoned, and the rubric 'a large fire is prepared' allows of any convenient means of producing a flame.[63] In *Lent, Holy Week, and Easter,* the new service-book of the Church of England, the rubric relating to the new fire contains no firm injunction, but merely states that 'According to ancient custom the light for the Easter candle was taken from newly-kindled fire and not from an already existing source of light' (p.226). It does, however, countenance the lighting of a bonfire outside the building and a procession of the faithful accompanying the new fire into church.[64]

---

[59]*MR 1474* (HBS 17 p.174).
[60]Ordo of P.Amiel (OPA) (PL 78.1321C).
[61]*Missale Romanum* (t.e. 1950) p.186.
[62]D.Schmidt I p.118.
[63]'Praeparatur rogus.' 1970 *Missale Romanum* (t.e.) p.267.
[64]The Anglican rite, as exemplified in the above-mentioned Church of

The Symbolism of the Flint. Medieval commentators were not slow to detect a symbolic significance in the use of the flint, in the action of striking, and in the generation of a spark. In his identification of the stone with Christ, Rupert of Deutz cites the authority of Psalm 117 (118).[65] The same author sees in the striking of the stone a symbolic reminder of the Crucifixion, and for him the production of the spark represents the release of the Holy Spirit.[66] The notion of the symbolic representation of Christ by the stone is mentioned by both Beleth and Sicardus.[67] The former adds that the Church has been built on the rock, which stands for Christ, and from that rock comes the New Law. He thus implicitly draws a parallel with Moses and the tablets of stone in Exodus 32. Durandus, by adding that the spark produced from the striking of the stone represents the fire of God's love and at the same time symbolises the piercing of Jesus' side, out of which flowed the blood and the water, enlarges upon the symbolism attached to the stone by these three writers.[68] In more recent times, Guéranger has likened the spark leaping from the flint to Christ rising from the rock-hewn sepulchre;[69] and Bouyer, expressing the notion more succinctly, writes that the new fire, drawn from the flint, symbolises 'the divine spark that God himself would cause to rise from the sepulchre of Golgotha to kindle the universe at the flame of Christ's own splendour'.[70] As late as 1956, in a preamble to his edition of the revised services of Holy Week, Dom Godfrey Diekmann describes the kindling of the fire from the flint as 'a vivid image of Christ's new presence among men : as the spark leaps

England service-book and in the 1979 American Book of Common Prayer, provides no prayer for the blessing of the new fire.

[65]Lapidem quem reprobaverunt aedificantes. *De Div.Off.* V (PL 170.149B).

[66]*op.cit.*

[67]*Rationale* (PL 202.111B); *Mitrale* (PL 213.323A).

[68]*Rationale* VI.80 fol.350.

[69]*Liturgical Year* (PTHW) p.554.

[70]*The Paschal Mystery* p.267.

from the flint, so He arose from His rock tomb'.[71] It is important to note that there is a twofold symbolism in the identification of Christ with the stone. For not only is He the *lapis angularis* of the psalm; Christ is also the stone through the medium of which God's brightness is brought to the faithful. The notion that it is the rock that stands for Christ is also mentioned by Thurston.[72]

With the simplification of the paschal ceremonies in the liturgical changes following the Second Vatican Council, much of the traditional symbolism associated with the new fire ceremony was omitted from the Missal of 1970. With the abandoning of the flint as the obligatory means of obtaining the new fire, it was almost inevitable that the reference to the flint in the benedictory *Formula A* should be removed from that prayer.

It is perhaps not out of place at this juncture to refer to the belief, recorded by Rupert of Deutz, that fire was inherent in certain types of rock, for example, flint.[73] John of Avranches implies that the spark released from the stone had been confined within it prior to the act of striking.[74] The use by a number of writers of the verb *elicere,* 'to draw out', within this context, reinforces the idea. It is beyond the scope of this work to discuss ancient and medieval notions regarding the nature and essence of fire. However, it is not difficult to understand that the act of generating a spark from a stone was regarded by the unscientific minds of primitive humans both as a miracle and as a mystery, so that the stone from which the fire leapt came to be held in reverential awe and the fire was believed to participate in the divine nature and to be the visible presence of God in the world. This belief is, of course, present in the Old Testament in the incidents of the Burning Bush and the Pillar of Fire. Christian thought had inherited

[71] *The Masses of Holy Week* p.127.
[72] *Lent and Holy Week* p.411.
[73] *De Div. Off.* V (PL 170.149A).
[74] *Lib. de Off. Eccl.* (PL 147.49A).

from Judaism the notion of conceiving the nature of God in terms of fire and light, had evolved a theology of light from the discourses of Jesus as recorded in the Johannine writings, and to a certain extent had adopted the pagan philosophical notion that fire was the underlying principle behind creation.

(ii) Fire by Refraction of the Sun's Rays

Throughout this section, 'lens' translates *cristallus*,[75] the term found in our sources to signify the semi-precious stones, such as beryl or rock-crystal, which were used to produce fire by the refraction of the sun's rays. There is good reason to believe that these stones, which were widely used for this purpose in the ancient world,[76] also featured in pagan religious new fire ceremonies, which were adopted by the Church into her liturgy. Although the word *vitrum,* 'glass', is not found within the context of the new fire rubrics, this material was probably used on occasions as a substitute for a translucent stone.

Since the use of a lens for the production of the new fire was dependent upon the shining of the sun at the required moment, it may be safely assumed that in those churches where the new fire was kindled by this method, alternative means of obtaining fire must always have been readily available in the event of a cloudy day. The obumbration of the sun is succinctly alluded to in the Missal of St-Martin d'Ainay.[77] Of the thirty-three instances, compiled from documentary sources and listed in *Table 37,* where a lens is stated to be a means of producing fire, six, including that of St-Martin d'Ainay, do not record an alternative method. To this group

[75]Or *cristallum.*

[76]See especially F.Dolger, *Das Karsamstag Feuer* pp.288–96.

[77]The phrase *si fieri potest,* 'if it is possible', both implies the use of an alternative means and also indicates the importance attached to the use of a lens.

belong the twelfth-century Ritual of Soissons and the eleventh-century Sacramentary of Holy Trinity on Mons Suavicinius.[78]

In the *Sacramentary*, Honorius of Autun refers only to *crystallum;* but in the *Gemma Animae*, we find that a flint is alternative to a lens.[79] This would suggest that the lens was the principal, but not the sole device for kindling the new fire in the liturgical milieu with which Honorius was familiar. Hugh of St-Victor refers only to the lens and also mentions the pieces of charcoal. In a somewhat forced analogy, he likens Christ to the mediatorial rays, which shine through the lens and bring back to life the 'dead' charcoals, which themselves symbolise the souls of men and women in bondage to sin.

In the Customary of Cluny, the lens is specifically stated to be a beryl. At St-Bénigne, Dijon, it was kept in the custody of an official called the *apocrisarius* (senior sacristan), who carried it in the procession for the blessing of the new fire. It was perhaps inevitable, therefore, in view of the importance attached to this translucent stone at Cluny, that reference to an alternative fire-kindling device was omitted from the rubrics relating to the new fire ceremony. In addition to the two above-mentioned monasteries, a beryl was used at Fleury, at Barking, and at York, and by the Gilbertines.

Unlike the identification of שִׁישׁ (taršîš) in the Old Testament,[80] there seems little doubt that the beryl referred to in the texts which relate to the new fire is to be equated with the aluminium silicate of beryllium ($Be_3Al_2Si_6O_{18}$), the chemical composition of the gemstone, which is still known

---

[78]The use of a lens here is suggested by the use of the benediction-formula *J*.

[79]PL 172.746A and PL 172.668A.

[80]In the Massoretic Text of Ex 28:20; 39:13; Ez 1:16; 10:9; 28:13; and Dan 10:6, שִׁישׁ is rendered throughout in the AV 'beryl'. The uncertainty of the LXX translators in their varying renditions of this word is reflected in modern English versions, where the Hebrew word is variously interpreted 'chalcedony', 'chrysolite', 'a precious stone', as well as 'beryl'.

by that name. For in an eighth-century or ninth-century description of the stone we read :

> Beryl is surrounded by a golden mist and has six facets. It is said to burn the hand of anyone who holds it.[81]

The vitreous and almost resinous quality of the beryl could well be said to give the impression that the stone was surrounded by a haze, and this particular silicate does indeed crystallise in the hexagonal system. Its reputation for burning the hand, if held, almost certainly arose partly from its use in kindling the new fire, partly from ignorance, and partly from its being endowed with wonderfully strange qualities by the superstitious and unscientific minds of medieval people. For the beryl which was used for the new fire almost certainly saw the light of day only once a year,[82] and remained safely locked away for the rest of the time. Beryls of various colours occur, but the colourless or white variety is sufficiently translucent to allow the rays of the sun to pass through and ignite combustible materials. The view that the term *beryllus* within the context of the new fire merely refers to glass of high quality cannot be sustained. For in addition to the evidence of Bede's *Pseudographia,* it must be stated that if the lens had been made of glass or rock-crystal, the writers who refer to *beryllus* would almost certainly have used *vitrum* or *crystallum;* and the importance attached to the lens in the procession at Cluny and other places can more readily be understood if that object were a stone both rare and of considerable value, rather than an easily-obtainable piece of glass.

The fact that no alternative means of kindling the new fire at Tours is recorded by Martène may well be explained by his desire to draw attention to the curious method involved in the use of the lens. For according to the thirteenth-century

---

[81]Beryllus, nube aure tegitur : et sex angulos habet, tenentem manu adurere dicitur. *Baedae Pseudographia* (PL 94.552A).

[82]And, presumably, on three days of the year, when the new fire came to be kindled on each day of the Triduum.

missal of that church, the new fire was produced 'by sunlight, a lens, and cold water'.[83]

It is clear that the fire was kindled by means of a translucent stone held above the tinder; but the mention of the third element, cold water, seemingly essential for the production of the fire, is baffling. This method involving water is also mentioned by Beleth, who, when describing how the new fire is kindled, writes :

> For if a lens is fitted in the mouth of a bottle filled with water and tilted towards the sun, fire is very quickly produced from the lens at that place.[84]

Beleth gives no indication as to the shape or the size of the bottle, although the use of water as well as a lens in a device intended to refract the rays of the sun strongly suggests that the bottle was made of glass or some other translucent substance.[85] Without more information, it is difficult for us at this point in time to understand why the lens alone was not sufficient to produce fire. One possibility is that the water-filled bottle with a lens for a stopper provided a double refractive surface and so, it was believed, enhanced the effectiveness of the device. The use of a translucent container for the production of the new fire is recorded in the tenth-century Sacramentary of Corbie. It refers to an *ampulla*.[86] We are not told whether this vessel was filled with water, but it must be presupposed that it was of a vitreous or crystalline composition and that part of its external surface was convex in shape.

---

[83]Sole et cristallo et aqua frigida. Martène, *DAER* 4.22.5 p.96 (M 324).

[84]Nam si crystallus supponatur orificio phialae aqua plenae ad solem sine mora ignis e crystallo illico excutietur. *Rationale* (PL 202.111B).

[85]The use of rock-crystal for the manufacture of containers for liquids is attested by Solinus (*Coll. Rerum Mem.* 15,29–31) cited by Dolger, *Das Karsamstag* p.294.

[86]Hora sexta cum ampulla a sole illuminatum. PL 78.336B. Originally and by derivation, an *ampulla* was a vessel with two handles. Even in classical times, the feature characteristic of this container was a convex or bulbous shape.

Church/Document	Date	Lens	Flint	Source
Poitiers	c.900	1	2	*Poitiers* p.138
PRG (MS C)	c.950	2	1	II p.94 §342
Corbie	10 C	1	2	PL 78.336B
Cluny	11 C	1*	—	PL 149.659A
St-Bénigne, Dijon	11 C	1*	2	*DAMR* 3.13.34 p.126
Fleury	11 C	1*	2	Albers V p.143
Sacramentarium Vetus	11 C	1	—	PL 151.846B
Avellana	11 C	1	2	PL 151.880D
Ripoll	1038	2	1	Sacramentary p.92
Gilbertines	1150	2*	1	HBS 59 p.39
York	12 C	1*	2	Missal p.109
Soissons	1180–1190	1	—	*DAER* 4.24 p.161
Tours	13 C	1	—	*DAER* 4.22 p.96
Albi	14 C	2	1	Feasey (1906) p.355
St Mary's, York	c.1400	1*	2	HBS 75 p.275
Barking	1404	1*	2	HBS 65 p.101
Prague	1498	1	2	Missal fol.xci
Copenhagen	1510	2	1	Missal fol.cv
Spires	1512	1	2	*Agenda* fol.xciii
Upsala	1513	1	2	Missal fol.lxxvi
Narbonne	1528	2	1	Missal fol.lxxxiii
St-Martin d'Ainay	1531	1	—	*DAER* 4.22 p.125
Burgos	1546	2	1	Missal fol.ciii
Osma	1561	2	1	Missal fol.lxxxix
Ratisbon	1570	1	2	Ritual fol.cii
Freising	1579	1	2	Missal fol.85
Sens	1715	1	2	Missal p.238
Commentator				
Rupert of Deutz	1111	2	1	PL 170.149A
Hugh (St-Victor)	c.1140	1	—	PL 177.889D
Honorius (Autun)	c.1150	1	2	PL 172.668A
Beleth	c.1180	2	1	PL 202.111B
Sicardus	c.1200	2	1	PL 213.322D
Bauldry	1762	2	1	*Manuale* p.189

*Signifies the use of a beryl.
The figure 1 in the third and fourth columns indicates that the rubrics give this method priority. The figure 2 indicates the alternative means.

Table 37. Evidence for the production of fire by refection[87]

The need for a translucent container which would allow the rays of the sun to pass through makes it extremely likely that the *phiala* referred to by Beleth was also made of glass or crystal.

Apropos of the glass phial or container, a choice of devices for refracting the sun's rays is attested in the Pontifical of Poitiers :

> Fire is obtained from a lens or from a phial. If neither of these can be used, it is struck from a stone.[88]

This choice of refractive devices would suggest that great importance and significance were attached to the kindling of fire in this way.

The use of a lens, in preference to a flint, at Barking, Copenhagen, Upsala, and York shows that its use was not confined to the generally sunnier and warmer parts of Southern Europe.[89] A hitherto largely-unnoticed passage in Bede's *De Tabernaculo* may well contain a reference to the use of a lens and if so, would antedate the first recorded instance of its use *(PRG)* by over two hundred years.

> It is permissible to offer for use in the temple of God oil which is made from only the fruit of the olive, just as the fire which burns in the sacred lamps or upon the altar of God should be only that which has come down from heaven. Accordingly let the oil, which the sons of Israel bring for the lamp of God, be not any kind of oil, but obtained from the fruit of the olive, of the best quality, and beaten with a stick.[90]

[87]In addition to the evidence in the table above, there are the two ordinaries cited in the 1856 Ritual of Soissons, and the evidence of Bede. This additional evidence is discussed in this chapter.

[88]Ignis de christallo sive de amula sumitur, vel etiam de cote, si neutrum horum fuerit, excutitur. *Poitiers* p.138. *Amula* is either mis-spelt, or a regional variation of *ampulla.*

[89]The writer has demonstrated by experiment that fire can be kindled with the use of a lens at an early hour on both a late autumnal and early spring morning at a latitude of 54° N.

[90]Nullum offerri licet tabernaculo Dei, nisi quod de lignis olivarum conficitur, sicut nec ignis alius quam qui caelo descendit, vel in lucernis sanc-

This reference to fire occurs in a passage containing regulations relating to the use of oil in church lamps. It is true that the passage contains Old Testament allusions and an attempt is made to justify the liturgical practices of the day by appealing to biblical precedents, but it is difficult to see any reference or allusion to an instance in the Old Testament of fire descending from heaven. For on those occasions when fire is said to have originated with the Lord, some (such as Leviticus 9:24 and 1 Kings 18:38) involve the consuming of the sacrifice upon the altar; others (such as Genesis 19:24, Leviticus 10:2, and Numbers 11:1) describe the punishment of those who had sinned against the Lord. In the passage under discussion, neither of these aspects of fire seems to be of relevance. It is rather the fire which burns in the lamps for illumination or on the altar for symbolic reasons that is of concern to Bede; and for this reason he almost certainly is referring to the source of the flame for those lamps. Moreover, since there was no tradition in Judaism of obtaining fire for liturgical lights from any particular source, as opposed to either the flint or lens in Christian ritual, it is tempting to see in the phrase *ignis . . . qui coelo descendit* an implicit but unmistakable reference to the kindling of new fire by means of a lens.

The compilers of the 1856 Ritual of Soissons claim that the mention and use of *crystallus* in the former period imply that the new fire had been formerly kindled by frictional means and that the historian Jean Cabaret is guilty of a very serious mistake when he writes that at Soissons the new fire was produced 'by means of a lens of crystal glass which they used to expose to the rays of the sun' (p.308 note xi). In support of their assertion they cite the rubric from the Ordinary of St-Martial, Limoges :

> igne de cristallo vel silice noviter excusso, 'fire newly struck from a lens or a flint',

tis vel in altari Dei debet accendi. Offerant ergo filii Israel oleum ad lucernam Dei, non qualecumque, sed de lignis olivarum, et hoc purissimum, piloque contusum. PL 91.463.

in which the participle *excusso* qualifies both nouns, and part of the corresponding instruction in the Ordinary of St-Pierre d'Orval :

> silice vel cristallo noviter cum calibe, 'newly (struck) from a flint or a lens with a steel'.

It is true that in the second instance, *cum calibe,* 'with a steel', appears to relate to both *silice* and *cristallo;* but the absence of a verb makes difficult the interpretation of the rubric, which, being incomplete, is therefore inadmissible as corroborative evidence. Moreover, the addition of *cum calibe* is very rare in other rubrics similar to this. The compilers would almost certainly be familiar with the rubric of the twelfth-century Ritual of Soissons, which prescribes the use of a lens *(Table 37);* but they may not be able to reconcile this information with the rubric of their 1745 Missal, which refers to the use of a flint, *silex* (p.163). It would seem, therefore, that they attempt to explain this inconsistency of practice by maintaining that the *crystallus* had formerly served the same purpose as the flint.

The compilers are apparently unaware of Beleth's statement, which we quoted a few pages previously, or of Rupert of Deutz's reference to the use of a lens 'on a cloudless day' or the evidence of Sicardus. Moreover, it would seem that the verb *excutere,* whose perfect participle *excussus* is used in the first of the above-quoted rubrics and which formerly suggested 'shaking out' or 'driving out' with the use of rapid or violent movement, had either extended its meaning to include other methods of kindling fire, as *Rubrics 1, 2, 4,* and *7* in *Table 38* would suggest, or was linking *cristallo* and *silice* in a sylleptic union. At first sight, the rubric in the Gilbertine Ordinal would appear to support the view of the nineteenth-century rubricians of Soissons :

> a cilice *(sic)* vel cristallo aut berillo excussus.

In classical Latin, the use of *vel* would have indicated that *silex* and *cristallus* were variants within the same category, as opposed to *beryllus,* which was contrasted with them by the use of *aut*. In medieval Latin, these niceties of distinction no longer obtained. Indeed, in the above-quoted instance and in the corresponding rubric in the Pontifical of Poitiers, the role and function of *vel* is reversed.

A number of observations may be adduced in favour of the traditional interpretation and understanding of the use of *cristallus* to show that the liturgists were themselves in error and that the word *cristallus* within the present context signified a lens used for generating fire by the refraction of the sun's rays. (i) In earlier documents, it is clear that two different methods are involved from the use of two separate verbs to express the actions of kindling fire by refraction and by friction : in *Poitiers, sumere* and *excutere* respectively and in the Customary of Fleury, *producere* and *excutere* respectively. (ii) The symbolic interpretation of the lens makes sense only if the principle of refraction is under discussion. (iii) There are clear references to the sun in the Sacramentary of Corbie and by John Beleth, and the Ordinal of St Mary's, York, refers to the possibility of cloud covering. (iv) It is very difficult to believe that a semi-precious stone was subjected to the violent impact of an iron bar. (v) Few semi-precious stones, such as beryl, will produce a spark if struck with iron. Moreover, their small size would have necessitated their being held in a clamp or other similar device.

The writer is of the opinion that in the rubric, the placing of the lens before the flint indicates that within the rite priority was given to the use of the lens. The inclusion of the alternative method of fire by friction was a prudent precaution designed to obviate the possible dismay or frustration likely to be experienced in the event of a cloudy day. In instances in which the rubric prescribes the use of the flint first, followed by the alternative of a lens, it should not be assumed that the frictional method of kindling fire had priority. In many instances, it is likely that a simple choice existed and that either method was valid liturgically. One suspects that in a number of rites, the existence of a choice represents a synthesis of ceremonial elements drawn from different cultural or religious traditions. The preference of most of the liturgical commentators for the frictional method of kindling fire reflects the fact that the use of the flint was far more common than the use of the lens throughout the Western Church.

The Symbolism of the Lens. Whereas the action of striking a steel against a flint was thought to result in the release of a spark contained in the flint, a lens was believed to be the means of transferring fire from the sun to the earth. Medieval writers seized upon the potential symbolism inherent in this method of obtaining fire, not only because of the obvious similarity in function between a fire-producing lens and the mediatorial role of Christ, but also because of the closeness in spelling and identical pronunciation of *Christ* with part of the Latin word for lens, *cristallus.* Commenting upon the method of obtaining fire by the refraction of the sun's rays, Rupert of Deutz compares the sun with God and the pieces of charcoal with men and women in bondage to death. The lens is Christ, who mediates between God and humans and who brings life to the latter.[91] Similarly, the fire, which the lens brings into being and which ignites the charcoal, is the Holy Spirit, which Jesus told His disciples He would send. In another sense, the lens brings the fire of God's love to human beings; for without the mediation of Christ, they would not exist without that love.[92] The symbolic interpretation of the lens as Christ the Mediator is also mentioned by Sicardus and Durandus.[93] The notion of the fire representing the Spirit of Christ spread amongst the faithful is found in the *Gemma Animae* of Honorius of Autun.[94] Beleth and Honorius both elaborate the idea of the lens representing Christ; for they see the translucent stone

[91]This notion is also found in the *Miscellanea* of Hugh of St-Victor (PL 177.889D).

[92]*De Div. Off.* V (PL 170.149C).

[93]*Mitrale* (PL 213.323A); *Rationale* VI.80 fol.350. Durandus says that the lens comes between the sun and the moon. It is almost certain that he, or a later copyist, should have written *earth* for the latter noun.

[94]PL 172.668B.

as symbolising the 'clear resurrection body of Christ'. Beleth describes the resurrectional flesh of Christ as 'pure and pellucid', a notion echoed in the Missal of Upsala.[95]

* * * * *

In some churches there was no new fire ceremony as such; instead, the new fire was 'taken from elsewhere' *(sumptus aliunde)*. We shall refer to this practice later.

---

[95]*Rationale* (PL 202.111B); 1513 Missal fol.lxxvi.

Chapter Fourteen
THE NEW FIRE AT ROME

(i) The Eighth-Century Evidence of Pope Zachary

The earliest explicit reference to the new fire ceremony at
Rome is found in the following extract from a letter which
Pope Zachary (741–752) wrote in reply to an enquiry from
Boniface, Bishop of Mainz.

> Now concerning the paschal fire about which you enquired :
> since the time of our saintly fathers of old, when the Church
> was established (*or* when the church was dedicated) through
> the grace of God and Our Lord Jesus Christ and by His pre-
> cious blood, on Thursday of Holy Week while the Sacrament
> is being consecrated, three large lamps, fuelled by a copious
> supply of oil which has been collected from the various lamps
> in church, will be tended with great care and will burn con-
> tinuously in a remote part of the church, recalling the flame
> of the inner tabernacle. There will be sufficient oil to last until
> the third day. From these lamps fire will be taken on Holy
> Saturday for the sacred Baptism at the font, and will be re-
> hallowed by the Bishop (*or* by a priest). As you have made
> mention of lenses, we have no tradition of using them.[1]

[1]De igne autem pascali quod inquisisti, a sanctis priscis patribus, ex
quo per Dei et Domini nostri Jesu Christi gratiam et pretioso sanguine
eius Ecclesia dedicata est, quinta feria Paschae, dum sacrum consecretur,
tres lampades magnae capacitatis, ex diversis candelis ecclesiae oleo col-

Before we discuss the practice of reserving fire and comment on the ceremonial details, we must first deal with a number of points of interpretation which this passage raises. The custom of reserving the fire at Rome on Maundy Thursday and *renewing* it on Holy Saturday was obviously of long standing. Zachary himself is writing in the 740s, and it is reasonable to suppose that the practice went back at least to the middle of the seventh century. The Pope himself is in no doubt that the ceremony was of very great antiquity, although precisely which era he is referring to in the above-quoted letter is debatable. From a temporal point of view, the first three lines of the extract from the letter are capable of two different interpretations. (i) The Latin text is taken from the nineteenth-century edition of J.-P. Migne. In the third line the Latin word for 'church' is printed with a capital E. The editor of the text clearly regards Zachary as here envisaging the universal church, which came into being after the Resurrection; and *sancti prisci patres* are presumably the Twelve Apostles. According to this interpretation, therefore, it would appear that Zachary is ascribing a venerable age to the custom of reserving the paschal fire and claiming an antiquity for the practice coeval with the Church itself. (ii) Alternatively, if *Ecclesia* refers to the Cathedral of St John Lateran and the *sancti prisci patres* are to be identified with the leaders of the Church in Rome at the time of St John's Constantinian foundation, Zachary is attributing an age of about four hundred years to the custom. This latter explanation has two serious drawbacks. First, the phrase *pretioso sanguine* can only be accommodated with difficulty within a fourth-century Roman context. Secondly, the identification of the *sancti prisci patres* with a fourth-century Roman bishop and his presbyters is strained.

lecto , in secretiore ecclesiae loco ad figuram interioris tabernaculi insistente indeficienter cum multa diligentia ardebunt, ita ut oleum sufficere possit usque ad tertium diem. De quibus candelis sabbato sancto pro sacro fontis baptismate sumptus ignis per sacerdotem renovabitur. De crystallis autem, ut asseruisti, nullam habemus traditionem. PL 89.951.

There is probably an element of credibility in both interpretations. For on the one hand, Zachary is specifically referring to the Church in Rome, since his description of the way in which the fire was reserved relates to Roman usage. Yet he is also claiming an apostolic descent and approbation for the practice in order, perhaps, to assert the prior claim of Rome to be the guardian of the Church's traditions. For the Roman Church had been established with the apostolic authority of St Peter; Mainz and the other churches of Gaul and Germany had no comparable foundation. Yet at the same time, one suspects that the Pope may be aware that the customs relating to the reservation of the paschal fire may have derived in part from pagan Roman ceremonial. The attribution of the new fire ritual at Rome to the Apostolic Age may be a deliberate attempt by him, or more likely one of his predecessors, to discountenance the suggestion or belief that the ritual surrounding the reservation of fire at Rome was inherited from a pre-Christian milieu. However, as we shall mention again, the custom of renewing the sacred fire at Rome at this time of the year antedates the Age of the Apostles by many centuries; for it was a feature of the ancient Roman religion. Zachary's claim, therefore, that the reservation and renewal of fire during Holy Week is a practice of the Roman Church dating from the first century, is not entirely without truth. It must be stressed, however, that the ceremonial surrounding the provision of paschal fire at Rome also contained elements drawn from the *Lucernarium,* and suggested by the events of the first Holy Week.

It is clear, from the words *insistente indeficienter . . . ardebunt* and from the fact that they were large, that the three lamps burned simultaneously and not singly in succession as the supply of oil in each one became exhausted. The size of these lamps can be estimated only by the amount of oil it was necessary for each to hold in its reservoir. It is known that half a *log* of oil was required for keeping alight the *Ner Tamid* in the Jewish Temple during a winter's night.[2] If we accept that a

[2]Babylonian Talmud, *Shabbath* 22b p.96 note 13.

log was equivalent to about one imperial pint or half a litre,[3] and that for the sake of our argument, a winter's night comprised twelve hours, each of the Roman lamps would have required an oil reservoir with a capacity of at least two pints in order to provide continuous illumination for the forty-eight hours between the evenings of Maundy Thursday and Holy Saturday. This accords well with the description of the lamps as being *'magnae capacitatis'*. The concealing of the lamps in a remote part of the basilica prompted Zachary to draw the analogy between the reserved fire at Rome and the *Ner Tamid* in Jerusalem. The phrase *cum multa diligentia* reveals the importance attached to keeping the fire alive and the concern felt that it should not go out. The phrase would imply that the lamps were constantly attended during this two-day period.

The phrase *in secretiore ecclesiae loco* clearly indicates that the lamps were placed in a little-visited part of the basilica. It is just possible that the sacristy was used for this purpose, although one might perhaps have expected Zachary to specify the sacristy if the fire had been reserved in that room. However, the sepulchral aspect of the occasion and the circumstances in which the fire was reserved demanded that the place of concealment should be as far removed as possible from the gaze of people; and although the Cathedral of St John Lateran remained unused for divine worship during the whole of Good Friday and for most of Holy Saturday, it is likely that the sacristy of the basilica received a number of visitors during that period. Moreover, the size of that church afforded a much more suitable location for the reserved fire than the sacristy.

It is true that the reservation of fire on Maundy Thursday was also a feature of some of the Gallican rites. However, in those rites, the fire was reserved on Maundy Thursday in order to replace that lost at Tenebrae on Maundy Thursday, Good Friday, and Holy Saturday. At Rome in the eighth century, the purpose in reserving the fire was partly functional—to provide light at Baptism on Holy Saturday after the Vigil—but

[3] De Vaux, *Ancient Israel* pp.202–03.

its principal function was to convey through the symbolism of the fire something of the death and resurrection of Jesus. This was facilitated by the use to which St John Lateran was put on Good Friday and Holy Saturday. Commenting on the later practice of illuminating the altar and church lights with a flame from the triple candle, Van Gennep stated, 'L'ensemble constitue une dramatisation visuelle du schéma des *Rites de Passages* : séparation, marge, et renaissance.'[4] His triple-phase theory is equally pertinent to the ceremonial of the Roman Church in the eighth century. For the fire was removed from view together with all the oil in the church lamps; it was kept in a state of limbo in its place of reservation; and it was subsequently reproduced for use at Baptism on Holy Saturday. However, it is not at all clear to what extent the new fire ritual of the Roman Church derived from pagan antecedents, since the events of the latter part of Holy Week provided a parallel historical setting for the evolution of a liturgical re-enactment and 'visual dramatisation' of the death, the burial, and the resurrection of Jesus, in which He was symbolically represented by the fire. It is true that Zachary does not mention any symbolic significance attached to the reservation of the fire; but it is our belief that by placing the old fire in a remote part of the church, concealed from sight and the living world in the same way the dead are hidden away in a tomb, the old fire was in a sense held to have died; and that the act of blessing performed by the Pope or priest accomplished the revivification of the dead fire, analogously to the way in which God had raised Jesus from the dead. Thurston calls the Roman method of hiding fire an image of the death of Christ and its reappearance 'a wonderful type of Resurrection'.[5]

There is some uncertainty as to whether the reserved fire was a newly-kindled flame or whether it was taken from an already-existing source of fire. The silence of Zachary on this

[4]*Manuel* 1.3 p.1257 note 2.
[5]*Lent and Holy Week* p.413.

matter leaves open both possibilities. It is true that in pagan Rome new fire had been kindled annually in March in the Temple of Vesta.[6] It is unlikely, however, that there was any continuity of practice in Rome itself, once that city had closed its temples. Paganism in Rome was suppressed more ruthlessly than in most rural areas, where pre-Christian rituals and traditions were often either Christianised or adopted into the life and liturgy of the Church.

Possible support for the view that the fire at Rome was newly kindled comes from the *Lucernarium* hymn of Prudentius, which was sung at that daily office. According to lines 7 and 8 of the hymn, the flame for the lamp which burned during that service was kindled anew each day.[7] Since the bringing of the reserved fire for the lighting of the baptismal candles, or Vigil-candles, at Rome represented the survival of the old office of the *Lucernarium* within the rite of that city's Church, and since it would seem that the act, if it took place, of kindling the new fire at Rome did not possess the same liturgical importance that it did in the Gallican and Spanish rites, it could be argued that reference to the source of fire did not merit inclusion in any rubrics and was therefore omitted. From this it follows that there is no good reason to believe that the flame for lighting the three large lamps was not obtained from newly-kindled fire.[8] The evidence of Prudentius in this matter, however, should be treated with extreme caution. For not only does a period of about three hundred and fifty years stand between Prudentius and Zachary; we cannot be sure that the lighting of the lamp for the *Lucernarium* was accomplished in Spain in the same way as in Rome, as-

[6]Ovid, *Fasti* III.143.

[7]Incussu silicis lumina . . . monstras saxigeno semine, 'At a blow of the flint you reveal the light with a rock-born spark'. *Liber Cathemerinon* V (Cunningham p.23).

[8]Zachary's silence concerning the source of the fire is perhaps comparable to the omission of reference to water in a baptismal font in the rubrics of service-books and manuals. Rarely is it stated that the font should contain water; for its presence is presupposed.

suming that as a Spaniard, Prudentius in his hymn was drawing on his experience of the Spanish form of the service.[9]

The final sentence of Zachary's letter provides weightier support for the view that the three lamps were lit with newly-kindled fire. Although we do not possess a copy of Boniface's letter and do not know the precise form of the question which prompted Zachary, in his reply, to mention the use of lenses, there can be little doubt that Boniface had referred to their use in the kindling of the fire for the Easter vigil.[10] In view of Zachary's denial of the Roman use of the lens, it would seem to follow that at Rome the paschal fire was kindled by means of a flint. However, his reply relates specifically to the use of a lens, as opposed to any other means of producing fire; and his silence concerning the use of a flint at Rome can be interpreted equally as indicating that there was no production of new fire at Rome, but that the three lamps were lit from an already-existing source of fire.

In favour of the view, already referred to above, that the three lamps were kindled with *old* fire is Zachary's silence regarding the source of the fire. For in view of his mention of the size and number of the lamps, the source of the oil that

[9]It is debatable whether in this instance a distinction should be made between what Kenneth Stevenson terms *Vesper-light* and *Paschal-light* (*The Ceremonies* p.178). For the paschal themes from Exodus figure prominently in Prudentius' *Lucernarium* hymn (ll.37–88 and 89–104).

[10]Boniface's letter appears to have contained a twofold request : for information concerning the new fire procedure at Rome and for papal approval for the use of a lens in Christian ceremonial. The Englishman was almost certainly familiar with the method of kindling the paschal fire by friction—Ordo 26, which attests the practice, is to be dated to the mid-eighth century—and the guidance which he is seeking in the matter of the lens may relate to the first occasion when that method of producing the new fire for Easter was permitted by the Church. Interestingly, the use of a lens for the new fire is allowed in *PRG,* which is thought to have had its provenance in Mainz, the city where Boniface was bishop. Zachary's non-commital reply suggests a grudging approval. A policy of toleration towards non-Roman ritual had characterised the pontificate of St Gregory (Bede, *A History of the English Church and People* 1.27 : the reply to Augustine's second question).

fuelled them, the time at which they were reserved, their location, and the care with which they were tended, his failure
to refer to the act of kindling anew the fire, assuming that
this act did occur, would seem somewhat surprising. A more
important consideration, however, centres around the interpretation of *renovabitur,* 'will be renewed', in the penultimate line of the passage. The verb obviously does not describe
the kindling of the fire, either prior to or following its reservation, since it refers to the act of renewal, which the already-
burning flame undergoes *(de candelis . . . sumptus ignis)*. It is
true that *renovare* may be interpreted 'change' or 'alter' and
that within the Roman context under discussion, it would indicate that the newly-kindled and therefore unconsecrated fire
in reservation was transformed by the Pope, or a priest
deputising for the Pope, on Holy Saturday into fire hallowed
for liturgical use. However, it is difficult to see why Zachary
did not write *benedicetur,* 'will be blessed', if he intended
renovabitur to have the sense of 'will be changed'. The usual
interpretation of *renovare* is 'renew' or 'restore'; and given the
circumstances in which the verb is being used, it is unnecessary to translate the word otherwise. For it is the view of the
writer that the flame for kindling the three lamps was taken
from an already-existing source of consecrated fire and that,
since the fire symbolised the Spirit of Jesus in this visual
dramatisation of His death and burial, it was held to be *dead*
during the time of its reservation. On Holy Saturday, when
the fire was brought out of its place of concealment, it was
necessary to revivify the flame for liturgical use by means of
a sacerdotal pronouncement of blessing. In this way, the old
fire which had died was restored to life and thus *renewed.*

The three lamps were lit during the Mass which commemorated the Last Supper. Dendy, perhaps because of the superficial connection between the collecting of the oil for the lamps
and the blessing of the chrism on Maundy Thursday, states
that the lamps were hidden during the Mass of the Holy Oils.[11]

---

[11]*The Use of Lights* p.133.

However, the fact that mention is made of the consecration of the *sacrum* rather than the chrism would suggest that Zachary is referring to the evening Mass of Maundy Thursday; moreover, the absence of Tenebrae on Maundy Thursday at Rome in the mid-eighth century would indicate that in the city at that time, the Triduum was held to begin with the Mass of the Lord's Supper on Thursday evening,[12] a time more suitable than one earlier in the day for the lighting and reservation of the three large lamps. Subsequently, on Holy Saturday, the reserved fire was used to light the two Vigil-candles, which were set close to the font as it was being blessed—a fact alluded to by Zachary.

The Pope does not comment upon the reservation of *three* lamps as opposed to one. It would not be unreasonable to believe that the simultaneous burning of the three flames was designed to minimise greatly the chances of losing the fire during this period. However, in the Gallican tradition, in which the reservation of fire also took place, only one lamp was used; and since it would seem that the flames were constantly attended by an official of the Lateran Basilica, as we have already suggested, it is clear that the three lamps were lit not as a precautionary measure. A symbolic significance seems to be the most likely explanation for the use of the three lamps. Either they were lit in honour of the Trinity; or more likely, they symbolised the three-day repose of Jesus in the tomb.

The absence of illumination at the all-night vigil of Good Friday/Holy Saturday at Poitiers in the sixth century and at Matins/Lauds of Holy Saturday in Rome, Milan, and parts of Gaul in the eighth century leads us to believe that in Rome before and including the time of Pope Zachary, no liturgical lights were lit on Good Friday.[13] This is further borne out

[12]Since the liturgical changes of 1955, this is now once more a feature of the Roman rite.

[13]The absence of any liturgical light at Rome on Good Friday may be assumed from the fact that the old fire was reserved in the three lamps during the whole of this day. Moreover, the Pope on that day used unconsecrated fire for his honorific lights.

by the fact that the old fire was reserved during the evening
of Maundy Thursday and remained concealed until its renewal on Holy Saturday. In any study of the Triduum at
Rome in the early Middle Ages, it is important to bear in
mind that not all the ceremonies of the last three days of Holy
Week took place in the same church. In other dioceses, the
ceremonies were necessarily confined to one building, at least
in the period of which we treat. At Rome the Good Friday
ceremonies, namely, the Mass of the Catechumens, the Passion, the Solemn Prayers, the Veneration, and the Mass of
the Presanctified, were held in the Church of S.Croce in
Gerusalemme, whilst those of Maundy Thursday and the Vigil
of Holy Saturday took place in St John Lateran. As a result,
no liturgical illumination was required in the latter church
on Good Friday since the Pope was officiating in S.Croce.
The three lamps would therefore have burned in a remote
part of the Lateran Basilica from the evening of Maundy
Thursday onwards, light not being required for any purpose
in the cathedral during the next forty-eight hours. For the
lamps used at the night office of Good Friday could have been
lit from the flame of a candle used at the *Lotio;* and the night
office of Holy Saturday was sung in total darkness at this period, as we have already noted.

(ii) The Ninth-Century Evidence

(A) THEODORE'S EVIDENCE (832). We have already discussed
Archdeacon Theodore's inconclusive evidence relating to the
provision of new fire at Rome during the Triduum.[14] We observed that if the new fire of Good Friday was also reserved
to light the two Vigil-candles later that day, the ritual involving the reservation of the three large lamps would have lost
its *raison d'être,* and presumably they would have ceased to fea-

---

[14]In ipsa die novus ignis accenditur de quo reservetur usque ad nocturnale officium. 'On that same day [Good Friday] new fire is kindled and
reserved for the night office.' Amalarius, *Lib.de Ord.Ant.* XLIV.2.

ture in the Roman rite. On the other hand, since the conversation between Amalarius and Theodore centred around the provision and the loss of light at the night offices of the Triduum, and since the supply of reserved fire could not be used for the supply of illumination at the night office of Holy Saturday in view of its unconsecrated state, there was no reason why Theodore should have mentioned the lamps, assuming that they were burning all the while in their state of reservation.

Although the evidence of Theodore is inconclusive by itself, Amalarius' statement that in the Roman Church *all* fire (*totus ignis*) was extinguished at midday and new fire was kindled at about the ninth hour would imply that the old fire was no longer reserved in the three large lamps, if *totus* here bears its all-inclusive meaning. However, if, as we have suggested, the reserved fire was held to exist in a state of limbo, as it were, it is unlikely that the fire considered to be dead was included in the extinguishing of all the fires that took place on Good Friday; and if the new fire was kindled during the afternoon of the same day for the sole purpose of providing illumination at the night office of Holy Saturday, we can but assume that the three large lamps continued to be reserved as before.

We saw earlier that the new fire at Lyon was kindled behind the high altar and suggested that that feature of the church's liturgy may have been inherited from the old Roman rite, which Leidrad of Nürnberg had introduced at Lyon in the early years of the ninth century.[15] We also suggested that the use of light at the night office of Holy Saturday may have been introduced into the Roman rite during the pontificate of Leo III (795–816). It would not be unreasonable to believe that the kindling of the fire for that office became part of Roman ritual at the same time. Since Leidrad was responsible for the adoption of the Roman rite by the Church in Lyon, he presumably also introduced the new fire ceremony,

---

[15]King, *LPS* p.11.

which would only recently have made its appearance in Rome itself. From this it would follow that the new fire at Rome was kindled behind the high altar of the Lateran Basilica, the church in which the night office of Holy Saturday was to be held.

(B) LEO'S EVIDENCE (*c.* 850). Some fifteen or twenty years after the date of Theodore's testimony, Pope Leo IV issued the following decree :

> On Holy Saturday let the old fire be extinguished and let the new fire be blessed. Let it be distributed amongst the people in the same way as the holy water.[16]

The uncertainty regarding the relationship of *extincto veteri* to the rest of the first clause and the absence of any reference to the kindling of the new fire render the first clause open to a number of different interpretations. For instance, the loss of fire may have taken place and the new fire may have been kindled on the previous day—the arrangement familiar to Theodore—or the old fire may have been extinguished on Good Friday and the new fire kindled shortly before it was blessed on the following day. The most likely meaning, however, is that the loss of fire, and the kindling and blessing of the new fire all took place on Holy Saturday. If this interpretation is correct, it would indicate that a significant development had occurred in the new fire ceremony of the Roman Church between the archidiaconate of Theodore and the pontificate of Leo IV.

In attempting to account for the change of day on which the new fire was kindled at Rome,[17] it is unnecessary to look for Milanese, Mozarabic, or direct Gallican influence. In view of Leo's keen interest in liturgy, it is not difficult to ascribe this development in Rome's new fire ceremonial to this pope.

---

[16]In sabbato Paschae extincto veteri novus ignis benedicatur, et per populum dividatur, et aqua benedicta similiter. PL 115.681/2. The exact date of the decree is not known. Leo was Pope from 847 to 855.

[17]That is, from Good Friday to Holy Saturday.

The reform survived the changes brought about by the introduction into Rome of the *Pontificale Romano-Germanicum (PRG);* for as we have already observed, the twelfth-century *Pontificale Romanum (PR XII)* gives priority to the practice of kindling the new fire on Holy Saturday. The performance of the ceremony on Maundy Thursday, as prescribed by *PRG,* is reduced to an alternative.

There is no evidence from the middle of the ninth century to show that the use of the Easter candle had been introduced into Rome by that date. Attestation of its use in the Roman rite is first provided by *PRG* a century later. It would seem, therefore, that the new fire, kindled on Holy Saturday, provided the flame for lighting the two Vigil-candles, which presumably continued to form a feature of the Roman rite.

(iii) The Use of a Lens in the Roman Rite

There is no firm evidence before the twelfth century for the use of a lens as the means of kindling the new fire at Rome. We have already seen that the mid-eighth century statement of Pope Zachary that 'we have no tradition of using lenses' related to the production of fire generally and not specifically to the new fire ceremony; and although in the evidence provided by Theodore and Leo there is no indication of how the fire was produced, Zachary's denial of the use of lenses would suggest that the frictional method was employed in ninth-century Rome. In assessing the evidence of *PRG,* which became the service-book of the Roman Church, we must take into account the fact that it is unknown which of the two traditions relating to the actual production of the new fire was adopted into the Roman rite.[18] The uncertainty is caused by the tradition, attested in Manuscript C, in which the choice of a flint or a lens is offered. This tradition, *vis-à-vis* the prac-

---

[18]*PRG* preserves two different traditions. According to Manuscript K, the fire was kindled from a stone. Manuscript C offers the choice of either a flint or a lens *(de silice vel christallo)* (II p.94 §342).

tice of the Roman Church, invites the consideration of two possibilities. (i) Assuming that prior to the introduction of *PRG,* the new fire at Rome had been kindled by means of a flint, did the existence of this choice of means, which is attested in Manuscript C, so influence the practice of the Roman Church that she abandoned the use of the flint and opted for the lens? (ii) Was the rubric enjoining only the use of the flint expanded to include the use of a lens as an alternative in order to accommodate those churches where the practice of using a lens was well established? The situation envisaged by the former suggestion is most unlikely. It requires much more than the alternative directive of a rubric to change radically a well-established practice. The latter possibility has more to commend it. However, the uncertainty concerning the precise origin of the double rubric, the fact that Manuscripts C and K relate to different liturgical traditions, and doubt that a lens was used for the new fire in Rome before the tenth century can lead in this instance only to conclusions which are based on speculation.

We previously suggested that, if in a new fire rubric a reference to the lens preceded the mention of a flint, priority was to be given to the refractive method of producing the new fire. This is well exemplified in *Rubric 1* in *Table 38,* which is also the earliest evidence for the use of a lens at Rome. That this method had priority at Rome is further intimated by the unspecified and almost vague alternative of *alio modo,* 'in any other way'. *Alio modo* probably implies the use of a stone; but the alternative device involving friction, namely, a wooden fire-drill, should not be completely ruled out. The use of a lens is attested in eight documents, which span a period of some two centuries; and the absence of any reference in *Rubrics 3, 5,* and *11* to the means leaves open the possibility that the use of the lens was allowed *(Table 38).*

It might be argued that although a lens may have been used at Rome in the twelfth century, its use did not extend much beyond 1200, and that mention was made of it in the fourteenth-century documents almost as a matter of course, the rubric having assumed a set form of words and the device itself having become by then an anachronism. For it is significant that the Lateran Missal makes reference only to the flint *(Rubric 6)*. An argument based upon this assumption cannot be sustained. To challenge the accuracy or validity of these rubrics is to call into question other liturgical rubrics which offer a choice of action. Moreover, if the practice of using a translucent stone had fallen into desuetude, it is almost certain that any reference to the lens would have been omitted from the relevant rubric. The apparent difficulty caused by the intrusion of the rubric from the Lateran Missal can best be explained by the circumstances in which medieval service-books were compiled. The compilation of a service-book, be it *ordo,* pontifical, or missal, was the responsibility of an individual; and the arrangement and content to some extent reflected the preference and revealed the mind of its compiler. It is possible, therefore, that the compiler of the Lateran Missal omitted any reference to the lens out of a personal preference for the use of the flint.[19]

We have previously referred to the influence of Cluniac practice upon the Roman rite. In view of the prominence given to the beryl in the new fire ceremony at that monastery, it is not difficult to believe that the Roman Church borrowed this liturgical feature from the new fire ceremonial of Cluny; for it is known that Pope Gregory VII and Pope Paschal II had close connections with that monastery.[20] The introduction of the lens into the new fire ceremony at Rome is probably to be dated to the latter part of the eleventh century or to the early years of the twelfth century.

[19]It is just possible that *de cristallo* has disappeared from *Rubric 6* in the transmission of the text.

[20]The duration of their pontificates were respectively 1073 to 1085 and 1099 to 1118.

Rubric	Date	Document
1. novus ignis . . . excutiatur . . . de crystallo vel etiam aliomodo	12 C	*PR XII*
	1214	Pontifical of Apamea
2. ignem de cristallo vel silice . . . noviter excussum	c.1140	*Ordo Ecclesiae Lateranensis*
3. efficitur novus ignis	c.1140	*Ordo Benedicti*
4. ignis excutitur de cristallo sive lapide	12 C	*PRC* = Ordo X
5. efficitur novus ignis	c.1190	*Ordo Albini*
	c.1190	*Ordo Cencii*
6. ignis excutitur de lapide	13 C	Lateran Missal
7. ignis novus de cristallo vel silice excutitur	c.1296	*PGD*
8. . . . de crystallo sive lapide	c.1310	*Ordo Caietani*
9. extrahitur novus ignis de crystallo vel alio lapide	c.1350	C.A. 1760
	1377	*Bindo F.*
10. extrahitur novus ignis de crystallo vel alio lapide	14 C	Ordo XV = *Ordo P.Amelii*
11. efficitur novus ignis	c.1451	Pontifical of G.Barozzi
12. ignis excutitur de lapide	1474	*Missale Romanum*

Table 38. The evidence for the kindling of the new fire at Rome[21]

[21] *References.* (1) *PRMA* I p.238, and *DAER* 4.24 p.160 (M 25). (2) *OEL* p.130. (3) *LPB* p.151. (4) *PRMA* II p.470. (5) *Liber Censuum* I p.296 and 2 p.130. (6) Schmidt II p.610 §108. (7) *PRMA* III p.587. (8) PL 78.1218A/B. (9) *ZRKM* p.213 and p.276. (10) PL 78.1321C. (11) *ZRKM* p.373. (12) HBS 17 p.174.

Chapter Fifteen

THE ANTECEDENTS
OF THE NEW FIRE CEREMONY

The incorporation into the liturgy of Holy Saturday and the development of the new fire ceremony were closely linked with the need for a supply of light at the paschal vigil. The antecedents of this ceremony are to be found in two distinct liturgical traditions.

(A) According to the older tradition, which derives from the fourth-century Jerusalem archetype, the flame which provided the light at the Easter vigil was obtained from an existing source of fire which burned in a darkened place that represented the Sepulchre of Jesus. At Jerusalem, a perpetual lamp burned within the Church of the Anastasis at the very place where Jesus had been buried. A flame was taken from this shrine in procession to the Church of the Martyrium, in which the Easter vigil at Jerusalem was held. This two-church arrangement also obtained at Milan, and the use of a darkened sacristy for the kindling of the new fire according to the Mozarabic rite is almost certainly an attempt to reproduce conditions comparable to those found at Jerusalem. The use of the darkened west end of the nave of Salisbury Cathedral may also ultimately derive from the Jerusalem setting for the production of the paschal light.[1] It is possible that a similar arrangement obtained at Auxerre, where the new fire was kindled in one church and subsequently blessed in another.[2] However,there is some uncertainty about the practice at Rouen, where the new fire was kindled in the Church of St-Etienne; for De Moléon informs us that the fire had previously been kindled in the porch of the cathedral.[3]

(B) The Gallico-Germanic tradition was derived from the pre-Christian new fire rituals of Northern Europe. Unlike the fire in the tradition which had its provenance in Jerusalem, the flame for the provision of light at the Vigil was taken from newly-kindled fire in a ceremony performed for that very purpose.

The study of the new fire rituals of pre-Christian Europe is beyond the scope of this work.[4] Suffice it to state that in addition to the fires lit in honour of the sun or the local deity, fire was also kindled for purificatory or sympathetic reasons. The attitude of the Church was at times hostile, if the use of fire posed a threat to the survival of Christianity or was at odds with the teaching of the Church. These were probably the reasons for the denunciation of certain practices involving the use of fire at a synod held *c.*745 under the presidency of Boniface of Mainz.[5] Generally, however, the Church seems to have been tolerant of pagan fire rituals, especially if they could be transformed and given a Christian orientation or incorporated into the liturgy of the Church. To the former category of rituals belong the Yule candles of England and Serbia, the bonfires lit on St John's Eve in Brittany and Spain, and those formerly lit in Belgium and North-

[1]Sarum Missal of ?1486 fol.lxxxiii.

[2]Martène, *DAER* 4.24.3 p.145 (M 39).

[3]*Voyages* p.299.

[4]J.G.Frazer's *Golden Bough,* researched in the earlier part of this century, still remains the standard work on this aspect of pre-Christian European religion.

[5]Frazer, *Golden Bough* 10 p.270.

ern France at the start of Lent.[6] Into the latter group may
be placed the former lighting of the candles at Candlemas in
parts of the Cotswolds, designed to strengthen the power of
the winter sun, and especially the lighting of fire on the eve
of 1 May in Scotland, Ireland, Wales, and Scandinavia and
in other parts of Europe.[7] In view of the need for the provision of newly-kindled fire for use at the Easter vigil, it would
seem that the production of fire for this pagan festival was
transferred to an earlier, though changeable, day before
Easter. Thus the fires, formerly kindled in honour of the Celtic
sun-god Bel or Beal,[8] were henceforth to be lit in the worship
of the Sun of Righteousness.

The toleration afforded by the Church to pagan fire festivals and other allied rituals depended on her control and
monopoly of the use of fire. The Pythagorean belief that fire
was at the centre of the universe manifested itself in many
of the religious systems of Europe and the Middle East. It
is found in the Rig Veda, in Zoroastrianism, in the worship
of Hephaestus amongst the Greeks and of Vesta at Rome,
and amongst the Celtic peoples of Northern Europe. In practical terms, it often meant that the lighting of a fire on a piece
of ground entitled the kindler either to the possession of that
ground or to rights on that land.[9] It was 'a ritual proclamation of the ascendancy of the one who lights it'.[10]

By adopting and incorporating this annual rite of kindling
the new fire into her own liturgy, the Church not only tacitly
accepted the theological implications of this understanding of
fire, but appropriated to herself the rights and responsibili-
ties that had formerly belonged to those who had previously

[6]Le Braz p.101; Herrera p.234; Frazer, *op.cit.* p.107.

[7]Briggs p.19; Ross p.138; Bolton p.215; Rees and Rees p.193; Frazer,
op.cit. p.159.

[8]Known somewhat tautologically as 'Beltane fires'. The element *tane*
signifies 'fire'.

[9]Wade-Evans 16 p.10. The custom survived in parts of Wales up to
the end of the nineteenth century.

[10]Rees and Rees p.157.

performed the new fire rites. The discharge of this duty provided a means by which the Church was able to consolidate or extend her authority both at a theological level and *vis-à-vis* each location in which Christianity had been established. For the authority which she possessed related to the places in which she had supervised the kindling of the new fire. This is clear from the directive of the Pontifical of Poitiers which states that the new fire should be kindled and blessed in the most recently-built church in the locality or in one at some distance from the cathedral.[11] The performance of this ritual established an ontological rapport between the church in which the new fire was kindled and the ground on which the church stood. It also bestowed the benefits of God's protection on those who availed themselves of the fire that had been kindled and blessed within the church.

The extinguishing of the old fire prior to the kindling of the new afforded the Church an opportunity to reassert each year that authority which she possessed by virtue of her role as administrator of that ritual, and to maintain a spiritual hegemony over the lives of those who owed her their allegiance. For the conversion of communities to Christianity did not result in the obliteration of existing pagan beliefs and rituals. These age-old pre-Christian religious practices continued to thrive, at times only just beneath the surface of an outwardly Christian culture. The Church, therefore, did not discourage the renewal of the fires, which were extinguished annually in the homes of the faithful,[12] with a flame taken from the fire newly kindled and hallowed by a Christian priest. For in a sense, the taking home of the new fire perpetuated the spiritual authority of the Church and enabled the faithful to enjoy the benefit of a life-giving element upon which God's blessing had been invoked.

[11]*In novissima sive forensi loci eclesia* [sic]. *Poitiers* p.138.

[12]Documentary evidence for this practice comes from Regensburg (Sacramentary p.126), Salzburg (1507 Missal fol.xcvii), and Auch (1836 Missal p.191).

Evidence for the taking of new fire to every home is plentiful throughout Western Europe from the eighth century onwards.[13] The custom survived in parts of France well into the present century.[14]

*   *   *   *   *

Grancolas' statement that the new fire was not kindled in some churches but was taken from another place relates to churches which obtained their new fire from a central supply, either from the cathedral or from a nearby monastery.[15] Although he himself does not give any instance of this procedure, we know from another source that the new fire in the churches of Evreux and its suburbs was obtained from Evreux Cathedral.[16]

*   *   *   *   *

The Symbolism of the Old and the New Fire. The extinguishing of all illumination during the afternoon liturgy of Good Friday was, it would seem, a practice originally confined to the Roman Church. Amalarius is the earliest writer to record the absence of light during this period and the symbolic interpretation attached to this Roman custom. For according to him, the absence of light during the Solemn Prayers and Veneration both commemorated and symbolised the period from the sixth to the ninth hour on Good Friday when 'there was darkness over all the earth'.[17] Moreover, those three hours of darkness were held to foreshadow the three days and nights when 'the creator and producer of light would cover himself with darkness in the tomb'.[18] Honorius of Autun also draws the

---

[13]Ordo 28.63; Ordo 32.21; *Poitiers* p.215; *PRG* II p.99 §348; John of Avranches, PL147.49A.

[14]Van Gennep p.1257.

[15]Non eliciebatur sed aliunde sumebatur. *Commentarius* p.316.

[16]1740 Missal p.187.

[17]*Liber de ord.ant.* XLIV.6.

[18]Ut praedicaret orbi tribus diebus et tribus noctibus creatorem et operatorem obscuraturum se in sepulchro *(ibidem)*.

same analogy between the liturgical darkness of the Passion and the solar eclipse that took place during the Crucifixion.[19]

Commenting on the extinguishing of all fires prior to the start of the paschal vigil on Holy Saturday, Sicardus likens the old fire to the Law of the Old Covenant, now fulfilled and superseded by Christ.[20] John Beleth records a similar interpretation of the old fire.[21]

In a general sense, the new fire is seen to represent different aspects of God's nature and gifts. For John of Avranches it symbolises the *lux deitatis* which remained concealed during the earthly life of our Lord, but which was revealed mystically to the Church and which shone forth in the hearts of the faithful during the Passion and after the Resurrection.[22] In the *Speculum Ecclesiae,* Honorius of Autun likens the new fire to the Holy Spirit, who illuminates the souls of all the faithful; but in the *Gemma Animae,* he compares the new fire with the new Christian teaching.[23] Robert Paululus, echoing Honorius, suggests that the new fire also represents the new grace that results from the Resurrection.[24] In his commentary on the ceremonies of the Roman Church,[25] Philippo Zazzera in more recent times compared the new fire with the life-sustaining flame with which Jesus is continuously kindling us, a notion expressed some centuries earlier by Bianco da Siena in his hymn *Discendi Amor Santo,* and also in a nineteenth-century commentary from Langres.[26]

In our discussion of the symbolic interpretation of the kindling of fire from flint, we suggested that in view of the medieval ignorance as to its physical nature, fire was regarded

[19]*Gemma Animae* (PL 172.667C).
[20]*Mitrale* (PL 213.322D).
[21]*Rationale* (PL 202.111B).
[22]*Lib. de Off. Eccl.* (PL 147.49A).
[23]PL 172.928C and PL 172.668A, respectively.
[24]PL 172.452.
[25]*SS. Ecclesiae Rituum* p.301.
[26]'(Le) feu nouveau, image de la lumière et de la charité que nous reçevons par Notre-Seigneur Jesus-Christ.' 1844 Langres Directory p.53.

as being essentially one with that aspect of God's nature which was manifest in the Burning Bush and at the Transfiguration, though present and visible in the world as perceived by humankind in an allotropic form, as it were. This is in contrast with the understanding of fire purely as a symbol of life and lacking any essential relationship with the divine nature, such as was held by the Gipsies and other peoples.[27] Using Johannine theological concepts, Durandus describes the new fire as the 'unfailing light' of God,[28] which comes into the world and illuminates our hearts and senses. It brings us from darkness to light and eternal life.

[27]Rao p.161.

[28]*Rationale* VI.80 p.350. This phrase occurs in the B-group of the benediction-formulas (Appendix 5). Used in the vocative case, it is both a title and an attribute of God.

Part Three

THE NEW FIRE PROCESSION

Chapter Sixteen

THE NEW FIRE
AND THE PROCESSION

This section describes the new fire procession on Holy
Saturday. In places where the new fire was kindled on Maundy
Thursday and Good Friday, the processions on those two days
were identical to that of Holy Saturday, except that they did
not culminate in the lighting and blessing of the Easter candle.

There can be little doubt that the new fire procession was
a feature of pre-Christian ritual which was adopted into the
liturgy of the Christian Church. The necessity of transferring
the new fire from its place of reservation on Maundy Thursday, or place of kindling on Holy Saturday, also perpetuated
a primitive element of the *Lucernarium,* namely, the bringing
in of the lamp, and within its revitalised Christian milieu,
resulted in the emergence of an elaborate ceremonial which
invested the procession with its own distinctive character.
From the evidence of the early *ordines,* we find that two main
traditions existed within the Romano-Gallican Church: (i) that
in which a small candle, lit with the new fire, was borne in
procession for the lighting of the Easter candle in church, and
(ii) that in which the Easter candle itself was carried in procession, having previously been kindled with the new fire. This
latter tradition is treated in Part Four.

The Gelasian sacramentaries do not state how the fire was
conveyed to the Easter candle. It is likely, however, that a

small lighted candle was carried from the place of reservation.[1] The practice of lighting the small candle from the new or reserved fire is first attested in the eighth-century Ordo 26.[2] It is also found in the ninth-century Ordo 29 and Pontifical of Poitiers, and in the *Regularis Concordia* of the tenth century.[3] Thereafter, this became the practice of the vast majority of churches in both the cathedral and monastic traditions. Information about the size of the small candle is meagre. However, it is recorded that at Canterbury the candle should weigh half a pound and that it should not have been previously used.[4] In some places the upper candle of the Tenebrae hearse was used.[5]

After the candle had been lit from the new fire, it was common practice to light another small taper and to place it in a lantern.[6] Gavanti tells us that this was done in case a high wind should extinguish the processional candle;[7] and this is confirmed by Lanfranc and the Gilbertine Ordinal, and by evidence from St-Lô and Nidaros. At St Paul's, Rome, at Besançon, and at Nidaros, the lantern was carried by a boy; but the *Decrees* of Lanfranc, implemented at St-Vedast's Abbey and at Durham, specify the *magister puerorum*.[8]

The processional candle was carried into church raised aloft.[9] A symbolic interpretation was subsequently attached to the raising of the light, but our sources give no indication as to why the candle was originally held on high. There are a number of possible reasons. (i) It was a feature of a corresponding pre-Christian ritual. (ii) It was done so that the

---

[1]If the fire was reserved beneath the altar, a small taper would still have been required to transfer the flame.

[2]OR 26.14, by inference.

[3]OR 29.59; *Poitiers* p.138; PL 137.349B.

[4]HBS 23 p.380.

[5]Feasey p.189.

[6]Or *sconsa*, 'a screened light', as at Fleury and Besançon.

[7]Vol. I p.234.

[8]For the references in this paragraph, see *Tables 39–41*.

[9]It was customary for this candle to be borne by the officiating deacon. Maigne-d'Arnis ascribes the duty to a subdeacon (*Lexicon* VII p.438).

fire would be visible to all those participating in the ceremony.
(iii) It was raised as a gesture of thankfulness that the minor
miracle of producing fire had been performed. (iv) The bringing of light into the gloom of the church symbolised Christ's
leaving the darkness of His tomb, as Van Doren observed.[10]
The candle raised on high would have visually expressed the
notion of His triumph and symbolised His victory over the
forces of darkness.

A number of different devices were used for supporting the
candle.

(A) THE POLE.[11] The use of the pole is enjoined in Lanfranc's
Decrees and in most of the early surviving monastic customaries.
In more recent times, a pole continued to be used at Amiens
and Le Mans, and most likely in other churches which clung
to their Gallican traditions *(Table 39)*. At Cambrai, the pole
was painted red, in sympathy perhaps with the colour of the
fire.[12]

(B) THE REED. In respect of the surviving documentary evidence, the use of a reed antedates that of a pole. It figures
in a number of early *ordines*,[13] and is found in some other early
sources.[14] Some of the later medieval Roman service-books
offer a choice between a reed and a pole;[15] others,[16] which
relate more closely to the ceremonial of the papal court, specify
'reed' alone. Similarly, the influential Pian Missal of 1570
specifies the sole use of a reed.

The length of the reed was traditionally three and a half
cubits or ten palms, both measurements being approximately

[10]*La cérémonie* p.78.

[11]*Baculus, pertica, virga*. All three terms are found.

[12]Compare the phrase *rutilans ignis* from the Romano-Gallican Preface.

[13]OR 26.4; OR 28.26; OR 29.15; OR 31.29. The last *ordo* records its
use only on Maundy Thursday, but it was presumably used on the other
two days of the Triduum.

[14]*Poitiers, PRG,* and *Alcuin*.

[15]Ordo XIV; Ordo XV; CA 1706; *Bindo F.*

[16]Haymo's *Ordo Missalis, PGD,* and *MR 1474.*

Church/Document	Date	Comment	Source
Fleury	10 C	*d*	Albers V p.143
Lanfranc	*c.*1070	*abc*	*Decrees* (PL 150.467B)
Besançon	11 C	*a*	*DAMR* 3.13 p.127 (M 56)
Cluny	11 C	*d*	PL 149.659A
Farfa	11 C	*acd*	Albers I p.48
Fruttuaria	11 C	*acd*	Albers IV p.54
Gembloux	11 C	*acd*	Albers II p.93
St-Bénigne, Dijon	11 C		*DAMR* 3.13.34 p.126 (M 1150)
St Paul's, Rome	11 C	*c*	*DAER* 3.22 p.124 (M 1184)
Nidaros	*c.*1210		*ONE* p.232
Haymo *(OM)*	1243	*b*	HBS 85 p.209
St-Denys	*c.*1273		*DAMR* 3.13.34 p.126 (M 1158)
PGD	*c.*1296		*PRMA* III xxxii.7 p.239
Reims	14 C	*a*	*DAER* 22.5.2 p.97 (M 261)
Missale Romanum	1474	*b*	HBS 17 p.175
Würzburg	1477		Ordinary np
Toulouse	1490	*b*	*DAER* 4.23.6 p.127 (M 311)
Austin Friars	1491		Missal np
Melk	1495	*b*	Missal fol.lxviii
Rouen	1640	*b*	Ritual p.305
Cambrai	1699		Gav./Mer. IV p.161
Amiens	1752		Missal p.182
Le Mans	1789		Ceremonial p.127
Bayeux	1790	*b*	Missal p.168

a Reference to the use of a small candle.
b Offers choice of device.
c Spare candle in lantern.
d Evidence for Maundy Thursday only.

Table 39. The use of a pole for the new fire

the height of a person.[17] More recent manuals have recommended a measurement of about five feet.[18] Some liturgical
commentators insist that the reed should not be a pole or a
rod, nor should it be an imitation reed.[19] According to Rupert
of Deutz, it represented the reed which the soldiers gave to
Jesus after His trial (Matthew 27:29).[20] Bisso, followed by
Desideri, also links the reed with the Passion;[21] but the symbolism is forced. Possibly alluding to the use of the serpent-
rod or the serpent-candle, which had all but disappeared from
the ceremonial of Holy Saturday by his day, Bisso claims that
the reed signified the Passion of Christ, and that, just as a
reed was used to kill serpents, so the Passion of Christ destroyed the Devil.

It became customary in some churches to decorate the reed
with flowers, thus paralleling the ornamentation of the Easter
candle. The earliest references to this practice come from two
writers in the middle of the seventeenth century.[22] Both state
that some of the actual reed should be visible, the latter adding that this is done 'because it (the reed) is not devoid of
symbolism'.[23] Van Gennep also writes that flowers were attached to the upper portion of the reed.[24] The importance of
leaving part of the reed free of flowers is mentioned in two
eighteenth-century ceremonials,[25] and by other commentators such as Merati and Desideri.[26] The last also mentions
its being decorated with other ornaments. At Constance, the

[17]Desideri p.150; Bisso I p.79. The former measurement is first recorded
in Ordo XIV *(Ordo Caietani)* (PL 78.1218B).

[18]For instance, Fortescue and O'Connell (6th edition) p.339

[19]Gavanti/Merati IV p.155; Desideri p.149; Loan p.283. The last admitted that in practice a thin pole 5 feet long was often used.

[20]*De Div.Off.* V (PL 170.169C).

[21]*Hierurgia* I p.78 and *Praxis* p.149, respectively.

[22]Corsetti (1656) p.316 and De Bralion (1657) p.247. Colti (1772) adds
that it may also be adorned with gold (II p.156).

[23]Id enim mysterio non caret (De Bralion p.247).

[24]*Manuel* 1.3 p.1257.

[25]Augustinian Friars (1714) p.307 and Capuchins (1775) p.128.

[26]Gavanti/Merati IV p.155 and *Praxis* p.150, respectively.

Document	Date	Comment	Source
Ordo 26	750–775	*a*	OR 26.6
Ordo 28	*c.*800		OR 28.26
Ordo 29	870–890	*a*	OR 29.15
Poitiers	*c.*900	*a*	Pontifical p.215
PRG	*c.*950	*a*	Vol. 2 §220 p.58
Alcuin	*c.*1000	*a*	*Lib.de Div.Off.* (PL 101.1205C)
Beneventum	11 C	*a*	Odermatt p.273
Vallombrosa	11 C		Albers IV p.249
CMG	11 C		Albers V p.32
Rupert	*c.*1111		*De Div.Off* V (PL 170.169C/D)
Ordo XII	*c.*1190		PL 78.1076C
Ordo Albini	*c.*1190		*Liber Censuum* II p.130
Monte Cassino	12 C		*Monte Cassino A* (*PRMA* I p.292)
PR XII	12 C		*PRMA* I.xxxii.7 p.239
Haymo *(OM)*	1243	*b*	HBS 85 p.209
Marseilles	13 C	*b*	*ILEM* p.84
Ordo XIV	*c.*1310		PL 78.1218B
CA 1706	*c.*1350		*ZRKM* p.213
Bindo F.	1377		*ZRKM* p.274
Arles	14 C	*d*	*DAER* 4.22 p.117 (M 30)
Ordo XV	14 C		PL 78.1321C
MR 1474	1474	*b*	HBS 17 p.175
Melk	1495	*b*	Missal fol.lxviii
Salzburg	1507	*ad*	Missal fol.lxxxvi
Aquileia	1519		Missal p.91
Cosenza	1549		Missal fol.115
Camaldolese	1634	*a*	Ceremonial p.82 and p.84
St-Lô	*c.*1700	*ac*	De Moléon p.403
Austin Friars	1714	*a*	Missal p.307 and p.309
Bayeux	1790		Missal p.168
Nantes	1837		Missal p.199

a Reference to the use of a small candle.
b Offers choice of device.
c Spare candle in lantern.
d Evidence for Maundy Thursday only.

Table 40. The use of a reed for the new fire

reed was in fact a pole, at the end of which was the effigy of a deacon bent backwards; above its head were the words 'Here (is placed) the twisted candle'.[27]

It might be argued that the reed was a development of the pole, suggested by the scriptural precedent of Matthew 27:29. Caution, however, is recommended here for two reasons. (i) The evidence for the reed antedates that for the pole by some 250 years, and (ii) there is only a tenuous link between the reed of the New Testament and that used for conveying the new fire. In all likelihood, the reed and the pole derive from different liturgical milieux. Moreover, it is tempting to see in the use of the reed an echo of the myth of Prometheus' theft of fire from heaven,[28] or at least a Gallican version of the myth, whose re-enactment in a pre-Christian religious context the Church incorporated into her own ceremonial. Corroborative evidence, however, to confirm direct continuity is lacking; but the pagan ancestry of the ritual seems almost certain *(Table 40)*.

(c) THE SPEAR. The use of a spear for the transportation of the candle is first attested in the tenth-century *Regularis Concordia;* and the fact that it also appears in Lanfranc's *Decrees* as an alternative to a pole may suggest that the spear was a development or refinement of the latter—unlike the reed, which we maintain was inherited from pre-Christian ritual. Its use may have been suggested by the biblical precedent of the soldier's lance of John 19:34 in the same way that the use of the reed recalled Matthew 27:48. Alternatively, the spear with its sharp point provided a suitable instrument for affixing the candle; and having become a feature of the new fire ceremonial, it may have been subsequently endowed with a symbolic interpretation. John of Avranches comments that the spear recalled the Crucifixion *(Table 41)*.[29]

[27]*Hic Cereus torquatus.* Ceremonial of Constance, cited in Gav./Mer. IV p.161.

[28]Interestingly, the plant fennel, in which the fire was stolen, grows to a height of 5 feet.

[29]*Lib.de Off.Eccl.* (PL 147.49A) : Christus in cruce suspensus.

The surviving evidence would suggest that in addition to the houses of the Benedictine order, the spear was used mainly in England and Northern France. In the romanised ceremonial at Palencia, the two small candles which were lit from the new fire were placed on small spears *(hastuli)*.[30] Somewhat surprisingly, the twelfth-century Roman *Ordo Albini* prescribes the use of a spear; other Roman *ordines* stipulate a reed.

Church/Document	Date	Comment	Source
Regularis Concordia	c.970	a	PL 137.491B
John of Avranches	c.1070	d	PL 147.49A
Lanfranc	c.1070	abc	*Decrees* (PL 150.467B)
Ordo Albini	c.1190		*Liber Censuum* II p.130
Gilbertines	12 C	c	HBS 59 p.39
Norwich	c.1265	acd	HBS 82 p.81
Canterbury	13 C		HBS 28 p.274
Hereford	13 C		Missal p.97
St-Vedast, Arras	c.1300	ac	HBS 86 p.160
Westminster	1370	c	HBS 5 col.574
Durham	14 C	ac	Missal p.185
Tongres	15 C		Ordinary p.164
York	14 C		Missal p.109
St Mary's, York	c.1400		HBS 75 p.275
Barking	1404		HBS 65 p.101
Salisbury	1502	a	Processional p.84
Palencia	1568	e	Missal fol.c
Rouen	1640		Ritual p.305
Chalons	1748		Missal p.178
Bayeux	1790		Missal p.168

a Reference to small candle.   d Evidence for Maundy Thursday only.
b Offers choice of device.   e Use of two small spears.
c Spare candle in lantern.

Table 41. The use of a spear for the new fire

(D) THE *ARUNDO SERPENTINA*. This device is discussed in the next chapter.

[30] 1568 *Missale Pallantinum* fol.c.

Chapter Seventeen
THE *ARUNDO SERPENTINA*

(i) Its Description and Use

The *arundo serpentina* was a reed or, more likely, a pole, the upper part of which terminated in the effigy or representation of a serpent.[1] Three variations of the device are known. (i) Either the end of the wooden pole was carved in the likeness of a serpent, or a graven image of this creature was attached to the end of the pole.[2] At Braga, the *arundo* was a bronze winged dragon with three candles issuing from its mouth.[3] Elsewhere, the candle which was inserted into the serpent's mouth terminated in a triple ramification.[4] The use of the serpent-reed is attested in the seventeenth century and also in the eighteenth century.[5] De Moléon refers to the *arundo*

[1]In addition to *serpens,* it was also known as *coluber (Poitiers* p.215), and *draco* (1790 Missal of Bayeux).

[2]The latter type is well exemplified in the woodcut illustration in the 1502 Sarum Processional (p.75). Also in Wordsworth, *Ceremonies and Processions* p.84.

[3]King, *LPS* p.224. At Worcester also, the serpent held three candles (Antiphonary p.69).

[4]For instance, in the Roman rite. See also *Table 43.*

[5]Feasey (*The Paschal Preconium* p.259) refers to an illustration of a boy, dressed as an angel with wings, lighting the Easter candle with a wax serpent twined about a rod, in *Le Tableau de la Croix représenté dans les cérémonies de la Sainte Messe,* printed by F.Mazot in 1653.

used at Rouen Cathedral at the beginning of the latter century but records that the carving of the serpent had disappeared.[6] Its use was still permitted at Bayeux at the end of
the same century.[7] (ii) The *arundo serpentina* was also a reed
or pole to the end of which was affixed a candle twisted to
resemble a snake. Examples of this type appear on some of
the *Exultet* rolls of Southern Italy and show the candle either
protruding from a spike or socket at the end of the pole or
entwined around the upper section of the shaft.[8] (iii) The tenth-
century *Regularis Concordia* attests the combination of the two
variants described above in the same device :

> ferentes hastam cum imagine serpentis . . . et . . . candela,
> quae more serpentis infixa est.[9]

The combination of serpent-reed and serpent-candle was also
familiar to Durandus :

> In some churches also during these seven days (Easter Week),
> when they go to the font for Baptism, the effigy of a serpent
> placed on a pole leads the procession. A twisted candle, lit
> with the new fire, is fixed on the head of the serpent. With
> this the Easter candle and all the other lights of the church
> are lit.[10]

And it is attested at Toulouse in the late fifteenth century.[11]
A triple twisted candle emerging from the serpent's mouth

---

[6] *Voyages Liturgiques* p.304.

[7] 1790 Missal of Bayeux p.168.

[8] Avery, *Plates LXXII, CXX,* and *CXXXIII.*

[9] 'Bearing a spear with an effigy of a serpent . . . and . . . a candle,
which is inserted to resemble a snake.' PL 137.491B.

[10] In quibusdam etiam ecclesiis, in his septem diebus, quando descen-
ditur ad fontes, antefertur quidam serpens imaginarius, super virgam; et
candela novo lumine accensa, super caput serpentis retorta affigitur, ex
qua cereus paschalis et omnes aliae ecclesiae accenduntur. *Rationale* VI.89
fol.377.

[11] Deferentes virgam sculptam in figuram serpentis . . . Nam ex igne
novo accendebatur cereus in modum serpentis efformatus. Martène, *DAER*
4.23.6 p.127 (M 311).

is found at Braga in the mid-sixteenth century. At Bayeux in the thirteenth century, the serpent held an unspecified number of twisted candles in its mouth : *habeat draco in ore candelas plures retortas (Table 42).*

The use of the serpent was not confined to the lighting of the Easter candle. We have already noted in the above-quoted excerpt from the *Rationale* that Durandus mentions the lighting of the lamps in some churches by means of the *arundo*—a practice attested by evidence from Vallombrosa.[12] Moreover, the serpent was used at other ceremonies and on other days. Its use at the blessing of the font and at Baptism is not only attested by Durandus in the same above-quoted passage from the *Rationale,* but is also found in the rite of Braga and in the revised Mozarabic rite.[13] It featured in the new fire processions on Maundy Thursday and Good Friday at Auch;[14] and at Bayonne, the serpent-candle was lit for the reading of St John's Passion on Good Friday, perhaps as a liturgical allusion to Jesus' reference to the raising of the serpent in the same gospel (John 3:14).[15] At Rouen, a winged dragon was borne in procession on Ascension Day by a verger in a purple robe and placed at the feet of the Blessed Virgin Mary.[16]

(ii) The Origin of the *Arundo Serpentina*

The origin of the serpent-reed or serpent-candle should not be sought in the emergence and development of the triple candle; rather, it was the triple candle which developed from the serpent-candle, as we shall show. In fact, the earliest reference to the serpent-candle is found in the ninth-century Pontifical of Poitiers (p.215); the earliest *ordines* are silent con-

[12]1503 Missal fol.xcv.

[13]King, *LPS* p.224 and *Missale Mixtum* (PL 85.470A), respectively.

[14]1491 Missal, cited by Feasey, *The Paschal Preconium* p.259.

[15]1543 Missal p.42. It was put to one side after the reading and taken to the sacristy at the end of the liturgy.

[16]Alleau, *Guide de la France Mysterieuse* p.814.

Document	Date	Comment	Source
Poitiers	*c.*900	C	Pontifical p.215
Regularis Concordia	*c.*970	CR	PL 137.491B
St-Vito, Verdun	10 C	R	Albers V p.122
John of Avranches	*c.*1070	C	*Lib.de Off.Eccl.* (PL 147.49A)
CMG	11 C	C	Albers V p.32
Fleury	11 C	R	Albers V p.143
Rupert	*c.*1111	R	*De Div.Off.* V (PL 170.169C/D)
Corbie	12 C		*DAMR* 3.13.34 p.126 (M 1146)
PGD	*c.*1296	R	III.iv.8 p.588
Bayeux	13 C		Ordinary p.135
Hereford	13 C	R	Missal p.97
Marseille	13 C		*ILEM* p.84
Worcester	13 C		Antiphonary p.69
Strasbourg	1364	C	*DAER* 4.24 p.162 (M 35)
Westminster	*c.*1370	R	Missal HBS 5 col.574
Arles	14 C	C	*DAER* 4.22 p.117 (M 30)
St Mary's, York	*c.*1400	R	HBS 75 p.275
Toulouse	1490	CR	*DAER* 4.23.6 p.127 (M 331)
Auch	1491		Missal, cited by Feasey, *The Paschal Preconium* p.259
Uzès	1495	R	Missal fol.lxiii
Salisbury	1502	R	Processional p.75
Spires	1512	C	*Agenda* fol.xciii
Coutances	1557	R	Missal fol.lxvii
Braga	1558		Missal fol.xcvi
Austin Canons	1579		Ordinary fol.137
Rouen	*c.*1700	R	De Moléon p.304
Bayeux	1790	R	Missal p.168

C   Use of serpent-candle.
R   Use of serpent-reed.
CR Use of serpent-candle and serpent-reed in combination.

Table 42. Evidence for the use of the arundo serpentina

cerning the shape of the candle. The presence of liturgical features and ritual elements of probable pagan provenance in this pontifical and in ceremonies described in other documents suggests a pre-Christian antecedent for the serpent-candle also.[17] For there can be little doubt that the ceremony of the new fire pre-dates the arrival of Christianity.

If the use of the serpent-candle derives from a pre-Christian religious milieu—the importance of the snake in northern European worship is widely recognised—it is difficult to see how it can represent the malign aspects of that creature within the context of the new fire. The fire-breathing serpents and dragons inherited from pagan folklore appear within the context of Christian theology as creatures symbolising vice or evil or paganism itself. Numerous are the instances of hermits, bishops, and saints who in times past had done battle with and vanquished such monsters.[18] One should not try to see a link between this type of serpent and that which bore the new fire. Nor should one try to find in the new-fire serpent an echo of an otherwise-irrecoverable myth relating to the conquest of the powers of darkness by the superior strength of the deities of heaven, represented by fire and light.

On the other hand, the fire-serpent may have been a tangible relic of the belief that this being symbolised the force of power and life, which was visually represented amongst the ancient Greeks by the *caduceus*. Again, it has been pointed out that in a *caduceus*-like device, the serpents may stand for the past and the future, whilst the wand represents eternity.[19] The weakness of both these theories is that no account is taken of the presence and use of fire; and since the ceremony under study revolves around the production of fire and its transportation, it is safer to look for the origin of the fire-serpent else-

[17]For instance, the three apotropaic weather-candles (§406) and the carved wooden model of a turret city (§407), both on p.216 of *Poitiers;* the circumambulation of the new fire at Breslau and Würzburg; and the noise at the conclusion of Tenebrae.

[18]For instance, St-Romain (Rouen), St-Vigor (Bayeux), St-Nicaise (Vaux), St-Julien and St-Leon (Le Mans), St-Bienheure (Vendôme), St-Clement (Metz), St-Martial (Bordeaux), St-Martha (Tarascon), St-Florent (Seaumur).

[19]Varley p.126.

where. If its origin is to be sought in mythology, a more plausible explanation would be to see in the fire-serpent a visual representation and re-enactment of the myth, found in many parts of the world, according to which, the thief of the fire stolen from the gods was a bird or a beast.[20] Interestingly, a woodcut illustration in the Sarum Processional of 1508 depicts the head of an animal, almost certainly a boar, with a candle protruding from its mouth, as the termination of the *arundo serpentina* (p.75). However, the lateness of the drawing, together with allowance made for artistic licence; the uniqueness of the creature; and the otherwise-universal use of a snake for the transportation of the new fire seem to rule out any direct connection between the Sarum device and the above-mentioned myth.

Apropos of this myth, it is appropriate to mention at this point those instances in which the Easter candle was lit by means of a dove. In an *Exultet* roll of the early twelfth century from Monte Cassino, there is an illustration of a dove lighting the Easter candle.[21] This may be the artist's own graphic means of expressing the symbolism suggested by the account of Jesus' baptism in the Jordan. On the other hand, the dove may represent the actual device used for the kindling—a sculptured bird atop a pole or even a contrivance which enabled a metal or ceramic dove to be lowered from the ceiling or to be swung in a lateral movement to the wick of the candle.[22] The former device was used to light the Easter candle at Tongres in the fifteenth century; a candle was placed in the dove's mouth.[23] A similar appliance may have been

[20]Frazer, *Apollodorus* II, Appendix III p.327.

[21]Avery, *Plate LXII*.

[22]The artificial descent of fire at Easter was not unknown in the East. At the beginning of the eleventh century, the Christian writer Abelfaragius records the allegation that at Jerusalem the iron chain which held the lamp above the Holy Sepulchre was probably greased with oil of balsam and ignited from the roof. Masudi, a Moslem historian, had previously alluded to the production of fire by a clever device. Goodrich-Freer pp.107–08.

[23]Ordinary pp.164–65.

in use at York in the fourteenth century. For we read in an inventory :

> He will find the Easter candle and all its accessories, namely, paints flowers and ribbons, as well as the accoutrements for the dove.[24]

We have previously referred to the likely scripturally-inspired origin of the reed and of the spear. In attempting to discover a biblical antecedent for the fire-serpent, we may with confidence dismiss the suggestion that it was inspired either by the Cherubim of Genesis 3:24 or by the Seraphim of Isaiah 6:2, since serpentine characteristics were attributed to neither beings, although fire was associated attributively with the former and circumstantially with the latter. Moreover, allusions to these creatures seem incongruous within the context of the new fire. Both John of Avranches and Rupert of Deutz state that the fire-serpent recalls the fiery serpent which Moses set upon a pole (Numbers 21:8-9). The former alludes to John 3:14; and just as Jesus compared Himself to the bronze serpent which Moses set up in the desert, he symbolically identifies Christ with the fire-serpent used in church.[25] However, he does not observe that just as the uplifting of Moses' serpent and of Christ brought salvation, so fire in a sense brings life to human beings. The identification of Christ with the fire-serpent represents an instance of secondary or expository symbolism, which characterised medieval interpretation of the liturgy and which to the mind of the modern person often seems inapposite and forced.

Rupert of Deutz offers a mystical and more explicitly allegorical interpretation of the fire-serpent and at the same time presents a symbolic interpretation of both the reed and the rod, and links both in a secondary comparison.[26] The reed,

[24]Inveniet cereum paschalem et omnia ad eum pertinencia tam in coloribus, floribus et cordis quam in aliis pertinentibus ad columbam. Bradshaw and Wordsworth II p.98. It is difficult to see what else *columbam* may refer to.
[25]*Lib. de Off. Eccl.* (PL147.49A).
[26]*De Div. Off.* V (PL 170.169C/D).

which represents that which the soldiers gave Jesus after His trial, was foreshadowed by the rod which Moses turned into a snake; so that, in the same way that the rod was transformed into a snake and then became a rod again, Jesus (prefigured by the rod) lives, will die, and then will transform the deaths of sinners by rising to life again.

It is possible that Rupert, though writing some decades later than John of Avranches, preserves an older tradition which relates, not to the origin of the serpent-candle, but to the reason for its adoption within the paschal liturgy. As we have noted elsewhere, the theme of the entire paschal liturgy is rooted in the Old Testament types and prefigurements of Exodus and Numbers : from the allusions and references to Moses and the Burning Bush in the formulas for the blessing of the fire at the start of the liturgy to the ceremony of Baptism, which recalls the entry of the Israelites, God's chosen people, into the promised land. The writer is therefore of the opinion that in view of the Mosaic motif running through the paschal liturgy, the rod on which the new fire was borne into church was seen to be foreshadowed in the rod which Moses used at the court of Pharaoh, and that the image of the serpent, borrowed possibly from a corresponding pre-Christian new fire ritual, became attached to the end of a pole to commemorate and to portray vividly the transformation of the rod as described in Exodus 4:3. It is significant that just as the rod was turned into a serpent shortly after the beginning of Moses' mission, so the serpent-rod was used in the early stages of the new fire ceremony. The writer also believes that the development of the serpentine candle emerging from the serpent's mouth was a visual portrayal and liturgical re-enactment of the swallowing of the snakes by Aaron's rod in Exodus 7:12.[27]

[27]A copper-gilt and enamel cross from the Meuse region, now in the British Museum, shows Moses and Aaron flanking a brazen serpent on top of a column. It dates from the third quarter of the twelfth century.

Chapter Eighteen
THE TRIPLE CANDLE

(i) Description and Construction

The use of the triple candle is first attested in the *Pontificale Romanum* of the twelfth century *(PR XII)*.[1] It refers to *triplicem candelam coniunctam,* 'a candle twisted into three branches', a device found in nearly all subsequent Roman documents up to and including the Pian Missal of 1570, as well as in the rites of some religious orders and of some churches outside Italy.[2] Corsetti refers to the triple candle as *'in calce unum';*[3] England, describing the papal ceremony of the last century, mentions that the three candles 'part from a common stock';[4] and Van Gennep, writing in the earlier part of the present century, refers to the candle with three branches.[5] With the eventual adoption of the Roman rite by most of the churches in the West, the use of the triple candle became almost universal. However, up to the liturgical changes of 1955, a single

---

[1]For this and other documentary references relating to the use of the triple candle, see *Table 43*.

[2]Its use was unknown in the Milanese and Mozarabic rites and in those of the Cistercian and Dominican orders.

[3]*Praxis* p.316.

[4]*Ceremonies of Holy Week* p.119.

[5]*Manuel* 1.3 p.1257. The Capuchin candle had one foot and three branches.

candle was still used for bearing the new fire in a number of French dioceses whose rites preserved features of their traditional ceremonial.[6]

It would appear that elsewhere three separate candles were arranged at the end of the reed or pole in a triangular formation. This is the arrangement prescribed in the Roman Missal of 1474. The Ritual of Evesham refers to three *cereoli;* and the mention of a three-branched candlestick, as opposed to a single candle, at Aquileia, Lyon, Vallombrosa, and St Mary's, York, indicates that three individual candles were used. At Tours, the candleholder was known as the *rastrum,* 'the three-pronged hoe'. In some instances, it is not clear whether it was the candle or the candlestick which was triple. The 1836 Missal of Auch refers to the triple *arundo,* whilst in a manual of the Augustinian Friars, the descriptive phrase *triangulo distinctis* is equally ambiguous.

Twentieth-century manuals permit the use of either three separate tapers or a triple candle with a single stock.[7] The disposition of the candles in a trident-like formation was prohibited,[8] even though the *Caeremoniale Episcoporum* of 1600 contains an illustration of the three candles arranged in this very way (p.298). The combination of serpent-reed and triple candle has been referred to in the previous chapter.

(ii) The Origin of the Triple Candle

No single explanation can adequately account for the emergence of the triple candle and its use within the new fire ceremony; surviving documentary evidence would suggest that its origins are to be sought in a number of different liturgical milieux. It is maintained that the small candle which bore the new fire into church became a triple taper to match the three-

---

[6]For instance, Agen, Autun, Bayonne, Carcassonne, Digne, St-Brieuc, St-Dié, and Vannes. 1984 Survey of France.

[7]O'Loan p.283; Fortescue and O'Connell (4th ed.) p.337.

[8]Fortescue and O'Connell *ibidem.*

Document	Date	Source
PR XII	12 C	*PRMA* I xxxii.7 p.238
Corbie	12 C	*DAMR* 3.13.34 p.126 (M 1146)
Bec	*c.*1200	*DAMR* 3.13.34 p.127 (M 1153)
Apamea	1214	*DAER* 4.24 p.160 (M 25)
Haymo *(OM)*	1243	HBS 85 p.209
Evesham	*c.*1250	HBS 6 col.80*
PGD	*c.*1296	*PRMA* III iv.8 p.588
Worcester	13 C	Antiphonary p.69
Bayeux	13 C	Ordinary p.135
Ordo XIV	*c.*1310	PL 78.1218B
CA 1706	*c.*1350	*ZRKM* p.213
Durham	14 C	Missal p.185
St Mary's, York	*c.*1400	HBS 75 p.275
Barking	1404	HBS 65 p.101
Missale Romanum	1474	HBS 17 p.175
Austin Friars	1491	Missal np
Tongres	15 C	Ordinary p.164
Vallombrosa	1503	Missal fol.xcv
Monte Cassino	1507	Missal fol.91
Aquileia	1519	Missal fol.91
Cosenza	1549	Missal fol.115
Braga	1558	Missal fol.xcvi
Missale Romanum	1570	1950 t.e. p.186
Austin Canons	1579	Ordinary fol.137
Camaldolese	1634	Ceremonial p.84
Carmelites	1664	Missal p.157
Cistercians	1689	Ritual p.245
Evreux	1740	Missal p.186
Cahors	1760	Missal p.173
Poitiers	1767	Missal p.245
Lyon	1771	Missal p.189
Poland	1819	Manual II p.473
Auch	1836	Missal p.192
Nantes	1837	Missal p.199
Vatican	19 C	England p.119

*Evidence for Maundy Thursday.

Table 43. Evidence for the use of the triple candle

fold cry of *Lumen Christi;*[9] and indeed this theory is difficult to discredit in view of the fact that the triple candle and the triple acclamation do occur together in *PR XII,* our earliest evidence for the former. Also in support of this view is the illustrated evidence of the *Exultet* rolls of Southern Italy : some of the poles have a single twisted termination, perhaps representing a serpent; and one has a double twisted end to the shaft.[10] It is not difficult to believe, in view of the evidence of the latter, that the number of candles may have been increased from one to three to match the number of cries or to symbolise the Trinity or to accommodate both. The objection that such an explanation does not satisfactorily account for the springing of the candles from a central stock is partially removed when one considers the relative difficulty of entwining three candles around a central pole compared with the ease of affixing a *candela triplex.*

The evidence of the slightly later *Ordo Ecclesiae Lateranensis,* however, does not support the theory that the number of candles was increased to *three* in order to achieve the abovementioned liturgical symmetry. For according to that document, the deacon, prior to chanting the triple *Lumen Christi,* carried into church on the reed

> several candles bound together, so that they might not easily be extinguished by the wind.[11]

The functional purpose of the several candles could not be more clearly stated. The mention of *plures* suggests that a definite number had not been fixed, but the fact that an indefinite number was used clearly shows that as far as the Lateran Church was concerned, their number had not been increased to correspond to the cries of *Lumen Christi.* The subsequent use of three candles in the Roman rite could just as easily have

[9]Bugnini and Braga p.189.

[10]Avery, *Plates CXX, CXXXIII,* and *CXXXVIII.*

[11]Plures candelas in unum glomeratas ne a vento leviter extinguantur. *OEL* p.61.

been determined by that number's symbolic representation of the Trinity as by a deliberate design to achieve numerical correspondence with the acclamations of *Lumen Christi*. Subsequently, the Trinitarian significance of the device in question was highlighted. Louis Thomassin comments that 'we light the tripartite candle in honour of the Trinity, believing that, bathed in the light of Jesus Christ, we have knowledge of the inner mysteries of the Trinity'.[12]

Indeed, the evidence of *OEL* and the service-books of other churches in which the three candles were lit at the same time strongly suggests that the close rapport which existed between each of the three candles and the corresponding cry of *Lumen Christi*, as exemplified in the Pian Missal—of which more presently—was unknown during most of the Middle Ages.[13] In support of this position, we can make two important observations. (i) The acclamation of *Lumen Christi* did not feature in the rites of a number of churches in which the triple candle was used.[14] (ii) The triple candle was borne in procession to the singing of the *Inventor rutili* at Evesham, Salisbury, York, and Tongres.[15]

The significance of the phrase *in unum* is not immediately clear.[16] It may indicate simply that the candles were bound together around the reed and not arranged at fixed intervals from each other; or it may signify that the candles sprang from a central stock—a method of arrangement more easy to ac-

[12]In Trinitatis honorem Cereum in tres divisum accendimus, rati nos Jesu Christi lumine fusos Trinitatis penitiora Mysteria nosse. *De Dierum Festorum* II.14 p.72.

[13]For instance, Monte Cassino and Coutances, and also the Carmelite Missal. See *Table 43* for all documentary reference to the triple candle.

[14]For instance, Bec, Braga, Lyon (all missals including that of 1904), and Rome, according to the testimony of Haymo's *Ordo Missalis*, and most pre-Tridentine missals. In twenty-two of these last service-books (from 1474 to 1561) which were examined by the writer, only two (1558 and 1560 Missals) contain the triple cry of *Lumen Christi*.

[15]See *Table 45*.

[16]From the above-quoted excerpt from *OEL*.

complish, as we suggested above. The serpentine theme involving the reed and the candles, which is attested in other documents, was unknown in the Roman rite.

Further support for the functional origin of the triple candle comes from England and Ireland. At Barking and Durham, an unspecified number of candles were affixed to the top of the spear for the reception of the new fire.[17] Similarly in the Old Irish Missal, the number of candles is not stated (p.126). However, in the Gilbertine rite, five candles were used.[18] In view of the reason given in *OEL* for the use of several candles, it is not difficult to see in the multiple use of candles attested by these four documents a precaution against the sudden quenching of the processional fire by the elements.[19]

There remain to be considered three further possible factors which may have contributed to the emergence and use of the triple candle. (i) The first has already been touched upon. We saw that the eighteenth-century liturgist Thomassin suggests that the processional candle became tripartite in honour of the Trinity.[20] Jean Grancolas also puts forward this explanation.[21] However, we cannot be sure whether the number of candles was fixed at three as a gesture to honour the Trinity or whether the Trinitarian association was subsequently added to this device. Corsetti points out that the three candles springing from a central stock signified both the Trinity and the unity of God.[22] Other writers comment upon the Trinitarian symbolism of the candles,[23] Dom Gaspar Le Febvre noting in the twentieth century that the device anticipated the Baptism in the Trinity which the catechumens in former times

[17]HBS 65 p.101 and Missal p.186, respectively.

[18]HBS 59 p.39. It is unlikely that this number was chosen to match the number of grains of incense inserted into the Easter candle.

[19]At Durham, a candle in a lantern was also used in case of an emergency (Missal p.186).

[20]*De Dierum Festorum* II.14 p.72.

[21]*Commentarius* p.316.

[22]*Praxis* p.316.

[23]Desideri, *Praxis* p.150; Thurston, *LHW* p.415.

had undergone.[24] Van Doren's claim that the use of the triple candle is purely allegorical is unwarranted. Moreover, his statement that this candle represents Christ in His divinity and in His humanity seems curious, as does his comparison of the reed bending in the wind with the humiliation of Christ during His Passion. (ii) It might be argued that the increase in the number of candles from one to three constituted an elaboration of the serpent-candle and symbolised more realistically the swallowing of the snakes as narrated in Exodus 7:12. However, while such a theory is attractive, it must be advanced tentatively in view of the absence of corroborative evidence. It is true that at Braga a triple candle emerged from the mouth of the serpent-reed; however, the late appearance of the device and the known influence of Cluny suggest that the use of the triple candle in this rite was a later development. (iii) In an eleventh-century *Exultet* roll from Bari, there is an illustration of the triple candle, which, if part of the original picture, would provide the earliest evidence for the device.[25] Significantly, the pole is tilted forwards, the position in which it should be held according to a number of early documents.[26] Moreover, it should be borne in mind that Bari was a Byzantine dependency until 1071; and though the local Italian rite was used in that city, the influence of Byzantine ceremonial, which included the episcopal triple hand-candle,[27] should not be completely ruled out.

(iii) The Lighting of the Triple Candle

The functional purpose of the triple candle necessitated the kindling of all three wicks at the same time.[28] There is no evidence before the sixteenth century to show that the three

[24]1928 Daily Missal p.828.
[25]Avery, *Plate XIX*. Avery is of the opinion that the pole is a later addition.
[26]OR 26.9; OR 29.17; *Alcuin* (PL 101.1205D).
[27]The τριχήριον is mentioned in Byzantine liturgical texts of the tenth century.
[28]1507 Missal of Monte Cassino fol.92; Ordinary of Tongres p.164.

candles were lit one by one in close conjunction with each cry of *Lumen Christi*.[29] Even after the practice of uttering the three cries intermittently during the procession into church had become established, the lighting of all three candles at the same time continued at Vallombrosa, at Cosenza, in the Carmelite rite, and possibly at Aquileia.[30]

The custom of lighting one candle in sympathy with each acclamation of *Lumen Christi* is first attested, perhaps surprisingly, as late as 1570 in the *Missale Romanum* of Pope Pius V and seems to have had its origin within the liturgy of that church. The practice was subsequently adopted by a number of diocesan churches, mostly French, and by some religious orders.[31]

The establishment of the close rapport between the candle and the cry of *Lumen Christi* resulted in the lighting of the first candle *inside* the church, and necessitated the transportation of the flame from the source of the new fire to the door of the church in readiness for the lighting of the first candle. A number of different devices are known to have been used to fetch the new fire. They included a small candle,[32] which was sometimes placed in a lantern if a strong wind was blowing;[33] a *busia,* which consisted of two wax-wicks twisted together for the better preservation of the flame;[34] and a *gossypium cera-*

[29]This practice has to be inferred in some manuals, for example, the 1634 Camaldolese Ceremonial (p.84) and the 1775 Cappuchin Ritual (p.128).

[30]1503 Missal fol.xcii; 1549 Missal fol.115; 1664 Missal p.157; and 1519 Missal fol.91, respectively.

[31]Missals of Evreux (1740) p.187; of Cahors (1760) p.173; of Poitiers (1767) p.245; of Auch (1836) p.192; and of Nantes (1837) p.199. Religious orders include Augustinian Canons (1579 Ordinary fol.137); Camaldolese (1634 Ceremonial p.84); and Capuchins (1775 Ritual p.128).

[32]*Caeremoniale Episcoporum* p.298; *Maison du Roy* p.400; Ceremonial of Lyon p.474. At Lyon, where there was no new fire procession, the triple candle was lit only at the announcement of the *Exultet*.

[33]Gavanti I p.234.

[34]Merati p.78.

tum, which was a length or roll of cotton covered with wax.[35]
A manual of ceremonies for Poland mentions a wax-coated
spill for lighting the triple candle or that in the lantern if necessary.[36] The use of *ligna sulphurata* first appears in the Camal-
dolensian Ceremonial of 1634.[37] They were sulphur-tipped
or sulphur-coated splints of wood whose original purpose was
to transfer the new fire from the burning woodpile or chafing-
dish to the small candle,[38] or to the triple candle in instances
where all three lights were kindled together.[39] They were subsequently used, it would appear, to bring the new fire into
church and to light one of the three candles prior to the singing of the first *Lumen Christi,* as at Auch and Nantes,[40] and
also to light the Easter candle itself.[41]

(iv) The Disposition and Disposal
of the Processional Candle(s)

Several commentators mention the stand for holding the
reed once the Easter candle had been lit.[42] This could be made
of marble or wood, materials also specified in a number of
ceremonials.[43] The Augustinian Ceremonial enjoined that it
should be placed on the Epistle side of the altar. At Uzès, the
serpent-reed was placed next to the archdeacon's seat.[44] According to the Pontifical of Poitiers, the deacon handed the

[35]Martinucci II p.241.

[36]1819 Manual II p.468.

[37]Page 82. The mention of them by Gavanti in 1652 (*Thesaurus* I p.233)
would suggest that their use in the sixteenth century was not confined to
the rite of this order.

[38]1634 Camaldolese Ceremonial p.82 and p.84; 1662 Ceremonial of Paris
p.375.

[39]For instance, in the Cistercian rite (1689 Ritual p.247).

[40]1836 Missal p.192 and 1837 Missal p.199, respectively.

[41]See Part Four Chapter 29.

[42]Gavanti/Merati IV p.155; Desideri p.144; Gattinari p.143.

[43]For instance, those of the Augustinian Friars (1714) p.311; of the Capuchins (1775) p.125; and of the Camaldolese (1634) p.82.

[44]1495 Missal fol.lxiii. The rubric adds 'or in a convenient place'.

reed to the sacristan after he had lit the Easter candle (p.215); and among the Cistercians, the small candle taper used for lighting the Easter candle was blown out after the singing of the *Exultet* and Preface.[45] At the Cathedral of St John Lateran, the reed was taken into the sacristy after the two standard candles and the seven lamps had been lit.[46] A rubric in the Sarum Missal states simply that the reed should be removed after the conclusion of the Preface, a direction enjoined by Corsetti.[47] Merati prescribes that a drip-pan should be placed below the reed-candle to catch the wax as it falls (p.77). Elsewhere, the extinguishing of the reed-candle or of the triple candles probably did not take place until the conclusion of the ceremony, as at Lyon.[48] The Augustinian Friars allowed their three candles to burn until after the end of Vespers on Holy Saturday.[49] At Vallombrosa, the church lamps were lit by using the triple candle.[50]

[45]*Nom. Cist.* p.105. A reed was not used in this rite.
[46]This took place during the singing of the Preface. *OEL* p.61.
[47]Dickinson, *Missale* p.343 and *Praxis* p.320, respectively.
[48]1838 Ceremonial p.418.
[49]Ceremonial p.314.
[50]1503 Missal fol.xcv.

Chapter Nineteen
THE PSALMS,
THE *INVENTOR RUTILI,*
AND THE *LUMEN CHRISTI*

The earliest documents record that the procession of clergy and people moved into church with the new fire in silence.[1] From the middle of the tenth century, the practice arose of singing one or more psalms, or Prudentius' hymn, *Inventor rutili.* Alternatively, the cries of *Lumen Christi* punctuated the silence of the procession in some churches.

(i) The Psalms

The chanting of psalms during the return of the procession with the newly-kindled fire was prescribed in Lanfranc's *Decrees.* It was also enjoined in a number of earlier Benedictine customaries, as well as in the Cluniac and Carmelite rites.[2] The tradition survived for several centuries in a number of cathedrals, mainly, it would seem, as a result of monastic influence. It is not difficult to believe that the return-psalms were

[1]OR 26.9; OR 29.17; OR 31.63; OR 32.17; *PRG* II p.97; *CMG* (Albers V p.32); the *ordo* of Corbie and Ordinal of Monte Cassino (*DAMR* 3.13.34 p.126 [M1145 and M1139 respectively]); and *Alcuin* (PL 101.1205D).

[2]For these and other relevant references, see *Table 44*.

Church/Order	Psalms	Date	Source
Farfa	53 56 66 69	c.1000	PL 150.1199
Fruttuaria	23 26 66 147	c.1000	Albers IV p.54
Vallombrosa	66	c.1040	Albers IV p.249
Dijon	53 56 66 69 119	c.1050	*DAMR* 3.13.34 p.126
Cluny	53 56 79	c.1060	PL 149.659A
Lanfranc	53 56 66 69	c.1070	PL 150.467B
Sigibert	26 27 53	c.1070	Albers II p.93
Bec	53 56 66 69	c.1200	*DAMR* 3.13.34 p.126
Norwich	26	c.1265	HBS 82 p.81
Evesham	26 27	c.1250	Ritual col.80
St-Vedast, Arras	53 56	c.1300	HBS 86 p.160
Carmelites	66	c.1312	Ordinary p.171
Lyre	53 56 66 69	c.1400	*DAMR* 3.13.34 p.126
Burgos	66	1546	Missal fol.ciii
Palencia	66	1568	Missal fol.c
Rouen	26	1640	Ritual p.307

(The numeration of the psalms is taken from the Septuagint.)

Table 44. The processional psalms after the new fire

introduced into the new fire ceremonial as a counterpart to those sung on the way to the new fire in an attempt to achieve a sort of liturgical symmetry. Psalms 26 (27), 66 (67), and 79 (80) were almost certainly chosen because of their mention of the light of the Lord. Psalms 23 (24) and 147 tell of the triumph of the Lord and of His glorification, the latter actually mentioning God's control of fire. The choice of Psalms 69 (70) and 119 (120), and to some extent Psalm 56 (57), seems somewhat obscure. Their penitential aspect makes them more fitting to have been sung *before* the kindling of the new fire, as indeed the Penitential Psalms were sung in a number of places.[3]

At Bayeux, the choir sang the antiphon *Clamaverunt ad Dominum cum tribularentur* as they returned into church, whilst at

[3]The *Consuetudines Cluniacenses* (Albers II p.47, *Antiquiores C*) record the older tradition of using the Penitential Psalms on the return.

Rouen, before the deacon began the *Exultet,* they sang the antiphon *Cum rex gloriae Christus infernum debellaturus intraret et chorus angelicus portas principum tolli praeciperet.*[4] This antiphon was also sung at Hereford at the Sepulchre on Holy Saturday night (Breviary p.324).

(ii) The *Inventor Rutili*[5]

The singing of this hymn of Prudentius after the kindling of the new fire is first attested in the Romano-Germanic Pontifical *(PRG);* but according to that document its use was geographically restricted.[6] Although Lanfranc refers to the *Inventor rutili* in his *Decrees,*[7] there is no evidence for its use in any monastery of Italy, Spain, or Switzerland. Indeed, with the exception of Aquileia, the hymn was sung only in churches to the east and north of the Alps.[8] It was particularly popular in Germany, as is clear from a glance at *Table 45.* According to Lanfranc, the *Inventor rutili* was sung by two choirboys who were standing close to the bishop's throne as the procession made its way from the place where the new fire had been kindled and blessed; but the practice developed in which the

[4]1780 *Semaine Sainte* p.495 and 1497 Missal np, respectively.

[5]For the implications of the internal evidence of the hymn, see Appendix 11 : *The* Inventor rutili *of Prudentius.* For a list of churches where this hymn was sung after the blessing of the new fire, see *Table 45.*

[6]*PRG* II §345 p.97. Manuscripts C and K both state that a procession in silence was the norm. It is only C which adds : *Aliqui tamen hic cantant hymnum Prudentii,* 'However some sing Prudentius' hymn at this point'.

[7]PL 150.467B. Since Lanfranc also mentions the singing of psalms after the kindling of the new fire, presumably the *Inventor rutili* was alternative to them, although Lanfranc does not refer to a choice.

[8]Since the singing of the hymn was not universal according to *PRG,* Dendy's statement (p.140) that the hymn was used in the Roman rite for a time must be challenged : ' . . . the Inventor rutili . . . at Rome only enjoyed a brief period of use during the ascendancy of the Ordo Romanus Antiquus [= *PRG*]'. Not all features of the new fire ceremony found in *PRG* passed into the Roman rite, for example, the kindling of fire on Maundy Thursday.

Church/Document	Date	Source
PRG (MS C)	c.950	II §345 p.97
Lanfranc	c.1070	PL 150.467B
Rupert of Deutz	c.1111	PL 170.149B
Magdelen College Pontifical	12 C	HBS 39 pp.169–70
Ireland	c.1200	Old Irish Missal p.126
Evesham	c.1250	HBS 6 col.90
Norwich	c.1265	HBS 82 p.91
Le Mans	c.1295	*DAER* 4.24.3 p.146 (M 89)
Salisbury	13 C	HBS 91
Worcester	13 C	Antiphonary p.69
Nidaros	13 C	*ONE* p.232
Exeter	1337	HBS 37
Strasbourg	1364	*DAER* 4.24.3 p.146 (M 35)
Anderlecht	14 C	Ordinary p.88
Westminster	c.1370	HBS 5 col.578
Durham	14 C	Missal p.187
York	14 C	Missal p.110
St Mary's, York	c.1400	HBS 75 p.292
Barking	1404	HBS 65 p.101
Würzburg	1477	Ordinary np
Verdun	1481	Missal fol.lxiiii
Breslau	1483	Missal np
Odense	1483	Missal fols.10–11
Freising	1487	Missal fol.cii
Basel	1488	Missal fol.xcii
Trier	1488	Missal fol.cii
Cologne	1494	Missal fol.cxxii
Prague	1498	Missal fol.xci
Hildesheim	1499	Missal fol.xcvi
Tongres	15 C	Ordinary p.164
Viborg	1500	Missal fol.E5
Esztergom	1501	Missal fol.lxxiiii
Passau	1503	Missal fol.lxxxiv
Halberstadt	c.1505	Missal fol.lxx
Bystorp	c.1505	Manual p.83
Mainz	1507	Missal fol.xcii
Saltzburg	1507	Missal fol.xciii
Hamburg	1509	Missal fol.xc
Copenhagen	1510	Missal fol.ci
Bremen	1511	Missal fol.lxxxv
Spires	1512	*Agenda* fol.xcvi
Slesvig	1512	*Agenda* pp.129–30
Minden	1513	Missal fol.ciii
Roskilde	1513	Manual pp.59–60
Lund	1514	Missal fol.xc

Church/Document	Date	Source
Aquileia	1519	Missal fol.91
Breslau	1519	Missal fol.lxxix
Meissen	1520	Breviary np
Abo	*c.*1522	Manual p.240
Auxerre	1537	*DAER* 4.24.3 p.146 (M 39)
Liège	1540	Missal fol.lxxvii
Ratisbon	1570	Ritual np
Sens	1715	Missal p.238
Périgueux	1782	Missal p.159
Le Puy	1836	Ceremonial p.376

Table 45. Evidence for the Inventor rutili

singers themselves joined the procession and a chorus, formed of those participating, repeated the first verse of the hymn as a refrain between the singing of subsequent verses. At Durham and Westminster, two brothers led the singing, at Exeter two boys, and at Barking the duty-priest for the week and a priest representing the Chapter; whilst among the Gilbertines, two candle-bearers *(ceroferarii)* or two others performed the duty. Instances of its use after the Council of Trent are few. It survived at Sens and Périgueux until the eighteenth century and is even found in a ceremonial for Le Puy as late as 1836.

(iii) The Cry of *Lumen Christi*

(A) ORIGIN. Dom Bernard Capelle, followed by others, would find the origin of the triple cry of *Lumen Christi* of the Roman rite, together with the complementary refrain of *Deo gratias,* in the corresponding Mozarabic ceremonial of Holy Saturday.[9] According to the latter rite, the bishop emerged from the sacristy with the lighted Easter candle and proclaimed '*Deo*

[9]*La procession* pp.116–17. See also Bugnini and Brage pp.189–90 and Dendy p.138.

gratias'; to which the congregation responded three times in like manner. As the procession moved into the choir, they sang the antiphon *Lumen verum inluminans omnem hominem in hunc mundum venientem.* Capelle argues that this ritual found its way to Rome by way of Gaul, Milan, and Central Italy (p.117), citing as evidence for this route a debatable instance of Mozarabic influence in the Old Gallican Missal,[10] and the testimony of what he believed to be an eleventh-century Milanese *ordo* (MS Vat.lat 10673), but which has been shown to be a Beneventan gradual.[11]

It is true that similarities do exist between the Spanish rite and that of Central Italy[12] : the lighting of the bishop's candle, the procession into church with that candle, and the three-fold acclamation of the congregation; but the greater number of differences which exist between the two rites should make us very cautious in trying to detect the influence or dependency of the one rite on the other. Moreover, it has yet to be shown what liturgical contact or interchange existed between Spain and Southern Italy in the period 700 to 900, when the Beneventan rite is most likely to have been susceptible to the liturgical influences of other churches, and when any importations of Spanish provenance are most likely to have occurred. Political conditions in Spain, however, during this crucial time would suggest that exchanges of liturgical forms and practices between Spain and Southern Italy were most unlikely, especially any issuing from Spain.

---

[10]It is true that the prayer in the *Vetus Missale Gallicum* (PL 72.363) entitled PRAEFATIONE CERAE 'does seem to indicate a procession where all carried lights' and may have originated in a liturgical milieu, such as the Mozarabic, where this ritual did take place. On the other hand, the references in the prayer to *vinculis . . . disruptis, illuminationem,* and *candoris* suggest a baptismal setting in which *accensa luminaria* will be the candles of the neophytes. Evidence for the existence of these lights at the time comes from Amalarius (*Liber de Ord.Ant.* 44.8).

[11]Hesbert p.189.

[12]As attested in the Beneventan Gradual and *Missale Antiquum.* For the text of these two documents, see Hesbert p.188.

The new fire ceremonies of the Beneventan and Mozarabic rites differed from each other in the following respects :

Mozarabic	*Beneventan*
1. Easter candle brought into church.	Easter candle already in position.
2. Bishop cries *'Deo gratias'* at the sacristy door.	Deacon cries threefold *Lumen Christi* at ambo.
3. Singing of antiphon *lumen verum* during procession.	Silent procession.
4. Fire kindled and Easter candle lit in a darkened room.	Fire not necessarily kindled inside the building.[13]
5. Lighting and blessing of a lamp.	No use of lamp.
6. No blessing of new fire.	Blessing of new fire.

If the Beneventan rite had been subjected to Mozarabic influence, we might have expected a greater correspondence of ceremonial detail and fewer divergences. The phrase *ex occulto* does not necessarily refer to a darkened sacristy, and even the congregational cry of *Deo gratias* is not completely parallel in the two rites. Moreover, although certain features of the Spanish rite are of a venerable antiquity, it is by no means certain that all the elements recorded in the tenth-century Antiphonary date from the time of Elipandus (*c.*718–802). In an appendix, we have argued in favour of the importation

---

[13]The rubric of the Gradual states : De quo igne accendetur cereus; et, quasi ex occulto, proferatur in publicum. 'From this fire the Easter candle will be lit; and just as the fire has been kept in a place of concealment, so let it be brought forth for all to see.' Dendy's claim (p.132) that this 'suggests the theatrical procession with lights from a darkened room' is unconvincing. Not only is there no evidence for the use of more than one light in the Beneventan procession; rather, the phrase suggests the *locus secretior,* familiar from the Roman rite, which was a place well hidden from view. Moreover, a rubric earlier in the Gradual prescribes the kindling of the new fire by means of a fire-stone 'or in some other way' *(alio livet* [= quolibet] *modo).* If the latter included the use of a lens, the ritual could hardly have been performed 'in a darkened room'.

of a number of Gallicanisms into the Mozarabic rite, including the cry of *Deo gratias*.

All the early evidence for the *Lumen Christi* is to be found in documents of Central Italian provenance.[14] Indeed, as we observed above, the threefold cry is found only outside Italy amongst the religious orders whose own rites closely followed that of Rome[15]—it is even absent from the ceremonial of many northern Benedictine houses, not being prescribed in Lanfranc's *Decrees*—and in churches which were influenced by Roman ritual, such as Marseille, or which used romanised Gallican missals, such as Chalons and Poitiers. Having discounted a Mozarabic provenance for this liturgical feature, it is not difficult to find its origin within the Romano-Gallican tradition. In Section 22 of the eighth-century Ordo 19 we read :

> If night comes while they are eating and it is necessary to kindle a light, as soon as the brother who carries the light enters, he says, so that all may hear, 'The Light of Christ'. All reply 'Thanks be to God'. After a blessing from the *senior* he puts the light in its place.

As Andrieu observes, Benedict's Rule provided for the evening meal to end before night-fall. However, the 'Strasbourg liturgical historian', who dated this *ordo* to the years 781–790, suggests somewhat carelessly that, in view of the climatic consideration relating to Section 22, the *ordo* may well have come from north of the Alps.[16] Bad winter evenings do occur in Italy; and presumably the evening meal was always taken at the same hour. This *ordo,* therefore, could equally have originated in Italy. Indeed, it seems difficult to escape the conclusion that this greeting with its response came to be used in

[14]For a list of rites in which the *Lumen Christi* was a feature and for the documentary references, see *Table 46.*

[15]In the Cistercian rite, there was only a single cry at the altar (1669 Missal p.155), whilst the *Lumen Christi* did not feature in that of the Premonstratensians (King, *LRO* p.190).

[16]*Les* Ordines Romani III p.212.

Church/Document	Date	Source
Beneventum*	c.1000	Hesbert p.188
Vallombrosa	11 C	Albers IV p.249
Lateran	c.1140	*OEL* p.61
Monte Cassino A *	12 C	*PRMA (PR XII)* I p.292
PR XII	12 C	*PRMA* I xxxii.7 p.239
Apamea	1214	*DAER* 4.24. p.160 (M 25)
Marseilles	13 C	*ILEM* p.84
Ordo XIV	c.1310	PL 78.1218C
CA 1706	c.1350	*ZRKM* p.214
Uzès*	1495	Missal fol.lxiii
Camaldolese	1503	Missal fol.89
Aquileia	1519	Missal fol.91
Cosenza	1549	Missal fol.115
Missale Romanum	1558	HBS 33 p.84
Missale Romanum	1560	HBS 33 p.84
Missale Romanum	1570	1950 t.e. p.188
Austin Canons	1579	Ordinary fol.137
Fréjus	c.1600	De Rubeis p.327
Cistercians†	1689	Ritual p.247
Evreux	1740	Missal p.187
Cahors*	1760	Missal p.173
Poitiers	1767	Missal p.245
Capuchins	1775	Ritual p.128
Auch	1836	Missal p.192
Nantes	1837	Missal p.199

*There was only one processional candle.
†*Lumen Christi* was acclaimed only once.

Table 46. Evidence for the acclamation of Lumen Christi

the Holy Saturday liturgy once the Vigil began to be held in the late afternoon or early evening.

(B) THE DEVELOPMENT OF THE RITUAL. The ritual of the *Lumen Christi* passed through a number of stages in its development before it reached the form familiar from the Pian Missal of 1570.

1. The oldest form of the ritual, and that from which subsequent variations of the ceremonial developed, is found in the Beneventan rite of the late tenth century, as attested in the Gradual and *Missale Antiquum*. According to these two documents, the threefold *Lumen Christi* together with the responsorial *Deo gratias* was acclaimed at the ambo by the deacon after the lighting of the Easter candle and just prior to his chanting of the *Exultet*.[17] *Monte Cassino A* may attest the same practice.[18]

2. In *Monte Cassino B,* the cry of *Lumen Christi* was directed by the deacon at the reed-candle which, lit with the new fire, had been brought into church by an acolyte. Only after the last response of *Deo gratias* was the Easter candle lit. The so-called suburbicarian practice, described in the twelfth-century *Pontificale Romanum (PR XII)*, suggests that the triple cry was uttered by the deacon standing close to the Easter candle near to the altar, again before that candle was lit.[19]

3. The next stage of development reveals an elaboration of ceremonial. For, whereas the deacon or acolyte had previously stood in the same position to utter the cries,[20] the proclamations of *Lumen Christi* became incorporated into the new fire procession in such a way that the first *Lumen Christi* was heard at the door of the church, the second in the nave, and

[17]As the bearer of the *Lumen Christi,* the deacon had the duty to proclaim its presence.

[18]The text of *Monte Cassino A* and *Monte Cassino B,* both of the twelfth century, is printed in Andrieu's edition of *PR XII* (I pp.292–93). The problem of the former document and in particular the interpretation of the clause : *Acolytus vero portat cereum ad ammonem,* is discussed in Appendix 10 : *Monte Cassino A.* If *cereum* refers to the Easter candle, this document attests Beneventan practice. If, however, the reed-candle is to be understood, the document relates to the second stage of the development, as does *Monte Cassino B.* In either interpretation, it is the acolyte's voice that is heard.

[19]*PRMA* I xxxii.10 p.241. So also *PGD* (*PRMA* III iv.8–9 p.588). For the so-called suburbicarian practice, see Appendix 14.

[20]Sicardus records that this took place at the doors of the church. *Mitrale* (PL 213.323B).

the final cry at the altar. This arrangement subsequently obtained until 1970, surviving the liturgical reforms of 1955, though with the Easter candle replacing the triple candle. In some rites, the stational norm of door, nave, and altar was not observed. The third acclamation occurred at the ambo, if it was customary to locate the Easter candle in that position. Ordo XIV prescribes the choir for the second station. This also took place at Fréjus and Cahors. At Marseille, the procession emerged from the sacristy door and stopped at the altar of the Blessed Virgin Mary, in the choir, and at the reading desk next to the Easter candle. In the Roman rite since 1970, the nave stopping has generally been omitted, the acclamations occurring at the new fire, in the doorway, and at the altar.

The processional chanting of the *Lumen Christi* is first attested at Vallombrosa in the eleventh century, and it may be that the practice originated within that very monastery. According to earlier practice, the procession had moved into the church in silence, as we noted at the beginning of this chapter. At Vallombrosa, however, the unique practice obtained of chanting a psalm *and* uttering the triple *Lumen Christi* during the procession. A glance at *Table 44* shows that contemporary monastic practice was to chant several psalms on the return into church; at Vallombrosa only one psalm was sung. It is the writer's belief that at this monastery in former times, more than one psalm was chanted during this part of the ceremony, and that the processional *Lumen Christi,* borrowed from a Central Italian monastic milieu, was deliberately included in the ceremonial, either as a musical feature additional to the psalms or as a replacement for those psalms which were previously chanted once the procession had entered the church. The triple acclamation of the *Lumen Christi* during the procession subsequently found its way into the Roman rite in the twelfth century. At Rome, the duty was performed by the junior cardinal deacon.[21]

[21]*PR XII (PRMA* I xxxii p.239) and *OEL* p.61. The history of the *Lumen*

4. The final stage in the development saw the utilisation of the triple candle to reinforce dramatically the significance of the threefold cry. It had formerly been the practice to light all three candles from the new fire at the same time. This is implied in Ordo XIV : with each successive cry of *Lumen Christi,* the deacon raised the candle higher. The practice is also attested in the two Roman missals of 1558 and 1560. According to the Pian Missal of 1570, the triple candle was carried into church unlit. The deacon who bore the candle then lowered the reed, and one of the candles was lit with the new fire; thereupon, the deacon chanted the first *Lumen Christi.* The ritual was then repeated in the centre of the church; and after the procession had reached the altar, the last candle was lit and *Lumen Christi* was announced for the third and final time. In prescribing the west end of the chancel, the centre of the chancel, and the altar steps as the three stations for the *Lumen Christi,* the compilers of the *Caeremoniale Episcoporum* were perhaps taking a realistic view of the small number of laity who were likely to attend the Vigil, then held on Saturday morning (II.27 p.297). The Roman Missal of 1574 and the Vallombrosan Missal of 1503 record that the triple candle was handed to an acolyte and subdeacon, respectively, after the

Christi in the Roman rite is not at all clear. In addition to the two above-mentioned documents, it is also found in Ordo XII (1192) (PL 78.1076C); *PGD* (*c.* 1296) (*PRMA* III p.588); Ordo XIV (1311) (PL 78.1121); CA 1706 (*c.* 1350) (*ZRKM* p.214); and *Bindo F.* (1377) (*ZRKM* p.276). It is not found in Haymo's *Ordo Missalis* or in the Dominican rite, both of which were modelled closely on papal ceremonial (*SMRL* I p.44; King, *LRO* p.338), or in the 1474 *Missale Romanum* and subsequent missals, except two printed in Venice in 1558 and 1560. It appears in the mandatory Pian Missal of 1570. Van Dijk (I p.82) attributed the omission of the *Lumen Christi* in Haymo's *ordo* to the fact that it was not known outside Rome; but this, as we have seen, is clearly incorrect, as is Dendy's claim that it was 'probably kept out by the popularity of the *Inventor rutili* (p.140)'. Both the 1558 and the 1560 Missals refer to the custom being observed 'in certain places' (HBS 33 p.84), one of which was presumably the papal court, and state that it was a priest, as opposed to a deacon in *MR 1474* and other Roman missals, who performed the duty.

chanting of the third *Lumen Christi.* They held it until it was time to light the Easter candle.[22] With each cry of *Lumen Christi* all genuflected except the cross-bearer.[23]

Thus a close rapport was established between the lighting of the three candles and the threefold acclamation. It inevitably resulted in directing the attention of the congregation away from the Easter candle, and in the close identification of the 'light of Christ' with the flames of the three candles. Nor did the Trinitarian significance of the number of candles go unnoticed.[24] Indeed, it might be said that a slight shift in emphasis occurred in the status and role of the triple candle *vis-à-vis* the aspect of God which the light represented. For the triple light and the threefold cry to some extent blurred the distinction between God's light and Christ's light as expressed in the Nicene Creed and detracted from the centrality of the latter within the Paschal vigil. Guéranger goes so far as to assert that the threefold cry of *Lumen Christi* expresses the revelation of the divinity of the Three Persons of the Trinity.[25] The greeting of the triple candle also had the effect of detracting from the significance of the Easter candle, especially since it was not kindled in the majority of churches until the singing of the Preface was half-completed. This had the result of marring the close relationship between the Candle

[22]HBS 33 p.85 and 1503 Missal fol.xcii.

[23]The genuflection of the deacon who held the reed is first attested in the Roman rite. Ordo XV (PL 78.1321C). The practice is also found at Cahors (1760 Missal p.172). According to the 1600 *Caeremoniale Episcoporum,* the deacon should both genuflect and raise high the triple candle simultaneously (p.298).

[24]The prominence of the triple candle and the superstitious awe in which it came to be held are referred to by two writers. Sir James Frazer records that at the end of the last century in the Abruzzi, fragments of the three candles were used as charms against lightning (*Golden Bough* 7.1 p.122); and well into the present century, Estella Canziani writes that at Isernia, 'If three drops of wax from the three candles lit by the priest from the new fire drop on anyone's hat, that person is safe against lightning, provided he keeps his hat on.' (*Through the Apennines* p.328).

[25]*Liturgical Year* pp.558–59.

and the flame, and of assigning to the column of wax almost the function of a totem.[26]

The practice of chanting the first *Lumen Christi* in a deep voice and the subsequent cries at a successively higher pitch is first found in the above-mentioned eleventh-century Customary of Vallombrosa. Apropos of our contention referred to above, this may suggest a Central Italian provenance for the custom, although there is no hint of this practice in the two Beneventan documents. The ritual is also attested in *PR XII* and *PGD,* and was subsequently adopted in the majority of churches in which the *Lumen Christi* was acclaimed.

The emergence of this liturgical feature may be explained in two ways. (i) If we are correct in our belief that the custom originated in a Central or Southern Italian liturgical milieu, the rise in pitch in the deacon's voice may have developed in correspondence with his ascent of the ambo in three stages. The weakness of this theory is that there is no evidence that his ascent of the ambo was a gradual one. (ii) More likely, perhaps, is the writer's own suggestion that the rise in pitch occurred so as to enable those standing at some distance from the deacon to hear his acclamation. A desire to make oneself more audible is usually achieved by an utterance or shout at a higher level of sound, especially if the first attempt at attracting attention was considered ineffective and the strength of the voice insufficient. Moreover, the twice-repeated cry of *Lumen Christi* would serve to emphasise the importance and significance of the flame which the deacon held in his hands.

[26]Harbert p.236.

Chapter Twenty

THE EASTER CANDLE
AND THE PROCESSION

The bringing in of the fire and the blessing of the light that it provided are the two principal elements which are derived from the *Lucernarium* and present in all the rites of the western tradition. The Milanese rite preserved the primitive practice of using a lamp for the bearing of the light. In other traditions in which the new fire ceremony was combined with the blessing of the Easter candle, three different practices developed of conveying the new fire to the place where the Easter candle was to be blessed. The most common method, that of employing a small candle or the triple candle to carry the fire, has been dealt with in Chapters 16–18. The second and third ways of bringing the new fire into church involved the same fundamental procedure, but admitted the use of the Easter candle as a characteristic feature of the procession.

(i) The Bearing of the Easter Candle : Lit

The tradition in which the Easter candle was borne in procession already kindled is first attested in the eighth-century Ordo 28 :

And after the Easter candle has been lit, they all accompany
it in procession into church in silence. There is no singing.
The Candle is placed in a candelabrum in front of the altar.[1]

There seems little doubt that the Easter candle has been substituted for the lamp of the *Lucernarium* in order to bear the
new fire into church. Interestingly, in the Mozarabic rite, in
which the new fire was also borne into church by means of
the Easter candle, the use of the lamp was also retained.[2] In
Appendix 10, *Monte Cassino A,* we will show that in the twelfth
century in Central Italy, almost the same ceremonial involving the procession with the lit Easter candle was still in use.
In that rite, the Easter candle was subsequently taken to the
ambo for the singing of the *Exultet* and for the Prophecies.
At Naples in the fourteenth century, the *cimiliarcha* carried
the lighted Easter candle into the church.[3] The same practice at Bourges as late as the eighteenth century was almost
certainly a survival of the same tradition attested in Ordo 28
and Ordo 31;[4] for that Gallican rite contained other primitive elements, such as the litany before the *Exultet* and the blessing of the Easter candle with the original form of the *Veniat
quaesumus.* The revival of this tradition following the liturgical reforms of 1955 was part of the attempt to emphasise the
importance of the Easter candle and to restore it to its former
position of centrality within the Vigil liturgy. The claim that
the Easter candle ceased to be carried in procession because
in some churches it had become too large and too heavy cannot be sustained.[5] (i) In some rites, such as the Ambrosian,
it seems unlikely that the Candle was ever carried in proces-

[1]Et, accenso cereo, procedunt simul omnes de sacrario cum ipso cereo
in ecclesia cum silentio, nihil cantantes, et ponitur in candelabro ante altare. OR 28.59. The practice is also attested in Ordo 31 (§63).

[2]The custom of using a lamp, probably the result of Mozarabic influence,
was also maintained at Ripoll (Sacramentary p.92).

[3]Mallardo p.33.

[4]1741 Missal pp.225–26.

[5]Bugnini and Braga p.189.

sion. (ii) We shall see in a later chapter that very large candles were carried during the course of the old Roman liturgy. (iii) The evidence would suggest that the Easter candles began to assume massive proportions long after the custom of bearing them in procession had generally fallen into desuetude.

(ii) The Bearing of the Easter Candle : Unlit

The custom of bearing the Easter candle in procession unlit appears to be a synthesis of traditions; for the small candle, lit with the new fire, was also carried in the same procession. The earliest mention of the bearing of the unlit Easter candle is found in the Sacramentary of Corbie and in the *Pontificale Romano-Germanicum (PRG)*, both of the tenth century.[6] It is not clear from the former document how the fire was taken to the altar where it was blessed. The evidence of *PRG* is discussed below. At Aquileia, the unlit Easter candle was borne along with the triple candle ablaze;[7] and at Palencia, two small candles on spears accompanied the unlit column of wax from the cloister.[8]

(iii) The Evidence of *PRG*

The composite character of the Pontifical is apparent from the variant rubrics recorded by its Manuscripts C and K, and the task of identifying the separate strands and elements which make up its new fire ritual is not made easy by the fact that the new fire ceremony took place on each day of the Triduum.

Sections 342 and 346 of *PRG* are of principal concern for our study. The former records that after the procession had assembled outside the church,

> cereus ponitur in loco mundo, 'the candle is set in a clean place'.

[6]PL 78.336B and *PRG* II §§342 and 346 pp.94 and 98.
[7]1519 Missal fol.91.
[8]1568 Missal fol.c.

Since we are informed later that the *cereus* was lit with the new fire and put on a reed (§345), it would seem to follow that this was the candle which was placed *in loco mundo*. There are, however, two difficulties over this interpretation. The sign of the cross was made over the candle and the benediction-formula, *Deus mundi Conditor,* was pronounced over the new fire. The ascription of undue importance to the small candle with this formula, is not only unique to *PRG,* but recalls the blessing of the Easter candle according to the Gelasian sacramentaries.[9] This fact and the setting of the candle 'in a clean place' strongly suggest that in §342 *cereus* is to be identified with the Easter candle and that the rubrics of this section relate to its consecration outside the church and presumably close to the source of the new fire. The structure of the ritual differs from that found in the Gelasian sacramentaries in that, whereas the latter comprises the bringing of fire, the sign of the cross, the lighting of the candle, and the blessing, *PRG* omits the kindling at this stage. It is not difficult to believe that at a former time, the Easter candle was lit outside the church and borne thus in procession into the building and that, with the merging into a combined ritual of this practice and the tradition in which the new fire was carried on a reed-candle, the bearing of the Easter candle, also ablaze, was seen as a superfluous duplication. Hence, it came to be borne unlit.

Now, it is true that the rubrics of *PRG* do not actually state that the Easter candle was borne unlit into church. However, we are informed that after the procession had entered the church :

> The seven lamps in front of the altar are kindled from it [the reed-candle]. They had previously been placed unlit in such a way that they could be lit without any hindrance. The great candle which is to be blessed *is placed* in the centre of the church and in front of the altar.[10]

[9]See Chapter 28.
[10]Et illuminatur ex eo VII lampades ante altare quae tamen prius sine

At first sight it might appear as though *ponitur* relates to the position of the Easter candle as a result of its being set in position prior to the start of the ceremony, and such a descriptive sentence would not be out of place within the context. However, *ponitur* bears a passive verbal force which relates to an action and not to a state, and should be interpreted 'they place'. Confirmation of this translation is provided by the use of another verb in the passive voice, also from the same rubric of §342 : *illuminantur*. This can only mean 'are lit', or expressed actively, 'they light'. Moreover, the use of the periphrastic verb *erunt compositae* to describe the lamps prior to their being lit makes it very likely that *erit positus*[11] or some equivalent expression would have been used instead of *ponitur,* if the Easter candle had already been in position before the start of the service.

We conclude that *PRG* contains sufficient information for the attestation of Stage 2 in the development of the use of the Easter candle, which is summarised below.

Stage 1 : Easter candle lit outside church with new fire.
Easter candle carried into church in procession.

Stage 2 : Reed-candle lit outside church with new fire.
Easter candle carried into church unlit.

Stage 3 : Reed-candle carried into church lit with new fire.
Easter candle already in position inside church.

lumine erunt ita compositae, ut absque ullo impedimento possint accendi. Cereus vero magnus qui benedicendus est, ponitur in candelabro ante altare in medio ecclesiae . . . .

[11]Literally 'will have been placed'.

Part Four

THE EASTER CANDLE
AND THE VIGIL

Chapter Twenty-one

THE EASTER CANDLE :
ORIGIN AND
EARLIEST REFERENCES

A. ORIGIN

It is generally believed that the lighting and blessing of the Easter candle was a liturgical development of the *Lucernarium* of Holy Saturday. It not only ensured the survival of that service, admittedly in an altered form; but without destroying the traditional structure of the *Lucernarium,* the incorporation of the new element transformed the old ceremony, which, combined with the ritual of the new fire, became integrated into the paschal vigil to produce the liturgy of Holy Saturday.[1] Elsewhere we have referred to the elements in the paschal vigil which survived from the *Lucernarium.* These were :

- the bringing in of the lamp
- the officiating deacon
- the offering of light to God.[2]

The carrying of the lamp survived unchanged in the Milanese and Mozarabic rites, and in other western rites, as

[1]The basic structure of new fire, blessing of Easter candle, Vigil-readings, and Baptism, which still obtains today, had been achieved in some parts of Gaul by 800.

[2]For the Dialogue and the Blessing of the Light, see Chapter 28.

the bearing of either a candle lit with the new fire and placed on a pole, spear, or reed, or of the Easter candle itself. It is the deacon who still officiates at the service; and the offering of light is a feature of the formula for the blessing of the Candle in all the western rites.

It is difficult to disagree with Gregory Dix's description of the *Lucernarium* as an 'originally utilitarian ritual' in which the purpose of the lamp was 'to give light to the lector'.[3] The functional use of the lamp, or the candle which later replaced the lamp in most rites, was first pointed out by De Vert.[4] However, a number of scholars have denied the utilitarian origin of the Easter candle. Berlière, either unaware of the antecedents of the Easter candle or choosing to ignore them, claims that its purpose was never functional because it could not provide enough light for illuminating the rest of the church building and that its origin was symbolic.[5] Likewise Thurston, in an uncharacteristic lapse of scholarship, asserts that the ceremony involving the Easter candle was designed from the beginning with a strictly mystical and symbolical meaning.[6]

It hardly needs to be mentioned that it was unnecessary to illuminate the rest of the church during the proclamation of the *Exultet* and the Preface. Indeed, in the Roman rite, it was intended that the *Exultet* and part of the Preface should be chanted in semi-darkness.[7]

To argue that the beeswax candle replaced the lamp of the *Lucernarium* as the source of light for the reader is correct to a point. It is true that the small taper or the Easter candle itself replaced the lamp as the means by which the light was introduced into church. In the Mozarabic and Milanese tra-

[3]*Shape* p.23.
[4]*Paschal* col.328.
[5]*Le cièrge pascal* p.107.
[6]*Lent and Holy Week* p.408.
[7]After the Vigil came to be held in the earlier part of Holy Saturday, a sufficient amount of natural daylight, especially on a sunny day, would have rendered the flame of the Easter candle unnecessary for the provision of light by which to read.

ditions, the lamp continued to feature in the ceremony. In the latter rite, it was present at the blessing of the font.[8] In the Spanish ceremony, however, it was carried into church along with the Easter candle and continued to burn throughout the remainder of the paschal liturgy, maintaining almost parity with the Easter candle.

In the next chapter, we will show that as early as the fourth century, the Easter candle emerged as the principal feature of the *Lucernarium* of Holy Saturday in the region of Northern Italy. Before we survey the early evidence for the Candle, two questions remain to be considered. (i) Why was the lamp of the *Lucernarium* replaced by a candle of beeswax as the means of illumination for the reader? (ii) Why did this development first take place in Northern Italy?

Since the origin of the Easter candle is shrouded in obscurity, it is perhaps understandable why liturgical commentators in the past have, without exception, avoided addressing themselves directly to answering the first question. It seems unlikely that the Easter candle was borrowed from a pagan religious milieu with a comparable ritual or that it was suggested by such features of pre-Christian worship as sky-pillars[9] or sacred trees.[10] The view that a large candle was used in order to provide a great light for the reader of the lessons merely side-steps the issue. For apart from the fact that there is no evidence to suggest that in the fourth century the Easter candle was especially large, a lamp of considerable dimensions would have been equally suitable for this purpose.

A clue to the solution of this problem may be provided by the internal evidence of the songs composed in honour of the Easter candle, the Prefaces. Now, it is true that there are prominent references and allusions to the Passover, to Baptism, and to the Resurrection in all the Prefaces; but the pre-eminent theme is the praise of the Candle itself and the sig-

[8]1768 Missal p.125.
[9]Cook, *Zeus* Vol.2 pp.36ff.
[10]Duval, *Les Dieux de la Gaule* pp.116–17.

nificance of this source of light. When we turn to study the two surviving *benedictiones cerei* of Ennodius, we discover that in addition to the allusion to the bees and the generation of beeswax, which is common to all the Prefaces, the composition of the Candle is for him of profound significance. In both *laudes,* he identifies the three constituent elements of the Candle, namely, the wax, the wick, and the light.

> (a) Elements, joined together in triple partnership, are united by the bond of an almost mystical fellowship. The virgin-born bee has prepared the wax for her nectareous parturition; the water has produced the papyrus for the sustenance of the fire; and light is admitted from the sky.

> (b) We offer to you, O Lord, a torch composed of elements to be revered, a union of three gifts : one, which from the plants of the rivers enables the fuel for the flames to burn, and another, which the unsullied fertility of the bees provides. Fire, sent from the sky, is also added.[11]

For Ennodius it is not the physical elements in themselves which are important; it is the hallowing of them by the direct intervention of God in the historical process of redemption recorded in Scripture. For the wax, produced parthenogenetically by bees—so it was believed—symbolised Jesus' birth from a pure virgin; the papyrus, which served as a wick in the Candle, grew in river-water, the element hallowed by Jesus through His own baptism; and the silent flame recalled the

---

[11](a) species trino conpaginatae consortio societatis propemodum mysticae glutino coniunguntur, quarum *ceram* paravit nectariis partubus feta virginitatis, *papyrum* ad alimenta ignium lympha transmisit, *lumen* adhibetur e caelo. (b) venerandis compactam elementis facem tibi, Domine, mancipamus in qua trium copula munerum . . . unum, quod de *fetibus fluminum* adcedunt nutrimenta flammarum : aliud quod apum *tribuit* interemerata fecunditas . . . *ignis* etiam caelo infusus adhibetur. The excerpts are from Preface I and Preface II, respectively. Pinell, *La Benedicció* p.93 and p.95. (The writer's italics.) The text is also in Hartel pp.415–22. In the latter passage *fetibus fluminum,* 'the produce of rivers', refers to the papyrus, which was obtained from the River Nile and the marshes of Egypt.

Burning Bush with its foliage still intact. The Easter candle, therefore, represents the God-hallowed material world, and by extension the whole of creation, which as a result of the Incarnation and the advent of end-time following the Resurrection, has now become potentially redeemable. Therefore, the offering of the Candle, this microcosm of the world, would symbolise and once more re-enact the union of heaven and earth in anticipation of the final redemption of all creation at the close of the Age, and reinforce the eschatological theme of the paschal liturgy. This union of human and divine is twice referred to explicitly in the Romano-Gallican Preface of the Tridentine Missal :

> A night in which heavenly things are united to those of earth. That this Candle may be mingled with heavenly lights.[12]

The latter reference, of which there is also an echo in the Beneventan Preface,[13] underlines and reinforces the importance of the Candle; and the eschatological significance of this particular source of light largely explains why a candle composed of beeswax was used, in preference to an oil-lamp, as the medium for the offertory of light in the Vigil liturgy.

It is very likely that its shape was not an inconsiderable factor in the adoption of a candle for the provision of light at the liturgy of Holy Saturday. For in contrast with a lamp, the column of wax provided a much more vivid and realistic symbol of the pillar of fire that featured prominently at the paschal vigil.

Any attempt to account for the Northern Italian provenance of the Easter candle must remain speculative in our present state of knowledge. This part of Italy was not especially noted for apiculture or for the production of a superior quality of beeswax.

---

[12]Nox in qua terrenis coelestia, humana divine coniunguntur *and* Ut Cereus iste . . . supernis luminaribus misceatur.

[13]Pinell, *La Benedicció* p.96.

B. EARLIEST REFERENCES

It would seem that the lighting and blessing of the Easter candle is a purely western liturgical development, and the earliest references to the ritual strongly suggest a geographical provenance in Northern Italy. The earliest reference to the Easter candle occurs in a letter,[14] written by Jerome in 384, to a deacon named Praesidius in the church at Piacenza. Praesidius had previously asked Jerome to compose a *carmen cerei* for him, but Jerome is unwilling to comply for two main reasons. His first objection is to the style of language which he is expected to use in composing this song of praise. Previous writers had used a florid form of language reminiscent of the fourth book of Virgil's *Georgics*.[15] This is all very soothing on the ear, says Jerome, but it is not in keeping with the office of a deacon, especially as on these occasions ecclesiastical superiors are listening in silence to a minister who does not possess sacerdotal authority; nor with the sacraments of the Church; nor with the season of Easter. His other and principal objection is to the whole notion of the ceremony involving the Easter candle. Anticipating in a way some of the reformers of the sixteenth century, he claims that the ceremony and some of its features are unscriptural. 'Read the Old Testament', he fulminates. 'There is no instance of the use of wax.[16] And where can you find a reference in the New Testament to a wax taper?' Elsewhere in the letter, he refers to the whole proceedings as a 'rather vulgar ritual'.

We must bear in mind, when assessing the evidence of Jerome, that in many ways he was not typical of his age. Therefore, we must disregard his undisguised antipathy to this ceremony and try to evaluate the evidence in an unbiased way.

---

[14]Epistola ad Praesidium : *de Cereo paschali* (PL 30.188–89).

[15]Interestingly, Virgil was born near Mantua, only 55 miles from Piacenza.

[16]The use of candles in Palestine was not widespread in pre-Christian times.

Four conclusions emerge. (i) At Eastertide in Piacenza, there existed a ritual involving the use of a wax candle, at which a *carmen cerei* was sung by way of a benediction. (ii) It had become traditional to compose the song in a recognised poetic style. (iii) The allusions in the *carmen* to bees and honey and beeswax, to which Jerome took so much exception, strongly suggest that the content and theme of these fourth-century *laudes cerei* were similar to those of the later extant examples. (iv) It was the officiating deacon who was responsible for the singing, though not necessarily the composition, of the *carmen* and who occupied a position of prominence during the ceremony, a feature of the rite that has survived to this day.

The existence of a recognised style of composition shows that the use of the wax-candle at the Easter vigil was well-established at Piacenza, and almost certainly at Milan, into whose liturgical orbit Piacenza and other cities in Northern Italy came. Indeed, Jerome, who was himself born at Strido near Aquileia, was clearly familiar with the ceremony, even if he found it distasteful. His sneer suggests that the rite was popular, and this may well indicate that it had been in existence for a number of years. Lack of evidence, however, prevents us from assigning even a rough date to the first appearance of the ceremony. Moreover, the situation is complicated by the fact that the use of the Easter candle emerged within the context of the well-established *Lucernarium,* so that even a date in the earlier part of the fourth century must remain conjectural.

The next firm evidence for the ceremony comes from St Augustine. His own words that he had written a short *carmen* in praise of the Easter candle clearly shows that he was familiar with this paschal ritual and may well have actively participated in it on one occasion.[17] The composition of his *laus cerei* must have been undertaken before 391, when he was still a deacon, since in that year he was consecrated bishop. We are

---

[17]Quod in laude quadam Cerei breviter versibus dixi. *De Civitate Dei* 15.22.

not told where the *carmen* was sung; but it may have been on the occasion of his visit to Milan, where we have suggested this paschal ceremony was well-known. However, it may have taken place in North Africa. It is unfortunate that we possess no evidence for the Easter candle in that region, unless Augustine's words are applicable to North Africa.

Indicative of the popularity of the ceremony and also of its early appearance in Central Italy is the decree of Pope Zosimus (417–418) :

> Per parrocia (sic) concessa licentia cereum benedici.[18]

It was generally[19] believed in subsequent centuries, solely on the strength of this statement, that the ceremony surrounding the Easter candle had been instituted throughout the churches of the West, except Rome, by this pope. However, we have already observed that the rite was well-established in Northern Italy in the fourth century. It was assumed that *paroccia* referred to the dioceses outside Rome and that the Church of Rome at this time was powerful enough to influence and even sanction the liturgies of other churches in the West.[20] The earliest evidence for the blessing of the Easter candle within the Cathedral of St John Lateran dates only from the tenth century.[21]

As additional evidence for the continuity, if not the provenance, of the ceremony in Northern Italy, there survive the two *laudes cerei* written at the beginning of the sixth century by Ennodius, who became Bishop of Pavia in 517.[22] Pope

---

[18]'Permission was granted to bless the Candle throughout the *parishes.'* (The writer's italics.) Liber Pontificalis I p.225.

[19]Amalarius, *Lib.Off.* I.18.1; Sicardus, *Mitrale* (PL 213.323B); *PR XII* (*PRMA* I xxxii.8 p.240); Durandus, *Rationale* VI.80 fol.350.

[20]For the attitude of the Church of Rome towards local customs elsewhere during the pontificate of St Gregory, see Chapter 14 n.10. For other interpretations of *paroccia,* see Appendix 15.

[21]*PRG* II p.97. Interestingly, the institution of the Easter candle according to the 1507 Missal of Salzburg (fol.xciiii), which derives directly from *PRG,* is attributed to Pope Gelasius (492–496).

[22]Pinell, *La Benedicció* pp.92–95 (Hartel's text). Also in PL 63.258–62.

Gregory also, writing *c.*595 to Marinianus, Bishop of Ravenna, has occasion to refer to the blessing of the Easter candle as performed in that northern Italian city.[23]

Evidence for the use of the Easter candle in the East is wanting. Feasey produces no corroborative evidence to support his extravagant claim : 'The rite [*of the Easter candle*] undoubtedly came from the East, either from Jerusalem or Antioch.'[24] Dendy would see a possible origin for the Easter candle in the East.[25] He adduces in support of his suggestion the statement of F.C.Burkitt : 'The Saturday of Annunciation has been the name of Easter Eve or Holy Saturday among the Jacobites ever since the middle of the sixth century : no doubt the name is derived from some "announcement" of Easter tidings corresponding to the Western *Exultet.*'[26] All this is clearly conjecture and guesswork. Neither can attempts to see any connection between the Easter candle and Constantine's lavish display of street illumination in Constantinople be taken seriously.[27] It is true that Egeria's evidence is ambiguous; for she wrote *c.*380 of the liturgy of the Church in Jerusalem that 'they keep the Vigil like us'.[28] If it could be shown that the Easter candle was known in Spain, Egeria's probable homeland, in the last quarter of the fourth century, it could be argued, as Thurston does, that it was a feature of the Jerusalem liturgy at that time.[29] However, there is no mention of the Easter candle by the Christian Spanish poet Prudentius, who wrote some twenty years after Egeria's visit to Jerusalem, in any of his poems; and in view of the fact that the Easter candle is so significant a liturgical feature, whose symbolism readily lends itself to poetic composition, his silence would seem to

[23]*Epistle* XI.33 (PL 77.1146).
[24]*The Paschal Candle* p.353.
[25]*The Use of Lights* p.131.
[26]In *JTS* (1923) p.425.
[27]Eusebius, *Vita Constantini* 4.22 (PL 20.1169).
[28]Wilkinson, *Egeria's Travels* p.138.
[29]*The Exultet* p.514.

be conclusive for its absence from the rites of Spain at that time. The earliest firm evidence for the Easter candle in Spain comes from the year 633.[30]

[30]Fourth Council of Toledo, Canon 9 (PL 84.369B).

Chapter Twenty-two

THE EASTER CANDLE : PREPARATION, COMPOSITION, COST, AND SIZE

A. PREPARATION, COMPOSITION, AND COST

Our sources tell us little about the preparation of the Easter candle. At Gembloux, it was set up after Sext on Holy Saturday.[1] However, at Barking Abbey, the Candle was prepared on Good Friday, and at Fleury on Monday of Holy Week.[2] At the two last-mentioned monasteries, it was necessary to inscribe the insignia on the Candle in readiness for the Vigil.

Traditionally the Easter candle has been made of beeswax, as the Preface following the *Exultet* proclaims. However, the advantages of beeswax, a more pleasant odour and a slower rate of combustion than tallow, are matched to some extent by its scarcity and inevitably its cost. Later in this chapter, we shall show how the use of the *Judas* to some extent curtailed excessive expense. At Lyon, the use of a wooden or metal Easter candle with a *bougie* inserted in a socket at its upper end was forbidden.[3] However, in some of the large churches

[1]Albers II p.99.
[2]HBS 65 p.101 and Novarinus p.17, respectively.
[3]1832 Ceremonial p.479.

of Paris in the last century, two Easter candles were used :
one was of wax, which was taken to the font; the other was
a tin or wooden candle-like fixture of great height placed in
the choir, which was supported by a large candlestick.[4]

The problem of obtaining candles of pure beeswax became
acute during the last century. For instance, in 1857, the Bishop
of Charleston in South Carolina asked Pope Pius IX for permission to use tallow candles because of the scarcity and price
of beeswax. 'Let the recent malpractice of making candles from
tallow be stopped', came the reply.[5] However, a decree of
the Sacred Congregation of Rites, dated 14 December 1904,
permitted the addition of other substances to the beeswax
provided that the proportion of beeswax was *in maxima parte*.[6]
Even then, some authorities still insisted on a beeswax content of 75%.[7] In the remote missions of *Oceania,* the use of
whale oil or blubber was allowed.

In England during the later Middle Ages, mention of the
charges for the preparation of the Easter candle is 'to be found
in every book of church accounts'.[8]

B. SIZE

It is not unreasonable to suppose that from its earliest appearance within the paschal liturgy, the Easter candle was always distinguishable from other candles by its size, however
modest the difference may have been. The first indication not
simply of its size but of its unusual size appears in the account of the fire that occurred in the Church of St Stephen
in Naples in the eighth century :

[4]Paschal col.333.
[5]Van der Stappen p.92 : Inductus abusus adhibendi candelas ex sevo
eliminetur.
[6]*DACSR. Maxima pars* was interpreted 65%.
[7]Van der Stappen p.89.
[8]Gasquet, *Parish Life* p.181. A useful list of churchwarden's accounts
is to be found on page xi of that work.

The Saviour's church, which is named after its founder, Stephanus, was destroyed by the fire of divine judgement. I weep as I write this. The Holy Candle stood extremely high as a mark of honour for the Lord's resurrection. It was customary for it to burn from the beginning of the blessing until the solemnities of the Masses on Easter Day were completed. During the night of one Holy Saturday, when the Candle was unattended as usual and all were resting, some drapery in the church caught fire; and after the fire had reached the roof, the whole building was eventually engulfed in flames.[9]

Mallardo refers to both the 'extraordinary length of the candle' and the height of the surviving column which had supported the Candle, and which he presumably had seen. However, even if the column does date back to the eighth century, there is no corroborative evidence to substantiate the claim that the Candle which caused the fire was of similar dimensions. The Easter candle at the not-too-distant Monastery of Monte Cassino was quite small; yet being atop a very tall stone column,[10] it could be said to be *'inormi mensura porrectus'* and was certainly impressive enough to honour the Lord's resurrection. In later Neapolitan practice, it was small enough to be carried in procession by the *cimiliarcha,* the cathedral treasurer.[11] Moreover, it is unlikely that the size of the candle envisaged by Mallardo had shrunk to quite the proportions of the port-

[9]Ecclesia Salvatoris, quae de nomine sui auctoris, Stephania vocitatur divino—quod flens dico—iudicio igne cremata est. Moris enim fuit, ut cereus sanctus, inormi mensura porrectus. propter dominicae resurrectionis honorem a benedictionis exordio usque ad alterius diei missarum expleta sollemnia non extingueretur. Nocte igitur quadam ipsius festivitatis, cum solito dimitteretur accensus, cunctis quiescentibus, ignis per aranearum forte congeriem in laquearia ipsius ecclesiae pervenit, et sic demum aestuavit in omne aedificium. *Gesta episcoporum Neapolitanorum* (Waitz's edition p.426). Text in Mallardo, *La Pasqua* p.22.

[10]Zarnecki p.17.

[11]The ceremonial of Holy Saturday according to the fourteenth-century Constitutions of John Orsini, in Mallardo, *La Pasqua* p.33.

able wax column of Orsini's *Constitutions,* even allowing for a reduction in its size as a result of the conflagration.[12]

An interval of more than two hundred years separates the incident at Naples from the palaeographic evidence of the *Exultet* rolls of Southern Italy. Even making allowances for some artistic licence in the execution of the detailed liturgical scenes, these eleventh-century and twelfth-century drawings record a considerable range in the size of the various Easter candles depicted. The above-mentioned Candle at Monte Cassino appears to measure between eighteen and twenty-four inches in height, and those at Bari and Mirabella about three feet,[13] whilst the Easter candle at Gaeta stands at about five feet from the ground.[14] All the Candles depicted in the rolls taper towards their apexes. Candles shaped in this way give the columns which support them a more aesthetically-satisfying termination; their lower centres of gravity give them greater stability; and their almost pointed ends render the wicks more accessible for kindling and less prone to inopportune failure and embarrassing extinction.

The practice of fashioning Easter candles of very large and, to the modern way of thinking, excessive proportions is well documented throughout the later Middle Ages and beyond, in both the cathedral and monastic (mainly Benedictine) liturgical traditions. Not all Benedictine houses, however, were extravagant in this respect. The Roman Church encouraged the use of a Candle of considerable proportions.[15] Feasey's statement that the Easter candle had of necessity to be of great size so as to last throughout the night vigil, is manifestly un-

---

[12]For us, the cause of the fire is a matter for speculation. The drapery or curtains (*aranearum congeries*—the meaning is uncertain) had caught fire and set the ceiling alight. The cloth could just as easily have been set on fire closer to the floor as at a point near the roof.

[13]Zarnecki p.17; Avery, *Plates XII* and *LVI.*

[14]Avery, *Plate XXX.*

[15]The *Caeremoniale Episcoporum* prescribes : Praeparetur cereus Paschalis *praegrandis* (II.27.1). The writer's italics.

true.[16] Some candles of very small proportions are able to burn for twenty-four hours.

At Lincoln, the Easter candle weighed forty-two pounds,[17] and those at Bury St Edmunds and in the Lateran Basilica both contained eighty pounds of wax,[18] whilst the use of *desuper* in the rubric of the Ordinal of Barking in connection with the fixing of the great candle in its candelabrum, seems to imply the hoisting and lowering of a great weight.[19] We are informed that at Westminster in 1558, the paschal column consisted of three hundredweight of wax.[20] The massive Easter candle which Emperor Maximilian presented to the church at Echternach in Luxembourg in 1512 weighed 354 pounds.[21] A seventeenth-century manual of Rouen, which recommended that the Easter candle should be *'grandioris formae'*, was given a generous interpretation in that city.[22] For at the beginning of the eighteenth century, it is recorded that not only was the Candle in Rouen Cathedral twenty-five feet in height, but that those in the Churches of St-Ouen, Notre-Dame de la Ronde, and St-Sauveur were also of a similar dimension.[23]

It is recorded that the Easter candle at Salisbury stood thirty-six feet high,[24] but the claims made for the colossal height of those at Durham and Norwich cannot be substantiated. The Candle at the former cathedral was probably not as tall as is generally believed, whilst the assertion by Feasey that the Easter candle at Norwich was as tall as that at Durham, that is, it almost reached to the roof of the cathedral, was based

[16]*Ancient English Holy Week Ceremonial* p.192.

[17]Bradshaw and Wordsworth II p.291.

[18]HBS 99 p.53 and Gavanti/Merati IV p.154, respectively. A solid beeswax candle of this weight could have the dimensions of 9'6"x5".

[19]HBS 65 p.97.

[20]Machyn p.169.

[21]Passmore p.216.

[22]1640 Ritual p.305.

[23]De Moléon p.318 and p.321.

[24]1508 Processional p.73.

on the mistaken belief that the circular aperture at the junction of the vault-ribs in one of the bays was used for lighting the wick of the Easter candle.[25]

Great care must be exercised when interpreting the statistical information relating to the height and weight of Easter candles. For instance, we learn that the Easter candle at Rouen stood twenty-five feet high and weighed forty pounds;[26] yet that at Seville, which stood only two feet higher, weighed fifteen hundred pounds.[27] It is clear from a comparison of these two sets of statistics that a number of factors must be taken into consideration in assessing the authenticity and value of the recorded data, before any firm conclusions can be reached. (i) There may be errors in the transmission of the text, or descriptions may contain oft-repeated mistakes which have not or cannot be verified. (ii) Heights, and sometimes weights, may be based on a visual assessment. (iii) Human nature is often prone to exaggeration, especially in situations in which large numbers are involved. (iv) Errors may occur when converting from one system of measurements to another. (v) The constitution of the Easter candle must be determined. (vi) The method of its manufacture and its composition must be known.

Of the six above-mentioned points for consideration, the last two probably account for most of the seeming discrepancies and exaggerations. Strictly speaking, the Easter candle consists only of a column of wax. However, a false candlestock, or *Judas,* may have been added below the Candle so as to increase the height of the Candle, and in some instances, to double its overall vertical dimension, thereby giving an impression of considerable loftiness. On the other hand, the candlestick may have been included in the estimation of the height of the Easter candle, especially if the former was columnar in design and of similar diameter to the Candle.

[25]*Ancient English Holy Week Ceremonial* p.193.
[26]Feasey, *ibidem* p.193.
[27]Doblado (p.299) records 80 arrobas. (1 arroba = 18.75 lbs avoirdupois).

Two aspects of the manufacture of the Easter candle deserve our attention. (i) The ratio of a candle's diameter to its height is disproportionate in that the halving of the former does not result in the doubling of the latter. For instance, the height of a candle measuring 9'11"x5" becomes 20'0" when the diameter is reduced, by only 1½, to 3½". (ii) The manufacture of very tall candles, especially those with a diameter insufficient to maintain the rigidity of the wax column, necessitated the insertion of a wooden (as at Bourges) or metallic core for a large section of its length in order to ensure its continuing vertical position.[28] It follows that the weight of the Candle would be substantially increased if its core were a metal rod of considerable diameter.

The great height of some Easter candles is also confirmed by a description of the manner in which they were lit. At Seville, a chorister climbed a gilt-iron mast which stood close to the Easter candle. At its summit was a railed-in platform, similar to a ship's crow's-nest, on a level with the top of the Candle. From this platform the Candle was both lit and trimmed, and the melted wax was also drawn off with a large iron ladle.[29] At the Lateran Basilica, a portable pulpit was wheeled into the church so that the deacon could light the Candle,[30] whilst at Durham, where we are informed the Easter candle was square, a long pole was kept in the triforium above the choir for the purpose of kindling.[31] At St Leonard's, Leau, also, where the candleholder was 5.68 metres high (18'7"), the deacon had to climb to the triforium for the same purpose.[32]

Since the Easter candle came to be fashioned in large dimensions either to represent the importance of the Resurrection

[28]Pascal col.333; 1838 Ceremonial of Lyon p.479. The insertion of a core also had the advantage of reducing the expense incurred by the use of beeswax, a costly raw material.

[29]Doblado p.299.

[30]Feasey, *The Paschal Preconium* p.254.

[31]The writer's interpretation of Fowler, *Notes on the Rites of Durham* p.9.

[32]Callewaert p.141.

or to symbolise the pre-eminence of the light of Christ, it is not surprising that the size and sturdiness of the holder were increased to counteract the increased weight superimposed thereon and to provide additional support. It also ensured that from an aesthetic point of view, the Candle and the candlestick maintained a satisfactory relationship with each other; and at the same time underlined even more forcefully the importance of the person and the event it commemorated.

Either the Easter candle was supported by a metal candelabrum, frequently of exquisite craftsmanship; or it rested on the top of a stone column, often embellished with suitably-appropriate sculptures and other decorations.[33] The use of the column to elevate the Candle is first reliably attested at Monte Cassino in the eleventh century;[34] but as we have suggested at the beginning of this chapter, a column may have been in use at Naples in the eighth century. There can be little doubt that its use in the paschal liturgy of the Romano-Gallican tradition was suggested by the reference in the Preface following the *Exultet* to the pillar of fire in the Book of Exodus,[35] and by the identification of the Easter candle with that pillar.[36] The significance of the column in this respect is noted by Macri.[37]

The great height of the column or candelabrum, rendering the Easter candle beyond the deacon's reach,[38] may in some instances account for the absence of the five grains of incense in the ritual—at Durham possibly, for example—or explain why the grains were inserted into the Candle during the preparations for the Vigil, as, for example, at Barking.[39]

[33]Perhaps the finest are those at St Paul's-outside-the-Walls in Rome, and in the Baptistery in Florence.

[34]Zarnecki p.17

[35]*'Columnae illuminatione'*.

[36]*'Iam columnae huius praeconia novimus.'* In the Ambrosian Preface we read : *'ecce iam ignis columna resplendet.'*

[37]*Hierolexicon* p.142.

[38]At St-Maurice, Angers, it stood above 12' high. De Moléon p.60.

[39]HBS 65 p.101.

However, the problems created by the use of a lofty support for the Candle were not insuperable. The Gilbertine Ordinal and the Sarum Missal both permit the choice of inserting the grains of incense either into the Easter candle or into the candleholder,[40] whilst a Parisian handbook of ceremonial and a Polish manual both enjoin that ladders should be provided for this ritual act.[41]

Without specifying a maximum size for the Easter candle, the Roman Church recommended moderation in smaller churches, chiefly, one suspects, for the avoidance of unnecessary expense. Commentators on the Roman liturgy state that the Easter candle should appear larger than ordinary candles, and suggest a weight of between eight and ten pounds.[42] Somewhat paradoxically, the Easter candle in the Mother of Cathedrals weighed eighty pounds, as we have already noted. At Paris, twelve pounds of wax was used,[43] whilst in some churches the candle weighed thirty-three pounds to commemorate the traditional age of Jesus.[44] The above-mentioned Polish manual of Roman ceremonies also mentions the use of a 'rather long rod' for lighting the Easter candle in the event of its being very tall. However, since the candlestick was presumably included in the height, we can gain no indication of the vertical dimension of the Candle itself. In the Cistercian rite, whose ceremonial was characterised by austerity, the recommended weight of the Easter candle was three pounds.[45] It need hardly be added that in many instances the size of the Easter candle would have reflected the wealth of a church or monastery and at times would have been determined by the availability of beeswax.

[40]HBS 59 p.40 and 1515 Missal fol.cxi, respectively.
[41]1662 Ceremonial p.374 and 1819 Manual II p.478.
[42]Desideri p.150; Gavanti/Merati IV p.154; *DHCR* I p.470 (about 10 lbs).
[43]1662 Ceremonial p.374.
[44]Grancolas p.318; Gavanti/Merati IV p.154.
[45]1689 Ritual p.244.

Today, the Easter candle is distinguishable from other liturgical candles by its size; but both in height and in diameter, it is generally of very modest proportions. In Great Britain and Ireland, the Easter candle rarely exceeds thirty-six inches. In parts of France, however, the tradition of tall candles is still perpetuated to some extent, although the giant columns of old are no longer to be seen. Of the thirty-six cathedrals for which the writer has information, a Candle of at least one metre (thirty-nine inches) in height is used in thirty; and in eleven of these, the Candle stands at one and a half metres (fifty-eight inches).[46] The reduction in the size of the Easter candle in modern times has rendered some of the tall marble columns obsolete. Moreover, since the Candle is now borne into church in the procession from the new fire, the placing of it on the top of the tall shaft during the ceremony is now impracticable, as at Lyon. In that church, a portable iron candlestick is also used for the ease of carrying the Candle to the font for Baptism.

The Judas. In some churches, a desire to increase the height of the Easter candle, either to enhance its significance or to offset to some extent the need to use a small beeswax candle or simply to render it more conspicuous, resulted in the utilisation of a device known as the *Judas*. This was a shaft of wood shaped and painted to resemble a candle and attached to the base of the Easter candle, thus forming a lower false stock and so increasing the height of the Candle.[47] The latter was attached to the *Judas* by means of a spike protruding from the end of the *Judas* or by a spring of wire[48] or, one might reasonably suppose, by inserting the end of the Easter candle, neatly chamfered, into a socket at the top of the *Judas*. Sometimes the lower false candle of wood was coated with wax

---

[46]1984 Survey of France.

[47]The use of metal for this purpose is unknown.

[48]As at East Cheap in the fifteenth century. Feasey, *Paschal Candle* p.364.

rather than painted. The *Judas* at St Mary-at-Hill in London in 1511 weighed seven pounds.[49]

There is much uncertainty about the origin of the term *Judas*. W.Cooke traces the origin of the word to Hebrews 7:14 : Christ, typified by the Easter candle, sprang out of (the tribe of) Judah.[50] Alternatively, since it is said that the stocks of other candles were also called *Judases*,[51] the connection, if it is biblical, is more likely to have been with Judas Iscariot : his false nature and his sham relationship with Jesus.

[49]Peacock p.163. He refers to the destruction of these *Judases* in the early years of the reign of Queen Elizabeth I (pp.106,163,164).

[50]Cited by C.Wordsworth, *Medieval Services in England* p.168.

[51]There is a reference in the accounts of St Christopher-le-Stocks in 1488 to the wooden stocks for processional candles : 'vi judas staves for torches painted' (Freshfield p.119). The decorated *Judases* at Epworth in 1566, mentioned by Peacock (p.77), were probably stocks of this type, and not intended for use in supporting the Easter candle.

Chapter Twenty-three

THE POSITION
OF THE EASTER CANDLE

Apropos of the position in which the Easter candle stood prior to the chanting of the *Exultet,* two main traditions can be identified during the later Middle Ages. Both are discussed regardless of whether the Candle was borne in procession. For if the Candle had previously been carried in procession, it continued to be placed in the same position it had formerly been set in, once it was no longer borne into church.

(i) The Gallican Tradition

The placing of the Easter candle in front of the altar is implicitly attested in three Gelasian sacramentaries and in two other documents.[1] The relevant rubric, quoted at the beginning of Chapter 24, which describes the arrival of the archdeacon *ante altare,* leaves us in little doubt that the Easter candle was also in this position. Since it is also known from five *ordines* that there were seven lamps in front of the altar,[2] it is not clear whether the Easter candle was placed between them and the altar or whether it stood to the west of those lamps.

[1]*GeV* p.68; *GeAng* p.52; *GePr* p.55; OR 30A.15; Gradual of St Gregory, cited in Schelstrate II p.142.
[2]OR 26.9; OR 28.30; OR 29.17; OR 31.13; OR 32.5.

However, the slightly later *Pontificale Romano- Germanicum (PRG)*, which also mentions the seven lamps, expands the rubric by adding *in medio ecclesiae* 'in the middle of the church' and clarifies the description of the Candle's position by adding that the clergy and the people gather around it.[3] Presumably, the seven lamps remained outside the circle formed by the congregation.[4] A number of documents state that the Easter candle was placed in front of the altar without indicating whether the location was in the sanctuary or in the choir. At Soissons, it was placed in the sanctuary; and according to the Cistercian rite, it stood on the sanctuary step.[5] It is possible that in some instances the rubric was left deliberately vague so as to allow some flexibility of position. Martène, writing at the beginning of the eighteenth century, mentions the sanctuary steps as one of the possible locations for the Easter candle.[6]

The practice of placing the Easter candle in the centre of the choir survived in France well into the nineteenth century, as *Table 47a* shows, and was re-established in the Roman rite following the liturgical changes of 1955. It is usual today to leave the Candle in the choir only for the duration of the Vigil and subsequently to remove it to the sanctuary or to the ambo if one exists. However, practice is flexible. Sometimes the

---

[3]The suburbicarian variant of *PR XII* has a similar phrase qualifying *ante altare* (*PRMA* I p.240).

[4]The twelfth-century Ritual of Soissons would appear to be exceptional in this respect (*DAER* 4.24 p.161 [M 305]). According to this servicebook, the Easter candle stood in the middle of the sanctuary, and the seven-branched candlestick was placed on the sanctuary step (*ad ascensum presbyterii*). It is unlikely that the middle candle of this *menorah* and the Easter candle were one and the same since we are informed that a lectern was placed next to the Candle; but its position between the altar and the *menorah* poses the interesting question of how visible the Easter candle and the officiating deacon were to the congregation, assuming that the seven-branched candelabrum was of no mean proportions.

[5]1689 Ritual p.244. In fact, the middle step, from which the Abbot gave his blessing.

[6]*DAER* 4.24.8 p.147.

Candle remains where it was blessed. At times, it is placed conveniently near the font, to be lit at the ministration of Baptism.

(ii) The Italian Tradition

Although the practice was not confined exclusively to the churches of Italy—see *Table 47b*—the placing of the Easter candle next to the ambo almost certainly had its origin in that country. The earliest evidence is palaeographic : the *Exultet* rolls of Southern Italy provide vivid testimony for the practice from the tenth to the twelfth centuries.[7] Indeed, the medieval ambo, together with its column or holder for the Easter candle, survives in a number of Italian churches, especially in the South. The choice of this position was perhaps inevitable since the prophecies, an important element in the paschal vigil, were read from this raised platform, so that the juxtaposition of the Candle and the Bible emphasised the link and visibly expressed the close rapport that existed between the Light of Christ and the Word of God.

Documentary confirmation for the ambo-position of the Easter candle is found in an eleventh-century Beneventan ritual[8] and in the twelfth-century *Monte Cassino A* and *Monte Cassino B*. Its position by the ambo is also enjoined by the twelfth-century *Pontificale Romanum (PR XII)* and other Roman service-books, including the Roman Missal of 1570, and by Guéranger in the nineteenth century, even though in some churches this custom was at variance with official directives. The Pian Missal of 1570, however, does not make recognition of or allowance for the fact that not all churches possessed an ambo. Ordo XIV, Ordo XV, and the 1474 *Missale Romanum* make mention of the *ornatum pulpitum* on which the missal was placed and next to which stood the Easter candle. The term almost certainly refers to the ambo, which in many Italian

[7]Avery, *Plates XII, XXX, XLIV,* and *LXXVIII.*
[8]Odermatt p.273.

churches was elegantly constructed and exquisitely adorned, and not to the *legile* or reading-desk, which was used of necessity for the *Exultet* and prophecies in churches which possessed no ambo. At Milan, the ambo was known as the *tribunum* (Beroldus p.110).

(iii) The Later Development

In the same way that the Book of the Gospels is regarded in the Orthodox tradition as a verbal icon of Christ, the column of wax and the flame of the Easter candle that symbolised the Word of God in the Trinity came to be identified closely with the reading of that Word in the Gospel lection. Hence, at the Gospel of the first Mass of Easter, the customary honorific lights accompanying the written Word were, and indeed still are, dispensed with, since the Light of the Gospel was held to be visibly present in the flame of the Easter candle. In churches which possessed an ambo from which the Gospel was read, this had always been the practice. Elsewhere, the Gospel was read to the north of the altar—to its left as one faces it. The earliest evidence for the Easter candle being set in this position is found in the Sarum rite of the thirteenth century.[9] Attestation of the practice in the Dominican rite, though from a later period, would suggest that the ceremonial of the Black Friars had influenced the English rite in this respect.[10]

The Gospel position is also found in Spain at Seville and was also a feature of the Mozarabic rite;[11] and Baldeschi and De Vert both mention that this was the usual position for the Easter candle.[12] The position is also found in a number of

[9]See *Table* 47c for references and other instances of this position.

[10]The Sarum rite contained other Dominican influences, for example, the reckoning of Sundays after Trinity, rather than after Pentecost as in the Roman rite.

[11]Martène, *DAER* 4.42 p.164.

[12]*Ceremonial* p.271 and *Explication* IV p.133.

French diocesan rites, some permitting the alternative position of *in medio choro*. Paschal, commenting on this very aspect of the ritual, states that the position on the Gospel side was found in country districts.[13] It is likely that in many small country churches, a central position in the choir was not always suitable. This consideration may have been in the minds of the compilers of the Ordinal of Nidaros, which prescribes that the Easter candle should be set 'in a convenient place'.[14]

The Easter candle was also set at the Gospel side of the altar at the conclusion of the Preface at Limoges, at Milan, and at Biasca and other Swiss towns which followed the Ambrosian rite.[15] In some churches, of both the Roman and Milanese traditions, in which the use of the ambo fell into desuetude, the Easter candle was set in this position before the start of the service,[16] and the *Exultet* was proclaimed and the prophecies read from a sanctuary lectern.

Paschal also mentions that the Candle was sometimes placed at the Epistle side of the altar.[17] Examples of this position occur at St Mary-in-Trastevere in Rome and in the Florentine baptistery. Other authors record only slight variations of position. De Vert refers to the Easter candle at the altar rail in some churches; and De Moléon informs us that at Rouen Cathedral, the Candle formerly stood between the Tomb of Charles V and the three sanctuary lamps.[18]

[13]*La Liturgie* col.329.

[14]*ONE* p.232. This directive may have been partly determined by the existence of small churches in the more remote parts of this far-flung diocese, which in addition to the whole of Norway, included Iceland, Greenland, and the Isle of Man.

[15]1830 Missal p.227; Beroldus pp.111–12 and King, *PLS* p.359; King, *Holy Week* p.98.

[16]Baldeschi p.271 and King, *LPS* p.359.

[17]*La Liturgie* col.329.

[18]*Explication* IV p.133 and *Voyages* p.318, respectively.

Church/Document	Source
PRG	II §346 p.98
Corbie	PL 78.336B
Alcuin	PL 101.1216B
Paris	1662 Cerem. p.374
Maison du Roy	*Sem. Sainte* p.401
Sées	1742 Missal p.185
Mende	1766 Missal p.199
St-Bertrand	1773 Missal p.209
Tours	1784 Missal p.191
La Rochelle	1835 Missal p.186
Autun	1845 Missal p.238

Table 47a. The Easter candle in the centre of the choir

Beneventum	Odermatt p.273
Milan	Beroldus p.110
Rome (12 C)	*PRMA* I p.239
Monte Cassino A	*PRMA* I p.292
Monte Cassino B	*PRMA* I p.293
Apamea	*DAER* 4.24 p.160
Ordo XIV	PL 78.1218C
Ordo XV	PL 78.1322A
MR 1474	HBS 17 p.175
Strasbourg	*DAER* 4.24 p.162
Chalons	1748 Missal p.178

Table 47b. The Easter candle at the ambo

Salisbury	HBS 91 p.22
Dominicans	1482 Missal fol.89
Vallombrosa	1503 Missal fol.xcii
Camaldolese	1634 Cerem. p.82
Amiens	1745 Missal p.182
Soissons	1745 Missal p.163
Carcassonne	1749 Missal p.194
Seville	Doblado p.299
Coutances	1825 Cerem. p.329
Verdun	1832 Cerem. p.313

Table 47c. The Easter candle at the Gospel side of the altar

Church/Document	Source
Périgueux	1782 Missal p.158
Le Puy	1783 Missal p.159
Metz	1829 Missal p.158
Toulouse	1832 Missal p.205

Table 47d. The Easter candle in the choir or at the Gospel side

Reg. Conc.	PL 137.494C
Gembloux	Albers II p.99
Vallombrosa	Albers IV p.249
Rome (Suburbic.)	*PRMA* I p.240
Soissons	*DAER* 4.24 p.161
Naples	Mallardo p.33
Mainz	1507 Missal fol.xcii
Aquileia	1519 Missal fol.91
Cistercians	1689 Ritual p.244
Angers	De Moléon p.80
Cahors*	1760 Missal p.172
Vienna†	1782 Missal p.214

*Or outside the sanctuary.
†Outside the sanctuary.

Table 47e. The Easter candle in front of the altar

Chapter Twenty-four
THE EASTER CANDLE
AND THE SIGN OF THE CROSS

(i) The Sign of the Cross Made with a Gesture of the Hand

The consecration of the Easter candle is first attested in the eighth-century Gelasian Sacramentary :

> The archdeacon comes in front of the altar, takes a light from the fire that was hidden on Good Friday, and, after making the sign of the cross over the candle, lights it. Then he completes the blessing of the Candle.[1]

This rubric is found with only slight variations of wording in two other Gelasian sacramentaries and the Sacramentary of Reims, and in two other documents.[2] That the act of consecration was achieved by making the sign of the cross is not in doubt; what is not clear is the manner in which this was done. Rabotin, followed by Capelle, suggests that it was achieved either by the archdeacon's hand raised in the act

---

[1]Veniens archidiaconus ante altare, accipiens de lumine quod vi feria absconsum fuit, faciens crucem super cereum, et illuminans eum. Et completur ab ipso benediction cerei. *GeV,* Mohlberg p.68 §425. The document is a Frankish recension of a Roman book, and the ceremonial described here relates to the Gallican Church.

[2] Angoulême p.52; Prague p.55; PL 78.336B; OR 30A.15; and the Gradual of St Gregory, cited by Schelstrate II p.142.

of benediction or with his hand holding the small candle which had been lit from the reserved fire and with which the Easter candle was kindled.[3] Both cite the practice at Poitiers *c.*900[4] and the custom observed by a number of bishops of the Greek Orthodox Church of performing this act of benediction with a lighted candle in their hand.[5] However, the absence of any reference in any of the above-mentioned documents to a small candle and to the sign of the cross being made in this way makes this argument difficult to sustain, although the silence of the rubrics is not conclusive in view of the fact that there are other details of the ritual which are unrecorded.

There is no good reason to doubt that the primitive practice was to make the sign of the cross with a simple gesture of the hand. An alternative reading in Ordo 30A adds *manu sua* to the phrase *faciens crucem super cereum* by way of clarification.[6] However, it is possible that the latter phrase without the additional *manu sua* in some instances came to be interpreted as an injunction to incise a cross into the wax of the Easter candle. For (i) the incision of a cross did eventually replace the tracing of one manually in most churches, and (ii) the very fact that the adjectival phrase in the above-mentioned reading of Manuscript R is qualified by *manu sua* may suggest that *super cereum* was capable of two interpretations. In classical Latin *super* bore the meaning of 'above', 'over', or 'on top of' regardless of whether physical contact was involved.[7] The preposition *in,* on the other hand, was normally employed to convey the notion of one object resting upon another. In later Latin, *super* was regularly used to express the higher position of one object in relation to another with physical contact, as in *super virgam, super caput,* and *super*

---

[3]*Les Grains d'Encens* p.224 and *Le rite de cinq grains* p.5, respectively.

[4]*Poitiers* p.215.

[5]Rabotin, however, has reservations: 'J'hesite cependant a interpreter le geste Gelasien par la rubrique poitevine' (p.225).

[6]OR 30A.15, Manuscript R.

[7]The use of *super* in the latter sense is found in Gregory's letter to Marinianus : *preces quae super cereum . . . dici solent.* PL 77.1146.

candelabrum. Even in modern French, *sur* may mean 'on' and 'above' or 'over'. The incision of a cross on the Easter candle, therefore, may have been partly the result of this somewhat ambiguous rubric. The writer has suggested below an instance of where the Candle may have been marked with a visible cross.

In the rubric quoted at the beginning of this chapter, there is no indication of any formula of benediction before the Easter candle was lit and prior to the chanting of the *Exultet.* Now, in addition to this initial consecratory gesture, the Sacramentary of Prague also records that the sign of the cross was made with the hand once during the *Exultet* and once during the Preface.[8] The performing of the two additional gestures raises the possibility that the initial cross was actually cut into the surface of the beeswax, the two subsequent gestures serving to reinforce or confirm that which had been visibly incised. The *Pontificale Romano-Germanicum (PRG),* with its synthesised ceremonial, records a hand-gesture over the candle at the new fire (II p.95 §342) and an incision prior to the lighting of the Candle (p.97 §346) followed by a hand-gesture at *incensi sacrificium vespertinum* during the Preface (p.98 §347).

Although the incision of the cross in the Easter candle was adopted by most churches, the tracing of a cross with the hand in the air survived at Vallombrosa,[9] and at Basel[10] where a choice of performing or omitting this act of benediction was given during the Preface. On the other hand, at Nidaros in the early thirteenth century, the deacon was forbidden to raise his hand during the Preface,[11] either because this action was considered to be a superfluous duplication of the act of benediction or perhaps because the deacon was held to be acting *ultra vires* in appropriating to himself the sacerdotal authority of which the making of the sign of the cross was expressive.

[8]At *sancti + huius* and *cereus + iste,* respectively. *GePr* p.55 §95. The Sacramentary of Gellone also attests the latter gesture. *GeGe* p.95 §678C.

[9]1503 Missal fol.xcv : at *in honore nominis tui* of the Preface.

[10]1488 Missal fol.xcii : at *cereus iste sit benedictus* of the Preface.

[11]*ONE* p.233. At the words *cereus iste sit benedictus.*

(ii) The Sign of the Cross Made by Incision

In the same way that there is some uncertainty over the interpretation of the phrase *super cereum,* so there exists some doubt about the precise meaning of the preposition *in* as it occurs in the phrases *in cereo* and *in eo* [= *cereo*]. For in classical as well as in medieval Latin, this preposition may be translated into English either as 'in' in the sense of 'existing within' or 'inserted in', or as 'on' in the sense of 'lying on' or 'on the surface of'. The sign of the cross made *in cereo* in the latter sense implies either a tracing with the finger or thumb which leaves no visible mark upon the wax, or a cruciform anointing with oil or chrism which leaves a visible cross on the candle, however faint, against the pale background of the beeswax. A cross made *in cereo* in the former sense ensures that a permanently visible mark will be incised into the candle.

In the tenth-century Antiphonary of Léon we read : (After he has been given the candle)[12]

> Faciens episcopus in ipso cereo A et Ω.

Now, whilst the possibility should not be ruled out completely that this cross was traced with chrism, the addition of the two Greek letters would suggest that both the cross and the letters were designed to be visible to the faithful, once the Candle had been mounted in a prominent position, and that all three markings were incised into the wax of the Candle. This view is reinforced by the omission of any reference to the use of chrism in the rubrics, which are quite detailed.

According to the contemporary *PRG,* a cross was the only marking on the Candle.[13] Again, there is no mention of chrism, and its use for the purpose of making the cross seems unlikely. It is tempting to see the rubric as evidence for the *incision* of a cross as opposed to one effected by chrismation, in view of the contemporary practice at Corbie, described be-

---

[12]Page 280. 'The bishop, making this cross *on* the Candle . . . . '

[13]*Archidiaconus . . . facit crucem in eo,* 'The archdeacon . . . makes a cross on it.' *PRG* II §346 p.97.

low, and in view of the subsequent practice of the Roman
Church, as recorded in later service-books.[14] It must be borne
in mind, however, that liturgical practice in the tenth century varied markedly even within the confines of a small area;
and the later Roman evidence of the twelfth century should
not necessarily be regarded as corroborative for the practice
of two centuries earlier.

The tenth-century Sacramentary of Corbie also records :

> Let them make a cross on the Candle out of incense, and let
> the year of the Lord be inscribed and the letters A and *Ω*.[15]

In the next chapter we will argue that a cross had been incised prior to and in readiness for the reception of the five
grains of incense. It is difficult to believe that at Gembloux
in the eleventh century, the pre-traced cross on the Candle
was not incised.[16] Similarly, the Customary of the German
Monasteries and *Alcuin* both record the presence of a cross
on the Candle, which is almost certain to have been incised.[17]
Apropos of the above-mentioned Mozarabic evidence from
Léon, there is no mention or suggestion of the use of chrism
for this purpose; and the incision of other marks on the Candle
makes it almost certain that the cross had also been engraved.

The earliest indisputable references to the incision of the
cross are to be found in the two Roman documents referred
to above. That contained in the twelfth-century *Pontificale
Romanum (PR XII)* relates to the ceremony as observed in the
suburbicarian churches of Rome. They state :

> He incises a cross in the Candle with a stiletto *and*
> (let him set the Candle in position) and let him inscribe a cross
> on it.[18]

[14]*PRMA* I pp.240–41 (Suburbicarian variant); *OEL* p.60.
[15]Faciant crucem de incenso in cereo in cereo et scribatur annus Domini, atque A et *Ω*. PL 78.336B
[16]Albers II p.99.
[17]Albers V p.38 and PL 101.1216B, respectively. Both date from *c.*1000.
[18] Cum stylo facit crucem in ipso cereo *(PR XII) and* (erigat cereum)
scribatque in eo crucem *(OEL).*

In both instances, it is the duty of the officiating deacon to carve the cross during the ceremony and in the presence of the congregation, in the same way that the sign of the cross was made by the archdeacon according to the Gelasian sacramentaries or by the bishop at Léon. According to an alternative tradition, the cross was incised before the ceremony began. This is attested in three of the documents we have already met,[19] and it can also be inferred with confidence at Rouen in the eleventh century and in those Benedictine monasteries which followed strictly the regulations prescribed by Lanfranc.[20] At Barking at the beginning of the fifteenth century, the cross was incised on Good Friday along with the chronological information.[21] This would suggest that it was incised as much to provide guidelines for the insertion of the grains of incense as to convey to an onlooker the fact that the Easter candle had been consecrated. For the cruciform arrangement of the five grains now provided this indication of the Candle's consecration and so rendered the incision of a cross a preliminary act prior to the insertion of the grains. Moreover, the practice of gouging the five holes in the Candle for the reception of the grains made the cutting of a cross completely dispensable even for the purpose of providing guidelines.

In the Milanese rite, the presence of a cross upon the Easter candle is first attested in the Ambrosian Missal of 1560 (fol.113). There is no reference to it in earlier missals of that rite. Since it was inscribed before the start of the ceremony and mentioned only in conjunction with the insertion of the grains of incense—which in that rite then occurred after the

---

[19]Namely, Sacramentary of Corbie, the Customary of Sigibert, and the Customary of the German Monasteries. PL 78.336B, Albers II p.99 and V p.38.

[20]*Acta Vetera* (PL 147.176C) and *Decrees* (PL 150.446D). According to both documents, the insertion of the grains of incense formed part of the preparation of the Easter candle.

[21]HBS 65 p.101.

conclusion of the Preface—its primary purpose may have been functional : to indicate the spatial disposition of the grains.[22]

The surviving evidence would therefore suggest that the incision of a cross on the Easter candle was a development of the earlier practice of tracing a cross with the hand in the air, a concretisation of the manual gesture, analogous perhaps to the materialisation of the incensation of the Easter candle which resulted in the implantation in the wax of the five grains of incense in a cruciform arrangement.

(iii) The Sign of the Cross Made with Fire

In the Pontifical of Poitiers of *c.*900 we read (p.215) :

> When he [the deacon] has approached the Easter candle, he bows towards the altar, and making the sign of the cross three times with the candle on the reed in front of the Easter candle, he lights it.[23]

Dom B.Capelle has no hesitation in finding the antecedents of this practice in the rubrics of the Gelasian Sacramentary. His claim that '[i]l est manifeste que le Pontifical s'inspire du Sacramentaire' is based on doubtful linguistic similarities between the two sets of rubrics and on the fact that in both rites there was no physical contact between the consecrator of the Candle and the Candle itself. Inevitably there will be elements common to both rites, such as the tracing of the cross in the air and the lighting of the Candle; but liturgical development that may have taken place over the period of about 150 years, which separates the two documents, and the incorporation of elements, such as the serpent-shaped candle, drawn from different religious and cultural milieu, should

---

[22]At Milan, the marking of the cross was probably borrowed from the Roman rite, as were the five grains of incense.

[23]Qui dum propter cereum venerit, inclinans se ad altare et ter signum crucis de ipsa harundine cum candela accensa faciens contra cereum, inluminat eum.

make us wary of speaking of the dependence of the Pontifical upon the Sacramentary in this respect.

Although the practice of placing a lighted candle on a reed is also found in three earlier *ordines,* in the contemporary *PRG,* and in many later documents,[24] *Poitiers* alone records the use of this candle to trace a cross in the air in front of the Easter candle as a gesture of consecration. It is true that the rubrics of the Pontifical are much more detailed than those of the *ordines;* but in view of the silence of the latter documents on this point, we must conclude that the use of the lighted candle for forming the sign of the cross was unique to Poitiers.

(iv) The Use of Chrism for the Sign of the Cross

The marking of the Easter candle with a cross of chrism is found in two manuscripts relating to the Beneventan rite : the late tenth-century *Missale Antiquum* and a mid-eleventh-century gradual.[25] They both record that a cross was traced on the wax after the Candle had been lit, but before the cry of *Lumen Christi* and the singing of the *Exultet.* The practice is also found in the Diocese of Valence,[26] where the Easter candle was anointed shortly before the insertion of the five grains of incense. It is just possible that a survival of this ritual action is to be found in the rite of the Church of Lyon. There the grains of incense were first anointed with chrism before being inserted into the Candle. However, in the following chapter, we will suggest that this may have been done for another reason.

[24]For the refernces see *Table 40.*

[25]Beneventum MS VI.33 and Rome MS Vat.lat.10673, respectively. The text describing the kindling of the new fire and the lighting of the Easter candle is given in R.-J.Hesbert, *Antiphonale Missarum* p.188. H.M.Bannister, who claims (*Miscellanea Ceriani* p.135) that the Gradual was a fragment of an *ordo ambrosianus,* which preserved the ancient usage of the Milanese Church, has been shown to be in error (Hesbert, *ibidem* p.189). Hesbert's conclusion is apparently unknown to Dendy (*The Use of Lights* p.132).

[26]1504 Missal fol.lvi.

(v) The Origin and Significance of the Chrismal Cross

It is not difficult to see in this act of chrismation a situation analogous to the consecration of a church or altar in the Romano-Gallican rite, which is attested as early as the tenth century, in which the anointing of inanimate objects formed part of the ceremonial;[27] and just as the anointing of the altar and the walls of a church was commemorative of the blessing which they had received, so the chrismation of the Easter candle recalled its consecration by the deacon and corresponded to the cross either incised into the wax or delineated by the grains of incense in other western traditions. At the same time, the anointing of the Candle must also have been interpreted in a powerfully symbolic way in that it reinforced the intimate connection between the Easter candle and Baptism, recalling the chrismation of the baptizands.[28]

Capelle finds a reference to the origin of this practice in Prudentius' poem *Inventor rutili, dux bone, luminis,*[29] which dates from the late fourth or early fifth century and which was sung at the daily, or possibly weekly, office of the *Lucernarium*. He cites lines 155 and 156 :

> Lumen quod famulans offero suscipe (1.155)
> Tinctum pacifici chrismatis unguine (1.156)

and comments, 'The fine candle, which is going to illuminate the evening prayer, now that the sun's rays have disappeared, has therefore first been anointed with "peaceful chrism". This blessing forms part of the ritual, for it is quite difficult to understand this text in a purely symbolic and spiritual sense.

---

[27]*PRG* I : §52 p.144 for the anointing of the altar; §57 p.145 for the anointing of the walls of the church.

[28]Interestingly, the Ambrosian Preface contains a reference to baptismal chrismation at the point where the grains of incense were formerly inserted : *Christi vero populus insignitur fronte . . . chrismate* (1934 Missal t.e. p.40 of *Repertorium*). This invites speculation that the word *chrismate* may once have functioned as an internal rubric; and the anointing of the candle may have taken place at this juncture.

[29]Hymn V of the *Cathemerinon*. Cunningham's edition pp.23–28.

'Let us mark the first stage : anointing—obviously in the form of a cross—with holy chrism on the wax itself. It concerns the ordinary candle. All the more does the same apply to the Easter candle.'[30]

That the couplet refers to the office of the *Lucernarium* and in particular to the deacon's offering of light, as Capelle says, there can be little doubt; but Capelle's interpretation of the second line is open to question, and in particular the precise nature of the deacon's offering. Moreover, he assumes that the *Lucernarium,* of which the Spanish-born Prudentius treats, is that form of the service as found in Spain, whereas there is no firm evidence to support a claim that the form of this service which Prudentius had in mind was exclusively Spanish.[31] There are a number of reasons why Capelle's conclusions should be challenged.

(i) It is generally believed that the office of the *Lucernarium* derived its name from the fact that the lighting of a lamp *(lucerna)* and the offering of the light of that lamp formed the central features of that service. If this office was celebrated daily and if the lamp was anointed at each celebration, the use of a new lamp each day is implied since the act of chrismation in all liturgical situations is normally performed only once.[32] This difficulty and the belief that chrismation took

---

[30]*Le beau cierge qui va illuminer la prière du soir, maintenant que se sont éteintes les clartés du jour, a donc été préalablement oint du 'chrême pacifique'. Bénédiction rituelle, car il est bien difficile d'entendre ce texte au sens purement symbolique et spirituel.*

Marquons ce premier jalons : onction—en forme de croix évidement—avec le saint chrême, sur la cire elle-même. Il s'agit du cierge ordinaire. A plus forte raison en est-il ainsi du cierge pascal. (Le rite de cinq grains p.4)

[31]Thus Capelle. His discussion of the blessing of the Easter candle according to the Mozarabic rite in the very next paragraph begins 'En Espagne encore. . . . ' Admittedly, Prudentius was a Spaniard by birth and wrote poems about Spanish martyrs but Capelle overlooks the possibility that what was true of the *Lucernarium* in Spain may well have been applicable to the form that the office took in Italy and in Gaul.

[32]In Baptism, Confirmation, Ordination, and Extreme Unction; in the consecration of churches, altars, and bells; and in the blessing of the Easter candle.

place forced Capelle to assume that a fresh *candle* was used each day for this service. Although the use of a candle at the *Lucernarium* should not be ruled out, his description of the daily candle as *beau* is somewhat extravagant.

(ii) It is unnecessary to translate *lumen* as 'candle' in line 156. It is true that the word may refer to the object from which the light emanates, and in later transalpine Latin it is synonymous with *cereus*.[33] However, the translation of *lumen* in the couplet as 'lamp' or as 'candle' focuses undue attention on the participial phrase which comprises the whole of line 156. This phrase will then refer to the consecratory cross of chrism and will bear the meaning of 'anointed with the unction of peace-bringing chrism'. To the present writer this seems to place the emphasis of the couplet on the fact that there is a chrismal cross on the lamp (or candle) rather than on the fact that the deacon is offering a lamp (or candle). If, on the other hand, *lumen* bears its primary meaning of 'light' in the sense of the emanation of illumination, *tinctum* may then be rendered 'diffused' and *unguine* will then refer to the impregnation of the air with balsam *(chrismatis)*. This is the language of poetry; and in this couplet we surely have a reference to the use of scented lights in divine worship, attested elsewhere by Prudentius and by other writers.[34] It would seem,

[33]Andrieu, *Les* Ordines Romani II p.266.

[34]Peter of Paris mentions a porphyry candelabrum which was brought up from the font and carried a vase of gold, from which a wick of *amianthus*, set in balsam, 'diffused a great light'. (Cited by Gaillard, *Holy Week* p.110.)

The use of scented candles is mentioned by Prudentius :

nectar . . . guttatim lacrimis stillat olentibus, *

and by Paulinus :

Lumina ceratis adolentur odora papyris, **

and is almost certainly referred to by the same author in :

Sed quis odor nares allabitur aethere manans
   Unde meos stringit lux inopina oculos. ***

*Cathermerinon V (PL 59.820A).

**Poem XIV (PL 61.467B).

***Poem XXV (PL 61.637D).

therefore, that Capelle's attempt to establish a fourth-century precedent for the anointing of the Easter candle is unwarranted.

Later evidence for the use of scented candles is to be found in Gregory of Tours' description of the baptism of Clovis :

Balsama diffunduntur, micant fragrantes odore cerei. ****

*****Historia Francorum* II.31 (PL 71.226B).

Chapter Twenty-five
THE FIVE GRAINS OF INCENSE

(i) The Development of the Ceremony

The practice of inserting five grains of incense into the Easter candle in the shape of a cross is first reliably attested in the tenth-century Sacramentary of Corbie :

> Let them make a cross on the Candle out of incense, (and let the year of the Lord and the Greek letters A and Ω be inscribed).[1]

Doubts about the interpretation of the phrase *de incenso* have been expressed by Capelle.[2] He argues that *de incenso* bore the meaning of 'with the fire'. He claims that *incensum* here retained its primary meaning of 'fire', and instances the use of the word with this meaning in two phrases, one in the Preface following the *Exultet* and the other in the prayer, *Veniat quaesumus*.[3] In both instances it had undergone a shift in meaning from 'fire' to 'incense'. He also cites, as corroborative

---

[1]Faciant crucem de incenso in cereo (et scribatur annus Domini, atque A et Ω PL 78.336B (= M106). The evidence of the Pontifical of Egbert is discussed in the next chapter.

[2]*Le rite de cinq grains* p.8.

[3]*Suscipe incensi huius sacrificium vespertinum* and *super hunc incensum,* respectively. The latter phrase is found in the original version of the prayer.

evidence, the practice at Poitiers in the ninth century of tracing a cross with a lighted candle in front of the Easter candle.

The interpretation of *incensum* as used in its original meaning in the Preface and in the *Veniat quaesumus* is generally accepted by scholars and is not in dispute here. However, it is difficult to accept Capelle's interpretation of *de incenso* within the context under discussion and to believe that the sign of the cross was made with a lighted candle, as at Poitiers. For this adjectival phrase will then have to bear the meaning of '*with* the fire', a translation of *de* which is, to say the least, forced. Similarly, the phrase *in cereo* will have to be rendered 'in front of the Candle' instead of 'on the Candle'.[4] Apart from the fact that the clause appears to have the literal meaning of 'let them make a cross of incense on the Candle', the close association of this rubric with the directive, quoted in parenthesis, in the second half of the sentence, strongly suggests that the cross also was physically imposed upon the wax of the Candle. Moreover, the use of the impersonal *faciant* makes it difficult to envisage the tracing of a cross in the air by one individual using a lighted candle. Again, the sign of the cross in *Poitiers* was made with the fire on a *reed*. In the absence of evidence to the contrary and in the light of later practice, it must be assumed that the cross was formed by the insertion of five grains of incense at the salient points familiar from later practice, as opposed to the embedding of two continuous lines of incense grains into the wax at right angles to each other.[5]

The insertion of the grains of incense as a preliminary act prior to the blessing of the Easter candle is also enjoined in Lanfranc's *Decrees,* in the contemporary *Acta Vetera* of Rouen, and in the Customary of Sigibert.[6] It was performed at Essen in the fourteenth century; and at Barking, also in that

---

[4]Compare the corresponding phrase in *Poitiers* (p.215) : *contra cereum.*

[5]That this method may have been used, however, still remains a possibility.

[6]PL 150.466D; PL 147.176C; Albers II p.99, respectively.

century, the grains were inserted into a pre-incised cross on Good Friday.[7] In all these instances, there is no suggestion of any benediction-formula prior to their insertion; and, as decorations, they were commemorative in a way which we shall discuss presently.

Two traditions existed relating to the point in the ceremony at which the grains were inserted : (i) before the blessing of the Easter candle—already noted in the previous paragraph—and (ii) during the Preface following the *Exultet*.[8] On account of the close rapport that existed between the insertion of the grains and the censing of the Easter candle, and because the Candle came to be censed during the Preface for the reasons we will advance in the next chapter, the latter practice became by far the more common and eventually the norm throughout the Western Church.

The censing of the Easter candle *vis-à-vis* grains of incense is found in three traditions, referred to, for convenience, as *modes,* and summarised in *Table 48.*

At first sight, the insertion of the five grains of incense into the Easter candle, immediately followed by the censing of the same *(Mode D),* appears puzzling; for the first action was in a sense an honouring of the Candle with incense, so that the second action would seem to be a superfluous reduplication of the first. A similar claim could be made for the ritual according to *Mode C,* where the two actions were separated by an unspecified interval of time. Bearing in mind that liturgical practice did vary from rite to rite, it is not difficult to see in the *modes* three stages in the development of the incensation of the Easter candle; and to recognise that in the course of liturgical development anomalies and duplications do arise : as a result of misinterpretations or reinterpretations of language, or as the result of attempts to harmonise biblical symbolism with liturgical practice, or as the result of synthesising

[7]Ordinal p.66 and HBS 65 p.101, respectively.
[8]Hereafter referred to simply as the 'Preface'.

Church/Document	Date	Source
Gembloux	11 C	Albers II p.99
Essen	14 C	Ordinal p.66
Barking	1404	HBS 65 p.101
Carcassonne	1749	Missal p.196
Périgueux	1782	Missal p.159
Le Puy	1783	Missal p.159
Meaux	1845	Missal p.169

Mode A. Grains of incense inserted before the *Exultet*. Easter candle not censed.

Church/Document	Date	Source
Evesham*	c.1250	HBS 6 col.92
Norwich†	c.1265	HBS 82 p.91
Marseille‡	13 C	*ILEM* p.84
Durham‡	14 C	Missal p.188
Westminster‡	c.1370	HBS 5 col.582
St-Germain-des-Prés*	1394	*DAER* 3.15.7 p.142
Jumièges (Ordinal)		De Vert II p.35
Pontivy (Ritual)		De Vert II p.35
St-Vincent, Metz		De Vert II p.35

*At *in huius igitur noctis.*
†At *sacrificium vespertinum.*
‡At *suscipe, sancte pater.*

Mode B. No grains of incense inserted into the Easter candle. Easter candle censed during the Preface.

Church/Document	Date	Source
Corbie (Sacramentary)	10 C	PL 78.336B
Rouen *(Acta Vet.)*	11 C	PL 147.176C
Lanfranc	c.1070	PL 150. 467C

Mode C. Grains of incense inserted before the start of the ceremony. Easter candle censed during the Preface.

Church/Document	Date	Source
Vallombrosa	11 C	Albers IV p.249
St-Bénigne, Dijon	11 C	*DAMR* 3.15.7 p.142
Lateran Church	c.1143	*OEL* p.61
Narbonne	1528	Missal fol.lxxxv
Vendôme		De Vert II p.35
Sées (Ordinal)		De Vert II p.35

Mode D. Grains of incense inserted and Easter candle censed during the Preface.

Table 48. The grains of incense vis-à-vis *the censing of the Candle*

or attempting to synthesise into one ritual ceremonial actions drawn from varying liturgical milieux.

Perhaps the most likely explanation for this double ritual act is to be found in the parallel development of another consecratory action involving the use of incense, which provides a credible analogy to the ritual of the grains. The Gelasian Sacramentary prescribes 'an offering of incense upon the altar' at the suggestion of and to underline the *spiritual incense* in the prayer for the consecration of an altar.[9] In practice, according to ninth-century and tenth-century sources, this offering entailed the tracing with the thurible of a cross above the altar. By the twelfth century, the ritual had undergone a transformation : a cross made of incense grains was burned upon the altar.[10] Rabotin calls this 'a kind of materialisation of a primitive rite'.[11] The writer believes that the censing of the Easter candle underwent a similar materialisation at an earlier period, but resulted in a transformed outcome. For, whereas the dedicatory cross of incense upon the altar was made to burn, the incense inserted into the Easter candle was, for obvious reasons, diverted from its natural use and transformed into a permanent and visible symbol; and it is not difficult to discern the two main contributory factors which helped to bring about this change. (i) From a distance, the visibility of a cross incised into a candle of bleached wax would be greatly enhanced if the arms of the cross were highlighted either by two continuous lines of incense grains arranged at right angles to each other in the incision or by the insertion of single grains of incense at the five salient points of the cross. (ii) The identification of the Easter candle with the body of Christ and the association of the cross, already incised into the Candle, with His suffering and death may have invited

---

[9]Mohlberg, *GeV* §692 p.108.

[10]Small heaps of incense were placed in the four corners and in the middle of the altar during the consecration, and ignited. *PRMA* I p.200.

[11]*Les Grains d'Encens* p.225.

the insertion of the five grains of incense, as symbols of His wounds, at the points of the cross just referred to.[12]

We therefore believe that the insertion of the grains of incense does comprise a duplication of the first act of incensation with the thurible, in that the second ritual action both reinforced and expressed the latter in a more permanent and material way, and that this duplication of censing, attested by the six documents of *Mode D,* represents an intermediate stage in the development of the rite. We now tentatively suggest an outline history of the ritual, showing the stages by which the development may have occurred.

Stage 1. The censing of the Easter candle before the *Exultet.* There is no documentary evidence for the censing of the Easter candle at this stage of the ceremony. However, a number of observations may be made in support of our view that at an earlier period an initial act of incensation took place before the Candle was blessed. (i) We know that the censing of other inanimate objects took place prior to their consecration, for instance, at the above-mentioned dedication of an altar in the Gelasian Sacramentary. (ii) According to the three Gelasian sacramentaries, Ordo 30A, and the Reims Sacramentary, the cross was traced *super cereum* and the Candle was lit *before* the blessing. It is difficult to believe that the Candle was not censed also. (iii) The relevant descriptions in the above-mentioned documents are short and contain only a minimum of detail. Mention of a routine action, such as incensation, is likely to have been omitted. (iv) It is difficult to account otherwise for the insertion of the grains of incense in the rites of those churches listed in *Mode A* and to believe that they were originally inserted merely as decorations.

Stage 2. We suggested above that the insertion of the grains of incense represented a materialisation of the act of incensation. The presence of the grains of incense on the Candle,

[12]Medieval writers compared the wax of the Candle with the human substance of Christ. See Chapter 31.

therefore, prior to its being blessed *(Mode A)* presupposed that an act of incensation had already occurred. The grains thus embedded as a permanent and visible indication that the Easter candle had been honoured with incense, the action of censing with the thurible was either seen to be superfluous, since in effect the Candle had been censed twice, with the result that it disappeared from the ceremonial; or it was transferred to another point in the ceremony—a situation which we find in *Stage 3.*

Stage 3. The censing of the Easter candle during the Preface and the reasons which led to the occurrence of that ritual act midway through the *laus cerei* are dealt with at length in a later chapter. In some churches, the grains of incense continued to be inserted prior to the blessing of the Candle; but having lost their close rapport with the former initial act of incensation, now assumed an almost-decorative function. This stage in the development of the ritual of the grains *vis-à-vis* the censing of the Easter candle is to be identified with *Mode C.* (In the churches included in *Mode B,* the cruciform materialisation of the act of censing the Easter candle had not taken place.)

Stage 4. Here the censing of the Easter candle and the materialisation of that action in the form of the insertion of the five grains of incense into the Candle both occur *during* the Preface. This corresponds to *Mode D.*

Stage 5. We now reach the final phase in the development of the ritual. Here we must envisage a situation in which the incensation of the Easter candle during the Preface was regarded as an unnecessary duplication, as it were, of the insertion of the five grains of incense. Since the presence of the grains in the wax provided visible and permanent evidence that the Candle had been honoured with incense, the censing of the Candle with the thurible ceased to be carried out. We believe that this development had occurred in the earlier

Romano-Gallican rite, from which the later medieval Roman rite derived.

(ii) The Significance of the Five Grains of Incense

It is possible to identify three main traditions relating to the use of the five grains of incense.

(A) THE NEGATIVE USE OF THE GRAINS OF INCENSE. Since liturgical development was never uniform and variety of practice could and did occur even within one small geographical area, it is perhaps not surprising to find that the ritual of the grains did not feature in the ceremonial of a considerable number of churches during the Middle Ages. *Table 49* lists some of the churches in whose service-books there is no mention of the grains of incense.

The insertion of the grains of incense was unknown in the ancient rites of Beneventum, Braga, Milan, and Toledo; and it is clear from the table below that the absence of this feature was not confined to any particular geographical area. The Missal of Breslau contains a prayer for the blessing of the incense (fol.lxxix). Interestingly, this prayer, *Veniat quaesumus,* is the second of the four prayers prescribed in that missal for the blessing of the fire and occupies the same position as the corresponding prayer in the Durham Missal. In the latter church, this was a prayer for the blessing of the incense in the thurible. It should be borne in mind that the absence of rubrics relating to the grains of incense does not necessarily imply that the ritual was unknown in that rite.[13] The presence of eight Benedictine houses in the above list shows that liturgical practice was not uniform in the monasteries of that order, a fact not unnoticed by Lanfranc.[14]

---

[13]It is just possible that the reason for the silence of some of the documents in the above list lies in the fact that the grains of incense had been inserted before the start of the ceremony.

[14]*Decrees* (PL 150.467B).

Church	Date	Document/Source
Léon*	10 C	Antiphonary
Mainz	c.950	*PRG*
Ripoll	1038	Sacramentary
Beneventum	11 C	*Missale Antiquum*
Evesham	c.1250	Ritual
Norwich	c.1265	Customary
Marseille	13 C	*ILEM*
Westminster	c.1370	Missal
St-Germain-des-Prés	1394	*DAMR* 3.15 p.142 (M 1165)
St Mary's, York	c.1400	Ordinal
Durham	14 C	Missal
Tongres	14 C	Ordinal
Milan*	1475	Missal
Braga*	15 C	King, *LPS* p.223
Saintes	c.1500	Missal
Passau	1503	Missal
Cambrai	1507	Missal
Hamburg	1511	Missal
Breslau	1519	Missal
Jumièges	†	Ordinal (De Vert II p.35)
Pontivy	†	Ritual (De Vert II p.35)
St-Vincent, Metz	†	Ordinal (De Vert II p.35)

*The ritual of the grains was subsequently introduced as a result of Roman or monastic influence into the rite of Toledo in 1500, of Braga in 1512, and of Milan in 1560, according to the respective missals for those years.
†De Vert does not mention the date.

Table 49. No mention of the grains of incense

(B) THE CROSS OF INCENSE GRAINS AS A DECORATION. We noted above that in churches in which the grains of incense had been inserted into the Easter candle before the ceremony began, they had come to be regarded almost as markers highlighting the five salient points of the cross, rather than as visible symbols recalling the incensation of the Candle. This is almost certainly borne out by the fact that there is no instance from those places where the grains were inserted prior to the blessing of the Easter candle where they themselves received a blessing. It is also significant that in five of the six medieval instances in which the insertion of the grains featured as a preliminary act,[15] other insignia were also placed on the Candle as part of its preparation. Only the *Acta Vetera* of Rouen is silent on this point. A number of churches, listed in *Table 50a,* record the insertion of the incense grains during the Preface as a decorative and commemorative act. There is no benediction-formula for these grains, which seem to serve chiefly as the means of delineating the cross on the Easter

Church	Date	Document/Source
Fruttuaria	11 C	Customary (Albers IV p.65)
Vallombrosa	11 C	Customary (Albers IV p.249)
Cluny	11 C	Customary (PL 149.663B)
Würzburg	1477	Ordinal np
Trier	*c.*1487	Missal fol.ciii
Cologne	1494	Missal fol.cxxv
Bremen	1511	Missal fol.lxxxvi
Spires	1512	*Agenda* fol.c
Meissen	1520	Breviary np
Tournai	1540	Missal fol.lxx
Sens	1715	Missal p.242

Table 50a

Church	Date	Document/Source
Cistercians	1119	*Nom. Cist.* p.105
Soissons	*c.*1185	*DAER* 4.24 p.161 (M 305)
Nidaros	13 C	*ONE* p.232
Exeter	1337	Ordinal (HBS 37 p.322)

Table 50b

Table 50. Evidence for the decorative function of the grains

[15]The documents are listed in *Mode A* and *Mode C*.

candle, and only secondarily as reminders that in former times the Candle had been censed during the Preface.

The documents in *Table 50b* prescribe the insertion of the grains during the Preface and do not include a prayer for their blessing. However, since they also omit any prayers for the blessing of the fire, they have been listed separately. It should be noted that the first, second, and fourth documents in *Table 50b* also enjoin the inscribing of other insignia on the Candle as part of its preparation.

(C) THE REPRESENTATIONAL FUNCTION OF THE INCENSE GRAINS. In a later chapter, we shall discuss the symbolism of the Easter candle and the shift in emphasis regarding the nature and significance of the Candle. In the same way that the whole Candle—flame, wax, and wick—came to represent different aspects of the human nature of Christ, in addition to symbolising His divine light, so the grains of incense, decorative attachments recalling the incensation of the Candle, assumed a more realistic function and became vivid representations of the wounds of Christ in the wax that was His 'flesh'. This developed from a modification or change in two aspects of the ritual. (i) A blessing came to be pronounced over the grains prior to their insertion into the Candle. (ii) It became the practice in some places to bear the incense grains in procession along with the new fire. As a result, they acquired greater prominence within the ceremonial, achieving an importance almost on a par with the new fire. At Lyon, the anointing of the grains almost certainly recalled the treatment of Christ's wounds.

The ritual involving the blessing and insertion into the Candle of the five grains of incense developed along three different lines.

MODE I

The grains were :

(a) blessed shortly after the commissioning of the new fire;

(b) carried in procession (in churches where a procession was held);

(c) inserted into the Candle at the words *suscipe, sancte pater . . . incensi* of the Preface.

This is the *mode* that was ultimately adopted by the great majority of churches in the West, mainly through Roman or monastic influence. It is first attested in the twelfth-century *Pontificale Romanum (PR XII)*,[16] though there was no procession according to that document, and in a contemporary Premonstratensian sacramentary.[17] The aspersion and censing of the grains, though absent from the 1474 *Missale Romanum,* feature in the Roman Missal of 1570 and entered the Ambrosian rite in the revised Missal of 1902.

Mode II

The grains were blessed and inserted during the Preface. This *mode* is found in the following rites :[18]

Evesham	(*c.* 1250)
St-Vedast, Arras	(*c.* 1300)
Seville	(1507)
Braga	(1512)
Rennes	(1523)
Troyes	(1736)

At Braga, the first of the two prayers used for the blessing of the grains began during the Preface at the words *in huius igitur noctis;* the second presumably finished in time for the grains to be inserted at the usual place *(suscipe, sancte pater).* At Rennes, the incense was also aspersed at this point. We are not told the precise point at which the incense grains were blessed in any of the other churches.

[16] *PRMA* I pp.238–40.
[17] Weyns p.69 (Manuscript B).
[18] Respective references : HBS 6 col.91; HBS 86 p.160; Missal fol.lxxviii; Missal np; Missal fol.lxxiii; Missal p.27.

MODE III

The grains were blessed and inserted before the *Exultet*. This third tradition occurred in the rites of the group of churches in France listed in *Table 51*.

Church[19]	Date	Benediction-formula	Source
Bourges	1741	*D.D.N.qui suscepisti*	Missal pp.225–27
Carcassonne	1749	*Veniat quaesumus*	Missal p.196
Le Puy	1783	*D.D.N.qui suscepisti*	Missal pp.159–60
Périgueux	1784	*D.D.N.qui suscepisti*	Missal pp.159–60
Meaux	1845	*Veniat quaesumus*	Missal p.169

Table 51

This variant recalls the practice of inserting the five grains of incense prior to the blessing of the Easter candle, which was attested in the six medieval instances in *Table 48 (Modes A and C)*, but derives from an older tradition in which the Easter candle was kindled before the singing of the *Exultet*.[20] All five churches listed in *Table 51* preserved this feature; and in all, except Meaux, the Easter candle was lit prior to the insertion of the grains.

The reformed Mozarabic rite, as authorised by the *Missale Mixtum* of 1500, strictly falls into this category, *Mode III*. However, since the ceremonial it prescribes was the result of an attempt to harmonise two different traditions, the insertion of the grains before the lighting of the Easter candle was deliberately contrived and not the result of normal liturgical development.

[19]Bourges, Le Puy, and Périgueux belong to a subgroup whose ceremonial was characterised not only by the use of the prayer *D.D.N.qui suscepisti* for the blessing of the grains of incense but by the survival of the *Veniat quaesumus* as a preliminary blessing of the Easter candle. Amiens, too, might be classed with these three churches, except that in the former churches the grains were inserted into the Candle *more Romano* during the Preface.

[20]The use of the *Veniat quaesumus* for the blessing of the Easter candle belongs to the same ancient tradition.

(iii) The Insertion of the Grains of Incense

The implantation of the grains of incense into the Easter candle prior to the commencement of the Vigil, or even prior to the chanting of the *Exultet*, enabled those involved in the preparation of the Candle to ensure that the grains were embedded securely in the wax. With the insertion of the grains during the *laus cerei*, the possibility always existed that one or more of the grains might fall from the wax through the failure of the resin to adhere to the Candle for one reason or another. We therefore find that the directions in a number of service-books state that the five small holes should previously have been gouged out of the side of the Candle in readiness for the reception of the grains;[21] and until 1955, this practice was officially sanctioned by the Church of Rome. Desideri adds the sensible advice that the holes should be lower than the part of the Candle which will burn.[22] A rubric from Magdeburg states that the incense should be inserted *sub signo crucis*.[23] This may be interpreted 'in the form of a cross' or 'under the sign of the cross'. The former interpretation is to be preferred in view of the almost-universal observance of the cruciform arrangement.

At Lyon, the grains were first warmed so as to soften the wax and then anointed with chrism before being affixed.[24] Rome also allowed the application of heat.[25] It is recorded that at Valence, the grains were embedded into the salient points of an incised cross which had first been anointed with chrism.[26]

This oil in the above-mentioned instances may also have acted as an adhesive, although we have suggested an alter-

[21]Ordo of Nidaros p.232; Strasbourg Ordinal (*DAER* 4.24 p.162); Besançon Ceremonial p.314; Paris Ceremonial p.374; 1488 Missal of Basel fol.xcii; 1498 Missal of Prague fol.xci.

[22]*Praxis* p.150.

[23]1503 Missal fol.xciiii.

[24]1838 Ceremonial p.481.

[25]Fortescue and O'Connell (6th ed.) p.343.

[26]1504 Missal fol.liiii.

native origin for the use of the chrism at Lyon. It was also recommended that the grains should be large or that several grains should be fused together so as to be conspicuous at a distance. In more recent times, the grains have sometimes been held in wooden or metal cases to which a spike has been attached for their insertion into the wax. As a result, the devices have been referred to as *nails*. The term is also used of the small spike of red wax with a grain of incense in its head, which is infixed into a specially-prepared cavity. Both the word *nail* and the colour of the wax, which highlights the grains against the pale background of the Easter candle, appropriately reinforce the symbolism of the incense.

As a result of the liturgical reforms of 1955, the primitive practice was restored : the grains were thenceforth to be inserted immediately before the Easter candle was lit, and subsequently blessed.[27] In the Roman Missal of 1970, there is no reference to the insertion and blessing of the grains. All markings on the Easter candle have now been made optional.[28]

Traditionally, the grains of incense have been inserted by the officiating deacon or the priest who acts for the deacon. According to the Customary of St-Bénigne, Dijon,[29] the *armarius* performed this task while the deacon was censing the Easter candle. At St-Vedast, Arras, and at Cordoba, the sacristan gave the deacon one grain to insert and himself infixed the other four.[30] At the Cathedral of St John Lateran, the grains had to be of the purest incense.[31]

According to the rubrics of the vast majority of provincial and diocesan rites, the grains began to be inserted following the words *curvat imperia* in the Preface. In the next chapter we shall observe why this was thought to be an apposite junc-

[27]Diekmann p.129.

[28]1970 *Missale Romanum* p.267; Harbert p.236. The Milanese rite follows Roman practice in this respect (1981 *Missale Ambrosianum* p.243), as does the recently-revised Anglican service (*Lent, Holy Week, Easter* p.229).

[29]Martène, *DAMR* 3.15.7 p.142 (M 1150).

[30]HBS 86 p.160 and 1561 Missal fol.cix, respectively.

[31]*OEL* p.61.

ture for carrying out the insertions. It also provided a suitable point in the Preface at which to pause. In some sources, the break is prescribed at the words *in huius igitur noctis*,[32] in others at *sacrificium vespertinum*,[33] whilst in a number of other service-books, it is enjoined at *suscipe, sancte pater*.[34] These slight variations did not substantially affect the performance of this ritual action, and different interpretations based on these variations are not justified. Since there is no indication to the contrary in the rubrics of any service-book, we must assume that the deacon interrupted his singing at the point indicated by the words, in order to insert the grains into the Candle; and that on the completion of this duty, he resumed his chanting of the *laus*. At Cologne, however, the rubrics in the Missal of 1495 specify a fixed point in the Preface for the insertion of each grain (fol.cxxv). Within the sentence beginning *in huius igitur noctis* the following arrangement is found :

1st grain inserted at *suscipe*
2nd grain inserted at *vespertinum*
3rd grain inserted at *oblationem*
4th grain inserted at *solemni*
5th grain inserted at *apum*

Subsequent missals of Cologne present a difficulty; for whilst they specify the moment for each insertion, they refer to only four grains.

1514 Missal	**1525 Missal**
1st grain at *suscipe*	1st grain at *suscipe*
2nd grain at *vespertinum*	2nd grain at *vespertinum*
3rd grain at *solemni*	3rd grain at *per ministrorum*
4th grain at *manus*	4th grain at *de operibus*

[32]For instance, Haymo *(OM);* HBS 85 p.205, and Customary of St-Germain-des-Prés; *DAMR* 3.15.7 p.142 (M 1165).

[33]For instance, *PRMA* I p.240; 1561 Missal of Cordoba fol.cix; Bystorp Manual p.94; Missals of Lund and Copenhagen, cited by Stromberg p.40.

[34]Ordinal of St-Vedast, Arras (HBS 86 p.160); 1481 Missal of Verdun fol.lxiiii; 1519 Missal of Aquileia fol.91.

The reduction in the number of grains from five to four is inexplicable from the evidence of the missals alone. The only other known instance where only four grains of incense were used occurs in a fourteenth-century ordinary of the Collegiate Church at Essen. Here four grains of incense occupied the outer points of the cross. However, although some connection could be argued on the grounds of the geographical proximity of the two cities, additional evidence is required before a liturgical link between the two churches can be established. Moreover, the central grain at Essen consisted of myrrh, not incense.[35]

Now, the 1518 Missal of Ratisbon records that the grains of incense were inserted at the words *in odore(m) suavitatis* (fol.xcvii). In the next chapter, we shall argue that the lighting of the Easter candle at *suscipe, sancte pater* indicated that *incensi* (the following word) had retained its original meaning of 'fire' within this context. It is, therefore, just possible that the Ratisbon Missal preserves the original point in the Preface at which the Easter candle was censed, since these words invited the incensation of the Candle almost as an internal rubric.

We have shown that the five salient points of the incised cross provided the obvious places at which to impress the grains into the wax of the Candle. Contemporary practice is to insert them in the form of a Greek cross; and illustrations from manuals of the past,[36] which prescribe the order for the insertion of the grains, would suggest that this shape has long been traditional. However, at Le Puy, Nantes, and La Rochelle, a Latin cross was used.[37] The grains were normally inserted in the order shown below, regardless of the shape of the cross. This corresponds to the personal sign of the cross in the Western Church in which the cross-stroke is made from left to right.

[35]Ordinary p.66.
[36]For example, Martinucci II p.242 and Merati p.81.
[37]1783 Missal p.160; 1837 Missal p.203; 1835 Missal p.191, respectively.

1

4   2   5

3

At Auch and at Toulouse, the grains were arranged in the form of a five-pointed star.[38] This shape was, according to De Vert (II p.37), suggested by the occurrence of *vespertinum* in the above-mentioned phrase from the Preface, the word being the adjectival form of *vesper,* 'the evening star'.

At Salisbury, Exeter, and in the Gilbertine houses, there existed a choice of affixing the grains either to the Easter candle or to the candelabrum which supported it.[39] The phrase *si attingi potest* in the Gilbertine Ordinal suggests that the Easter candle might have been beyond the reach of the deacon's hands if the candlestick was very tall. The practice of affixing the grains to the false stock of the Candle was forbidden according to a nineteenth-century ceremonial of Lyon.[40] It maintains that the union of the grains with the wax was a prerequisite of a valid benediction of the Candle; and that the drops of wax that fell into the baptismal waters were inefficacious since the Easter candle had not received an authentic blessing. At Salisbury, Angers, and in the churches of the Diocese of Lyon, grains were also inserted into the *cereus minor,* the smaller Easter candle that was carried to the font.[41]

(iv) The Grains of Incense at Milan

The ceremony of the grains of incense in the Ambrosian rite has an interesting history in that we plot its gradual adop-

---

[38]Feasey, *The Paschal Preconium* p.252; De Vert II p.37. The latter refers to some other churches without specifying them.

[39]Sarum Missal (Warren) p.270; HBS 37 p.322; HBS 59 p.40, respectively.

[40]1838 Ceremonial p.479.

[41]Sarum Missal (Warren) p.270; 1731 Ceremonial p.261; 1838 Ceremonial p.479, respectively.

tion from the Roman rite in three stages. (i) In the Missal of 1475, the Easter candle is censed at the conclusion of the Preface (fol.lxxxi). There is no mention of the grains of incense. (ii) According to the Missal of 1560, five grains of incense are inserted into the salient points of a pre-traced cross after the incensation of the Candle, which follows the deacon's song (fol.113). (iii) In the Missal of 1594, we find that the grains are now inserted during the Preface at the words *chrismate, non cruore* (fol.95). This is almost certainly the result of Roman influence; for the Candle, formerly lit before the singing of the *Exultet,* now receives its flame also during the *laus.* The Preface in the Roman rite had been characterised by these ritual interruptions since the twelfth century.[42]

(v) The Symbolism of the Grains of Incense

Medieval commentators were not slow to find biblical echoes in the use of the five grains of incense and to attach symbolic interpretations to them. We therefore encounter symbolism at two levels : that which recalled and was suggested by two incidents in the Gospel narrative and that which had wider theological implications.

[42]Unlike the interruptions in the Roman Preface, which follow each other at fairly short intervals and which are largely determined by words acting almost as internal rubrics, those in the Ambrosian Preface occur at the end of well-defined sections and divide the *laus* into four more or less equal parts. The wording of those phrases in the Preface at which the three actions occur (namely, the lighting of the Candle, the affixing of the grains, and the illumination of the church lights) is not unrelated to the nature of those actions. Of particular relevance here is the action involving the grains and the sentence from the Preface which invites that action : *Christi vero populus insignitur fronte, non inguine; lavacro, non vulnere; chrismate, non cruore.* Here, this Roman-derived ritual action of inserting the grains bears little, if any, relationship to the post-prefatorial act of incensation that occurred in the Milanese rite. The cross formed by the grains of incense is symbolic and anticipatory of the chrismal cross of Baptism.

(A) Writing *c*.1111, Rupert of Deutz, followed by Sicardus and later Durandus, sees represented in the grains of incense the spices and ointment which the women brought to the grave of Jesus.[43] In general, detractors of medieval symbolism, such as Capelle, have not been slow to point out that the body of Jesus was anointed with myrrh and aloes, and not with incense (John 19:39).[44] Their criticisms, however, have been largely unjustified on two counts. (i) A symbol is but one object representing another object, and by the very nature of a symbol cannot be that which it represents. The incense was understood to represent the women's myrrh because of the redolent properties characteristic of both substances, and its use was all the more apposite in those churches in which the grains of incense were carried in procession from the new fire to the Easter candle. (ii) Incense and myrrh are not dissimilar substances. In fact, in some types of incense myrrh is an ingredient. The correspondence between the incense and the myrrh and aloes brought by the women was further suggested by the relative points during the Roman Preface at which the grains were inserted and the Easter candle was lit. For the Resurrection, symbolised by the lighting of the Candle, did not take place until after the embalming.

The infixing of the five grains of incense into the Candle also recalled the five wounds of Jesus. The symbolism, which is still associated with the grains, is first mentioned by Durandus *c*.1280;[45] but it is difficult to believe that the identification of the grains with the wounds was not made much earlier. For the increase in the ceremonial importance of the grains, noted earlier in this chapter, is almost certainly linked with

[43]*De Div. Off.* V (PL 170.173C); *Mitrale* (PL 213.324A); *Rationale* VI.80 p.351.

[44]*Le rite des cinq grains* p.11. Van Doren, on the other hand, was equally dogmatic   :
'Ils ne doivent pas réprésenter les clous de la croix. Ils signifient, d'après les liturgistes, les onguents précieux dont on entoura le corps du Seigneur.' *Le cièrge paschal* p.75.

[45]*Rationale* VI.80 fol.351.

the symbolic identification of the wax of the Easter candle with the human flesh of Christ. Again, Capelle's objection to the symbolism on the grounds of the lack of positional correspondence is somewhat unjustified. A symbol does not necessarily mirror an object in every small detail.

(B) At a theological level, the grains of incense had a more profound and also a double significance. For, since they were inserted at the words *sacrificium vespertinum,* they not only recalled the evening sacrifice in the Temple under the dispensation of the Old Law, which itself prefigured the sacrifice of Christ;[46] they also vividly suggested the sacrifice of Christ Himself for three reasons : the grains were inserted into His *body;* they were disposed in a cruciform arrangement and recalled the Cross; in the Middle Ages, the ceremony had come to take place at the time of day corresponding to the hours of the Crucifixion. From a less objective point of view but still within a sacrificial context, the grains of incense, together with the flame of the Candle, symbolised the sacrifice or offering of the people to God by the people and on behalf of the people.[47]

---

[46]Beleth, *Rationale* (PL 202.11D); Zazzera p.299.
[47]Parvio, *Manuale* p.213.

Chapter Twenty-six
THE INCENSATION
OF THE EASTER CANDLE

The use of incense in the ceremony of the Easter candle belongs strictly to a study of the history of that element; but the prominence of the five grains of incense in the ceremonial necessitates some study of the use of incense in order to account for the presence of those grains within the ritual. The attempt to trace the history and development of the use of incense within the ceremonial from the surviving documentary evidence is fraught with difficulties. Practices involving its use, inherited from differing liturgical traditions, could vary markedly even throughout one small geographical area. At times, a document has few rubrics and much has to be understood. At times the rubrics, because of their brevity, are either vague or ambiguous. With regard to the latter type of directives, perhaps the greatest difficulty has been in deciding how to interpret the stark instruction *'A prayer for the blessing of the incense'*, where it is not clear whether *incense* relates to the substance in the thurible with which the new fire or the Easter candle is to be censed, or whether the word refers to the five grains later to be inserted into the Easter candle.

In the previous chapter, we looked at the close and intimate connection which the writer believes existed between the censing of the Easter candle and the affixing of the five grains of incense, and traced the development that occurred in the use of the grains of incense *vis-à-vis* the incensation of the Candle. In this chapter, we shall consider the incensation of the Easter candle, noting the three points during the ceremony when this ritual act is known or is thought to have occurred, namely, prior to, during, and following the blessing of the Easter candle.

(i) Incensation before the *Exultet*

Direct evidence for an initial act of incensation is wanting; but we have tried to show in the previous chapter that the insertion of the five grains of incense prior to the blessing of the Easter candle presupposes that this ritual act at one time occurred at this stage of the ceremony. Although evidence is again lacking, it is possible that an initial act of incensation of the Candle was transferred to the newly-kindled fire, if a distinction is made between the censing of the fire and the censing of the Easter candle. Such a transfer could explain why the new fire was censed *after* it had been aspersed. In all other instances of blessings, incensation preceded aspersion. For, if a situation had formerly existed in which the censing of the Candle had been followed by the insertion of the five grains of incense and if, as we argued in the previous chapter, this was seen as a duplication of the act of incensation, it is not unreasonable to believe that the action involving the thurible was transferred to the new fire, whilst the presence of the grains on the Candle was held to be tantamount to its being censed.

(ii) Incensation during the Preface

Evidence for the incensation of the Easter candle during the Preface is plentiful,[1] and dates from the eleventh century,

---

[1]For the eighteen instances of this practice, see *Modes B, C,* and *D* in *Table 48.*

if not the tenth.² It must be assumed that the incense was first

²There are two documents from this century which may attest the practice. (i) According to the Sacramentary of Corbie (PL 78.336B), the bishop blesses both the new fire and the incense while the deacon is consecrating the Easter candle. Unfortunately, there is no indication as to whether the incense was used to cense the new fire or the Candle, or both. (It is true that a cross of incense had been placed on the Candle prior to the start of the ceremony, but it is most unlikely that it is this incense which the bishop blesses.) (ii) The evidence of the Pontifical of Egbert is more problematical. It contains the following rubric (p.130) :

> Benedictio incensi in Sabbato Sancto antequam benediceris cereum, et ipsum debes mitti in cereum in ipso loco ubi dicitur suscipe incensi.

and is followed by Formula (b) for the blessing of the incense (Appendix 4). The rubric is generally cited as an early instance—Thurston claims it was the earliest (*Holy Saturday* p.14)—of the practice of inserting the five grains of incense into the Candle (Rabotin p.222; Capelle, *Le rite des cinq grains* p.9); but if so, it antedates the next oldest rubric for the blessing of the grains by about two hundred years. Now it is not impossible that an isolated piece of evidence such as this should have survived from a minor liturgical milieu; but the interval of time which separates it and the evidence from Corbie raises some doubt about its authenticity. Since, however, the *terminus post quem* for this document is 1000, even allowing for the possibility that this rubric is an interpolation, a closer examination of the language of the rubric would not be out of place. For the use of the second person singular strongly suggests that the directive is the addition of a later hand.

The second part of the rubric is generally rendered : ' . . . and you ought to put it *(ipsum)* into the Candle at the very point where the words *suscipe sancte* occur' on the assumption that *ipsum* refers to the five grains of incense. The writer, however, would suggest that *ipsum,* which is singular, refers, not to the grains, but to the thurible of incense, since he is of the opinion that *mitti* here has its basic meaning of 'send' or 'direct' and that *in cereum* should be rendered 'towards the Candle' or 'against the Candle'. Moreover, the rubricist has distinguished carefully between the use of the preposition *in* meaning 'in' or 'on' and suggesting position, and *in* governing the accusative case and conveying the notion of forward movement.

The clause *ipsum debes mitti in cereum* will then be interpreted 'you ought to cense the Candle'. If the suggestion is correct, the Pontifical should now be cited as evidence for the censing of the Easter candle in the tenth century, but not for the insertion of the grains.

blessed before it was used to honour the Candle, but this is not always stated in the sources. For instance, it is not mentioned by Lanfranc. However, according to the eleventh-century *Acta Vetera* of Rouen, the incense was blessed with the *Veniat quaesumus* after the procession had returned into church;[3] and at Durham and St-Germain-des-Prés,[4] and almost certainly at Norwich and Westminster,[5] the incense was hallowed at the same time as the fire. At Evesham, the blessing took place during the Preface.[6] At St-Germain-des-Prés and at Evesham, the deacon circumambulated the Easter candle as he swung the censer.[7]

Apropos of the censing of the Easter candle during the *laus cerei,* it is Claude de Vert who first draws attention to the fact that in the following invocation in the Preface :

> suscipe, sancte Pater, incensi huius sacrificium vespertinum

incensi had come to be interpreted 'incense' as a result of a shift in meaning which the word had undergone.[8] There seems little doubt that, at the time that the Preface was composed, *incensum* signified 'fire';[9] and that this is how the word was originally interpreted within the above-quoted context. Confirmation of this view is to be found in the 1518 Missal of Ratisbon (fol.cxvii), in which we encounter what appears to be an intermediate stage in the development of the ceremonial. For the rubric states that the Candle was to be lit at *suscipe, sancte Pater,* and that the grains of incense were to be inserted at *in odore(m) suavitatis.* We suggested that the incensation of the Candle may originally have occurred at the latter point in the Preface and may have subsequently been transferred

---

[3]PL 147.176C.
[4]Missal p.186 and *DAER* 4.24 p.158 (M 250), respectively.
[5]HBS 82 p.91 and HBS 5 col.576, respectively.
[6]HBS 6 col.90, at the words *Haec nox est in qua.*
[7]*DAMR* 3.15.7 p.142 (M 1165) and HBS 6 col.92, respectively.
[8]*Explication* II p.35.
[9]Literally, 'that which has been kindled'.

under the influence of *incensi* to the earlier position. Only at Ratisbon, it would appear, did the earlier practice survive. According to the Ordinary of Tongres, the Easter candle was lit at *suscipe, sancte Pater;* but it contains no rubrics relating to the grains of incense.

In the *laus cerei,* the dominant theme of Christ's resurrection is vividly supplemented by the contrast between the darkness of night, which symbolises the evil and wickedness of the old order, and the re-emergence and triumph of the light of Christ, of which the Easter candle with its bright flame is the symbol. The change in the interpretation of *incensi* not only detracted from the centrality of the Candle's light,[10] but introduced into the blessing of the Candle the offering of incense in addition to the offering of the Candle and its light—and this occurred at the beginning of a new section of the *laus.* The offering of incense having been introduced into the text of the Preface, the way was now open for an act of incensation to take place at the words which made reference to that element; and this in turn resulted in the insertion of the five grains of incense into the Candle at this precise point.

It was perhaps inevitable that *incensi* should undergo this shift in meaning from 'fire' to 'incense'; for according to Amalarius, the altar at Vespers was censed at the second verse of Psalm 140 (141) :[11]

> Dirigatur oratio mea sicut incensum in conspectu tuo : elevatio manuum mearum sacrificium vespertinum.

The verse was particularly apposite *vis-à-vis* the invocation in the Preface since (i) the deacon's prayer was being offered *in conspectu tuo;* (ii) the words of the psalm, *incensum* and *sacrificium vespertinum,* were directly paralleled in the Preface; and

[10]The English translation of *OHS* 'this evening sacrifice of burning light' restored the original and correct interpretation of *incensi* (Diekmann p.135). Sadly, ICEL was content with 'the sacrifice of praise' for the Roman Missal of 1970 (*PJSM* p.322).

[11]De Eccl.Off. IV.7 (PL 105.1181C).

(iii) as we noted in Chapter Twenty-four, in some churches the sign of the cross was traced in the air at the word *incensi*—an action possibly echoing the *elevatio manuum* of the psalm.[12]

(iii) Incensation after the Preface

The censing of the Easter candle after the Preface occurs in the Ambrosian rite at Milan. Though not mentioned by Beroldus in the twelfth century, it is prescribed in the Ambrosian Missal of 1475 (fol.lxxxi) and in the revised Missal of 1902.[13] In the revision of the Ambrosian rite following the Second Vatican Council, the incensation of the Easter candle still takes place at the conclusion of the Preface.[14] This contrasts with the revised Roman rite, in which incensation takes place prior to the *preconium*. The Milanese practice is also found at Essen in the fourteenth century,[15] and may also have featured at Ripoll and at Saintes. For at the Spanish monastery, a prayer for the blessing of the incense follows the Preface,[16] whilst at Saintes, a rubric indicates that the benediction of the element occurred at the same juncture.[17]

[12]*PRG* II §347 p.98.
[13]*Repertorium* p.47, t.e.
[14]1986 *Messale Ambrosiano* p.59.
[15]Ordinary p.66.
[16]Sacramentary p.92.
[17]Missal of *c*.1500 fol.lxxxi.

Chapter Twenty-seven
THE INSIGNIA
ON THE EASTER CANDLE

(i) Alpha and Omega

The delineation of the two Greek letters A and Ω on the Easter candle is attested in surprisingly few documents. It is found in the Sacramentary of Corbie and in the contemporary tenth-century Mozarabic Antiphonary of Léon,[1] in the twelfth-century *Pontificale Romanum (PR XII)* and in two other closely-related Roman documents,[2] and in the fourteenth-century Ordinal of Essen (p.58). Their occurrence in the so-called suburbicarian tradition recorded in *PR XII* and their presence in the Sacramentary of Corbie point to a Gallican provenance for the practice.

It is generally believed that the A and Ω were depicted on the Easter candle to indicate that Christ was Lord of the Ages and 'potentate of time'; and to a point this is true. However, the inclusion of the date, that is, the number of years from the Incarnation, also on the surface of the Candle, rendered the two Greek emblems superfluous, in that the date also came

---

[1]PL 78.336B (M 106) and Antiphonary p.280, respectively.
[2]*PR XII (PRMA* I xxxii.10 p.241, suburbicarian variant); *OEL* p.60; Pontifical of Apamea (*DAER* 4.24 p.160).

to represent the same concept and to signify Christ's sovereignty over time. It is almost certain that for this reason the depicting of A and Ω on the Candle generally fell into desuetude, surviving only in isolated instances in the later Middle Ages, such as at the Collegiate Church in Essen.[3]

Although it is unknown when the two Greek letters were first inscribed on the Easter candle, it is not difficult to discern the reason for their delineation. In earlier times, the paschal vigil was observed in an expectation of the second coming of Christ and in commemoration of the Resurrection, the event which had ushered in the New Age. Nor is it difficult to realise why, within the other-worldly context of the paschal liturgy, the eschatological name or attribute of Christ, found in St John's Revelation (20:6), should be chosen and used both to identify the Candle with Christ within this eschatologically liturgical context and to indicate to the faithful the identity of the Candle.[4] The depicting on the Candle of this title from Scripture is reminiscent of the practice within the Orthodox tradition of including the name or an abbreviation of the name on the icon of a saint. The inscribing of the earthly name of Jesus may have seemed inapposite within the futuristic context of the liturgy, being evocative of the inscription above the Cross, and thus in some way diverting attention towards the Passion rather than anticipating the Resurrection and the Second Coming.

In two manuscripts, a pictorial representation is preserved of the two letters in a spatial relationship to the Cross.[5] Presumably they bear some likeness to the devices actually delineated on the Easter candles. The later and more elaborately-designed device from Essen also incorporates the Chi-Rho monogram and a trio of crosses, symbolising the Trinity rather than echoing Golgotha.

[3]Ordinary p.58.
[4]Especially if the Candle was of very modest proportions.
[5]Antiphonary of Léon p.280 and Ordinal of Essen p.58.

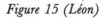

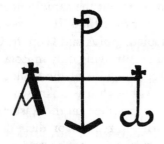

Figure 15 (Léon)   *Figure 16 (Essen)*

The similarity of the position of A and Ω in both devices suggests that the two crosses derive from a common ancestor in spite of the differences in time and location which separate their respective delineations. The position of the letters at the extremities of the arms of the cross suggests that they represent the notion that time belongs to and is held in the hands of Christ, even when he is on the cross.

(ii) The Year

Earlier liturgical commentators cite the following passage from Chapter 7 of Bede's *De Temporum Ratione,* written in 725, as early evidence for the inscribing of the year on the Easter candle :[6]

> The holy and apostolic Roman Church bears witness that she keeps this faith even by the very marks which it is her custom to inscribe on her candles each year. For in order to remind the people of the season of the Lord's Passion, she registers (on the candles) the number of years less thirty-three, which Dionysius calculated from the Incarnation. Accordingly, in the seven hundred and first year from the Incarnation by Dionysius' reckoning, our brothers who were in Rome at the time said that on Christmas Day, they saw written on the candles of St Mary's Church [S.Maria Maggiore] and made

[6]For instance, Novarinus p.17 (*c.*1635); Martène, *DAER* 4.24.7 (*c.*1700).

a note of the following : 'From the Passion of our Lord Jesus Christ 668 years'.[7]

Martène's comment is, 'It is clear that the inscription was formerly applied at Easter, and kept on the Candle throughout the whole year'.[8] The French liturgist is correct in finding the origin of the custom of inscribing the year in the practice of the Roman Church; but in the mistaken belief of his time that the Easter candle was known at Rome in 701, he interprets Bede's *in cereis* as though the noun were in the singular form *in cereo* and thus avoids a difficulty, as Dendy points out (p.138). Since the candles in S.Maria Maggiore, which Bede's fellow monks visited on Christmas Day, were not Easter candles—he clearly refers to the existence of more than one candle in this basilica—we must try to establish which were the candles in that church that bore the inscription. A number of preliminary observations must be made. (i) We may at once eliminate this as a reference to all the candles of the basilica since it is unlikely that all of them were made of beeswax *(cera)*. (ii) The candles in question were either used only on rare occasions, since the date was still visible at the end of December, or were exceedingly large, so that even with constant use they had not burned down to that part of the stock which bore the inscription. Moreover, the wording of Bede's reported inscription, if authentic, would have required the use of candles of no mean diameter. (iii) Bede informs us that the candles

---

[7]Sancta quidem Romana et apostolica Ecclesia hanc se fidem tenere et ipsis testutur indiculis, quae suis in cereis annuatim scribere solet, ubi tempus dominicae passionis in memoriam populis revocans, numerum annorum triginta semper et tribus annis minorem quam ab eius incarnatione Dionysius ponat, adnotat. Denique anno ab eius incarnatione iuxta Dionysium septingensimo primo, indictione quarta decima, fratres nostri qui tunc fuere Romae, hoc modo se in natali Domini in cereis sanctae Mariae scriptum vidisse, et inde descripsisse referebant : 'A passione Domini nostri Jesu Christi anni sunt DCLXVIII'. PL 95.494B–495A.

[8]Patet inscriptionem olim in Paschate adhibitam, per totum annum in cereo conservatam fuisse. *DAER* 4.24.7.

were renewed every year; and if this is so, they lasted for the whole year, as Martène conjectures. (iv) The candles were closely associated with the events of Holy Week, and in particular the Triduum.

In view of these observations, it is difficult to escape the conclusion that the wax candles to which Bede is referring are none other than the two candles, the size of a human being, which figured prominently in the Roman paschal vigil. It is significant that in the Pontifical of Poitiers, which contains elements from both the Roman and the Gallican Vigil traditions, both these large candles bear an inscription (p.215). The writer believes that the imprinting of information on these candles was a practice of some antiquity, even when the Pontifical of Poitiers was compiled. The objection that the paschal vigil at Rome was held only in the Cathedral of St John Lateran is not insurmountable. The early *ordines Romani* relate primarily to papal ceremonial in the Mother of Cathedrals; and there is no evidence to suggest that a Vigil was not held in the other basilicas of Rome, apart possibly from S.Croce in Gerusalemme.

With the fusion of ceremonial elements from both the Roman and the Gallican Vigil traditions in the region of northern Gaul and the resulting diminished importance of the two-Vigil-candles, it is not difficult to envisage the transference of the inscription from the two large candles of the Roman tradition to the single Easter candle and to understand why the date, previously reckoned from the Passion, subsequently expressed the number of years from the Incarnation. For the former were the visible symbols of the Passion that characterised the Roman Vigil; the single Candle represented the Light of the world and the moment the Light entered the world.[9]

[9]It may be significant that in the earlier *laudes cerei* we encounter a close connection between the supposed parthenogenesis of the bee and the production of wax on the one hand, and the birth of Jesus and the Virgin Mary on the other.

The inscribing on the Easter candle of the year reckoned from the Incarnation is first attested *c.*900 in the Pontifical of Poitiers. In addition to the Sacramentary of Corbie, it is mentioned in the Customary of the German Monasteries (*c.*1000) and in Lanfranc's *Decrees;*[10] whilst its appearance in three Roman documents[11] may be the result of the Benedictine influence of Monte Cassino, unless we have at Rome a survival of the above-mentioned custom of dating the candles, described by Bede. Apart from these documents, but excluding *Poitiers,* there are very few instances in which the *annus Domini* alone was inscribed on the Easter candle. In the vast majority of instances, it formed the *point de départ* or nucleus for the development of the *charta,* which provided additional chronological and liturgical information. For this reason, we have deferred a discussion of its subsequent history and survival until the next section.

The inscribing of the year disappeared from the Roman rite sometime after 1250, probably as a result of the liturgical influence of the Franciscans, in whose service-books this ritual act does not appear, and perhaps also as a result of a wish on the part of the Roman Church that this symbol of the risen Christ should be devoid of decorative excess. It is not found in the Roman Missal of 1474. Likewise, it must have disappeared from the ceremonial of churches which were influenced by or had adopted the Roman rite. The instance of Salzburg at the beginning of the sixteenth century is a rare and late survival of this practice.[12]

The Church has always stressed that Christianity is an historical religion and that its founder was born at a specific point in time. The dating of the candles, which Bede refers to, belongs to that tradition, first found in the Gospels, of rooting the message of salvation firmly in history, and serves to

[10]PL 78.336B; Albers V p.38; PL 150.446D.

[11]Namely, *PR XII* I p.241; *OEL* p.60; Pontifical of Apamea (*DAER* p.160 [M25]).

[12]1507 Missal fol.xciiii.

remind the faithful of this fact within the context of the liturgy.[13] With the development of the *charta,* this functional purpose was underlined by means of the inclusion of additional information, as we shall observe presently. The medieval mind, however, was not slow to endow the practice of dating the Easter candle with a symbolic interpretation. John Beleth explains that the practice conveyed the notion that time belongs to Christ and at a different level of interpretation, observes, in a comparison that relates to saintliness or intensity of faith rather than to actual numbers, that in the same way the year symbolises Christ, the divisions of the year stand for the Twelve Apostles and the days represent the Christian faithful.[14] Honorius of Autun designates Christ as the acceptable year of the Lord and extends Beleth's symbolism to include baptised children, who are equated with the hours.[15] The symbolism is echoed by Sicardus, who refers to Christ as both the summation and the consummation of time, 'the ancient and the fullness of days'.[16] Sicardus, in the same passage, also refers to *fertilitas fructuum in anno,* perhaps echoing the words of Psalm 64 (65) : 'You crown the year with your bounty'.

(iii) The *Charta*

It is said that the *De Temporibus* of Bede 'did much to establish the practice of dating events from the Incarnation' (DCC). It is therefore significant that the dual method of dating events used by Bede, that is, the year from the Incarnation and the *indictio,* was also found on the Easter candle at Poitiers in the ninth century and at a number of other churches.[17] The inclusion of this second item of information,

[13]*'In memoriam populis revocans.'* PL 95.667D.
[14]*Rationale* (PL 202.112A).
[15]*Gemma Animae* (PL 172.667D).
[16]Maximus annus antiquus et plenus dierum. *Mitrale* (PL 213.323D).
[17]*Poitiers* p.215. Also at Gembloux (Albers II p.99); Essen (Ordinal p.58); and Nidaros (*ONE* p.232).

which, it may be argued, was both superfluous and of relevance only within a fifteen year period, may be attributable to Bede. It is significant that in 701 the inscription on the candles at Rome, as recorded by Bede, did not mention the *indictio*.

The inclusion of the epact—the age in days of the moon on 1 January of a given year—from the eleventh century onwards not only provided an additional piece of chronological information,[18] but underlined the prominence and importance of the Easter candle at Eastertide, almost as a subtle reminder. Although in this respect it recalls the purpose of the inscription on the eighth-century Roman Vigil-candles, there is no direct evidence to link the recording of the epact with the earlier Roman practice. As with the inscribing of the year, medieval commentators attach a symbolic interpretation to the *indictio* and to the epact.[19] Sicardus writes that the *indictio* epitomised the actions of human beings, and the epact the succession of ages and the passing of time.[20] Both, he declares, were ordained and disposed by Christ.[21] Later instances of churches which confined the information to the year, the *indictio*, and the epact are rare. In the influential Roman rite, the insignia were absent. Elsewhere, and especially in France, the inclusion of additional information resulted in the emergence of the *charta*. However, at Barking at the start of the fifteenth century, the custom of recording only the year, the *indictio*, and the epact was maintained,[22] whilst at the end of that century, it was still observed in the Cathedral of Prague.[23]

The numerals and letters of the insignia may have been incised into the wax like the cross. If so, the incisions would have to have been filled in with some form of colouring in

---

[18]According to the Customary of Farfa, the *indictio* was not included. Albers I p.54

[19]Beleth also refers to the *indictio* as the '*aera*'. *Rationale* (PL 202.112A).

[20]So also Durandus, *Rationale* VI.80 fol.351.

[21]*Mitrale* (PL 213.323D).

[22]HBS 65 p.101.

[23]1498 Missal fol.xci.

order to make them conspicuous and visible from a distance. It is equally likely, however, that the information was painted onto the wax of the Candle. For not only could the information then have been read with ease; should the same Candle have been required for use the following year, the alteration of the numbers could have been much more easily accomplished. At the beginning of the twelfth century, Cistercian practice was to write the year, the *indictio,* and the epact on a *cartula* or small piece of parchment.[24] In all probability, this was done because the surface available for inscribing moderately-large letters was inadequate for the representation of the necessary information since the Cistercians used only a small Easter candle. This is the earliest recorded instance of the use of a *charta.*

The precedent having been set, the *charta* was not only adopted into the rites of other religious orders and churches; but within a relatively short space of time, it was realised that it was possible to include more liturgical and religious information on the parchment by increasing its size. Merati informs[25] us that the cycle of liturgical feasts for the whole year[26] was originally incised into the wax of the Candle and only subsequently transferred to the parchment. This is borne out by the Customary of Fleury, according to which fourteen items of information were inscribed on the surface of the Easter candle,[27] and by the 1512 Missal of Spires.[28] Merati also tells us that the *charta* was known as *Breve anni,* 'the summary of the year', as well.

Chartae varied enormously in length and correspondingly in the range of information they conveyed. All retained the

---

[24]*Nom. Cist.* p.104. The number of entries was subsequently increased to eleven. It was customary for the *armarius* (treasurer) to produce the *charta* (Martène, *DAMR* 3.15.8 p.142), as at Farfa (PL 150.1203C) and Fleury (Martène, *ibidem*).

[25]Gavanti/Merati IV p.155.

[26]*'Officii ordo per totum annum. '*

[27]Novarinus p.17.

[28]*Agenda* of Spires fol.xciii.

original nucleus of the year, the *indictio,* and the epact. The Dominican chart had two additional entries relating to the order and the dominical letter,[29] whilst the Premonstratensians displayed the names of the Pope, the abbot, the bishop, and the king,[30] as well as the movable feasts. In post-Tridentine times, some of the charts became even longer and in addition to a large amount of biblical, liturgical, and astronomical information, included events of both medieval and recent history. For instance, at the Church of St Gudila in Brussels, the victory of John, Duke of Brabant, on 5 June 1288 at the Battle of Woeringen, was recorded.[31] As mentioned above, the chart at the Monastery of Fleury had fourteen entries, whilst there were eighteen at Reims Cathedral, thirty-five at Chalons, and forty-eight at Rouen.[32] At the last-mentioned cathedral, the deacon read aloud the contents of the chart at the conclusion of the Preface.[33] In many churches, the names of the treasurer or sacristan and precentor were also written on the vellum plaques.[34] It was also common practice to place at the head of the *charta* a formula of benediction or consecration, introduced by *benedictus est cereus . . .* or *consecratus est cereus. . . .*

The custom of affixing the *tabula paschalis* to the Easter candle survived within the cathedral tradition until recent times. At Amiens, where a *charta* was in use until 1969, it was the responsibility of the *Secrétaire Général* to make a new one each year. The custom survives in some houses of the Dominican Order, but disappeared from the Cistercian and Premonstratensian rites after the Second Vatican Council.

[29]Ceremonial of 1520 in King, *LRO* p.357. The *indictio,* epact, and dominical letter have disappeared from the present-day chart, but the year in which the Order was formally sanctioned and the year of St Dominic's death still survive.

[30]Missal of 1578, cited by King, *LRO* p.190.

[31]Zazzera p.300.

[32]For the years 1585, 1708, and 1678, respectively. Martène, *DAER* 4.24 pp.146–17. The full text of all three appear in Appendix 13.

[33]De Moléon p.318.

[34]Paschal col.329.

There were a number of reasons for the demise of the *charta,* foremost of which was perhaps its absence from the Roman rite and, over the years, the growing influence of that rite in France, where the tradition of affixing a chart to the Easter candle seems to have been very strong and to have lasted longest. The holding of the paschal vigil on the morning of Holy Saturday detracted from the ritual and ceremonial in general and must also be regarded as a contributory factor in its disappearance. Beaudin's assertion that the display of information on the parchment destroyed the *'rapport intime'* between the message and significance of the information, and the Easter candle, is justified in the same way that the insertion of the grains of incense into the candlestick rather than the Candle detracted from their significance and reduced their purpose to the level of mere ornamentation.[35] On the positive side, it could be argued that this loss of rapport resulted in the chart's acquiring an identity independent of the Easter candle and an informative role comparable to the depiction of biblical scenes in stained glass windows. It must be remembered that the Cistercians used a chart for more than eight hundred years and that many of the French churches employed this device for centuries.

The chart was normally affixed to the lower part of the Easter candle, the central portion of the stock being reserved for the grains of incense. Paschal's statement that the charts were not always fastened to the Candle is both vague and frustrating since he does not elaborate.[36] Presumably, some were fixed to the candlestick; and perhaps it was not unknown for some to be displayed in a prominent place in close juxtaposition to the Easter candle, for instance, on the ambo. The parallel which Durandus draws between the chart and the superscription above the Cross should not be adduced in support of the view that the chart was affixed to the upper part

[35]*Le cièrge pascal* p.27.
[36]*La Liturgie* col.329.

of the Candle.[37] Such a position would clearly not have been practicable. The large chart at Rouen was fastened at a person's height to the huge column of wax that was the Easter candle,[38] so that it could be read with ease. At Essen, the chart completely encircled the Candle,[39] whilst the custom at Spires recalled earlier practice. For in that church, the four entries, namely, the year, the golden number, the day of the cathedral's consecration, and the name of the bishop or burgomaster *(presule),* were written on the wax rather than on the parchment.[40]

Evidence for the physical appearance of the chart is meagre. The rubric in the Ordinal of Essen states that the information should be written 'in large and beautiful letters' (p.58); and De Moléon refers to the chart at Rouen as a *fine parchment.*[41] It would appear that the chart resembled the page of an illuminated manuscript. Those executed until recently at Amiens belonged to this tradition. From the lower edge hung two seals. One was made of green wax, the episcopal colour, and impressed with the arms of the diocese; the other, of purple wax, indicating that the status of Amiens Cathedral was that of a minor basilica, was stamped with the arms of the cathedral chapter. The seals were attached to the chart by ribbons of corresponding colours. These devices are still preserved in the Treasury of Amiens Cathedral.[42] For their chart, the Dominicans use the black and white shield of their order, and inscribe it with lettering of contrasting colours. That in use at Blackfriars in Oxford measures about eight by six inches.

---

[37]*Rationale* VI.80 fol.351.

[38]De Moléon p.318.

[39]Ordinal p.58.

[40]1512 Missal fol.xciii.

[41]*'Beau velin'. Voyages liturgiques* p.318.

[42]The writer is indebted for this information to the *Secrétaire Général* of that diocese, L'Abbé P.Grey.

(iv) Portraits and Decorations

Bernado Bisso records that it was the custom of some churches to paint the likeness of the bishop or of the patron saint or of any saint on the Easter candle;[43] but he does not give any indication of the extent of this practice. However, a French source in the early part of the last century informs us that the Easter candle was usually decorated with different portraits of saints.[44] The same writer adds that edifying 'objects' made of gold were also used as decorations.

The practice of painting candles is of long standing.[45] It is mentioned by St Paulinus in the fifth century.[46] Mention of colours *(coloribus)* in an inventory of accoutrements for the Easter candle at York in the thirteenth century probably relates to the paints that were used to decorate the Candle. Bellotte records that painted candles were frequently used in the former ceremonies of the Church of Laon, but he does not mention the Easter candle.[47] However, we are informed that at Seville, paint was applied to the newly-cast column of wax.[48] Illustrations in some late nineteenth-century and early twentieth-century missals depict zig-zags and other geometric patterns on the central portion of the Candle's stock. It is probably these that Van Doren has in mind when he criticises the candlemakers of his day for hiding the fragrant symbol of Christ's 'pure and glorious flesh' behind strips of coloured paper.[49]

[43]*Hierurgia* I p.180.
[44]*DHCR* I p.470.
[45]Candle-painting was formerly a trade in its own right. Pierin del Vaga was one such craftsman.
[46]*De S. Felice Natalatium, Carmen* VI (PL 61.491B) : *Ast alii pictis accendant lumina ceris.*
[47]*RELR* p.812.
[48]Doblado p.299.
[49]*Le Cièrge Paschal* p.75. In a communication dated 1 August 1988 with a leading firm of candlemakers in England, the present writer was informed that the handmade-candle foreman could not recall such designs in the forty-two years of experience in his craft.

(v) Flowers

The adornment of the Easter candle with flowers is first attested in the Mozarabic rite of the tenth century.[50] The Candle was festooned with flowers or garlands during the reading of the first prophecy. In Central and Southern Italy the surviving *Exultet* rolls provide pictorial evidence for the practice in that part of the world during the eleventh and twelfth centuries;[51] and at York in the thirteenth century, flowers appear in an inventory of accessories for the Easter candle.[52] Rock cites a reference in Pamelius' *Liturgicon* to the twining of flowers around the Easter candle in an old Ambrosian missal.[53] Their use as adornments of the Easter candle has survived to modern times—so great is the force of tradition that, although not prescribed by any of the manuals of Roman liturgy for this occasion, the *Memoriale Rituum* 'suggests their use "if customary" on certain days'.[54] In former times at Dixmude, Nieuport, Veyrne, and other places in West Flanders, branches were fastened to the candlestick in addition to the flowers and leaves. Known as the 'Paschal Tree', it was a visual expression of the *arbor decora et fulgida*.[55] Today, at Annecy not only is the candelabrum festooned with garlands; a vase of flowers is placed in front of it to show the importance of the Easter candle. In most cathedrals and churches, it is usual to leave the Candle adorned with flowers for the whole season of Easter. At Vannes Cathedral, however, flowers are used only at the Vigil itself, whilst at Lyon, they remain in position only till the end of Easter week.[56]

---

[50]Antiphonary of Léon p.284.

[51]Avery, *Plates XLVI, LXV,* and *LXIX.*

[52]Bradshaw and Wordsworth II p.98.

[53]*Church of Our Fathers* I p.167. The present writer has failed to locate this reference in either the cited or the original work. It is just possible that it existed as a marginal annotation in one of the above-mentioned books.

[54]Fortescue and O'Connell (11th edition) p.29.

[55]Callewaert p.140.

[56]1984 Survey of France.

Their use in pre-Christian religious rites may have been a contributory factor in the adornment of the Easter candle with flowers. However, it is much more likely that the practice of decorating the Candle with flowers was an internal liturgical development, suggested by references in the *laudes cerei* to the source of the beeswax. For not only did the presence of flowers fulfil a decorative function in furnishing a floral setting or foil for the Candle; it provided a physical and tangible complement to the floral allusions of the Song, a visual representation of one of the themes of the Preface, and served as a forceful reminder of the origin and source of the beeswax. In later centuries, when references to the bees and the flowers had been all but excised from the *laus cerei* in some churches and the rapport between the wording of the Preface and the flowers was subsequently lost, the floral decorations survived.[57]

[57]References to flowers are found in four different Prefaces in the Western rites. The clause *aliae vertunt flores in ceram* of the Gallican Preface (Vich Sacramentary p.3; *Miss. Gall. Vet.* p.36; Bobbio Missal p.77; S.Gall 348 p.83; Jumièges Missal p.92) is particularly apposite in view of the juxtaposition of the flowers and the beeswax. In the Milanese Preface (*Manuale Ambrosianum* p.201 and subsequent Ambrosian missals), not only is the importance of the flowers mentioned, but Christ is identified with both the wax of the Candle and with the flowers : *Quid enim magis accommodum magisque festivum quam iesseico flori floreis excubemus et tedis? praesertim cum et sapientia de semetipsa cecinerit : Ego sum flos agri, et lilium convallium.* ('What is more fitting and more festive than that we keep watch for the Flower of Jesse with floral torches? especially when even Wisdom has sung of herself : I am the flower of the field, and the lily of the valleys.') Similarly in the Beneventan Preface (Pinell, *La Benedicció* p.96), the importance of the flower to the bee is stressed : *flore utuntur coniuge, flore funguntur genere, flore domos instruunt, flore divitias convehunt, flore ceram conficiunt.* ('They use the flower as a spouse; they gain their offspring from the flower; they construct their homes from the flower; they gather their riches from the flower; they make their wax from the flower.') There is also a reference to flowers in the Mozarabic *benedictio cerei* (Pinell, *ibidem* p.117). In this last Preface, it is unlikely that the flowers, which were placed around the Easter candle during the reading of Genesis 1, represented nature or creation.

In former times in Hertfordshire in England, Holy Saturday was one of the great flower gathering days of the year. Particularly sought after was the rare Pasque flower *(anemone pulsatilla)* with its purple petals.[58]

(vi) Crucifix

C.Callewaert records that in some Belgian churches, an image of the Crucified was attached to the Easter candle.[59] Like the grains of incense, this emblem of the Passion, fastened to the waxen symbol of the Resurrection, betokened the mystery of the Cross and bore witness that the Crucified had risen from the dead, in the same way that the crown of thorns, which encircles some Easter candlesticks, signifies the triumphal kingship of Christ.

(vii) Branches

At St Maartenskerk in St Ghislain there is a fifteenth-century candlestick near to the crown of which three small branches spring from the main stem so as to form candle-holders vertical with and parallel to it. There is a copy in a church in Bruges. It is said that the three candles represent the three Marys, who went to embalm the body of Jesus and who were the first witnesses of the risen Lord.[60] At Capua, the three candles on a similar device were said to represent the Trinity.[61] In addition to three, Callewaert also mentions candlesticks with two, four, and six branches, but does not elaborate. It is not difficult to see in the latter type the survival or development of the *menorah*.

[58]Jones-Baker p.133.
[59]*De Paaschkandelaar* p.141.
[60]Callewaert, *ibidem*.
[61]Feasey, *The Paschal Preconium* p.259.

Chapter Twenty-eight
THE BENEDICTION-FORMULAS

(i) The Romano-Gallican A and Milanese Traditions

The structure of the formula found in both these traditions is tripartite :

    (i) The invitatory proclamation or *preconium*
    (ii) The Dialogue
    (iii) The Preface or *laus cerei*.

In view of the survival of other elements from the *Lucernarium* in the ceremonial surrounding the lighting and blessing of the Easter candle, it is not difficult to discern the origin of the Dialogue and Preface in the latter ritual, and to recognise that the dialogue and prayer of thanksgiving in the *Apostolic Tradition* are liturgical features expanded and transformed into the second and third sections of the later formula.[1]

It is not known when the structure of the formula achieved its present form. The scheme of *Exultet*/Dialogue/Preface, which still obtains today, had already been fixed by the eighth century; but the inclusion of this non-Roman ceremony into

---

[1]The Dialogue, followed by the prayer of thanksgiving for light, divine, natural, and that made by humans, lacks ' "Up with your hearts" because that is said only at the offering' (Cuming, *Hippolytus* p.23 §25). With the development of the *Lucernarium* into the blessing of the Easter candle, which included the offering of light, the omitted couplet was incorporated.

both the Gregorian and Gelasian Sacramentaries must have been of recent occurrence in that century. The first element, the *preconium* proper, serves as an introduction to the Preface; but the date of its incorporation into the formula as a whole cannot be placed before the eighth century by surviving documentary evidence. An earlier date, however, can be inferred with confidence in view of the age of Ennodius' *laudes cerei*.[2] We have seen that the Dialogue was a feature of the *Lucernarium*. With regard to the third element, the Preface, there can be little doubt, to judge from the surviving Beneventan, Gallican, and Milanese Prefaces, with their expansive references to flowers and bees, that poetic language was a characteristic of the *laudes cerei* to which Jerome took exception. If so, the Prefaces must have achieved their final form and contained the same themes, familiar from later compositions, well before the end of the fourth century.

There is evidence in the fourth century that the *laus cerei* could be composed either in prose or in verse. Capelle has shown that the Preface of the Romano-Gallican tradition was in all likelihood written by St Ambrose.[3] On the other hand, we have St Augustine's own clear testimony that his *laus cerei* had been written in verse.[4] The three extant lines of his Preface show that he had composed it in dactylic hexameters. Archdale King, amongst others, is of the opinion that the hymn *Ignis Creator Igneus,* found only in the Antiphonary of Ban-

[2] The close similarity between the Romano-Gallican and Milanese *preconia* and their omission from the beginning of both of the Prefaces of Ennodius (to be dated to *c.*510) would suggest that the wording of the *Exultet* had become fixed in a formula common to a number of western rites at an early date.

[3] *L'* 'Exultet' *Pascal* pp.219–46. The 1488 Missal of Basel attributes the work to the bishop (fol.xcii), but both M.Huglo and Dom B.Fischer (whom Huglo cites on p.88) contest its Ambrosian authorship (*L'Auteur* p.87).

[4] *De Civit.Dei* 15.22. On the strength of this remark, the Church for centuries regarded Augustine as the author of the Romano-Gallican Preface, as is evidenced, amongst other testimony, by the Sacramentary of Fulda (Schmidt I p.425), Grancolas (p.319), and even the 1830 Missal of Limoges (p.220). Huglo (p.81) casts doubt on the authenticity of the three verses.

gor,[5] is the sole remaining example of a *laus cerei* in verse and may have been written by St Ambrose, himself a no mean composer of hymns.[6] There is also in existence the *Escorial* Preface, a *laus cerei* composed in verse;[7] and the poem of Drepanius Florus, *De Cereo Paschali*, with its references to the composition of the wick and the apian origin of the wax, has also survived.[8]

A study of the composition and content of the Preface is strictly beyond the scope of this work; but it has to be observed that the Prefaces of the Romano-Gallican, Milanese, and Beneventan liturgies, and also the *laudes cerei* of Ennodius contain the same themes or motifs, and that the offering of light and the eulogy of the bees are elements peculiar to the Paschal Preface and represent a development and expansion of the simple prayer of thanksgiving found in the *Apostolic Tradition*.

Romano-Gallican	Milanese	Beneventan	Ennodius I	Ennodius II
Passover/	Lamb/	Resurrection	Mystery of	Mystery of
Resurrection	Sacrifice		Creation/	Creation/
			Resurrection	Renewal
Offering of	Offering of	Light	Offering of	Offering of
Light	Light		light of candle	light of candle
Eulogy of bees	Bees	Bees	Bees	(Bees)
Eschatology	Eschatology	Divine Protection	Divine Protection	Renewal

Similarly, the *Ignis Creator Igneus* incorporates the themes of Passover/Resurrection, the Candle, Light, and Bees. The three ritual Prefaces and the two *laudes cerei* of Ennodius differ from one another in that each seems to place a greater emphasis on one particular theme, or aspect of a theme, but without detriment to the overall structure and recognised pattern of composition. Prominent in the Romano-Gallican Preface are the references and allusions to the Passover and the Crossing of the Red Sea. A strong eschatological tone charac-

[5]HBS 10 p.11.
[6]*LRC* p.417.
[7]Reconstructed text in Pinell, *La Benedicció* pp.97–100.
[8]PL 61.1087–88.

terises the Milanese *laus cerei,* whilst in the Beneventan Preface, the theme of flowers and bees is particularly conspicuous. We have already observed that Ennodius dwells on the physical characteristics and composition of the Easter candle *vis-à-vis* the instances of God's intervention in history. In what could be interpreted as a posthumous vindication of Jerome's strictures, the Roman Church excised from the Roman Preface the offending and incongruous Virgilian language, leaving only two short references to the bee : *de operibus apum* and *apis mater eduxit.* It was left to the revisers of the post-Vatican II Missal to remove all references to that creature, in view of the modern composition of Easter candles which, it was thought, rendered allusion to the bee meaningless.[9]

(ii) The Romano-Gallican B Tradition

(A) THE *DEUS MUNDI CONDITOR.* Archdale King refers correctly, in the opinion of the writer, to two types of Preface within the Romano-Gallican tradition, which he designates *Type A* and *Type B.*[10] The latter has been discussed in the previous section. *Type A* comprises the single prayer *Deus mundi Conditor.* It is found as the *laus cerei* in the Gelasian Sacramentary, the Sacramentary of Autun, and Ordo 30A;[11] but as the sole formula for the consecration of the Easter candle, it is found nowhere else. In spite of its clear reference to the Easter candle, Pinell calls the formula an *oracio Romana;*[12] and Deshusses excises it from the supplement[13] to the Gregorian Sacramentary as one of those blessings in *codex R* 'which are scarcely recognisable'.[14] A brief examination of the contents of this

[9]See, Harbert p.240.
[10]*LRC* p.417.
[11]*GeV* (Mohlberg) p.68; *GePh* p.63; OR 30A.15.
[12]*La Benediccio* p.85.
[13]Considered by that author to have been compiled by St Benedict of Aniane *c.*810–815.
[14]*Le Sacramentaire Grégorien* p.42.

prayer, however, reveals that its structure closely resembles that of the Romano-Gallican Preface. It is true that the offering of light is placed first; but the formula is not strictly a Preface in that the opening words do not suggest a continuity of the Dialogue, a characteristic of the standard Preface. Rather, it resembles the initial invocations of later prayers for the blessing of the new fire. After the prologue, there are three sections, introduced respectively by *igitur, ergo,* and *igitur,* whose themes are the Resurrection, light, and bees. It closes with a further invocation recalling the eschatological themes and language of both the Romano-Gallican Preface and Ennodius' *laudes cerei.*

This last pericope, here linked to the preceding section by *ergo,* became detached from the rest of the prayer and came to constitute a formula of blessing in its own right, the *Veniat quaesumus.* [15] The *Deus mundi Conditor* (without the *Veniat quaesumus*) subsequently became a prayer for the blessing of the new fire on Holy Saturday within the Germanic tradition. [16]

(B) THE *DEUS MUNDI CONDITOR* AND THE ROMANO-GERMANIC *EXULTET*/PREFACE. The presence of both these benediction-formulas for the Easter candle in the Sacramentaries of Angoulême and Gellone would, at first sight, appear to constitute an unnecessary duplication of consecration. [17] As with the so-called double blessing in the Mozarabic rite, the difficulty largely disappears when it is realised that the *Deus mundi Conditor* is an invocatory blessing, whilst the *Exultet*/Preface formula has much in common with the notion of *berakah.* In the Spanish rite, an interval of time and space separated the two blessings. In the Gallican tradition, since both formulas were pronounced consecutively, it was perhaps inevitable that one

---

[15]Also found as a blessing for the new fire, as a blessing for the grains of incense, and as a blessing of the *cereus minor.*

[16]As such, it is found in *PRG* (II p.95), and was used at Abo (Manual of *c.*1522 p.238), at Mainz (1507 Missal fol.xcii), at Salzburg (1507 Missal fol.xciii), and at Ratisbon (1570 Ritual np).

[17]*GeAng* p.52 and *GeG* pp.92–93, respectively.

of them should disappear as a prayer of consecration—as indeed did happen—or be diverted to serve some other purpose.[18] In fact, within the Germanic tradition, the *Deus mundi Conditor* became a formula for the blessing of the new fire on Holy Saturday, as we have already noted, though in that development it shed its final pericope.

(c) THE *VENIAT QUAESUMUS*. The final pericope of the *Deus mundi Conditor*, once linked to that blessing by *ergo*, subsequently became either a prayer for the blessing of the new fire, or in the majority of churches including that of Rome, the prayer for the blessing of the five grains of incense. However, in a small number of churches within the Gallican tradition, it survived as the formula for the blessing of the Easter candle, once the major portion of the *Deus mundi Conditor* ceased to fulfil this function. These French churches thus represented the survival of the tradition attested above in the Sacramentaries of Angoulême and Gellone. At Bourges, Périgueux, and Le Puy,[19] the Easter candle was blessed, by means of invocation by the celebrant, with the *Veniat quaesumus*, after it had been kindled with the new fire, but prior to the chanting of the *Exultet* by the deacon. This double benediction was comparable to Mozarabic practice. At Amiens, where the Easter candle was consecrated according to the Roman rite, the *Veniat quaesumus* was used to bless the *cereus minor*.[20]

(iii) The Mozarabic Tradition

Mention has already been made of the double blessing of the Easter candle in the Mozarabic rite, reminiscent of the

[18]According to the Pontifical of Poitiers, the prayer was used to commission the three apotropaic candles lit at the 'altar of the fonts' (p.216).

[19]1741 Missal p.225; 1782 Missal p.159; 1783 Missal p.159. Apropos of this prayer used in the same context, Atchley (p.139) cites the 1845 Missal of Pamiers. He is in error, however, to include the Pontifical of St-Germain-des-Prés.

[20]1752 Missal p.182.

practice attested in the Sacramentaries of Angoulême and Gellone. In the former rite, the lamp was also blessed with the use of both an invocatory formula and a *berakah*-type benediction. Neither the blessing of the lamp nor the blessing of the Candle is preceded by a *preconium* corresponding to the *Exultet*, and the Dialogue appears as the detached triple acclamation of *Deo gratias*. The themes of the Candle-Preface are light, Baptism, and the composition of the Easter candle. The latter recalls the *laudes cerei* of Ennodius.

(iv) The *Exultet*/Dialogue/Preface as a Blessing

Within the Roman rite, the chanting of the *Exultet* and the Preface by the deacon is analogous to the reading of the Gospel. During the performance of this blessing, which has thus acquired the status of a Gospel-passage, the congregation remains standing,[21] those in the choir turning to face the deacon. At Milan, prior to the liturgical revisions that followed the Second Vatican Council, a lengthy interruption occurred at the end of the first pericope of the Preface. During this, a subdeacon and the sacristan withdrew to the sacristy to fetch the lamp containing the new fire. On their return, the Easter candle and the two Vigil-candles were lit.[22] This, in effect, divided the Preface into two distinct blessings, as is clear from the rubric which follows the words *in veritate proveniunt* at the end of the first pericope : *hac benedictione finita*,[23] and from the fact that at that juncture the congregation sat down and remained seated until the conclusion of the Preface.[24]

At Lyon, the *Exultet* was chanted after the reading of the prophecies.[25] This practice recalled the arrangement attested

[21]Fortescue and O'Connell (11th ed.) p.306. It is also prescribed in the 1669 Cistercian Missal p.155.

[22]1560 Missal fol.110.

[23]'When this blessing is finished.' 1475 Missal fol.lxxx.

[24]1560 Missal fol.110.

[25]1771 Missal p.226.

in Ordo 29.[26] Immediately prior to the *Exultet,* the first litany was sung.[27] This also occured at Paris, Besançon, and Luçon, and at Bourges.[28] At Coutances, Bayeux, Rouen, and Norwich, an antiphon preceded the *Exultet.*[29] At Lund, the *Exultet* was sung by a *lector,*[30] whilst at Slesvig the duty was performed by a *sacerdos.*[31]

There may be some link between the Milanese ritual and the practice attested in the *Pontificale Romano-Germanicum (PRG).* According to the rubrics of the latter (II p.97), the *Exultet* was termed the first blessing of the Candle and was *read* by the archdeacon 'as if in the manner of one reading'.[32] He then raised his voice for the Dialogue and presently began to chant the Preface.[33]

[26]OR 29.48.

[27]1510 Missal of Lyon fol.lxix.

[28]The first three churches are cited by Jounel, *La Semaine Sainte* p.147. 1741 Missal of Bourges p.226.

[29]1557 Missal fol.lxviii; *Semaine Sainte* p.495; 1497 Missal np; and HBS 82 p.91, respectively.

[30]1514 Missal fol.xci.

[31]Freisen p.131.

[32]Quasi in modum legentis.

[33]Inde vero accedit in consecrationem cerei, decantando quasi canonem : 'Then he began the blessing of the Candle in the same way that he would chant the Canon (of the Mass).'

Chapter Twenty-nine

THE LIGHTING
AND EXTINGUISHING
OF THE EASTER CANDLE

A. THE LIGHTING OF THE EASTER CANDLE

(i) Before the *Exultet*

Two traditions are found within the primitive practice of lighting the Easter candle *before* it was blessed. (i) The procession into church with the Candle previously kindled at the new fire has already been discussed.[1] (ii) Within the second tradition, the Easter candle was lit just prior to the commencement of the *Exultet;* and to this tradition belong all those churches in which the Easter candle was either borne into church unlit or was already in position by the altar or the ambo prior to the start of the ceremony. This tradition is attested in a number of early sacramentaries and pontificals, in *Alcuin* and the *Regularis Concordia,* and is mentioned by *Micrologus* and Honorius of Autun.[2] The latter adds that the kindling occurred at this point because 'Christ has the light from the beginning'. The practice was also observed at Monte Cassi-

---

[1]Chapter Twenty.

[2]*GeV* p.68; *GePr* p.55; *GeAng* p.52; OR 29.48; *PRG* II p.97 §346; *Poitiers* p.215; PL 101.1216B and PL 137.494C; PL 151.1016B and *Gemma Animae* (PL 172.668C).

no in the twelfth century.[3] At the beginning of the eighteenth century, De Vert found that the Easter candle was lit prior to the start of the blessing in a large number of churches;[4] and this is borne out by the rubrics of a number of French diocesan missals.[5] Thurston draws attention to the fact that the clause in the Roman Preface

(columnae) . . . quam in honorem Dei rutilans ignis *accendit*[6]

is a form of internal rubric, and implied at the time the *laus* was composed that the Easter candle was already lit.[7] The lighting of the Candle prior to the blessing meant that the *Exultet* and Preface were sung without interruption. For in the older documents, the ritual involving the grains of incense was unknown, whilst in the rites of the first four French cathedrals mentioned in note 5, Carcassonne, Périgueux, Le Puy, Meaux, the grains of incense were inserted before the deacon began the *Exultet*. In these four French cathedrals, the lighting of the Easter candle prior to the *Exultet* vis-à-vis the insertion of the grains of incense, also at a point before the blessing of the Candle, represents the first stage in the development of these two ritual actions as features which subsequently interrupted the Preface in most western rites, according to the scheme below.

According to two twelfth-century Roman pontificals, the Easter candle was also lit before it was blessed.[8] These documents are representative of Stage 2 in the scheme below, since they both attest the insertion of the grains of incense *during*

---

[3]*PRMA* I p.293 (= M 1139).
[4]Paschal col.330.
[5]Carcassonne (1749) p.196; Périgueux (1782) p.159; Le Puy (1783) p.159; Meaux (1849) p.169. Additional evidence for the practice comes from Albi (*DAER* 4.24.8 p.147 and Lyon [1487 Missal cited by King, *LPS* p.61]) and from Ordo XIV (PL 78.1218).
[6]'Which the ruddy fire has kindled to the honour of God.' Another interpretation of the word italicised by the writer is discussed below in (ii).
[7]*The* Exultet *and the Paschal Candle* p.517.
[8]*PR XII* (*PRMA* I xxxii.8 p.240) and the Pontifical of Apamea (*DAER* 4.24 p.160, M25).

the Preface. The evidence of later Roman service-books, however, is confusing. The twelfth-century Ordo of the Lateran Church, Durand's pontifical, and the slightly later *Bindo Fesulani* place the kindling and insertions during the Preface,[9] as does the *Missale Romanum* and all subsequent Roman Missals up to and including the Tridentine Missal of 1570. Ordo XIV and CA 1706, on the other hand, concur with the twelfth-century *Pontificale Romanum (PR XII)*.[10] As we noted when we discussed the triple *Lumen Christi*, a certain fluidity of ceremonial existed within Roman ceremonial up to 1570.

One of the most noticeable alterations to the paschal ceremonies, resulting from the liturgical revisions of 1955, was the restoration of the primitive practice, which had survived in the four above-mentioned cathedrals as late as the eighteenth century, of singing the *Exultet* and Preface without interruption, the lighting of the Candle being transferred to the beginning of the ceremony, its position of old. The following scheme illustrates the three stages of development :

Stage 1 : Easter candle lit before *Exultet*.
          Incense grains inserted before *Exultet*.
Stage 2 : Easter candle lit before *Exultet*.
          Incense grains inserted during Preface.
Stage 3 : Easter candle lit during Preface.
          Incense grains inserted during Preface.

(ii) During the Preface Following the *Exultet*

The practice of lighting the Easter candle at *ignis accendit* in the Preface is first attested in the tenth-century Sacramentary of Corbie.[11] In almost all other rites which perpetuated this tradition, it is at this same point that the Candle is lit.[12]

[9]*OEL* p.61; *PGD* III p.588; and *ZRKM* p.214, respectively.
[10]PL 78.1218C and *ZRKM* p.214, respectively.
[11]PL 78.336B.
[12]In Haymo's *Ordo Missalis* (Van Dijk II p.246) the Candle is lit at *divisus in partes;* in the 1543 Missal of Bayonne (p.46) at *sed iam columnae;* in

Mention of the practice at Rouen in the following century[13] and its inclusion by Lanfranc in his *Decrees* and by Ulric in the Customary of Cluny,[14] together with the evidence from Corbie, strongly suggest a monastic provenance in Northern France. Its adoption and use within the monastic tradition ultimately led to its appearance in most of the cathedral rites in the Romano-Gallican tradition, including that of Rome,[15] and in the rite of Milan.[16]

It is not difficult to see why the practice of kindling the Easter candle during the Preface developed. Elsewhere, we have observed that the censing of the Easter candle and the insertion of the five grains of incense during the Preface were the result of the ambiguous interpretation of *incensi huius sacrificium,* a phrase which invited the opportunity to match word with action. The intrusion of the ritual action into the Preface was further facilitated by the fact that the words which had come to be regarded as an internal rubric occurred at the start of a new section of the Preface, introduced by *igitur.* The break having occurred in the Preface for the incense, the precedent was now set for a further interruption, suggested, so the writer believes, by another ambiguity of language. For at the conclusion of the very next sentence occurs *accendit,* 'has kindled', which, as we have already seen, indicated that the Easter candle was alight before the start of the *Exultet.* Since, however, *accendit* could equally be construed as being in the present tense of the verb, it is the belief of the writer that the

the 1568 Missal of Palencia (fol.cvi) at *reddit ecclesia;* in the 1543 Missal of Paris (fol.lxxx) at *praeconia novimus;* and in the Ordinary of Tongres (p.165) and the 1518 Missal of Ratisbon (fol.cxvii) at *suscipe, sancte pater.*

[13]*Acta Vetera* (PL 147.176C).

[14]PL 150.467C and PL 149.663B, respectively.

[15]By the eleventh century, it featured at Fruttuaria and Vallombrosa in Northern Italy (Albers IV p.65 and p.249, respectively).

[16]Beroldus p.110. In the Milanese rite, the opening words of the second pericope *ecce iam ignis columnae resplendet* were acclaimed three times by the deacon, the congregation responding *Deo gratias* after each cry. Martène, *DAER* 4.24.11 p.148. For four Gallican exceptions, see (i) above.

alternative translation 'kindles' invited the lighting of the Easter candle at this point and created a materialisation, as it were, of the primary concept inherent in this verb. It thus became an internal rubric or cue for the deacon or another official who applied the fire to the wick of the Candle.

(iii) The Agent

As a rule the Easter candle was lit by the officiant, usually a deacon, who chanted the *Exultet* and Preface; and it is likely that the deacon performed these two duties in the fourth century, when the ceremony is first recorded. According to some early sacramentaries and other service-books, the officiant was the archdeacon.[17] This dignitary also functioned in this capacity at Vienne and Soissons,[18] whilst at Troyes, it was the senior archdeacon.[19] At Naples and in the Mozarabic rite, the bishop lit the Easter candle,[20] whilst Beneventan practice allowed either the bishop or a priest to perform the task.[21] In the churches listed below in *Table 52,* the Candle was lit by a variety of other officials and clerics.

Official	Church	Source
Acolyte	Monte Cassino	*DAMR* 3.15.10 p.143 (M 1139)
	Lisieux (possibly)	1752 Missal p.193
Serjent	Le Mans	1789 Ceremonial p.127
Subdeacon	Rome	HBS 17 p.175
	Albi	*DAER* 3.24.8 p.147 (M 1)
Sacristan	Lanfranc	PL 150.467C
	Chartres	13 C Ordinal p.111
Provost	St-Germain-des-Prés	*DAMR* 3.15.7 p.142 (M 1165)
Precentor	Premonstratensians	King, *LRO* p.190

Table 52. Some officials other than deacon who lit the Easter candle

[17]*GeV* §425 p.68; *GePr* p.55; *GeAng* p.55; OR 30A.15; *PRG* II p.97.
[18]De Moléon p.23 and Martène, *DAER* 4.24 p.161 (M 305), respectively.
[19]1736 Missal p.228.
[20]Mallardo p.33; Léon Antiphonary p.280.
[21]Hesbert p.188.

In none of the above-listed rites and documents is there any indication as to why the officiating deacon did not light the Easter candle. In some instances, it may have been thought that the deacon would be distracted from his chant if he performed this duty. In other churches, the height or location of the Easter candle would have rendered this task difficult for the deacon.[22] However, according to the service-books of the vast majority of the churches within the Roman, Gallican, and Germanic traditions, as well as in the Milanese rite, the lighting of the Easter candle was performed by the officiating deacon. In the papal ceremonial, the task fell to the junior cardinal deacon.[23] Although the Roman Missal of 1474 mentions a subdeacon,[24] the Tridentine Missal specifies the officiating deacon.

(iv) The Means

In the Milanese rite, the bringing in of the lamp lit with the new fire was almost certainly a survival from the *Lucernarium*. Within the Romano-Gallican tradition, the Easter candle was lit with either the serpent-candle, the reed-candle, or the triple candle. In France, the practice emerged of transferring the new fire from the single processional candle or one of the triple candles to the wick of the Easter candle by means of a sulphur-coated splint *(sulphuratum)*. None of the missals which attest this procedure[25] states the precise point at which the fire was transferred. The mention of the triple candle in

---

[22]As at Durham and Leau. Both Gavanti (p.166) and Bauldry (p.191) state that the Easter candle could be removed from its holder to allow its being kindled. The Polish Manual also permitted this concession to facilitate the insertion of the grains of incense (p.477). In the Hereford Missal, *accendit* is sustained for several notes, thus allowing time for the Candle to be lit at that very word (p.102).

[23]*PR XII (PRMA* I.xxxii.7 p.239); C.A.1706 (*ZRKM* p.213).

[24]HBS 17 p.175.

[25]Besançon (1707) p.317; Toulouse (1832) p.211; La Rochelle (1835) p.191; Auch (1836) p.192; Nantes (1837) p.203; Meaux (1845) p.169.

two of the missals (Auch and Nantes) again demonstrates how this functional means of bringing in the new fire had developed into a vivid and symbolic presentation of the Trinity with an almost separate existence and purpose of its own.

B. THE EXTINGUISHING OF THE EASTER CANDLE

In the history of the rite before 1100, two traditions existed relating to the length of time the Easter candle continued to burn following the paschal vigil: (i) that in which the Candle burned either continuously or intermittently until it was disposed of at the end of Easter week, and (ii) that in which the Candle was lit at certain services throughout the whole of the Easter season.

We shall have occasion to refer to the evidence of *Micrologus* and Honorius in the next chapter when we consider the fragmentation of the Easter candle at the end of Easter Week. Suffice it to state here that neither writer gives any indication as to whether the Easter candle burned continuously or intermittently during that period. At Rouen in the eleventh century, the Candle was lit at every mass in Easter Week.[26] It is very difficult to know whether the practice at Vienne *c.*1700, where the Easter candle was kept alight day and night until Easter Saturday, had survived over the centuries, or whether the custom was a recent neo-Gallican revival.[27] The alternative tradition, in which the Easter candle was lit at every major feast until Ascension Day, is first encountered *c.*1150 in the Gilbertine rite;[28] but it may have been known in the Cistercian rite some fifty years earlier.[29]

[26]*Acta Vetera* (PL 147.176C).
[27]De Vert II p.38. At Tours Cathedral and the Collegiate Church of St-Martin, also in Tours, the Easter candle burned continuously until Low Sunday. (Guyet p.294.)
[28]HBS 59 p.40.
[29]According to Guignard (p.117), the Easter candle should remain where it was blessed until Ascension Day. It is difficult to believe that it remained unlit during the whole of this period.

The disastrous results of leaving the Easter candle at Naples unattended during the night of Holy Saturday have already been described. Evidence elsewhere for the continuous burning of the Easter candle during the remainder of Holy Saturday and throughout all of Easter day is plentiful; and though the majority of it is late, it is likely that in nearly all instances it attests a centuries-old tradition. The custom of extinguishing the Candle after Compline on Easter Day became established. Some of the churches where this practice is attested are listed in *Table 53*.

At Vallombrosa, it remained lit *usque mane;*[30] and the Ordinal of St Mary's, York, refers to the Candle's being extinguished the followng day without specifying at which service this took place.[31] At Naples in the eighth century, it was put out after Mass on Easter Day.[32] The 1845 Missal of Meaux enjoins that the Easter candle should burn at each service on Easter Day (p.173). This could be interpreted to mean that the Candle was extinguished after every service on that day; but the significance of the Easter candle *vis-à-vis* the importance of Easter Day makes this unlikely. Moreover, there is no other recorded instance of such a practice.

In some churches, the Easter candle remained alight beyond the evening of Easter Sunday. At Sens, it was extinguished after Lauds on Easter Monday,[33] whilst it burned continuously until Tuesday, presumably until after Compline had been sung, at Verdun[34] and Clermont-Ferrand.[35] The Sarum rite, followed by that of Exeter, prescribed that the Candle be lit for Mass, Matins, Vespers, and Compline on

[30]Albers IV p.220.
[31]HBS 75 p.292.
[32]Mallardo p.22.
[33]Missal of 1715 p.244.
[34]Albers V p.123. The Customary of St Vitus states that the Easter candle is not extinguished 'until the third day'. De Vert mistakenly interprets this 'Wednesday' (*Explication* II p.38).
[35]De Vert II p.38.

Church	Date	Source
Rouen	11 C	PL 147.176C
Cistercians	1119	*Nom. Cist.* p.105
Gilbertines	*c.*1150	HBS 59 p.40
St Augustine's, Canterbury	13 C	HBS 28 p.274
Salisbury†	13 C	HBS 91 p.24
Exeter	1337	HBS 37 p.322
Bursfeld	*c.*1500	*DAER* 3.15.7 p.142 (M 1179)
Paris	1662	Ceremonial p.379
Amiens	*c.*1700	DeVert II p.38
Angers	1731	Ceremonial p.261
Evreux	1740	Missal p.194
Bourges	1741	Missal p.233
Sées	1742	Missal p.193
Lisieux	1752	Missal p.194
Poitiers	1767	Missal p.253
Reims‡	1770	Missal p.213
Lyon	1771	Missal p.203
Tours	1784	Missal p.200
Coutances	1825	Ceremonial p.329
La Rochelle	1835	Missal p.193
Nantes	1837	Missal p.205
Autun	1845	Missal p.247

†According to the Sarum Missal (Warren I p.270), it was extinguished at Vespers on Easter Day, the office also prescribed by Lanfranc (PL150.476C) and enjoined in the Premonstratensian rite (Missal of 1578, cited by King, *LRO* p.190).

‡The rubric of this missal banishes any doubt that the Easter candle burned throughout the night of Holy Saturday : 'The Easter candle should burn during the whole of Saturday, the night which follows, as well as on Easter Day continuously until Compline.' Direct evidence for the burning of the Candle during the night of Holy Saturday also comes from Laon (Bellotte p.814) and the 1597 Missal of Metz, in which the rubric is a quotation from the Preface : *flammas eius Lucifer matutinus inveniat,* 'let the morning star find her flames'.

Table 53. Evidence for the burning of the Easter candle from the Vigil until the end of Easter day

Easter Day, Monday, and Tuesday.[36] Roman practice, defined in the decree of the Sacred Congregation of Rites

[36]Warren I p.270; HBS 37 p.322.

(S.C.R.) dated 19 May 1607, stipulated that the Easter candle should be lit, on the three days of Easter, only at Mass and at Vespers.[37]

In the period between Easter and Ascension Day, universal practice, which included the Roman as permitted by the above-mentioned decree, was to light the Easter candle on all intervening Sundays. The decree of 1607 added that other customs, if occurring during Eastertide, should be kept. A considerable number of churches did in fact light the Candle on all major feast days between Easter and Ascension Day.[38] After Compline on Easter Day in the Cistercian rite, the Easter candle was not lit again until Vespers of Ascension Day.[39]

It was perhaps inevitable that the time during which the Easter candle remained in church should be increased from seven to forty days, seeing that the Candle had come to represent the visible presence of Christ on earth after His Resurrection.[40] Its removal from church symbolised His disappearance from human sight. In the majority of churches, including those of Rome, Lyon, Braga, and Milan, the Easter candle was extinguished at the end of the Gospel on Ascension Day, and removed from church at the end of the service. In some churches, variant traditions had grown up over the years, so that we find that the Easter candle was extinguished finally at other times :

1. End of Mass on Ascension Day—Old Carmelite rite (King, *LRO* p.268).

2. Friday after Ascension Day—Salisbury (Warren I p.270) and Exeter (HBS 37 p.322).

3. Compline on Friday after Ascension Day—Premonstratensians (King, *LRO* p.190).

[37] *DACSR* and Philippeau p.146.
[38] For instance, Exeter (HBS 37 p.322); Gilbertines (HBS 59 p.40); Bursfeld (*DAMR* 3.15.7 p.142 [M 1179]); St Augustine's, Canterbury (HBS 28 p.284); Poitiers (1767 Missal p.253).
[39] King, *LRO* p.104.
[40] Desideri p.151.

4. Compline of Ascension Day—Cistercians (King, *ibidem*).

5. After None on Ascension Day—Portuguese custom mentioned in decree of S.C.R. dated 20 December 1783.

6. Trinity Sunday—Worcester (Feasey, *The Paschal Candle* p.357).

7. Vigil of Pentecost—Albi, Paris, Rouen (Feasey, *ibidem*).

8. 'At Pentecost'—Bursfeld (Martène, *DAMR* 3.15.7 p.142).

9. Compline of Pentecost—Nantes (1837 Missal p.205).

10. At *assumptus est in coelum* in the Gospel for Ascension Day—Soissons (1745 Missal p.169) and Cahors (1760 Missal p.173).

11. At the 11th hour on Ascension Day—Tulle (Martène, *DAMR* 3.15.7 p.142).

12. Wednesday after Ascension Day—Durham (Raine p.9).

Chapter Thirty
THE DISPOSAL
OF THE EASTER CANDLE

Five different ways are known in which the Easter candle was disposed of, after it had served its purpose, either at the conclusion of Easter Week or at the end of the Season of Easter.

(i) In places, such as Spires, where the Easter candle was large, or where only a small portion of the wax had been consumed, the use of the same Candle was permitted for the following and even for subsequent years.[1] At Lyon, it was prescribed that if the same Candle were to be used the following year, it should not be blessed a second time.[2] Presumably this entailed only the omission of the *Exultet* and Preface from the paschal vigil. A sentence in Sicardus' *Mitrale* should not be cited as contemporary evidence for the reuse of the Easter candle.

> The Candle, renewed and lit, signifies Christ.[3]

At first sight *renovatus* appears to mean 'renewed' and to suggest that the Easter candle from the previous year was being used. However, the use of *renovatus* in this sense would imply

[1] *Agenda* (1512) fol.xciii.
[2] 1838 Ceremonial p.479.
[3] Cereus renovatus et illuminatus Christum significat. PL 213.323C.

that the same Candle was used year after year—possible, but unlikely; and his reference to the disposal of the Candle in a later passage shows that he does not intend us to understand that the wax of the previous year's Candle was reworked to provide the Candle for the following year.[4] It is much more likely that *renovatus* here refers to the changed state of the Candle, from a mass of lifeless beeswax to the consecrated and spirit-charged column in the focus of the paschal vigil.

(ii) In some places, such as at Westminster, the old Easter candle was reworked with the addition of new wax,[5] whilst at Seville, the huge column of wax was broken up and recast.[6] This corresponds to the contemporary practice of a number of churches where the unused portion of the Candle is returned to the manufacturer for recasting.

(iii) According to the Constitutions of Walter Cantilupe, the remainder of the Easter candle was used for the manufacture of small altar candles and of candles for the use of the poor, and for providing tapers at the funerals of paupers.[7]

(iv) The making of *Agnus Dei*'s from the wax of the previous year's Easter candle and their distribution was a physical counterpart or an extension in a material dimension of the practice, first encountered in the West in the Mozarabic rite, of sharing the light of the Candle with the assembled faithful. The receiving of the light on the candle of each man and woman was thus paralleled by the distribution of the wax of the Easter candle *via* the *Agnus Dei,* which imparted to each recipient whatever inherent virtue the Candle was held to possess.

The making of these medallions is attested in Rome and the dioceses outside Rome as early as the eighth century.[8] However, firm evidence for their production from the remains

---

[4]PL 213.325A.

[5]Feasey, *The Paschal Candle* p.361.

[6]Doblado p.299.

[7]Feasey, *Ancient Holy Week* p.204. The funeral tapers are also mentioned by Wilkins I p.571.

[8]OR 26.7–8.

of the Easter candle is relatively late.[9] It is true that Sicardus draws an analogy between an *Agnus Dei* and a fragment of the Easter candle, but he does not actually state that the former was composed of wax from the Candle.[10]

(v) An earlier form of the custom from which the above-mentioned practice almost certainly developed demonstrates the awe in which the Easter candle came to be held and the almost magical properties with which it was supposed to be endowed. It also shows clearly that the superstitious beliefs of pre-Christian Europe, far from being extinguished by the advent of Christianity, lived on vigorously as part of the sub-culture of medieval Christian society. In the early part of the eleventh century, *Micrologus* records that during Easter Week fragments of the Easter candle were distributed to the people 'for the fumigation of their possessions'.[11] Sicardus also states the purpose of the fragments to be *'ad fumigandos'*.[12] Small pieces of wax were presumably broken off the Easter candle and burnt in the homes of the faithful to render, it was believed, through the permeation of the smoke both the house and its contents immune from the assaults of the Devil. The purificatory theory of J.G.Frazer,[13] that fires were supposed to avert hail, thunder, and lightning caused by witches, is not new to that anthropologist. Grancolas writes in the eighteenth century that the lighting and blessing of the Easter candle was held to be sovereign against lightnings, tempests, and the many dangers in life.[14] In fact, the apotropaic virtues of the Candle were recognised as early as the time of Ennodius. In his longer surviving Preface, the request is made that a fragment of the wax candle may be sovereign 'against blasts of wind and

[9]Piccolomini I p.137 and Grancolas p.319.
[10]*Mitrale* (PL 213.325A).
[11]*Ad subfumigandum rebus eorum.* PL 151.1016B.
[12]*Mitrale* (PL 213.325A).
[13]*Golden Bough* 10 p.342.
[14]*Commentarius* p.319.

buffetings of storms' and 'a wall for the faithful should an enemy attack'.[15]

It is claimed that an allusion to the practice of distributing fragments of the Easter candle to the faithful as talismans is contained in the prayer *Veniat quaesumus*,[16] which, as we already noted, was originally the concluding pericope of the *Deus mundi Conditor* :

> Into whatever place a portion of this sanctifying mystery shall be carried, may the evil of Satan's guile be driven thence and may the power of your majesty be present.[17]

However, the evidence is ambiguous since the medium of sanctification is not stated and could be either the wax or the fire. For the practice of distributing the new fire is well-attested.

Honorius of Autun, who also mentions the practice, adds that the possession of a fragment of the Easter candle, which represented Christ, symbolised a share in Christ for the faithful at the general resurrection.[18]This teaching also gives us a small insight into how the Church achieved a sort of *modus vivendi* with some pagan beliefs and practices, and at the same time reveals how the Church in her turn was to some extent influenced by superstitious beliefs.

The tradition of fashioning talismans from the wax of the Easter candle survived into the twentieth century. Bisso describes the use of charms in the house or in the fields against *illusiones diabolicae* (amongst other evils) as a practice of the past;[19] but at Bourges in the eighteenth century, *globuli* of wax stamped with a cross were distributed after Mass on Ascen-

---

[15]Pinell, *La Benedicció* p.93.

[16]Van Doren, *La cérémonie du feu nouveau* p.77 note 3.

[17]In quocumque loco ex huius sanctificationis mysterio aliquid fuerit deportatum, expulsa diabolicae fraudis nequitia, virtus tuae maiestatis assistat.

[18]Quia Christus in resurrectione ultima fidelibus in premio tribueretur. *Gemma Animae* (PL 172.667D).

[19]*Hierurgia* I p.180.

sion Day and placed above the thresholds of houses as a protection against storms.[20] More recently, wax crosses made from the Easter candle were fastened to the doorposts of the churches of Capua, a practice still observed at the Monastery of Monte Cassino at the beginning of this century.[21] In his *History of Reims*, Flodoardus (894–966) records a story which further illustrates the supposed miraculous potency of the Easter candle. When the bodies of Rufinus and Valerius were being transferred to the cathedral, the Easter candle caught fire—a form of divine recognition of their saintliness.[22]

[20]1741 Missal p.233.
[21]Latis p.127.
[22]PL 135.326A/B.

Chapter Thirty-one

THE SYMBOLISM
OF THE EASTER CANDLE

We have suggested that a beeswax candle was used at the Vigil of Holy Saturday in preference to the traditional lamp of the *Lucernarium* because it held cosmic significance and its shape and size vividly symbolised the column of fire in Exodus.[1] We noted that in Ennodius' *laudes cerei* the lighted beeswax candle not merely symbolised, but actually existed as a tangible microcosm of creation. Although the Romano-Gallican Preface contains two eschatological allusions, it has as its pre-eminent theme the Passover and the passing of the Israelites through the Red Sea. These events were understood to be prefigurations of the Christian Vigil and Baptism.

It was perhaps inevitable, therefore, in view of the dominant references in the Romano-Gallican Preface to the events in Exodus, that the Easter candle, which provided the visual symbolic link between the Old Testament narrative and the liturgical re-enactment of that narrative at the paschal vigil, should undergo an elaboration of symbolism which emphasised the significance of the Easter candle both in its Old Testament setting and especially within the immediate context of the Vigil liturgy.

[1]See Chapter Twenty-one.

As early as Amalarius, we find an intensification of that typology, characteristic of medieval biblical interpretation, which sought to find the face of Christ present throughout the whole of the Old Testament.[2] Apropos of the paschal vigil, the Easter candle readily lent itself to its being interpreted as a symbol of Christ, since the pillar of fire in the Book of Exodus was seen to foreshadow the coming of Christ during the Christian Passover. The identification of Christ with the Easter candle was made by a number of medieval writers, who elaborated the symbolism and significance of the large burning column of wax.[3]

Just as the Easter candle symbolised the presence of the Lord in the fiery column[4] which led the Israelites through the Red Sea from bondage into a new life, so within a Christian liturgical context in which it was carried before the catechumens to Baptism, the Candle was seen to represent Christ leading the Christian faithful to a new life. The spread of light from the Easter candle imparted a share in the merits effected by Baptism, not only to those who received the light, but to the inanimate lamps and candles of both the church building and the hearths and homes of the faithful, and foreshadowed and anticipated the ultimate redemption of all creation, the doctrine familiar from the *laudes cerei* of Ennodius.

Beauduin draws attention to the fact that the Easter candle symbolised both the person and the work of Christ,[5] and this is well borne out by the above-mentioned medieval commentators and in particular by Durandus.[6] For the latter the Easter candle has a threefold significance. At one level, it represented both the new teaching of Christ and the new life

[2]*Liber Officialis* 1.1.18 : Columna ista [*of Exodus*] Christum praefigurabat.

[3]Hugh of St Victor, *De Off.Eccl. (PL 177.451–52); Rupert of Deutz, De Div.Off.* (PL170.171B); Honorius of Autun, *Gemma Animae* (PL172.668C); Robert Paululus (PL177.451); Sicardus, *Mitrale* (PL213.324B).

[4]Macri p.142; Thurston, *The* Exultet p.509.

[5]*Le cierge pascal* p.24.

[6]*Rationale* VI.80 fols.350–51.

in Christ, available to all and symbolised in the sharing of the light of the Candle. Like Rupert of Deutz and Honorius of Autun before him, Durandus identifies the light of the Easter candle with the Holy Spirit. In the same way that the disciples received the Holy Spirit from Christ, so all the candles should be lit from the Easter candle.

Durandus also echoes Rupert when he writes that the light of the Easter candle symbolised the Resurrection. Since the unlit Candle conveyed the notion of Christ in death and repose,[7] so the actual kindling of the wax column's wick represented the very instant that Christ arose from the dead. We noted above that at Naples, the Easter candle was fashioned to a great height in honour of the Resurrection, the size reflecting the magnitude of the One who rose. Thurston, commenting on the largeness of the Candle, adds that a great light should typify the True Light.[8]

The third symbolic aspect of the Easter candle was suggested by the three physical components of the lighted candle, not according to Ennodius' conception of the Candle as a microcosm of creation, but in the analogy which Augustine draws between a candle and a human being.[9] According to the African Doctor of the Church, the beeswax, the wick, and the flame of a candle corresponded to the flesh, the soul, and the intelligence of a human being. With the identification of the Easter candle with Christ, it was perhaps inevitable that the Ennodian conception of the Candle at a higher and cosmic level should yield to the more readily-grasped personal Augustinian view of the Candle. Since the analogy already existed between the supposed parthenogenetically-produced wax of the bee and the human flesh of Christ, who was born of a virgin, a tripartite identification of the wax, the wick, and the flame of the Easter candle with the person of Christ was readily made.

[7]Rock, *Hierurgia* p.407.
[8]*Lent and Holy Week* p.408.
[9]*Sermones Inediti* I (PL 46.819). There is some uncertainty over the authorship of this work.

In a wider sense, the beeswax, which symbolised Christ's flesh, was also held to represent his humanity, an analogy suggested perhaps by Clement of Alexandria, who states that wax was symbolic of human frailty.[10] Durandus also follows Augustine in likening the wick of the Candle to the soul of Christ, but identifies the flame of the Candle with Christ's divinity rather than his intelligence or intellect. Augustine had viewed the candle in light of human existence. In more recent times, it has been pointed out that for Christians the Augustinian view of the candle is a salutary reminder of their own position and standing *vis-à-vis* the Easter candle as the symbol of Christ. For they should find in the Candle an image of themselves, since the wax, the wick, and the flame symbolise respectively their bodies, their souls, and their faith.[11]

Elsewhere we have observed how the custom of extinguishing the Easter candle on or near Ascension Day considerably narrowed its significance and how the directing of the cries of *Lumen Christi* at the triple candle detracted from the importance of the paschal column of wax. It was generally regarded that the Candle represented the visible resurrected presence of Christ,[12] and for that reason was extinguished at Ascensiontide. One of the aims of the liturgical reforms of 1955 was to restore the Easter candle to its former status as a symbol of the timeless and universal presence of Christ.

* * * * *

Amalarius is also our earliest authority for attaching a symbolic interpretation to the smaller candle which was associated with the Easter candle.[13] This single candle stood for the Twelve Apostles, who accompanied Christ during his ministry and were responsible for the spread of Christ's light. For Christ had said to them, 'You are the light of the world'; and the second candle was a liturgical reminder of Christ's words.

---

[10]*Stromateis* 4, cited by Novarinus p.19.

[11]*Le cierge pascal* p.114.

[12]*DHCR* I p.471.

[13]Followed by Sicardus, *Mitrale* (PL 213.324B), and Durandus, *Rationale* VI.80 fol.352.

Chapter Thirty-two

THE PROVISION OF LIGHT
AT THE PASCHAL VIGIL

Little is known about the provision of light at the primitive paschal vigil in the West. The evidence of the eighth-century and ninth-century *ordines,* however, shows that prior to the commencement of the Vigil, the church was in total darkness.[1] Subsequently, it has been the universal practice throughout the western Church, even when the Vigil came to be anticipated and held in the morning light of Holy Saturday, to extinguish all the lights of the building prior to the start of the service. This is still a feature of the 1970 Roman and 1986 Church of England rites. In the Middle Ages, it was sometimes the practice to extinguish the lights after the kindling of the new fire.[2]

The darkened church provided a congruous ambience and created an appropriate atmosphere for the reading of the lections, which formed the principal feature of the Vigil. At one level, the reading of the Word in the gloom of night was viewed as a liturgical re-enactment of John 1:5;[3] and at another, the darkness of the church symbolised the sin of the world soon

---

[1]OR 26.9 and OR 29.17; OR 31.67, respectively.

[2]Missal of Lesnes (HBS 95 p.47); *MR* 1474 (HBS 17 p.175).

[3]With the emergence and use of the Easter candle, the symbolism became more appropriate.

to be dispelled by the light of the Resurrection, signified by the lamps and candles rekindled with new or rehallowed fire. With the anticipation of the Vigil in the afternoon and subsequently in the morning of Holy Saturday, these dramatic and atmospheric results were lost.

There are no grounds for believing that the paschal vigil was conducted in total darkness. It is true that the Vigil-lections could have been memorised and recited without the aid of the written word, so allowing the service to be conducted in a complete absence of light; for we saw that in sixth-century Gaul, Matins of Holy Saturday was held in such circumstances. However, a comparison between the two services is invalid, since at that office of Matins well-memorised psalms were chanted by a relatively small group of monks. During the Vigil, however, lengthy portions of Scripture were read to a congregation which included children. The difficulties attendant upon holding this service in total darkness seem obvious.

Nevertheless, the service was not held in an abundance of light. In the next chapter, we will show that at the old Roman Vigil, illumination for the purpose of reading was provided by two candles, the size of a grown person, lit from fire either reserved on Maundy Thursday,[4] or kindled on Good Friday and reserved until the following day. We learn from the Pontifical of Regensburg that the two large candles were blessed prior to the reading of the lections (p.125). Their benediction at this point can also be inferred from Zachary's letter and from Ordo 29.[5] The church thus remained in semi-darkness throughout the readings and the blessing of the font, until the cry of *Accendite,* following the *Agnus Dei* after Baptism, instructed the neophytes to light their candles and the sacristans to kindle the lamps of the church. The sudden appearance of light at the conclusion of the Vigil, heralding the Resurrection and symbolising the triumph of the Light of the

---

[4]Letter of Zachary (PL 89.951B).
[5]OR 29.45.

World over sin and death, provided a vivid contrast with the sepulchral atmosphere which pervaded the ceremonial that had just ended.[6] The faithful were now able to participate in the milieu of both physical and eschatological light in which the first Mass of Easter was celebrated.

The incorporation of the Easter candle and its ritual into the Roman Vigil resulted in a diversification of the ceremonial relating to the provision of light *vis-à-vis* the reading of the Vigil-lections and the blessing of the font. Whilst in some rites the tradition persisted of reading the Vigil-lections in semi-darkness, in some churches the provision of an abundance of light, that is, the illumination of the whole church, occurred either at the beginning or close to the beginning of the Paschal vigil.

(i) The Vigil in Semi-darkness

We have already observed that with the increasing anticipation of the Vigil in some churches in the West, the dependence on liturgical light for both reading and dramatic effect had largely disappeared.[7] The churches, listed in *Tables 54, 55,* and *56,* which perpetuated the tradition of holding the Vigil in darkness had the following scheme for the provision of light :

1. The new fire procession.

2. The lighting of the Easter candle at *ignis accendit.*

3. The general illumination of the church after the blessing of the font, cued (in some churches) by the cry of *Accendite.*

---

[6]The large candles recalled the two angels of Luke 24:4 (see Chapter 33). The darkened church obviously suggested the Tomb. The aspect of death is further reinforced by the remark of St Ambrose that 'the font has the shape and appearance of a sort of tomb' (*Sermons on the Sacraments* III.1).

[7]Nevertheless, there are a number of cathedrals whose unlit interiors on a dull late-March morning would have provided a fitting atmosphere of gloom.

The replacement or displacement of the two Vigil-candles by the Easter candle as the principal source of liturgical light ensured the continued supply of sufficient functional light necessary for the reading of the prophecies. However, the substitution was also a highly significant development; for whereas the two Vigil-candles suggested sepulchral light and the mourning of the Church for the dead Christ, the light of the Easter candle was both paschal and resurrectional. For given the prominent Exodus-typology, especially in the Romano-Gallican Preface, the fire of the Candle symbolised historically the presence of God in the Burning Bush and in the Fiery Column and, within the immediate eschatological context of the paschal vigil, anticipated the inrush of light at the dawn of the New Age, which would banish the darkness of this world's oppression and sin. At the same time, while the first chapter of Genesis was being read, the burning of the Easter candle, 'consecrated in honour of your name', demonstrated that the Word of God was in existence even at the Creation. The Easter candle 'burning over the pages of the Old Testament is a sign of the presence of Christ from the beginning'.[8]

Although only six of the documents listed in *Tables 54–56* specifically mention the kindling of the altar lights, it is safe to assume that most of the other documents include them in their mention of 'all the lights of the church'. Lanfranc's injunction includes the lights both *ante* and *circa* the altar, that is, both the functional and cultic lights of the choir and sanctuary. Further support for the implied inclusion of the altar lights comes from the alternative tradition, outlined in the next section, in which these liturgical lights were kindled prior to the start of Mass.

[8]Harbert p.241. The symbolism is valid regardless of when the Easter candle is lit, providing it precedes the reading of the prophecies. The weakness of the recent form of service, produced by the Joint Liturgical Group (Gray pp.76 ff.) and incorporated into *Lent, Holy Week, Easter,* produced by the Liturgical Commission of the Church of England (pp.223 ff.), in which the Vigil-lections precede the ceremony of light, is the necessity of providing 'essential' light for the reading of these lessons.

Church/Document	Date	Source
Lanfranc's *Decrees**	c. 1070	PL 150.468A
Carcassonne	14 C	*DAER* 4.24 p.150 (M 56)
Rosslyn Missal	c. 1300	HBS 15 p.35
Arles	14 C	*DAER* 4.24 p.150 (M 31)
Durham	14 C	Missal p.191
Mende	14 C	*DAER* 4.24 p.150 (M 187)
Bazas	1503	Missal fol.lxi
Narbonne	1528	*DAER* 4.24 p.150 (M 203)
Auxerre	1537	*DAER* 4.24 p.150 (M 39)
Tournai	1540	Missal fol.lxxiii
Bayonne	1543	Missal p.49
Osma	1561	Missal fol.c
Besançon	1766	Missal p.234

*Indicates that the altar lights were also lit.

*Table 54. Evidence for the illumination of the church
at the conclusion of the Vigil following the triple cry of* Accendite

The cry of *Accendite* can be traced back to the eighth-century Stational Mass of Easter Day at the Cathedral of St John Lateran, where the subdeacon issued the order to kindle the lights of the basilica before the start of the service, once the ceremonies of the Vigil had ended.[9] It was heard at Lyon, Regensburg, and in other churches where a Roman-influenced Vigil was held,[10] and survived in numerous French dioceses long after it had disappeared from the Roman rite.[11]

[9]Ordo I (PL 78.940D).

[10]One of the features of the old Roman Vigil, which survived at both Lyon, where the Roman rite was introduced by Leidrad c.800, and Beneventum, was the position in the liturgy of the Vigil-lections. At Lyon, the prophecies were read by natural light because of anticipation and without the use of liturgical light before the Easter candle was blessed. In the latter rite, the kindling of the new fire and the blessing of the Easter candle took place between the eleventh and final readings (Hesbert p.188).

[11]It is not found in *PR XII* or in subsequent Roman service-books.

Church/Document	Date	Source
Ordo 27	750–800	OR 27.62
Ordo 28	c.800	OR 28.81
Poitiers	c.900	*Poitiers* p.220
PRG	c.950	II p.110
Regularis Concordia	c.970	PL 137.494D
Regensburg	c.980	Pontifical p.130
Alcuin	c.1000	PL 101.1221C
Cluny*	11 C	PL 149.663C
Cluny	1510	Missal fol.liiii
Farfa	11 C	Albers I p.56
Fruttuaria*	11 C	Albers IV p.68
Fleury	11 C	Albers V p.146
Vallombrosa*	11 C	Albers IV p.250
Gembloux	11 C	Albers II p.101
CMG	11 C	Albers V p.38
St-Vito, Verdun	11 C	Albers V p.146
Besançon	11 C	*DAER* 4.24 p.150 (M 56)
Reims	c.1200	Ordinary p.130
St-Martin, Tours	13 C	Ritual p.58
St-Vedast, Arras	c.1300	HBS 86 p.160
Strasbourg	1364	*DAER* 4.24 p.163 (M 35)
Westminster	c.1370	HBS 5 col.589
Hereford	1502	Missal p.112
Camaldolese*	1503	Missal fol.94
Vallombrosa	1503	Missal fol.xcv
Lyon	1510	Missal fol.ci

*Indicates that the altar lights were also lit.

*Table 55. Evidence for the illumination of the church
at the conclusion of the Vigil following a single cry of* Accendite

The earliest sources attest a single cry of *Accendite*. There
is no evidence of any link between the twice-repeated order
enjoined by Lanfranc and the triple acclamation of *Lumen
Christi* when the new fire was brought into church. In the two
instances where both the *Lumen Christi* and the *Accendite* fea-

Church	Date	Source
Salzburg	1507	Missal fol.ciii
Liège	1540	Missal fol.lxxxv
Paris	1666	Missal p.260
Angers*	1731	Ceremonial p.267
Sées	1742	Missal p.204
Lisieux	1752	Missal p.203
St-Bertrand	1773	Missal p.226
Périgueux	1782	Missal p.171
Metz	1829	Missal p.175
La Rochelle	1835	Missal p.203
Autun	1845	Missal p.258

*Indicates that the altar lights were also lit.

Table 56. Evidence for the illumination of the church at the conclusion of the Vigil without the cry of Accendite

tured within the same rite, the latter was proclaimed only once.[12] In places, the threefold *Accendite* was announced by the choir *alta voce*.[13] At Bayonne, the deacon held the serpent-candle, whilst at Osma, the deacon ascended an altar step with each subsequent cry. In these two churches, the choir made the response of *Deo gratias* after each shout. At Arles and Narbonne, the response of *Lumen Christi* followed the first two acclamations and *Deo gratias* the third. In Auxerre Cathedral, a white-robed choir boy raised his voice with each subsequent cry of *Accendite*. In the rites of the churches listed in *Table 56*, there is no indication that the cry featured in the ceremonial.

[12]The Customary of Vallombrosa and the Camaldolese Missal. For these and subsequent references, see the Tables.

[13]In Lanfranc's *Decrees* and in the Missal of Bazas.

(ii) The Vigil in the Light

(A) ILLUMINATION *BEFORE* THE BLESSING OF THE EASTER CANDLE.

1. *The Mozarabic Tradition.* It is generally agreed that a number of elements in the Mozarabic new fire ceremony had their origin in the fourth-century liturgy of Jerusalem. Certain features, such as, the striking of the new fire and the blessing of the Easter candle together with its Preface, were importations from Gaul. However, there seems to be little doubt that the following had their provenance in the rite of Jerusalem :

- the sacristy in total darkness
- the lighting of the lamp by the bishop
- the lighting of the clergy candles
- the entry of the bishop into church
- the sharing and spread of light from candle to candle.

The initial ceremony completed, the Easter candle was consecrated and the Vigil-lections were read in a blaze of light from the candles of the faithful. This Jerusalem-derived Vigil, in which the congregation participated throughout in the newly-blessed light, contrasts markedly with the type of Vigil held in semi-darkness, which was described above in Section (i).

2. *Other Traditions.* The custom which obtained in the churches of Cordoba, Bourges, and Carcassonne resembled Mozarabic practice in that the Vigil-lections were read with the church lights ablaze. With these three churches should be included Uzès and Passau, where the church lights were kindled at the conclusion of the Preface *(Table 57)*. It is possible that at Cordoba, the influence of the Mozarabic rite may be detected, although, somewhat strangely, the Easter candle was lit only during the Preface at *ignis accendit*. The antecedents of this feature at Bourges and Carcassonne are more difficult to explain. Spanish influence seems very unlikely. One possible explanation is that we have in these two churches a survival and development of the ceremonial of the *Pontificale Romano-Germanicum (PRG)*. For according to that pontifical,

---

(i) Church illumination before the *Exultet*

Mozarabic rite	7 C		Léon Antiphonary pp.280–81
Cordoba	1561		Missal fol.ciiii
Bourges	1741		Missal p.226
Carcassonne	1749		Missal p.196

(ii) Church illumination after the *Exultet*

| Uzès | 1495 | all lights | Missal fol.lxiii |
| Passau | 1503 | other candles | Missal fol.lxxxiv |

---

*Table 57. Evidence for the illumination of the church
either before or after the blessing of the Easter candle*

both the seven lamps in front of the altar and the Easter candle
were kindled before the archdeacon began the *Exultet*.[14]

(B) ILLUMINATION *DURING* THE BLESSING OF THE EASTER CANDLE.
From about the middle of the eleventh century, there emerged
the practice of kindling, in addition to the Easter candle, other
lights during the Preface. It is first attested in the *Acta Vetera*
of Rouen : the two small Vigil-candles were lit during the Preface at the words *divisus in partes*.[15] The lighting of these candles
at this point is also found in the 1511 Missal of Nîmes and
in an Ordinary of the Regular Canons of St Rufinus, and
in the Dominican rite.[16] The practice suggests a liturgical
representation and visual interpretation of the subsequent
clause *mutuati (tamen) luminis detrimenta non novit*.[17] It is not difficult to realise why this practice was first extended to include

---

[14]II p.98 §346. The practice is also attested in *Alcuin* (PL 101.1216B).
[15]PL 147.176C.

[16]The first two documents are cited by De Vert, *Explication* II p.37; 1504
Dominican Missal fol.lxxxix and 1908 Missal p.169. According to Dominican practice, the two acolytes' candles were lit at *divisus in partes,* and a
further dissemination of light (for general illumination) occurred at *apis
mater eduxit.*

[17]'Suffers no detriment from its light being borrowed.'

the seven altar lamps,[18] and subsequently all the lights of the church, as at Salisbury.[19]

Later development, centring around the point at which the lights, both functional and liturgical, were kindled, resulted in a diversity of practice. One suspects that alternative points were adopted because the cue of *divisus in partes* was separated by only three words from *ignis accendit,* the point at which the Easter candle was lit. Three separate traditions developed involving this point.

1. *At* Suscipe, sancte Pater. In most other rites, the five grains of incense were inserted at this point. That the following phrase *incensi huius sacrificium vespertinum* originally related to the light of the Candle, and not to the incense, strongly suggests that the tradition of lighting other candles at this point was very old. Regrettably, the only known instance of its occurrence is at Tongres in the fifteenth century. Here, the other candles mentioned presumably included those of the acolytes, and the church lights.

2. *At* Ignis accendit. In a number of churches, the kindling of the other lights occurred at the same point at which the Easter candle was lit. These lights may have been kindled here because it was felt that, once the new fire had been used to kindle the Easter candle, there was no obvious reason to delay further acts of illumination; or because it demonstrated visibly the truth of the assertion, soon to be heard by all : *luminis detrimenta non novit;* or possibly because it avoided a further interruption in the chanting of the Preface.

3. *At* apis mater eduxit. A pause for the secondary act of illumination at this phrase was favoured by an even larger number of churches, including Rome, and by the majority of the monastic orders. These words, which closed the short pericope eulogising the bee, provided a suitable break in the Preface, in the same way that the insertion of the grains and

[18]*OEL* p.61 and *PR XII* (*PRMA* I.xxxii.8 p.240).
[19]For references, see *Table 58.*

the lighting of the Easter candle also occurred at the end of a section. In churches which retained the Preface containing the lengthy eulogy of the bees, the interruption for this secondary act of illumination occurred at *virgo permansit*. Other points during the Preface where secondary illumination is known to have occurred are listed in *Table 58*.

(i) At *suscipe, sancte pater*

Tongres	15 C	'other candles'	Ordinary p.165

(ii) At *ignis accendit*

St Mary's, York	c.1400	other lights	HBS 75 p.292
Carmelites	c.1312	acolyte and church	Ordinary p.31
Exeter	1337	other church lights	HBS 37 p.322
Langres	1492	other church lights	Missal fol.lxv
Seville	1507	other lights	Missal fol.lxxviii
Würzburg	1509	acolyte only	Missal fol.244
Cologne	1514	other church lights	Missal fol.lxxv
Coutances	1557	other church lights	Missal fol.lxx
Palencia	1568	church and altar	Missal fol.cvi
Chalons	1748	acolyte and lamps	Missal p.183
Lyon	1771	acolyte and church	Missal p.195
Bayeux	1790	other candles	Missal p.170
Meaux	1845	acolyte and lamps*	Missal p.169

(iii) At *mater eduxit*

Haymo *(OM)*†	c.1243	lamps*	Van Dijk II p.246
Rome	1477	lamps*	Miss. Rom. np
Würzburg	1497	other lights	Ordinary np
Coimbra (AC)	1597	lamps*	Ordinary fol.137
Camaldolese	1634	lamp of high altar and church lights	Ceremonial p.85
Rouen	1640	church lights	Ritual p.306
Carmelites	1664	church lamps	Missal p.162
Paris	1666	acolytes and hang-lamps in choir	Missal p.244
Cistercians	1669	all the lamps*	Missal p.159
Besançon	1682	all lights	Ceremonial p.333
Evreux	1740	lights	Missal p.192
Amiens	1752	lamps*	Missal p.79 (Suppl)

Maison du Roy	1741	lights	*Sem.Sainte* p.401
Mende	1766	other lights	Missal p.205
Poitiers	1767	all lights	Missal p.251
Capuchins‡	1775	nearby lamps	Ceremonial p.129
Bayeux	1790	altar lights	Missal p.170
Poland	1819	(As Camaldolese)	Manual p.479
Coutances	1825	acolyte and church	Ceremonial p.333
Luçon	1828	acolyte and lamps*	Missal p.220
Limoges	1830	church lights	Missal p.255
Toulouse	1832	candles and lights	Missal p.211

(iv) At *divisus in partes*

Salisbury	*c.*1300	church lights	Legg p.118
Salisbury	*c.*1486	church lights	Missal fol.lxxxiv

(v) At *virgo permansit*

Burgos	1546	church lights	Missal fol.cvii
Cosenza	1549	all lamps	Missal fol.118
Braga	1558	other lights	Missal fol.xcvi

(vi) At *non novit*

Braga	1558	2 other candles	Missal fol.xcvi

*Lampades.
†Actually at *O vere beata nox.*
‡Other lights at *O vere beata nox.*

Table 58. Evidence for illumination during the Preface

In a large number of service-books the rubrics are silent regarding the point at which additional illumination occurred. In the rubrics of a number of church rites it is not clear which lights were kindled during the Preface. The word *lampades* without a qualifying phrase or adjective may signify either the altar lights or the church lights or both. For instance, the rubric at *mater eduxit* in the 1762 Missal of Paris relates to the acolytes' candles and the *lampades* (p.239). The Missal of 1666, however, specifies 'the lamps hanging in the choir' (p.244).

That development and flexibility of practice could and did occur within the same rite is perhaps best exemplified in the various Roman documents which attest the various points at which the church, the acolytes', and the altar lights were kindled in the period 950 to 1574. As we observed at the beginning of this chapter, in the primitive Holy Saturday rites of the Roman Church, the two large Vigil-candles had been lit before the reading of the lections; and the church lights, together with the candles of the neophytes, were kindled after the cry of *Accendite*. Subsequent changes came about as follows.

(a) *The Church Lights*. PRG is silent on this score. The twelfth-century Ordo of the Lateran Church, however, states that all the lights of the church should be lit by the sacristan at the *Kyries* which introduce the Mass of Easter.[20] This procedure is also enjoined in Lanfranc's *Decrees* : after the cry of *Accendite* all the church lights should be kindled, including those in front of and around the altar.[21] Now, according to Haymo's *Ordo Missalis* of *c*.1243, 'lamps' were lit during the Preface at *mater eduxit*.[22] In view of the later reference in the same document to altar lights (p.248), the *lampades* referred to during the Preface are almost certainly the lamps which hung in the choir. Late fifteenth-century and early sixteenth-century Roman missals retain the rubric : *(accendunt) lampades ante altare;*[23] but the majority of later books, including the

---

[20]*OEL* p.73 : *omnia luminaria et lampades ecclesiae.*

[21]PL 150.468A : *ante et circa altare.* The evidence of later Roman missals strongly suggests that the phrase (in the missals) *lampades ante altare,* which formerly referred to the liturgical lights that subsequently became altar candles, indicates the functional lights of the choir. These, viewed from the nave, did indeed hang in front of the altar. Those disposed *circa altare* were the cultic lights. The evidence, such as it is, would suggest that in Lanfranc's time lights were not placed upon the altar, rather around it.

[22]Van Dijk II p.248.

[23]For instance, *MR* 1500, *MR* 1501, *MR* 1506, *MR* 1520. The corresponding mid-prefatorial rubric in the Roman Missals of 1474, 1477, 1484, and 1491 (HBS 33 p.85, np, np, fol.93, respectively) seems to present a difficulty; for it states : *Hic accenditur lampas ante altare,* 'Here a lamp is lit before the altar'. The use of the singular *lampas* may be explained in three ways. (Its appearance in successive missals seems to rule out an error.)

(i) It is used generically and is here to be interpreted 'light'. (ii) It refers

Tridentine Missal of 1574, omit the phrase *ante altare* and state simply : *Hic accenduntur lampades.* The vagueness of the rubric, which may relate to the church lights,[24] the choir lights, or even the altar lights, thus allowed some flexibility of practice.[25] In more recent times, all the lights and lamps in the church, except the altar candles, were kindled at *mater eduxit.* The latter were lit after the Litany.[26]

(b) *The Altar Lights.* Reference has been made in the above section to the practice of kindling the altar lights prior to the start of Mass. The Lateran Missal and Durand's Pontifical also provide evidence for the practice in the thirteenth century.[27] Earlier practice had been to light the seven lamps before the *Exultet.*[28] Subsequently, they were lit during the Preface. According to the twelfth-century *Pontificale Romanum (PR XII)* and the Lateran Ordo, the kindling of these lights took place at *luminis detrimenta non novit.*[29] This tradition survived at Palencia.[30]

to the first of the chancel lamps to be lit. (iii) The sanctuary lamp is intended.

The interpretation of *lampas* as 'light' is poetic and would be very unusual within a rubrical context. The second explanation implies that one of the chancel lights was in some way special. Support for the third possibility is to be found in the 1634 Camaldolese Ceremonial, in which we read that at the words *mater eduxit,* the lamp of the high altar was lit by an acolyte (p.85). The church lights were also lit at this point.

Somewhat surprisingly, the rubrics of *MR* 1477, *MR* 1484, and *MR* 1491, which form the preamble to the *Exultet,* state that at the words *mater eduxit :* Hic accendunt lampades.

[24]As in the 1509 Missal of Würzburg fol.244.

[25]This is further illustrated by the fact that the *Caeremoniale Episcoporum* of 1600 enjoins that the church lights should be lit during the Litany (p.303) and the Ceremonial of Benedict XIII states that this should occur just before the start of Mass.

[26]Fortescue and O'Connell (6th ed.) p.344.

[27]Schmidt II p.610 §112; *PGD (PRMA* III p.588). Bauldry in the eighteenth century also prescribes this point (p.193).

[28]Thus *PRG* II p.98 §346.

[29]*PRMA* I.xxxii.8 p.240 and *OEL* p.61, respectively.

[30]1568 Missal fol.cvi.

(c) *The Two Candles*. Custom varied regarding the moment at which the two candles, which had survived from the old Roman-influenced Vigil,[31] were lit. The displacement of the two candles, the size of a grown person, from the centrality of the liturgy resulted either in their assuming a very minor role in the ceremonial or in the merging of their function with the honorific episcopal candles in some churches or the acolytes' candles in others. Largely, one suspects, because they had acquired different functions within the liturgy, it is perhaps not surprising to find a variation in the points at which they were kindled during the ceremonial. At Chartres, the two bishop's candles were lit probably during the Preface,[32] whilst at St-Germain-des-Prés, the two Vigil-candles, their status reduced, were lit immediately after the conclusion of the Preface.[33] This is the point at which they were lit at Salzburg, where even in the fifteenth century, the two candles were of considerable dimensions.[34] At Vallombrosa, however, the two candles were lit after the cry of *Accendite*.[35] The lighting of the two acolytes' or torch-bearers' candles is unrecorded in many documents. At Périgueux, Meaux, and Odense, for instance, they were lit before the *Exultet*, as was the Easter candle.[36] Elsewhere, the kindling of the church lights presupposed that these two candles were already ablaze. The Sarum Missal of *c.*1486 states that the illumination of the church was the responsibility of the torch-bearers : the torch-bearers kindle the lamps throughout the church.[37]

(d) *The* Cereus Minor. Evidence for the point at which the *cereus minor*, or smaller Easter candle, was lit is confined to the *Regularis Concordia*. According to this document, the lighting

[31]For these candles, see Chapter 33.
[32]Ordinary p.111.
[33]Martène, *DAER* 4.24 p.159 (M 230).
[34]1507 Missal of Salzburg fol.xcvii.
[35]Albers IV p.250.
[36]1782 Missal p.159; 1845 Missal p.169; 1483 Missal fol.10 (Stromberg p.34).
[37]Ceroferarii accendunt candelas per ecclesiam. Fol.lxxxvi.

of this candle took place at the conclusion of the Preface.[38] At Salisbury, it seems to have been lit as soon as the larger Candle was aflame.[39]

(e) *The* Sanctissimum *Light.* Few service-books or manuals refer to the light before the reserved sacrament. The rubric of the fourteenth-century Customary of Laon seems to imply that the lights before the *Corpus Christi* were relit immediately after they had been extinguished.[40] This momentary loss of light is also attested by De Bralion and Gavanti.[41] The nineteenth-century Polish Manual states that the sanctuary lamp was lit during the Preface at *mater eduxit,* but does not indicate at what point it was extinguished (p.479). The 1775 Capuchin *Memoriale* concurs with the foregoing manual, but adds that the lamp was extinguished before None (p.130). On the other hand, Desideri[42] and more recent liturgical handbooks insist that this light ought never to be extinguished.[43]

(C) ILLUMINATION *AFTER* THE BLESSING OF THE EASTER CANDLE. At Passau and Uzès the church lights were lit at the conclusion of the Preface.[44] We noted above that according to the *Regularis Concordia,* the *cereus minor* and the two Vigil-candles were lit at this point during the service; but the fact that that document enjoins the kindling of the church lights after the cry of *Accendite* makes the influence of Benedictine practice unlikely.

(iii) The Rites of Lyon and Milan

The ceremonial of the primatial church of France has undergone a number of changes in respect of the provision of

[38]PL 137.494C.
[39]Implied from Dickinson p.341.
[40]Martène, *DAMR* 3.15.7 p.142 (M 1164).
[41]*Caeremoniale* p.255 and Gavanti-Merati p.166.
[42]*Praxis* p.144.
[43]For instance, Fortescue and O'Connell (11th ed.) p.301.
[44]1503 Missal fol.lxxxiv and 1495 Missal fol.lxiii, respectively.

light at the Paschal vigil. From *c.*800, when the Roman rite was first introduced at Lyon, until 1771, the cry of *Accendite* at the conclusion of the Vigil signalled that the lights of the cathedral should be lit. In 1771, the contemporary Roman practice was adopted : the acolytes' candles and the church lights were kindled during the Preface and the altar candles after the blessing of the font.[45] The traditional cry of *Accendite,* which had been excluded at that time, was restored to the liturgy in 1904, immediately before the *Agnus Dei.*[46] Present practice is modelled on the Roman reforms of 1955 and 1970.

The earliest evidence for the Ambrosian rite dates from the twelfth century. The Easter candle and the diaconal candles were lit at the words *Ecce iam ignis,* which introduce the second pericope of the Ambrosian Preface.[47] According to the Missal of 1594, the *lampades* were kindled at the closing words of the third pericope, *ut coruscus adveniet* (fol.97). To that rubric, the Missals of 1669 and 1901 add 'and the lights of the church'.[48] Contemporary practice is to kindle all the church lights and candles as the procession with the Easter candle moves into church.[49]

[45]1771 Missal p.195.
[46]1904 Missal p.221.
[47]Beroldus p.110 and all missals up to that of 1901.
[48]Martène, *DAER* 4.24 p.169 and 1934 Missal t.e. *Rep.* p.40.
[49]1986 Missal p.54.

Chapter Thirty-three
THE ROMAN VIGIL
AND THE GALLICAN RITE

(i) Outline Description and the Vigil-candles

The evidence for the older Roman Vigil is contained in five of the *ordines Romani,* which range in date from *c.*600 to *c.*800.[1] None of these five documents describes the service in great detail—the information supplied by Ordo 11, for instance, is extremely meagre; nevertheless, collectively they provide sufficient details to enable us to reconstruct with confidence the structure of the ceremony which took place during this period on the night of Holy Saturday in the Cathedral of St John Lateran.

After the clergy had donned their vestments in the sacristy,[2] they moved thence in silent procession into church escorting

[1]OR 11, OR 16, OR 23, OR 24, and OR 30B. All five documents attest papal practice. Ordo 11 contains what appears to be an anachronistic rubric relating to the blessing of the Easter candle : *postea impletur ⟨ cerei ⟩ benedictio* (Andrieu's parenthesis), 'afterwards the blessing (of the candle) is completed'. It is tempting, in view of the uncertainty over *cerei,* to emend the text by reading *cereorum* for *cerei.* This would accord well with the mention of the two candles in the next section and possibly account for the substitution of the singular form of the noun by a scribe who, perhaps familiar with the blessing of a single candle, had superscribed *cerei* above *cereorum* by way of a query.

[2]OR 16.36. From the evidence of OR 23.24 and OR 30B.37, it would

427

the two Vigil-candles, the size of a grown person,[3] and making their way to the altar to take up their appointed positions. The two candles were borne in procession by two junior officials or clerics in minor orders[4] and held by their bearers who stood one either side of the altar.[5] From the evidence of Ordo 23, it is not clear whether the two candles were lit in the sacristy. However, Ordo 24 leaves us in little doubt that the kindling took place in the main body of the church and in all likelihood in the sanctuary.[6] Elsewhere, we have seen that the fire used to light the candles had been reserved for that purpose either on Maundy Thursday or, in the ninth century, after its kindling on Good Friday.

We shall refer later in this chapter to the size and to the significance of the size of the two baptismal candles or Vigil-

---

appear that only deacons (including the archdeacon and subdeacons) were present at this ceremony. OR 30B.30 adds that the archdeacon presided. According to the same authority *(ibidem),* the Pope made his appearance at the paschal ceremonies only after the *Agnus Dei.*

[3]OR 16.36. It is true that only OR 11.90 mentions the size of the candles *(staturam hominis habentes,* 'having the size of a grown person'); but this phrase describing the two candles at the paschal vigil is also found in *PRG* (II p.99 §348), *Poitiers* (p.215), *Alcuin* (PL 101.1216C), and the 1507 Missal of Salzburg (fol.xcvii). It can be reasonably inferred that these lights were present at the Vigil described by the other *ordines,* even though they are not specifically mentioned.

[4]OR 23.24 mentions *regionarii;* OR 24.41 *notarii;* and OR 30B.37 subdeacons. The difference in title or status is here not significant. Both *regionarii* and *notarii* may well have been subdeacons during this period; and under the canons of the Roman Church, it may have been possible to hold the offices of *notarius* and *regionarius* concurrently. Alternatively, the discrepancy may be attributed to the different era which each ordo attests. Moreover, the mention of subdeacons in Ordo 30B may well be a Gallican substitution for a church where papal *notarii* and *regionarii* were unknown.

[5]OR 30B.37 adds that they stood to the rear of the altar.

[6]*Sabbato sancto veniunt omnes in ecclesiam et tunc illuminantur duo cerei, tenentibus duobus notariis, unus in dextro cornu altaris et alter in sinistro.* OR 24.41. The evidence is also found in the *Sacramentary of St Eligius* §88. *Ecclesiam* is almost certainly referring to the main body of the church, although the inclusion of the sacristy in the term should not be ruled out.

candles. Regarding their physical appearance, there is no good reason why the descriptive phrase *staturam hominis habentes,* 'the size of a grown person', should not be interpreted literally. The argument that a five or six foot high candle of solid wax could not have been carried in procession because of its weight cannot be sustained. A candle, the height of a human being, can be manufactured without an excessively wide diameter,[7] making quite feasible its transportation by one person over the short distance covered by the procession during the course of the Roman Vigil.[8] Moreover, the very use of the phrase *staturam hominis habentes* to describe these candles indicates that they were unusually large;[9] and there is other evidence for the existence and use in church of very large candles. At Assisi, there is a thirteenth-century fresco depicting a server at Mass holding a five or six foot high candle; and in a document from Haughmond Abbey, dated 1341, there is mention of twelve candles, each weighing six pounds, which burned around the tomb of Richard, Earl of Arundel.[10] However, candles half as tall as those indicated by this phrase and set in candle-holders standing two or three feet from the ground would have given the impression from a distance of attaining the height of an adult. The use of the verb *tenere* in two of the *ordines* to indicate that these candles were held during the course of the Vigil is inconclusive,[11] since these large candles would have rested on the ground, whilst those who held them were stationary, regardless of whether they were mounted in candlesticks or not. It is true that the *Romano-Germanic Pontifical (PRG)* states that these candles stood in

[7]Modern candles measuring 24" and 36" can be manufactured with diameters of as little as 0.75" and 1.25" respectively. A tallow candle measuring 5'x 2" would weigh approximately 6.44lbs. A beeswax candle would be slightly heavier.

[8]Even allowing for the fact that the baptistery of St John Lateran was a building detached, as now, from the cathedral itself.

[9]This phrase is not found outside the context of the paschal vigil.

[10]Document 1245 in Rees, *The Cartulary* p.227.

[11]OR 24.41 : *cerei tenentibus duobus notariis;* OR 30B.37 : *tenentes faculas.*

candleholders;[12] but in view of the centrality of the Easter candle in the rite described by this document, it was perhaps inevitable that the size of these two candles should be reduced as their role and status in the Vigil diminished. The use of holders to increase the overall height of the two Vigil-candles would continue to justify their description of 'the size of a grown person' and furnish a reminder of their former size.

(ii) The *Lucernarium* at Jerusalem

Egeria's mention of the importance of the *Lucernarium* in the cycle of daily offices at Jerusalem should not be taken as evidence that her readers would have been unfamiliar with the service, or that the office was unknown in Egeria's native Galicia or Aquitaine.[13] For the service which Egeria witnessed in Jerusalem had undergone a unique development under the direction of that city's innovative and dynamic bishop, Cyril, who utilised its topography and historic sites for liturgical experimentation and change. The Jerusalem *Lucernarium* must have contrasted strongly with the lamp-lighting service familiar to Egeria in her own native land.[14] That a close relationship existed in the Jerusalem rite between the *Lucernarium* of Holy Saturday and the paschal vigil is clear from the *Peregrinatio;*[15] but the entry of the bishop into the *cave* of the Anastasis,[16] the lighting of the candle he held from the lamp that burned perpetually at the Tomb, and the sharing of the fire with the

---

[12]*PRG* II p.99 §348.

[13]Wilkinson pp.66–69 and p.123. For Egeria's country of origin, see Wilkinson p.3.

[14]Her statement : Vigiliae autem paschales sic fiunt quemadmodum ad nos, 'They keep their paschal vigil like us' (Duchesne, *Christian Worship* p.512), relates only to the Vigil itself and not to any ritual that preceded it. There is no evidence that the *Lucernarium* in the western Church was other than a simple daily ceremony involving the lighting and blessing of a lamp.

[15]Wilkinson pp.66–69.

[16]Egeria uses *spelunca* to denote the Sepulchre (Duchesne, *ibidem* p.493).

faithful were features of a *Lucernarium* which were peculiar to Jerusalem and which together formed a preliminary ceremony in themselves, but were not an integral part of that office. This introductory service provided an opportunity for each of the participants to have a share in the blaze of light in which the readings from Scripture were proclaimed.

(iii) The Development of the Roman Vigil from the *Lucernarium*

When we examine the structure of the Roman paschal vigil of the seventh and eighth centuries, we find that whilst there are features inherited from the local Roman tradition, some elements which are common to both the Roman and Jerusalem ceremonies strongly suggest the influence of the latter church's liturgy on the former. The most striking similarity is the sepulchral nature of the place in which the fire is reserved for the lighting of the candles at the Vigil. At Jerusalem, a flame burned continuously at the Tomb, symbolising the undying and unquenchable Spirit of Jesus. At Rome, the unique topographical conditions of Jerusalem could obviously not be reproduced; nevertheless, it is our contention that the pattern of services at Rome during the Triduum reflected the topographical and liturgical conditions that obtained in Jerusalem. For the services at Rome during the latter part of Holy Week were not confined to one ecclesiastical building, as they were in most other churches. The main services of Good Friday, including the night office of Matins/Lauds, were held in the Church of S.Croce in Gerusalemme, with a result that no lights burned in St John Lateran from the conclusion of the *Pedilavium* on the evening of Maundy Thursday until the start of the paschal vigil during the evening of Holy Saturday. The absence of illumination in the cathedral for the duration of nearly two days perhaps inevitably suggested the gloom and silence of a tomb, especially at this time of the liturgical year. Moreover, we have already observed that the fire for the lighting of the two baptismal candles (or Vigil-candles) was reserved *in secretiore loco;* and in this remote chamber, where the fire was so carefully tended, it is possible to see a parallel derived from the cave or chapel in the Anastasis in Jerusalem.[17] Further evidence in support of the view that during Good Friday and Holy Saturday, the Cathedral of St John Lateran liturgically represented the Holy Sepulchre in Jerusalem will be presented later in this chapter.

As in the Jerusalem rite, on the evening of Holy Saturday, the liturgy of Rome began with a ceremony of light, which in the latter city appears to be a survival of the primitive *Lucernarium,*[18] the short description of which we find in *Hippolytus.*[19] According to this account, after the onset of evening, a deacon brought in a lamp 'and standing in the midst of all the faithful who are present', he exchanged an initial greeting with them and uttered the prayer of thanksgiving for the light.[20] Allowing for liturgical developments over a period of about four centuries, the preliminary ceremony to the Roman Vigil contained elements in common with and recognisably derived from the *Lucernarium.* (i) The ceremony took place late in the day. The start of the service at the ninth hour, or at the eighth hour, seems to confirm the generally-held view that by the eighth century the Vigil in the West had come to be anticipated.[21] (ii) Light was carried into church from without. The increase in the number of lights from one in the *Apostolic Tradition* to the two of the Roman *ordines* will be

[17]Whether the number of lamps, that is, three, can be attributed to the influence of Jerusalem is open to question. For whilst Egeria in the fourth century and Antonius of Placentia in the sixth mention that only one lamp burned at the Sepulchre (Duchesne, *Christian Worship* p.493 and Geyer p.171, respectively), Arculf, writing *c.*700, refers to twelve (Wright p.2).

[18]As a daily office this service had disappeared from the Roman liturgy as a result of the replacement of the old cathedral tradition by the monastic one. Bradshaw p.123.

[19]Cuming's text, p.23 §25.

[20]The writer disagrees with Cuming, who has argued that the prayer was said by the bishop. Both the sense and certainly the grammar demand that the understood subject of 'shall give thanks' should be the deacon.

[21]OR 16.38; OR 30B.37.

discussed presently. The difference does not alter the fact that light was carried. (iii) The deacons were prominent in the ceremony. From Ordo 23 and Ordo 30B,[22] it would appear that only deacons and subdeacons were present at this ceremony. We suggested in note 4 of this chapter that the *regionarii* of Ordo 23 and the *notarii* of Ordo 24 were members of the diaconate. Ordo 30B.30 adds that the archdeacon presided. Even allowing for development within the liturgy, the association of the diaconate with the lighting of the evening lamp seems to have been perpetuated throughout the centuries.

The similarity between the two services referred to above leads us to draw a number of conclusions. (i) The procession and the blessing of the candles prior to the start of the Roman Vigil was a development of the primitive *Lucernarium* in which the evening lamp was carried and blessed by a deacon. At Jerusalem, the unique conditions had resulted in the bishop's appropriation of the deacon's function. (ii) The anticipated hour for the Vigil was a Roman development. In Jerusalem, the Vigil continued to take place in the evening. (iii) The bringing in of the light, which had been in the primitive Roman *Lucernarium* both a functional and a symbolic act, had become primarily a symbolic ritual.

In the paschal vigil according to the Ambrosian and Mozarabic rites, the preliminary ceremony also preserved the central feature of the primitive *Lucernarium,* namely, the bringing in of light.[23] The Roman ceremony differed from the Jerusalem and Mozarabic rites in one significant respect : in the ceremonies of the last two, one light was *carried* in procession, whereas in Rome, and possibly at Milan, there were two.[24] The divergence of Roman practice (and possibly the Milanese) in this respect is not easy to account for in view of the likely influence of Jerusalem on all three western rites.

[22]OR 23.24 and OR 30B.37, respectively.

[23]The use of a lamp survived in both rites. See Appendix 12.

[24]It is very significant that at Vespers in the (former) Ambrosian rite, two *cantari* or candlesticks were placed beneath the table next to the altar and removed at the start of the evening hymn. (Borella p.251.)

One might have expected the use of only one lamp or candle at Rome, as at Milan and in Spain. The Roman exception may be explained in a number of ways.

(i) Since the two large candles were carried in procession to the baptistery later the same evening for the blessing of the font, and subsequently brought back to their former position behind the altar in readiness for the start of the Easter Mass,[25] it could be argued that the number of lights was deliberately increased from one to two so as to provide the escort of two lights for the Pope,[26] who officiated both at the blessing of the font and at the Mass which followed. This theory presupposes a change from the use of one baptismal lamp at an earlier period to the use of two candles by the seventh century.[27]

(ii) The evidence of Tertullian and the *Apostolic Tradition* shows that in some churches in the West, more than one lamp featured at the *Lucernarium.*[28] Two lamps, therefore, may originally have been used at Rome; and with the fusion of the *Lucernarium* and the Vigil proper into a single ceremony, they may have been replaced by the two candles which escorted the Pope.

(iii) A third suggestion would also explain why the Vigil-candles were so large—neither of the previously-mentioned theories can account for their size. The phrase describing the two candles, *staturam hominis habentes,* is significant. The language of liturgical rubrics and directives, unlike the language of prayer, has never been characterised by florid or poetic turns

---

[25]OR 30B.44 and .61.

[26]According to the solecistic Ordo 4, the Pope enjoyed two honorific lights at every liturgical occasion : Deinde oblationarius inluminet duos cereos ante secretario pro luminaria pontificis, quod est consuetudo omni tempori (§7).

[27]A baptismal lamp was formerly used at Milan (1768 Missal p.125).

[28]*Apology* 39; Cuming, *Hippolytus* p.23 §25. This evidence, which may well relate to the Roman Church, is admittedly ambiguous. The plural *lamps* appears in the title of the chapter; but the direction in the text states that the deacon should bring in *a lamp.*

of phrase. We should perhaps have expected a term such as *magni cerei* to indicate in a rubric candles of great size. For this reason the writer believes that the phrase in question should be understood in a literal sense to indicate that not only were the candles as tall as a human being, but they were also intended to represent human beings—or, as we shall see presently, beings in the form of people—and their height was thus increased deliberately to achieve this intention. Support for the theory comes from the ninth-century Pontifical of Poitiers :

> After this [the blessing of the Easter candle] two candles, the size of a grown person, are immediately lit from the Easter candle and held by two *notarii* on either side of the altar. The candle on the right has been marked by the *notarius* who holds it 'The angel sitting at the head'. The left one is marked 'The angel sitting at the feet'. The candles symbolise the two angels in the sepulchre. . . . (Luke 24:4).[29]

If the use of the two large candles and the symbolism associated with those candles were derived from Roman practice, then the two large candles lit at the Roman Vigil also represented the angels 'in dazzling apparel'. To this claim there are two immediate objections: (i) *Poitiers,* the Gallican pontifical of *c.*900, should not be used as evidence for the practice of the Roman Church nearly three hundred years earlier. (ii) The symbolism was suggested by the size of the candles and became attached subsequently.

Although both objections must be examined carefully, neither is fatal to our theory. Two observations should be made regarding the first. It is true that a period of about three hundred years separates the earliest mention of the two candles in Ordo 11 and the description of them in *Poitiers.* However,

---

[29]Qua expleta, statim illuminantur duo cerei staturam hominis habentes de cereo benedicto, et tenentur altrinsecus a duobus notariis in dextra parte et leva. Et dexter quidem habet sibi impressum a notario *Angelus ad caput sedens.* Sinister vero a suo *Angelus ad pedes sedens.* Quique in typo duorum angelorum in sepulchro domini . . . (p.215).

the evidence of Ordo 30B, which is to be dated to *c.*800, shows that the two candles still figured prominently at the Vigil; and although *Poitiers* itself was compiled *c.*900, the description of much of the ceremonial would have been valid for an earlier period. This pontifical is mainly Gallican in respect of the new fire ceremony and the use of the Easter candle. Two features, however, namely, the reservation of fire from Good Friday and the use of the two large candles, derive from Roman practice. There is, therefore, a strong possibility that this symbolic interpretation was not only known at Rome, but that it had originated from a Roman milieu, although it must be admitted that there is no documentary evidence from the Roman *ordines* to support this contention.[30]

The case for the Roman origin of the symbolism of the two angels gains support from a closer look at the circumstances surrounding the emergence of the symbolism. As a rule, a symbol is attached subsequently to the object it represents; and there are many instances where the Church has found in the minutiae of Christian ceremonial allusions and prefigurations in the Scriptures. The representation of the two angels by the two large candles seems to be a typical example; but the circumstances of the liturgy in which the candles were used also invites the possibility that it was not the size of the candles which suggested the symbolism. Rather, it was the mention of the two angels in Luke 24:4 which resulted in their representation by two candles *staturam hominis habentes* and their presence in the Roman ceremonies of the Triduum. Then again, it is possible that this symbolism, already attached to two smaller lights, brought about an increase in their height in order to achieve a more accurate and meaningful relationship between object and symbol.

On the other hand, if it was the size of the candles which suggested the symbolism in the first instance, it is necessary

---

[30]This is perhaps not surprising in view of the laconic style of the five *ordines* cited at the beginning of this chapter and the brevity of their rubrics, compared with, for example, *PRG* and *Poitiers*.

for us to ascertain not only why the candles were so large, but why they numbered two. With regard to their number, we have already referred to the Pope's two honorific lights and suggested the possibility of two *candelae lucernales*.[31] However, it is difficult to believe that either of these two sets of lights would have attained the height of a human being, had it not been for the existence of some potentially-influential aspect of the paschal liturgy. Later writers associate the two candles with the Apostles,[32] but the application of that symbolism in this instance is not valid since in later times there is a clear contrast between the two candles and the single Easter candle representing Christ. The possibility that the candles stood for the two natures of Christ is both an unlikely and an unsatisfactory explanation. There is no hint of this in any of our sources, and such mystical symbolism is more characteristic of Orthodox theology. Moreover, the fact that both candles were lit with the same fire makes this interpretation awkward. In the five papal *ordines* cited at the beginning of the chapter, there is no hint of what the candles represented; nor can any assistance be derived from the Milanese and Spanish rites, in which a single light was used.

Since we cannot readily account for either the number or the size of the candles which represented the angels, we must examine the possibility that the desire to represent visually the angels at the Vigil resulted in the introduction of the two large candles into the liturgy of Holy Saturday, from which illuminations had hitherto been absent. If so, this would assign the ceremony with its additional luminous feature to that category of services envisaged by Herbert Thurston when he writes (of the Easter candle) : 'In this case we have, I believe, a ceremony that was really designed from the beginning with a strictly mystical and symbolical meaning.'[33] However, it is doubtful if any religious ceremonies have such origins—

[31]'*Lucernarium*-lamps'.
[32]For instance, Honorius of Autun, *Sacramentary* (PL172.748B).
[33]*Holy Saturday* p.4.

even Thurston admits that there were not many—and this is true of many elements and features of Christian ritual which have a functional or utilitarian origin and subsequently become endowed with a symbolical interpretation. Such, we believe, is the origin of the presence, as opposed to the height, of the two large candles. Once, however, a ritual or an element within a ritual has been endowed with a symbolical significance, that ritual or element may undergo a development which will result in a closer approximation between it and the object that it represents.

Such a development appears to have occurred within the ritual involving the two candles at the Roman Vigil. It would satisfactorily account for both their size and their number. Two small lights were carried into church at the start of the Vigil, a surviving feature of the primitive *Lucernarium*, which at Rome had disappeared on every other day of the year. These lamps or candles were placed, or more likely held, one each side of the altar while the Vigil-lessons were read. We have already noted that the only service to have taken place since the evening of Maundy Thursday in the Cathedral of St John Lateran, wherein the Vigil was held, was the night office of Holy Saturday. The latter service was conducted in darkness. We suggested above that because of the absence of illumination during this period,[34] the entire church was held to symbolise the Tomb of Jesus. The sepulchral atmosphere was further emphasised by the use of the dim light in which the Vigil-lections were read. This would have recalled the time of day when the women visited the Tomb on the first Easter morning. Furthermore, the announcement of the two angels was of a prophetic nature, as was the content of the Vigil-lections. It is our contention, therefore, that suggested by the content of Luke 24:4, the two lights which had survived from the primitive *Lucernarium* were increased in size to convey the impression of human height. Moreover, if the two large candles, which were held either side of the altar, had the same

---

[34]Apart from the reserved fire, which was hidden from view.

significance as those in *Poitiers,* the altar coming between the two candles would have represented the Tomb; and although documentary evidence is lacking for the altar at St John Lateran, the hiding of the fire behind or under the altar at St Remigius' Abbey possibly shows that the notion of the altar as a tomb was not unknown.[35] The increase in the size of the candles would have resulted in the provision of more light for those who read. The candles were subsequently carried in procession to the font. Since the Pope was honoured with two smaller candles in the normal course of events, it does not seem unreasonable to suppose that at the blessing of the font, the two large candles served a dual purpose and that when they had been returned to the altar for the start of the Easter Mass, they then symbolised the presence and authority of the Pope.

* * * * *

In the earlier chapters of Part Four, we saw that our knowledge of the Easter candle in this early period[36] is derived almost exclusively from references in letters and from surviving *laudes cerei.* In the period between the earliest reference to the Candle and the first mention of it within the context of a service,[37] the ceremony in which the Easter candle figured prominently had been adopted by churches throughout a considerable part of Europe north of the Alps, almost certainly as a result of Milanese or Aquileian influence.[38] However, during this same period, Roman influence was also at work; and the results of this we shall note in the following sections. However, sufficient purely Gallican documentary evidence is extant for us to observe the main features of the Easter candle ceremony in Gaul before the importation of Roman elements.

[35]It would satisfactorily explain the practice at this monastery.
[36]That is, *c.*400–700.
[37]That is, from the late fourth to the mid-eighth century.
[38]By the fourth century, Milanese jurisdiction extended as far as Rhaetia; and by the fifth century, Chur, Augsburg, and Ratisbon were subject to Aquileia. As late as the eleventh century, these three cities were still using Ambrosian liturgical books. (Borella p.105).

(iv) The Eighth-century Gallican Rite : Mode A

All of our sources refer to the Easter candle as *cereus* without any adjectival qualification.[39] None of them mentions its
being brought into church as part of a procession, though Ordo
17 records the entry into church of the deacons 'without lighted
candles' (§102). The possibility, therefore, should not be ruled
out completely that it was carried into church, in view of the
evidence of later centuries and in view of the fact the sources
in question concern themselves primarily with the lighting and
blessing of the Candle. The officiant at the ceremony was a
deacon or the archdeacon,[40] who, after making the sign of
the cross, lit the Candle with the fire which had been reserved
for that purpose the previous day and began his benediction.
The fire was obtained from the candle, or more likely the lamp,
which had been concealed from view at the conclusion of the
night office in the early hours of Good Friday morning, or
from fire reserved on Maundy Thursday.[41] It is the writer's
belief that at St Remigius' Abbey, the fire was reserved behind or under the altar. This would explain why the officiant
moved to the rear of the altar :

> Then the prayer ended, the *priest* goes behind the altar and
> receives a light from the fire which had been concealed on
> Good Friday.[42]

[39]OR 17.103; OR 30A.15; *GeV* p.68; *GeAng* p.52; *GePr* p.55; Sacramentary of St Remigius' Abbey p.328; and the Gradual of St Gregory. A fragment of this last-mentioned source is to be found in Macri, *Hierolexicon* p.142.
These references also relate to the ceremony as a whole.

[40]Five of the documents cited in the previous note mention the archdeacon. Ordo 17 refers to *ille qui cereum benedici* (sic) *debet*, 'he who has to bless
the Candle'—presumably, a deacon. The Sacramentary of St Remigius'
Abbey states that the duty was performed by the *sacerdos,* who may have
been a priest, the abbot, or even the bishop. This is the only recorded instance of the ceremony being performed by someone other than a deacon
or an archdeacon. The preceding rubric rules out the possibility that *sacerdos* is here used to indicate any member of the clergy.

[41]*Quinta feria.* Thus the Gradual of St Gregory (Macri p.142).

[42]Deinde veniens sacerdos ab oratione vadit retro altare, accipiens de
lumine quod sexta feria absconsum fuit. Sacramentary p.328.

This location would also be most convenient for the concealing of a lamp at the conclusion of the night office of Good Friday. We have observed in Part One that in the Roman rite, the last candle at Tenebrae was hidden in this very place. As to the position of the Easter candle, all our sources, except the Sacramentary of St Remigius, state that the officiant stood *ante altare*. In view of this, it is almost certain that the Candle was placed also in front of the altar, presumably in a central position.

(v) The Later Gallican Rite : Mode B

An alternative Gallican tradition, also free from Roman influence, is contained in the tenth-century Sacramentary of Corbie.[43] Although the document relates to a period some two hundred years after that which the documents in the previous section attest, elements present in this rite are also found in the ninth-century Ordo 31 and in the eighth-century Ordo 26 and Ordo 28, and this would suggest that the tradition recorded by the sacramentary was much older than the tenth century.[44]

The ceremony described in this document differed from the eighth-century Gallican rite in Section (iv) in five important respects. (i) The service was presided over by the bishop with all orders of clergy in attendance. (ii) The Easter candle was borne in procession into church before being set down *in medio choro*.[45] (iii) The Easter candle was then consecrated by a deacon who sang the *Exultet* after he had received a blessing from the bishop. The blessing of the Candle by the deacon preserved the primitive practice of the Church, first found in the fourth century,[46] and suggests that its performance by

[43]PL 78.336B/C = M 106.

[44]The blessing of the Easter candle is not contained in Ordo 26, only alluded to. Ordo 28 and Ordo 31 should be used as corroborative evidence with some caution because of their Roman accretions.

[45]Also attested in OR 28.59 and OR 31.63.

[46]Also attested in OR 28.60.

the archdeacon was a later development. (iv) The fire for lighting the Easter candle was that newly kindled on Maundy Thursday and reserved until Holy Saturday, unlike the fire of Mode A, which was reserved on Good Friday. The reservation of fire newly kindled with a flint is first attested in Ordo 26 (§3). The sacramentary also contains the first recorded instance of the blessing of the new fire (and the incense) by the bishop (or a priest),[47] but does not include the prayer of consecration. The fire and the incense were blessed while the deacon was chanting the *Exultet.* (v) The lighting of the Easter candle during the Preface at *ignis accendit* contrasted markedly with the practice in Mode A, where the Candle was already alight at the start of the benediction, and marked the beginning, as far as documentary evidence is concerned, of that process of liturgical development which caused the *laus cerei* to undergo a series of interruptions.

Although most of the documentary evidence for the ceremonial surrounding the Easter candle in tenth-century Gaul attests the presence of the two Roman Vigil-candles and the lighting of the Easter candle prior to the chanting of the *Exultet,* the significance of the practice at Corbie should not be underestimated; for the twin candles ultimately either declined in liturgical importance or disappeared completely from the paschal rites, and it became universal practice to light the Easter candle at *ignis accendit.* With some confidence, we can attribute to Lanfranc the triumph of these two features of the Corbeian rite : the absence of the two Vigil-candles and the lighting of the Easter candle during the Preface. For in spite of the liturgical development which took place elsewhere in the century which intervenes between the Sacramentary of Corbie and Lanfranc's work, both these features are to be found in the elaboration of ceremonial set out in his *Decrees;* and Corbeian parentage seems very likely. For on the one hand, Corbie was a very influential Benedictine centre in Northern France *c.*1000; and on the other, Lanfranc was

---

[47]On the assumption that the sacramentary antedates *PRG.*

for a time Abbot of St Stephen's Monastery at Caen, and the local or regional liturgical variations of the area may well have been assimilated by him during his sojourn in that part of France. Certainly, the directions for the ritual surrounding the blessing of the Easter candle according to the Benedictine *Regularis Concordia* of the previous century are quite different from those enjoined by Lanfranc.[48]

(vi) The Roman Vigil in Gaul

In Section (i) of this chapter, we discussed the evidence of the five Roman *ordines* in an attempt to make a partial reconstruction of the form the paschal vigil took at the papal court in Rome. There seems little doubt that this Roman form of the Vigil was in use in a number of churches in Gaul since all five *ordines* have their provenance in that country, though they attest Roman practice, and since the Roman form of services was encouraged by Charlemagne in his desire to impose liturgical uniformity throughout the length and breadth of his vast domains. In addition to these five *ordines,* the Sacramentary of Autun also contains the Roman form of the paschal vigil. Like some of the other Gelasian sacramentaries, it includes the *Deus mundi Conditor,* the benediction-formula for the Vigil-candles.[49] We do not know how widely the Roman form of the Vigil was adopted in the regions to the north of the Alps. Charlemagne's only-partial success is reflected in the emergence of the Romano-Gallican synthesis from the liturgical disorder of the eighth and ninth centuries.

[48]A certain amount of ceremonial variation existed from one Benedictine house to another, a fact Lanfranc himself commented upon in his *Decrees* (PL 150.467B).

[49]*GePh* p.63. The Sacramentary was formerly referred to as the Phillipps Gelasian Sacramentary.

Chapter Thirty-four
THE ROMANO-GALLICAN SYNTHESIS

(i) The Diversity of Practice

It was perhaps inevitable that with the importation of the Roman form of the Vigil into Gaul, its fusion with the local Gallican rites not only took place but was achieved with differing results. The diversity of practice was known to Amalarius; and the recommendation in his *Liber de Ordine Antiphonarii*, written *c.*830, should be seen as an attempt by him to promote the synthesis of Roman and Gallican ceremonial practices.

> This is my recommendation : let fire be reserved from Good Friday to light the Candle which represents the column of fire and which is set in position to be blessed. It is lit at the beginning of the blessing, and after it has been consecrated, a second candle is lit from it.[1]

However, a compromise along these lines was bound to be forced—in fact there is no evidence that his suggestion was

---

[1]Hoc est quod dico : reservetur ignis de sexta feria, ut inluminetur cereus qui ponitur in vice columnae ignis benedicendum, qui ab initio benedictionis inluminatus est, et cum benedictus est, ab eo inluminetur secundus cereus. *LDOA* XLIV.8.

adopted by any church at the time, since the significance of the two Vigil-candles would have been lost if one had been converted into the Easter candle and the other had been made subordinate to it. It is true that at Aquileia in the sixteenth century, the status of the two candles corresponds to that prescribed by Amalarius;[2] but we cannot be certain that the presence of these two candles was the result of the recommendations of Amalarius. However, it is very likely that the candle lit at the conclusion of the *laus cerei* in the Benedictine rite, which we shall discuss in Section (ii), corresponded to the *secundus cereus* enjoined by Amalarius.

That the two candles envisaged by Amalarius were of unequal status is clear both from the symbolism which he attaches to each and from their use at the blessing of the font. For him, the larger candle was Christ, whilst the smaller one, which took its light from the larger, represented the company of apostles to whom Christ said, 'You are the light of the world'.[3] After the Vigil-lections, both candles were to be borne in front of the catechumens to Baptism, but only the larger one was immersed in the water.[4] The Benedictine development took place probably as a result of the influence of Amalarius' writings, but there were practical considerations also.

The diversity of practice, which had prompted Amalarius' solution for a synthesis of ceremonial, manifested itself in a number of different ways. Again for convenience we will refer to them as *modes*.

Mode 1

The description of the lighting and blessing of the candles in the late ninth-century Ordo 29 shows, not a fusion of two traditions, but a juxtaposition of two quite separate services.[5] The two Vigil-candles of the Roman rite were lit with fire

[2]1519 Missal fol.98.
[3]*Liber officialis* 1.20.2.
[4]*Liber officialis* 1.20.2 and 1.26.1-4.
[5]OR 29.45-48.

newly kindled on Holy Saturday, and were placed one either side of the altar. After the reading of the Vigil-lections, the clergy departed, together with the two candles. On their return, the Easter candle was lit with fire kindled on and reserved from Maundy Thursday. The separate performance of both the ceremonies on Easter Eve would appear to be a transitional stage in the fusion of both rituals. Ordo 29 is also unique in that it is the only early Roman *ordo* to record a separate kindling of fire on all three days of the Triduum.

MODE 2

This variation has features in common with the eighth-century Gallican rite but belongs more to the Roman than the Gallican tradition. It is found in the tenth-century Pontifical of Wolfgang, Bishop of Regensburg :

> Let the deacon receive some of the fire which had been kindled from a stone on Good Friday; and let him light the two large candles; and after making the sign of the cross let him bless them.[6]

It would appear from this pontifical that the Easter candle was unknown at Regensburg in the tenth century. Alternatively, the section relating to the Easter candle may be missing from this document. The two large candles, which later escorted the bishop,[7] and the new fire kindled from a stone on Good Friday were clearly Roman elements; but the blessing performed by the deacon and the sign of the cross would appear to have come from the Gallican tradition.

MODE 3

Mode 1 and *Mode 2* may represent isolated instances of attempts to harmonise the different liturgical traditions. In *Mode 3*, however, we have what appears to be a fusion of the Galli-

---

[6]Diaconus . . . accipiat de igne qui sexta fuerat excussus de lapide. et incendat duos magnos cereos. et faciens crucem benedicat eos. Pontifical p.125.

[7]These candles recall the Pope's honorific lights. Pontifical p.130.

can and Roman uses of light, in which the principal features of both would appear to have retained their original importance and significance. Thus in the eighth-century Gelasian Sacramentary of Gellone, it was the Easter candle which was kindled and blessed,[8] whilst at the blessing of the font, only the two Vigil-candles are mentioned.[9] Although there is no indication in the rubrics of this sacramentary, it is reasonable to assume that these two candles were also alight during the reading of the lections. Support for this view comes from the late ninth-century Pontifical of Poitiers, which also records the very point in that rite at which these candles were lit.[10] We learn that the two candles, the size of a grown person, were held by *notarii* who stood one either side of the Easter candle or the altar, and that they were kindled with fire taken from the flame of the Easter candle at the conclusion of the *laus cerei*. *Poitiers* concurs with the Sacramentary of Gellone in attesting the presence of only the two Vigil-candles at the blessing of the font (*ibidem* p.216).

Evidence for the widespread use of the Romano-Gallican synthesis throughout Western Europe is plentiful. At Mainz in the tenth century, the two large candles in candlesticks stood one either side of the altar and were lit at the conclusion of the *laus cerei*.[11] This arrangement is also found in the slightly-later *Alcuin;*[12] but it is possible to detect in that document a decline in the importance of the two Vigil-candles, since at the blessing of the font, the choice is permitted of immersing either the two large candles or the Easter candle. The placing of the two candles in candlesticks also indicates a reduction in their physical size.[13] The use of two smaller candles

---

[8]*GeGe* pp.92–93.

[9]*GeGe* p.99.

[10]*Poitiers* p.215.

[11]*PRG* II p.99 §348.

[12]PL 101.1216C.

[13]Evidence for this is to be found in *PRG* and *Alcuin, op.cit.; PR XII* (*PRMA* I.xxxii.8 p.240); Pontifical of St-Germain-des-Prés (*DAER* 4.24 p.159 [M 230]); and at Marseille in the thirteenth century (*ILEM* p.84).

placed either side of the Easter candle is documented as early as the eleventh century at Rouen,[14] and by Beleth,[15] Honorius of Autun,[16] and Durandus.[17] The last informs us that this practice obtained 'in most churches'.

At Milan in the twelfth century, two small candles were held by deacons, one either side of the Easter candle, and two large candles stood at the font.[18] By the seventeenth century, the use of the latter had been discontinued.[19] At Braga, the Missal of 1512 refers to the two candles lit during the Preface (np), but they are not mentioned in the Missal of 1558. We referred above to the practice at Aquileia and noted that the use of two candles in that church corresponded to the prescription of Amalarius. In the primitive Mozarabic rite, no additional candles were lit to accompany the Easter candle. However, according to the *Missale Mixtum* of 1500, two candles were to be lit from the flame of the Easter candle.[20] Of these, Martène informs us that one stood to the left of the altar, whilst the other was placed behind.[21] No reason is given for this arrangement. At the Benedictine monastery of Monte Cassino in the twelfth century, the two additional candles were placed *ad altare.*[22] Since the Easter candle stood next to the ambo, the phrase should perhaps be interpreted 'on either side of the altar'. This is the position mentioned in the contemporary Pontifical of St-Germain-des-Prés.[23] Here the Easter candle may also have stood by the ambo.

We mentioned above the statement of Durandus that in most churches two small candles stood either side of the Easter

---

[14]*Acta Vetera* (PL 147.176C).
[15]*Rationale* (PL 202.110C).
[16]*Sacramentary* (PL 172.748B).
[17]*Rationale* VI.80 fol.352.
[18]Beroldus p.110.
[19]They appear in Ambrosian missals of the sixteenth century, but not in the Missal of 1669.
[20]PL 85.442C.
[21]*DAER* 4.24 p.164.
[22]*PR XII* (*PRMA* I p.293) and Martène, *DAMR* 3.15.10 p.143.
[23]Martène, *DAER* 4.24 p.159 (M 230).

candle. Their absence from the minority of churches may be explained in three ways. (i) As (originally) baptismal candles, they would have lost their *raison d'être* if the ceremony of the blessing of the font no longer took place, as happened in some monasteries. (ii) There may have been some churches in which the use of the two candles was unknown, especially if these churches preserved a Gallican rite free of Roman influence in this respect. (iii) We have already observed that the function of the two small candles and the function of the two acolytes' or torch-bearers' candles may well have been merged, or they may have disappeared if the bishop was accorded two honorific candles.

(ii) The Benedictine Development

There can be little doubt that at the Monasteries of Monte Cassino and St-Germain-des-Prés, the ceremonial surrounding the kindling and blessing of lights at the Easter vigil followed the injunctions of the tenth-century Benedictine *Regularis Concordia*. This enjoined upon the houses of that order the principal features of the Romano-Gallican synthesis, namely, the lighting and blessing of the Easter candle and the kindling of the two candles, which were held by acolytes one each side of the altar. In addition to these lights, the *Regula* also directs that another smaller candle should be kindled at the conclusion of the *laus cerei*,[24] but gives no indication as to its purpose. Since its function was not to provide a source of fire in an emergency,[25] it either constituted the second candle, which, we saw at the beginning of this chapter, had been enjoined by Amalarius, albeit reduced in size, or it acted as a surrogate for the Easter candle, which for one reason or another remained in front of the altar or next to the ambo while

[24]PL 137.494C.

[25]In the event of the failure of the reed-candle or serpent-candle, an additional source of fire would have been available from the candle in the lantern or from one of the candles of the acolytes.

the font was being blessed. In later times, it had the latter function, as is evidenced at Worcester, where it was known as the *cereus fontium*,[26] and at Barking.[27] The Gilbertine Ordinal suggests that this small candle was used only where the blessing of the font took place.[28] The use of the *cereus minor* was not confined to the monastic tradition. Sicardus refers to it, again in a baptismal context.[29] For him, the small candle signifies the Order of the Apostles since Christ, who is symbolised by the larger Easter candle, addressed his disciples, 'You are the light of the world', and since the Apostles, like Christ, illuminate the Church. Durandus mentions its existence but does not comment upon its purpose.[30] It featured in the rites of Salisbury[31] and Aquileia;[32] and at the Church of St-Agnan in Orléans, it accompanied the Easter candle in the procession to the font as late as the eighteenth century.[33] There is also a reference to this candle at Reims.[34] In the older rite at Braga, this candle was lit with the serpent-candle before being dipped into the font.

[26]Antiphonary p.69.
[27]HBS 65 p.101.
[28]HBS 59 p.40.
[29]*Mitrale* (PL 213.324D-325A).
[30]*Rationale* IV.80 fol.352.
[31]13 C Missal (Warren) p.270.
[32]1519 Missal fol.98.
[33]De Moléon p.209.
[34]1770 Missal p.224.

APPENDIX 1

The Omissions

Since the eighth century in the Gallican Church and the tenth in the Roman rite, the night offices of Matins/Lauds on Maundy Thursday, Good Friday, and Holy Saturday were distinguished from the night offices of the rest of the days of the year by the omission of the customary versicles and responses. The *Deus in adiutorium* and the Invitatory were not said at the start of the service; no blessing was requested at the start of the lessons; and the *Kyrie eleison* was omitted at the conclusion of Lauds. Above all, the *Gloria Patri* doxology was omitted at the close of each psalm.[1] These same omissions, which are also found in the Office for the Dead and represent the funereal aspect of Tenebrae, were 'made designedly to mark the deep mourning in which the Church is plunged',[2] and seem to point to the great antiquity of the office.[3]

[1]Sicardus, *Mitrale* (PL 213.297A). In the now-superseded night office of Holy Saturday according to the Ambrosian rite, the *Gloria Patri* was omitted from the end of the twenty-three psalms and one canticle. *Breviarium Ambrosianum*, Pars Prima.

[2]Thurston, *LHW* p.243.

[3]Batiffol p.93.

In the Middle Ages, these omissions of the beginnings and endings were given an allegorical interpretation. According to Rupert of Deutz, Christ, who is the A and Ω, the beginning and the end, is *dead* during this period.[4] Hence they are omitted. This explanation is also to be found in the Ordinal of St Mary's, York.[5] Durandus also mentions that the *Gloria*'s etc. are not said because Christ is lying in the tomb.[6]

[4] *De Div. Off.* V (PL 170.148A).
[5] HBS 75 p.271.
[6] *Rationale* IV.72 fol.331.

APPENDIX 2

The Roman and Gallican Traditions

There has been a tendency in the past amongst some
writers, when dealing with the development of the Roman
and Gallican liturgies in the period 700 to 950, to assume the
existence of a uniform Roman rite and similarly a uniform
Gallican rite. The picture of two contrasting and at times
mutually interacting liturgies could not be further from the
reality of the situation.

It is probably true that as the temporal power of the papacy
increased, the pressures towards conformity were considerable in the areas which were subject to the Roman Church;
but in the areas of so-called Gallican influence, particularly
in the decades before the reign of Charlemagne, the existence
of several liturgically-independent churches and the absence
of a central unifying force inevitably resulted in a variety of
differing local rites. It is beyond the scope of this work to in-
vestigate the ancestries and origins of the Gallican liturgies.
It seems quite likely, however, that the various Gallican
rites—ultimately deriving from the same parent ancestor as
the Roman rite and developing independently, at times under
the pressure of local pagan customs—were influenced to a
greater or lesser degree by the liturgies of Aquileia and Milan, depending on their geographical proximity to those

453

centres, probably more than is generally recognised; and even in the period of increased Roman influence, from 789 onwards, the Milanese Church in all likelihood continued to be influential, especially in those areas where the boundaries of the Gallican and Milanese churches were coterminous.

It can be safely said that prior to the Decree of Conformity in 789, there was considerable variety in the forms of service found throughout the Gallican Church. When St Chrodegang, after a visit to Rome in 751, introduced the Roman rite at Metz, that church became 'a Roman lighthouse in a sea of liturgical disorder' (A.A.King). In view of the state of political unrest in Gaul and Western Germany in the preceding centuries, liturgical conformity had not been possible. It was Charlemagne who attempted to impose throughout his vast domains the Roman rite, which he had introduced into the royal chapel of his capital at Aachen, as part of his attempt to unify his extensive empire.

The attempt can be described as only partially successful and slow, if his intention was to replace completely the Gallican rites with the Roman. For it was not until *c*. 810 that the Roman rite was introduced at Lyon by Leidrad; and in 832, the night offices of the Triduum with which Amalarius was familiar were decidedly non-Roman.

After the death of Charlemagne, the Treaty of Verdun in 843 destroyed the political unity which had facilitated the partial imposition of liturgical uniformity. The next hundred years or so witnessed the gradual gallicanisation of the Roman rite, especially in the region at the centre of which lay Mainz, whence originated the *Pontificale Romano-Germanicum*, the ancestor of the future Tridentine Missal and Breviary.

APPENDIX 3

The Non-observation of the New Fire and Easter Candle Ceremonies

In view of the simplicity and austerity of its rite, the ceremonies of the new fire and the Easter candle have never been observed in the houses of the Carthusian order. Following the Second Vatican Council, some members of the order felt that the Easter candle ought to be adopted; but the idea was not accepted.[1]

Formerly, the Easter candle was not blessed in the Church of St Stephen and the Church of the Holy Cross in Lyon, the congregations of those churches repairing to the cathedral for the ceremony.[2] There was a similar custom for the faithful of the parochial churches of Evreux and its suburbs to attend the mother church, and subsequently to take some of the new fire home.[3]

In spite of the restoration of the paschal rites to their former times following the liturgical reforms of the Roman Church in 1955, the ceremonies are not observed in all parish churches; and only a small number of Anglican churches ob-

[1] Letter to the writer from Fr Bernard O'Donovan O.C. of St Hugh's Charterhouse, Horsham, England.
[2] 1771 Missal p.194.
[3] 1740 Missal p. 187.

serve the ceremonies of Holy Saturday, which closely follow those of the Roman rite. At Amiens Cathedral, they fell into desuetude in 1969, having been revived in 1955. This was mainly the result of poorly-attended services during those fourteen years.[4]

[4]Letter to the writer from L'Abbé P.Grey, *Secrétaire Général* of that diocese.

APPENDIX 4

The Formulas for the Blessing of the New Fire

A. Deus, qui per Filium tuum, angularem scilicet lapidem, claritatis* tuae ignem fidelibus contulisti : productum e silice, nostris profuturum usibus, novum hunc ignem sanctifica : et concede nobis, ita per haec festa paschalia coelestibus desideriis inflammari; ut ad perpetuae claritatis, puris mentibus, valeamus festa pertingere. Per.

A1. Deus, qui per Filium tuum claritatis tuae ignem fidelibus contulisti, novum hunc ignem + sanctifica, et concede nobis, ita per haec festa paschalia caelestibus desideriis inflammari, ut ad perpetuae claritatis puris mentibus valeamus festa pertingere. Per.

B. Exaudi nos, lumen indeficiens, Domine Deus noster, unici luminis lumen; fons luminis, lumen auctor luminum, quae creasti et inluminasti; lumen angelorum tuorum, sedium, dominationum, principatuum, potestatum et omnium intelligibilium, quae creasti; lumen sanctorum tuorum. Sint lucernae tuae animae nostrae; accedant ad te et inluminentur abs te; luceant veritate, ardeant caritate; luceant et non tenebrescant, ardeant et non cinerescant. Benedic hoc lumen, o lumen, quia et hoc, quod portamus in manibus, tu creasti,

---

PRG has caritatis.

tu donasti. Per haec lumina, quae accendimus, de hoc loco expellimus noctem; sic et tu expelle tenebras de cordibus nostris. Simus domus tua lucens de te, lucens in te; sine defectu luceamus et te semper colamus; in te accendamur, et non extinguamur.

B1. Dominus Deus, Pater omnipotens, lumen indeficiens, qui es conditor omnium luminum : benedic hoc lumen, quod a te sanctificatum atque benedictum est, qui illuminasti omnem mundum : ut ab eo lumine accendamur, atque illuminemur igne claritatis tuae : et sicut illuminasti Moysen exeuntem de Aegypto, ita illumines corda, et sensus nostros; ut ad vitam et lucem aeternam pervenire mereamus. Per.

B2(a). Domine Deus noster, Pater omnipotens, exaudi nos, lumen indeficiens : tu es sancte conditor omnium luminum, benedic, Domine, hoc lumen quod a te sanctificatum atque benedictum est. Tu inluminasti omnem mundum, ut ab eo lumine accendamur et illuminemur igne claritatis tuae, sicut ignem inluminasti Moyse, ita illuminabis cordibus et sensibus nostris, ut ad vitam aeternam pervenire mereamur. Per.

B2(b). Domine Deus noster, Pater omnipotens, exaudi nos lumen indeficiens : tu es sancte conditor omnium luminum, benedic, Domine, hoc lumen quod a te sanctificatum atque benedictum est. Tu inluminasti omnem mundum, ut ab eo lumine accendamur et inluminemur igne claritatis tuae, sicut igne inluminasti Moysen, ita inluminatis sensibus et cordibus nostris ut ad vitam aeternam pervenire mereamur. Per.

B2(c). Exaudi nos, lumen indeficiens : tu es sancte conditor omnium luminum, benedic, Domine, hoc lumen quod a te sanctificatum atque benedictum est. Tu inluminasti omnem mundum, ut ab eo lumine accendamur et inluminemur igne claritatis tuae, sicut ignem inluminasti Moyse, ita iluminabis cordibus et sensibus nostris, ut ad vitam aeternam pervenire mereamur. Per.

B2(d). Dominus Deus noster, Pater omnipotens, exaudi nos lumen indeficiens : Tu es sanctus conditor omnium luminum; bene + dic, Domine, hoc lumen quod a te sanctificatum et benedictum est, ut ab eo lumine accendamur, et illuminemur igne claritatis tuae. Sicut ignem illuminasti in rubo tempore Moysis, ita illuminare digneris corda nostra et sensus nostros, ut ad vitam aeternam pervenire mereamur. Per.

B2(e). Deus pater omnipotens, exaudi nos, lumen indeficiens; tu es sancte conditor omnium luminum, benedic, domine, hoc lumen, quod a te sanctificatum atque benedictum est. Tu illuminasti omnem mundum, ab eo lumine accendimur et illuminamur igni claritatis tuae; igni ergo quo illuminasti Moysen illumina quaesumus corda et sensus nostros ut ad vitam aeternam pervenire mereamur. Per.

B3. Domine Iesu Christe lumen indeficiens exaudi nos tu qui es sancte conditor omnium luminum. benedic domine hoc lumen quod a te sanctificatum atque benedictum est : tu qui illuminasti omnem mundum : ut accendamur et illuminemur igne claritatis tuae, sicut illuminasti domine Moysen legiferum tuum. ita illumina corda nostra et sensus. ut ad vitam eternam pervenire mereamur. Per.

B4. Domine Deus noster Pater omnipotens, lumen indeficiens conditor omnium luminum, exaudi nos famulos tuos et benedic hunc ignem : qui tua sanctificatione atque benedictione consecretur. Tu illuminans omnem hominem venientem in hunc mundum illumina conscientias cordis nostri igne tuae caritatis ut tuo igne igniti tuo lumine illuminati : expulsis a cordibus nostris peccatorum tenebris : ad vitam te illustrante pervenire mereamur aeternam. Per.

B5(a). *The first part of this prayer is identical with* B4 *above. After* aeternam *it continues :* Et sicut illuminasti ignem Moysi famulo tuo per columnam ignis ambulanti in mari rubro : ita illustra nostrum lumen : et candela quae de eo fuerit accensa in honore maiestatis tuae semper perserveret benedicta : ut quicumque ex eo lumine portaverit sit illuminatus lumine gratiae spiritualis. Per.

B5(b). Domine Deus Pater omnipotens lumen indeficiens, exaudi nos famulos tuos et benedic hunc ignem qui tua sanctificatione atque benedictione consecratur : tu domine qui illuminas omnem hominem venientem in hunc mundum illumina conscientias cordis nostri igne tuae caritatis. ut tuo igne igniti et illuminati expulsis a cordibus nostris peccatorum tenebris ad vitam te illustrante pervenire mereamur aeternam. Per.

B5(c). Domine Deus Noster Omnipotens, lumen indeficiens, conditor hominum, exaudi nos famulos tuos et bene + dic hunc ignem, qui tua sancti + ficatione et bene + dictione consecratus est. Tu qui illuminas omnem hominem venientem in hunc mundum, illumina tenebras cordis nostri, et conscientias nostras igne tuae caritatis, ut tuo lumine illuminati, expulsis a cordibus nostris peccatorum tenebris, ad vitam, te illustrante, pervenire mereamur. Per.

B5(d). Domine Deus Noster Omnipotens, Lumen indeficiens, conditor omnium luminum, exaudi nos famulos tuos et benedic hunc novum ignem qui tua sanctificatione consecretur. Tu illuminas omnem hominem venientem in hunc mundum, illumina quaesumus conscientias cordis nostri igne tuae caritatis ut tuo igne igniti tuo lumine illuminati expulsis a cordibus nostris peccatorum tenebris ad vitam te illustrante pervenire mereamur aeternam.

B5(e). Domine Deus noster audi nos pater omnipotens lumen indeficiens qui es sanctorum splendor luminum : et bene + dic domine hoc lumen quod a te conditum est : qui illuminas omnem hominem venientem in hunc mundum : ut a te vero lumine accendamur : et illuminemur igne claritatis tuae : illumina etiam corda et sensus nostros ut ad vitam aeternam pervenire mereamur. Per.

B6. Domine Deus noster Pater omnipotens qui es lumen indeficiens et conditor omnium luminum, benedic et sanctifica hunc ignem : ut per te sancificatum et benedictum, qui illuminasti omnem mundum, ab eo accendamur atque illuminemur igne claritatis tuae, quo illuminasti Moysen famulum tuum : ut, illuminatis cordibus et sensibus nostris, ad vitam aeternam pervenire mereamur. Per.

B7(a). Dominus Deus omnipotens, lumen indeficiens et conditor omnis luminis, exaudi nos indignos famulos tuos, et benedicere huius novi ignis lumen, quod a te vero lumine nobis donatum est, ut et tui amoris accendamur illustratione,

et verae caritatis illuminemur igne : et sicut Moysen famulum tuum mirabili illuminasti splendore, ita corda et sensus
nostros illuminare digneris; ut peccatorum labe expiati, ad
te, qui aeterna vita es, pervenire mereamur. Qui cum Deo
Patre et Spiritu Sancto vivis.

B7(b). Dominus Deus omnipotens, lumen indeficiens et
conditor omnium luminum, exaudi nos famulos tuos, et
benedicere digneris huius novi ignis lumen, quod a te vero
lumine nobis donatum est, ut et tui amoris accendamur splendore, ita corda et sensus nostros illuminare digneris, ut expiati peccatorum labe, ad te qui vita aeterna es pervenire
mereamur. Per.

B8. Dominus sancte pater, omnipotens aeternus deus, exaudi nos lumen indeficiens. Tu es enim, domine deus noster,
conditor omnium luminum. Benedic, domine, et hoc lumen,
et hanc caeram, quod a te incensum, sanctificatumque ac
benedictum est. Tu qui inluminasti omnem mundum, ab eo
lumine accendamur, et illuminemur igne claritatis tuae. Tu
es ignis qui famulo tuo moysi in rubo apparuisti. Tu es columna ignis qui populum israhel in nocte defendebas et in-
luminabas. Tu enim tres pueros de fornaci ignis liberasti,
domine, cum filio tuo ihesu christo et sancto spiritu tuo, qui
in igne super apostolos singulos die pentacosten, et post tempus super Cornelium, cum omni domo suo, tibi primum ex
gentibus credentem de celo descendisti, ut sicut eos omnes
conseruasti et inluminasti, ita sensus nostros cordaque et animas nostras in hac paschali sollempnitate et omni vitae nostrae tempore inluminare igne spiritus sancti digneris, ut ad
vitam aeternam pervenire mereamur in caelis. Per.

B9. Domine Deus, Pater Omnipotens, lumen indeficiens,
qui es conditor omnium luminum, qui illuminasti omnem
mundum, benedic lumen hoc, quod a te sanctificatum est atque benedictum, ut ab eo accendamur et illuminemur lumine
claritatis tuae et sicut illuminasti cor Moysi ad rubum arden-
tem et non comburentem, quando eum misisti in Egyptum
ad Pharaonem et cum ad te ascendisset in montem Synai,
ita illuminare cordibus nostris et sensibus, per te qui via, veri-

tas et vita es, ad vitam permanentem et lucem aeternam pervenire mereamur. Per.

B10. Dominus Deus noster pater omnipotens lumen indeficiens : exaudi nos qui es sancte conditor omnium luminum et benedicere digneris hoc lumen quod a te sanctificatum est atque benedictum et sicut illuminasti omnem mundum tuo lumine ut ab eo accendamur et illuminemur lumine claritatis tuae : ita illumina corda nostra et sensus nostros et ideo deprecamur te domine deus noster : ut sicut illuminasti ignem Moysi famulo tuo per columnam spiritualem ambulantem in mari rubro ita intelligentias nostras illustra : ut ad vitam aeternam pervenire mereamur et candela quae de hoc lumine fuerit accensa in honore maiestatis tuae : semper perseveret benedicta et quicumque acceperit de eodem lumine sit illuminatus lumine spiritualis gratiae. Per.

B11. Domine Deus noster, Pater omnipotens, qui lumen indeficiens omniumque creator es luminum, hunc ignem bene + dicere et sanctificare digneris, ut per Filium tuum, qui lux vera est mundum illuminans universum, ab isto, sicut Moyses, accendamur tuaeque claritatis igne sic iugiter illustremur, ut tamquam lucis filii ad vitam perveniamus aeternam. Per.

C. Domine sancte, Pater omnipotens, aeterne Deus : benedicentibus nobis hunc ignem in nomine tuo, et unigeniti Filii tui Dei ac Domini nostri Jesu Christi, et Spiritus Sancti, co-operari digneris; et adiuva nos contra igniti tela inimici, et illustra gratia coelesti : Qui vivis et regnas cum eodem Unigenito tuo, et Spiritu sancto, Deus : per omnia saecula saeculorum.

C1. Domine sancte, Pater omnipotens, aeterne Deus : nobis qui hunc ignem in nomine tuo, et Filii tui, Dei et Domini nostri Jesu Christi, et Spiritus Sancti, bene + dicimus, et sanctifi + camus, co-operari digneris, et nos adiuvare, Qui vivis, et regnas cum eodem Unigenito tuo, et Spiritu Sancto Deus.

D. Domine sancte, Pater omnipotens, aeterne Deus, benedicere et sanctificare digneris ignem istum, quem nos indigni per invocationem Unigeniti Filii tui Domini nostri Jesu Christi benedicere praesumimus : tu clementissime, eum tua benedictione sanctifica, et ad profectum humani generis provenire concede. Per eundem Dominum nostrum Jesum Christum Filium tuum, qui tecum vivit et regnat in unitate Spiritus Sancti Deus per omnia saecula saeculorum.

E. Domine sancte, Pater omnipotens, aeterne Deus, quia in nomine tuo et Filii tui Dei ac Domini nostri Iesu Christi et Spiritus Sancti benedicimus et sanctificamus hunc ignem, adiuva nos per eundem Dominum qui tecum vivit in unitate eiusdem Spiritus Sancti.

E1. Domine sancte Pater omnipotens aeterne Deus in nomine tuo et Filii tui ac Domini nostri Iesi Christi et Spiritus Sancti, benedicimus et sanctificamus lumen hoc. Adiuva nos. Qui vivit.

F. Domine Deus, Pater omnipotens, conditor omnium rerum, te invocamus ut benedicas et consecres hunc ignem sicut benedixisti rubum in quo apparuisti Moysi. et sicut illuminasti cor eius per visibile lumen maiestate tua invisibili ita et corda nostra potencia divinitatis tuae invisibiliter per hunc visibilem ignem illuminare digneris. Per.

G. Coelesti lumine quaesumus, domine, semper et ubique perveni, ut misterium cuius nos participes esse voluisti, et puro cernamus intuitu et digno percipiamus affectu. Per.

H. Domine sancte, Pater omnipotens, aeterne Deus, in nomine tuo et filii tui domini nostri Iesu Christi et spiritus sancti, benedicimus hunc ignem et eum cum cera, et omnibus eius alimoniis sanctificamus et signo crucis Christi Iesu filii tui altissimi signamus, ut intus vel foris, non quod nocet incendat, sed omnia ad usus hominum necessaria calefaciat sive illuminet et quae ex hoc igne fuerint conflata vel calefacta, sint benedicta et omni humanae saluti utilia, ut non, cum Nadab et Abiu ignem tibi offerentibus alienum, incendamur, sed cum Aaron pontifice et filiis eius Eleazaro et Ithamaro, hostias tibi pacificas, sancti spiritus igne assatas immolare valeamus et semper eiusdem spiritus sancti igne vitia nostra ure, cordaque luce scientiae tuae illumina et animas nostras fidei calore clarifica. Per.

I. Benedictio Dei + Patris omnipotens et Fi + lii et Spiritus + Sancti descendat et maneat super hoc lumen et incensum istud.

J. Omnipotens sempiterne, aeterne Deus Creator omnium rerum, te humiliter deprecamur, ut hunc ignem novum, caelo terrae largitum, sanctificare et benedicere digneris, et sicut in adventu tuo elementa contagione peccatorum polluta purgare polliceris; ita et hic ignis novus tabernaculis fidelium tuorum habendus purgationem perfectam obtineat, et obstaculis invictus contra omnem nequitiam maligni spiritus perficiatur.

K. Rogamus te domine deus omnipotens ut digneris benedicere hunc ignem ne impediat domum hanc in qua accenditur. Per.

L. Domine sancte, Pater omnipotens, eternus Deus, benedicere et sanctificare digneris ignem istum qui nos indigni suscipimus per invocationem hunigeniti filii tui domini nostri Iesu Christi quem hodie in templo presentatum, iustum Simeonem diu expectantem in ulnas suscepisse novimus et salutare tuum ante faciem omnium populorum, esse lumen scilicet gentibus et gloriam plebi tue Israel pro prophetico spiritu docuit, te quaesumus domine ut benedicere digneris lumen istud et omnibus illud manibus gestantibus verum lumen tue majestatis concede, ut ad te cognoscentes per viam virtutum ad te valeamus pervenire, qui in trinitate perfecta unus et gloriaris deus per omnia saec. saeculorum.

M. Adesto, quaesumus Domine, supplicantibus, tuaque praeferentia consecrare ac benedicere huius incrementa ignis dignare, ut omnibus in te sperantibus fugato daemonico phantasmate tribuas lumen et colorem spiritus tui saluberrimum.

N. Domine Deus noster, lumen indeficiens, benedicere, + sanctificare, + et consecrare digneris hanc ignis creaturam : ut eo in tui honorem utentes, expulsis a cordibus suis peccatorum tenebris, ad vitam, te illustrante, pervenire mereantur aeternam. Per.

O. Domine sancte Pater omnipotens aeternus Deus, lux et splendor universarum creaturarum, qui ex nihilo cuncta producere dignatus es, te humiliter deprecamur : ut hanc creaturam ignis benedicere et sanctificare digneris in nomine dilectissimi Filii tui, et in virtute Spiritus sancti : ut nobis ad obsequium et ad lumen esse facias tam animae quam corporis, et ut nihil in eo nobis adversarius damni irrogari possit; sed sit nobis in adiutorium per virtutem et potestatem tuam, salvator mundi. Qui vivis et regnas.

P. Deus qui Moisi famulo tuo in specie ignis, rubo ardente, apparuisti : quique etiam Sanctum Spiritum tuum Dominum nostrum de caelo promissum super apostolos igneis linguis descendere fecisti : nobis quoque famulis tuis caritatis ignem tribuere dignare; et hunc novum ignem de lapide prosilitum nobis in usum profuturum sanctifica : et concede nobis ita per haec festa paschalia coelestibus desideriis inflammari, ut ad perpetua festa purgatis mentibus pertingere valeamus. Per.

Q. Oramus te, domine deus noster, ut caereus iste in honorem nominis tui consecratus ad noctis huius caliginem destruendam indeficiens perseveret. In odorem suavitatis acceptus supernis luminaribus misceatur. Flammas eius lucifer matutinus inveniat, Ille, inquam, lucifer qui nescit occasum, Ille qui regressus ab inferis humano generi serenus inluxit.

R. Domine Deus, Pater Omnipotens, lux vera et fons omnium; benedic + et sanctifica Cereum istum, ut ab eius lumine accendamur atque illuminemur igne claritatis tuae : et sicut illuminasti Moisen exeuntem de Aegypto, ita illumines corda et sensus nostros, ut ad vitam et lucem aeternam pervenire mereamur. Per.

S. Domine Omnipotens, Eterne Deus, benedicentibus nobis hunc ignem novum productum e silice : nostris perfecturum usibus quem nos indigni invocatione unigeniti filii sui tui domini nostri Iesu Christi benedicere persumimus; tu clementissime deus cum tua benedictione sanctifica ad perfectum humani generis pervenire concede ut nos celestibus desideriis inflammati ad festa ventura purgatis mentibus pertingere valeamus. Per.

T. Domine Jesu Christe qui filios Israel egyptiaca servitute depressos : moyse famulo tuo ductore per columnam nubis in die ad terram repromissionis perduxisti benedic hunc ig-

nem benedictione tua coelesti : ut per tui amoris ignem spiritualiter mentibus nostris infusum conburat in nobis omne
viciorum incendium : ut tua ineffabili luce illuminati : ad il-
lius esum perducamur agni qui passionis suae vulnere pot-
ens est totius mundi peccata delere. Qui tecum vivit. . . .

U. Omnipotens sempiterne deus mundi conditor luminis
siderumque fabricator : per cuius ineffabilem potentiam omnis claritas sumpsit exordium : te in tuis opibus invocamus :
aperi nobis quaesumus labia nostra ad confitendum nomine
tuo et ad laudem gloriae tuae ut dignere celebrare mereamus
sacrum officium : qui in hac sacratissima nocte vigilia de do-
nis tuis cereum tuae suppliciter offerimus maiestati.

V. Veniat, quaesumus, omnipotens Deus, super hunc (hoc)
incensum larga tuae benedictionis infusio : et hunc nocturnum splendorem invisibilis regenerator accende; ut non solum sacrificium, quod hac nocte litatum est, arcana luminis
tui admixtione refulgeat; sed in quocumque loco ex huius sanctificationis mysterio aliquid fuerit deportatum, expulsa diabolicae fraudis nequitia, virtus tuae maiestatis assistat. Per.

W. Domine Sancte Pater Omnipotens Aeterne Deus, lumen quod in nomine tuo et filii tui dei ac domini nostri iesu
christi et spiritus sancti benedicimus et sanctificamus, quaesumus ut a te benedictum sit et sanctificatum, eoque utentes
exterius, interius spiritualiter calefieri mereamur. Per.

The Formulas for the Blessing of the Incense

A. Domine Deus noster, qui suscepisti munera Abel, Noe
et Abraham, sacrificium Aaron, Samuelis, et Zachariae, et
omnium sanctorum tuorum, incensum istud bene + dicere,
et de manibus nostris in odorem suavitatis recipere digneris;
ut omnes gestantes, tangentes, et adorantes illud, virtutem
et auxilium Spiritus sancti percipere mereantur.

B. Deus omnipotens, Deus Abraham, Deus Israel, Deus
Jacob, immitte in hanc creaturam incensi vim odoris tui vel
virtutem, ut sit servulis tuis vel ancillis munimentum tute-

laque defensionis, ne intret hostem in viscera eorum, aditumque et sedem habere non possit.

APPENDIX 5

The Sepulchre[1]

The placing of a light by the Sepulchre is first attested in the eleventh century by John of Avranches, at Rouen, in Lanfranc's *Decrees,* and in the Customaries of Sigibert and Fruttuaria.[2] The practice may be considerably older,[3] although the reposition of the *Sanctissimum* after the Mass of Maundy Thursday is attested no earlier than the tenth century.[4] Two traditions relating to the presence of lights at the Sepulchre may be identified : one, in which the light or lights were extinguished on Good Friday, and the other, in which the Sepulchre remained illuminated until the conclusion of the Vigil on Holy Saturday or until Easter Day.

---

[1] Usually known today as the 'altar of repose' or 'place of reposition'. Here the Host, consecrated on Maundy Thursday, is reserved for use at Communion (the Mass of the Pre-sanctified) on Good Friday.

[2] *Lib. de Off. Eccl.* (PL 147.50B); *Acta Vetera* (PL 147.173C); PL 150.460A; Albers II p.93; Albers IV p.58.

[3] The practice of honouring the dead with lights has a venerable antiquity. For pagan practice, see, for example, Dennis II p.388; Marwick p.93; Briggs p.72; and Hare, *Days* p.248. For its use in Christian worship, see, for example, Canziani p. 105, Lees p.168, and especially Dendy pp.99–107.

[4] *Regularis Concordia,* PL 137.495.

(A) According to the tradition recorded by the five above-
mentioned documents, a light burned continuously from the
reposition of the *Sanctissimum* until the conclusion of Lauds
on Good Friday.[5] This practice survived at Notre-Dame in
Rouen until at least the beginning of the eighteenth century.[6]
Subsequently, it became customary to relight the candle with
the new fire on Good Friday; and eventually, to allow the
candle to burn continuously[7] from the reposition on Maundy
Thursday to the consuming of the Sacrament on Good
Friday.[8]

A number of churches attest the use of two or more candles
during the presence of the *Sanctissimum* in the Sepulchre.[9] With
the elaboration of ceremonial following what Jounel calls the
'eucharistic triumphs' of the Counter-Reformation, the adornment of the Sepulchre with both lights and other decorations
became what might today be considered excessive.[10] This emphasis on magnificence was positively encouraged by the
Caeremoniale Episcoporum in its recommendations for the preparation of the chapel of repose.[11] In the last century, nearly
six hundred lighted candles surrounded the Pauline Chapel
of St Peter's in Rome. The diarist Samuel Rogers comments

[5]*Acta Vetera* and Lanfranc *(op.cit.)* : *lumen continue ardeat.*
[6]De Moléon pp.300–01.
[7]As at Laon *(DAMR* 3.15.7 p.142 [M 1164]) and St-Martin d'Ainay,
Lyon *(DAER* 4.22 p.125 [M 175]).
[8]This occurred at Nidaros *(ONE* p.226), Lund (1514 Missal fol.lxxxiiii),
Magdeburg (1503 Missal fol.lxxxvii), and Cambrai (1507 Missal fol.lxvi).
[9]2 CANDLES : Canterbury (HBS 23 p.380), Coutances (1825 Ceremonial p.315), Liège (1492 Ordinary np), and Rome (Ordo XV, PL 78.1306).
4 CANDLES : Barking (HBS 65 p.93). At Lyon, Mende, Salzburg, and
Vienna, four candles were held temporarily during the reposition of the
Corpus Christi. An unspecified number burned at Burgos (1546 Missal
fol.xciii), Cosenza (1549 Missal fol.104), Hildesheim (1499 Missal fol.xcvi),
Poitiers (1767 Missal p.240), and in the Cistercian rite (1699 Missal p.139).
[10]At Palencia in the sixteenth century, there were 'very many candles'.
1568 Missal fol.lxxxviiii.
[11]*Quo pulchrius magnificentiusque poterit, multis luminibus ornatum* (II.23.2).

that the arrangement was 'elegant in the highest degree'.[12]
Following the liturgical changes of 1955, the 'traditional simplicity of the Roman liturgy' was restored. It was enjoined
that the Sepulchre should be moderately adorned,[13] and that
a single light should burn at the conclusion of the Adoration
of the *Sanctissimum* at midnight on Maundy Thursday.[14]

(B) According to the alternative tradition, the Sepulchre was
honoured with light until the conclusion of the Vigil on Holy
Saturday. It is possible that in some churches the Sepulchre
may also have served as a place of reservation for the older
unconsumed Hosts. However, by the thirteenth century, it
had become customary in some churches to place a cross in
the same Sepulchre as the Host.[15] Its presence in the Sepulchre
invited and resulted in its being honoured by light also. At
Hereford one candle and at York two candles burned from
Maundy Thursday to Easter Day,[16] whereas at Salisbury one
of the two candles was extinguished after the removal of the
Sanctissimum while the other remained alight until the procession on Easter Day before Matins.[17] This procession is also
attested in Hungary.[18]

[12]Hale p.274.
[13]Pastoral Instruction 11.8; Jounel, *Le nouvel ordo* p.29.
[14]Fortescue and O'Connell (11th ed.) p.287.
[15]At York (Missal p.107) and Durham (Raine pp.10–11).
[16]HBS 26 p.324; Missal p.107.
[17]Missal (Dickinson) p.337.
[18]1815 Ritual pp.440–41.

APPENDIX 6

Illumination on Good Friday at the Passion and at the Adoration of the Cross

Two traditions relating to the use of light at the Good Friday liturgy existed within the rites of the Western Church. The use of liturgical light when the Passion was read and the Cross was venerated in the Gallican Church is attested by documentary evidence[1] and can be inferred with confidence for the Mozarabic rite.[2] Moreover, Amalarius' statement concerning the practice of the Roman Church implies that he was familiar with the use of light at the Good Friday liturgy. Both at Salzburg and in the Camaldolese rite, two altar candles burned during the reading of St John's Passion.[3]

The absence of illumination during the Good Friday liturgy of the Roman rite is attested in the ninth century by Amalarius, who writes that in the Roman Church on Good Friday all fire was extinguished from the sixth to the ninth hour in commemoration of the Crucifixion.[4] In its liturgical application, this entailed extinguishing the altar lights before

---

[1]*PRG* II p.86 §304.
[2]Léon Antiphonary pp.275 ff.
[3]1507 Missal fol.lxxxvii; 1503 Missal fol.82.
[4]*Liber Officialis* 4.22.2.

the reading of St John's Passion and rekindling them after the Adoration of the Cross.[5] Roman practice was generally followed throughout the western rites, including those of Braga and Lyon.[6] In the Ambrosian rite, however, the altar lights and the candles of the acolytes were extinguished at *emisit spiritum* during St Matthew's Passion, and were not rekindled until after the Easter candle had been lit the following day.[7]

[5]*Caeremoniale Episcoporum* p.278 and p.284.
[6]1558 Missal fol.xciii and 1771 Missal p.178, respectively.
[7]King, *Holy Week* p.98.

APPENDIX 7

The Paschal Column and Candelabrum

Many of the surviving paschal candlesticks in the churches of Rome are twisted shafts of verd-antique with bases of gilt bronze or white marble. Amongst the most impressive are the voluted columnar candlesticks of S.Clemente and S.Lorenzo, both inlaid with mosaics and bearing a spike on their summits to receive the Easter candle; that of S.Maria Cosmedin with its cosmatesque ornamentation; and the twelfth-century column in St Paul's, embellished with a series of *bassi-rilievi* depicting the Passion and the Resurrection. Other examples of paschal pillars with well-executed sculpture are to be found in the monastic church at Farfa, in the Capella Palatina of Palermo Cathedral, in the Church of SS.Nereus and Achilleus in Rome, and in the Baptistery at Florence.

The practice of using a pillar was not confined to Italy. At Spires, a choice existed between a column and a candelabrum,[1] whilst at Angers in the eighteenth century, a tall column of marble stood in front of the altar.[2] Likewise, at Lyon, a tall spiral column of marble stands by the ambo. Indeed, the rubrics of a number of French diocesan missals

[1]*Agenda* fol.xciii.
[2]De Moléon p.80.

473

recommend that the paschal candelabrum should resemble a column.[3]

The paschal candlestick has been characterised by two attributes, size and beauty. That at Barking in the fourteenth century was described as large,[4] as was that at Besançon in the seventeenth century,[5] whilst the Easter candle at Autun stood in a candelabrum that was both *grandius* and columnar.[6] It need hardly be stated that the candlestick was to be as tall, if not taller, than the Easter candle. Likewise, it was only fitting that the importance and significance of the Candle should have been matched by a holder made with noble skill. It was even recommended that the candelabrum of a country church should be *pulchre elaboratum*.[7] We are also informed that the candleholders were artistically worked, often in the form of an angel, even in smaller churches.[8] Most of these appear to have been replaced by candlesticks of a much simpler design.[9] At Ushaw College in England, there are four angels at the base of Pugin's elaborately-executed eight-foot high candelabrum, the fingers of the raised right hands pointing upwards towards the light, a vertical movement which also characterises the postures of the ceramic figures of pilgrims at St John's Cathedral in Portsmouth.

There is little evidence from previous centuries to make us believe that paschal candlesticks were generally fashioned from wood rather than metal, although it is likely that the use of the latter often reflected the financial resources of a church. Of those in use in thirty-five French cathedrals, eighteen were made of copper or bronze, four were of iron, and the rest were made of wood.[10]

[3]Sées (1742) p.185; Mends (1766 p.199; Périgueux (1782) p.158; Tours (1784) p.191; Metz (1829) p.158; La Rochelle (1835) p.186.
[4]HBS 65 p.97.
[5]1682 Ceremonial p.329.
[6]1845 Missal p.238.
[7]Desideri p.150.
[8]*DHCR* I p.470; Gattinari p.142.
[9]1984 Survey of France.
[10]1984 Survey of France.

At Durham, the central branch of the enormous seven-branched candlestick was used to hold the Easter candle.[11] According to a description of this candelabrum recorded in 1593, many years after its destruction, its feet were flying dragons; there were representations of the four evangelists; and it was studded with precious stones and embellished with intricately-wrought metalwork. 'The Paschall in latitude did containe almost the breadth of the Quire, in longitude that did extend to the height of the lower vault, wherein did stand a long piece of wood reaching within a man's height to the uppermost vault roofe of the church.'[12]

[11]These candelabra, made in imitation of the *menorah* in Solomon's Temple, became common in Western Europe as a result of the Crusades (Zarnecki pp.134–35). Although there were a number of them in use in the cathedrals of England, the only surviving examples are to be found in Central Europe—for instance, at Essen, Brunswick, Klosterneuburg, and Prague—and in Scandinavia at Århus, Lund, and Ribe.

[12]Raine, *Rites of Durham* p.9. It is generally believed that the 'long piece of wood' refers to a *Judas* which was inserted into the central holder to increase the size of the Easter candle. It is more likely, however, that this length of wood was a pole with a small candle at one end, used for lighting the Easter candle. If there was a hole in the roof of the cathedral—the description was based on the memory of an old man—it is unlikely to have been used for lighting the Candle. The writer believes that the presence of an aperture in the roof may have been linked to the use of a block and tackle, or similar device, which may well have been necessary for hoisting the large Easter candle into its holder.

APPENDIX 8

The Blessing of the Font and Baptism

The use of light at the blessing of the font is first attested in the Roman rite *c.* 600.[1] Ordo 11 informs us that the two Vigil-candles, the size of a grown person, were taken in procession to the font in front of the Pope.[2] Two later *ordines* state that the two candles were lowered into the baptismal water when the Pope or presiding priest uttered the prayer *Descendat in hanc plenitudinem*.[3] The practice is also attested in two eighth-century Gelasian sacramentaries[4] and in an eleventh-century baptismal *ordo* from Northern Italy.[5] It is also alluded to in Zachary's letter to Boniface.[6] The presence of the two large candles in the Ambrosian rite of the twelfth century is mentioned by Beroldus (p.111), but there is no evidence that they were lowered into the water.

[1]It is true that at the baptism of the Jews of Auvergne *c.* 500, Gregory of Tours refers to the flickering of the candles and the burning of the lamps (PL 71.326). The description, however, is too imprecise for us to comment with confidence upon the use of light from a liturgical point of view.

[2]OR 11.90.

[3]OR 23.24ff. and OR 30B.46.

[4]*GeGe* p.99 and *GePh* p.69.

[5]Lambot p.xxxv.

[6]PL 89.951B.

The immersion of the Easter candle into the font, which in the churches of Gaul and Germany replaced the immersion of the two Vigil-candles, is first found in the tenth-century *Pontificale Romano-Germanicum (PRG);*[7] and the practice became widespread throughout the western rites. *Alcuin* records a transitional stage in which the choice of immersing either the two Vigil-candles or the Easter candle was allowed.[8] By the end of the fifteenth century, it had also become customary for the priest to dip the Easter candle three times into the font, withdrawing it twice and sinking it to a lower level each time, and repeating in an ever-higher tone *Descendat in hanc plenitudinem.*[9] In many churches, some of the molten wax of the Easter candle was allowed to drop onto the surface of the baptismal water in the form of a cross. At Reims, the choice of using either the Easter candle or another candle was allowed. Presumably, the latter was the *cereus fontium* and was used if the Easter candle was too large to carry in procession.[10]

The Sacramentary of Ripoll enjoins that the candles be placed in the water (p.97). It is not clear whether *cer[e]os* refers to the two Vigil-candles or to the candles of the baptizands. Support for the latter comes from the Pontifical of Poitiers, which quite clearly states that the unlit candles of the children about to receive Baptism were placed in the water.[11] At Salisbury, the Easter candle, which was present at the font, was not lowered into the water. Instead, drops of wax dripped onto the surface of the fontal water.[12] The silence of Berol-

[7]*PRG* II p.104. Although the two Vigil-candles were present at the ceremony described by *PRG,* there is some uncertainty as to whether they also were dipped into the water.

[8]*De Div. Off.* (PL 101.1219A/B).

[9]Thus a very large number of missals. The silence of a few missals (for example, those of Valence (1504) fol.lxiii and Narbonne (1528) fol.xcv) on this score would suggest that a single immersion obtained in a number of churches.

[10]1770 Missal p.224.

[11]Deponunt in fontem cereos baptizandorum infantum non illuminatos (p.216).

[12]Missal of *c.*1300 (Legg) p.129.

dus would suggest that at Milan in the twelfth century, the Easter candle was not carried to the font. Its absence on this occasion is also attested at Biasca *c.*900[13] and at Nidaros in the early thirteenth century.[14]

The earliest reference in the West to the baptismal candles held by the neophytes occurs in a work formerly attributed to St Ambrose.[15] Martène cites the letter of Marcus of Gaza to Arcadius on the occasion of the baptism of Theodosius the Younger,[16] and we had occasion above to refer to the conversion of the Jews of Auvergne.

In the period from *c.*500 to 1000, the custom of handing an unlit candle to each baptizand is recorded only three times. In the ninth century, Amalarius states that the neophytes' candles were lit after the last litany;[17] and *Alcuin* records that they were lit after the precentor had proclaimed *'Accendite'*.[18] The plunging of these candles into the font at Poitiers has been referred to above. At what point during the service or during their period of preparation the catechumens received their candles is unknown. According to the Northern Italian baptismal *ordo,* they brought their candles to the scrutinies.[19]

Attestation of the use of a formula, which subsequently became widespread throughout the western rites, to accompany the presentation of a candle first occurs in the Missal of Robert of Jumièges.[20] It reads : 'Receive the irreproachable candle; guard your baptism; so that when the Lord comes to the wedding-feast, you may meet him in the court of heaven for ever and ever.' The twelfth-century Ritual of Soissons and the thirteenth-century Sarum Missal contain slight variations. The former begins : 'Receive the irreproachable, burning

[13]Sacramentary p.70.
[14]*ONE* p.234.
[15]*De Lapsu Virginis* (PL 16.372).
[16]*De Antiquis Ecclesiae Ritibus* Vol.1 p.54.
[17]*Liber de Ord.Ant.* XLIV.8.
[18]*De Div.Off.* (PL 101.1221C).
[19]Lambot 12, 14, 29.
[20]Wilson, *The Missal* pp.99–100.

candle . . . ',[21] whilst the latter starts : 'Receive the irreproachable candle; guard your baptism; keep the commandments . . . '.[22]

[21]*DAER* 4.24 p.161 (M 305).
[22]Missal of *c.*1300 (Legg) p.131.

APPENDIX 9

Anticipation

Reference has already been made to the anticipation of the new fire ceremony and the Easter vigil in the afternoon of Holy Saturday as early as the eighth century. The singing of Tenebrae at Rome in the fourteenth century in the late afternoon of Wednesday, Thursday, and Friday of Holy Week would suggest that the blessing of the Easter candle took place much earlier in the day.[1] Evidence from the late-fifteenth and sixteenth centuries for the kindling of the new fire at noon has been presented in *Table 27*, and for the performance of the same ceremony at about 9.00 A.M. in *Tables 24* and *26*.

However, we also observed that in the seventeenth century, some Benedictine houses continued to sing Tenebrae in the early hours of the morning, a practice that the Cistercians maintained until the time of the Second Vatican Council.[2] As late as the sixteenth century at Braga, the liturgy of Holy Saturday continued to be performed at night.[3] Jounel suggests that the anticipation of the services of the Triduum was

[1]Ordo XIV (PL 78.1204B).

[2]The writer is grateful to the Rt Rev. John Moakler, Abbot of Mount St Bernard Abbey, Coalville, for this information. Letter dated 21 June 1984.

[3]King, *LPS* p.223.

not universal in France until after 1600, but he does not instance any church where anticipation did not occur.[4]

In the cathedrals of the Catholic areas of Eastern Europe,
the liturgy of Holy Saturday has always been celebrated during the late evening of that day. Patrick Leigh Fermor graphi-
cally describes the ceremony at Esztergom in 1933.[5] The writer
is given to believe by eye-witnesses that a similar situation
obtained in the larger churches of Poland.

[4]*La Semaine Sainte* p.146.
[5]*Between the Woods* pp.15–16.

APPENDIX 10

Monte Cassino A

We hope to show that in respect of the ceremonies of Holy Saturday, the first of the two twelfth-century rites of Monte Cassino, referred to here as *Monte Cassino A*,[1] belongs to the same tradition as that recorded in the late eighth-century Ordo 28. For both attest a procession which accompanied the lighted Easter candle. The evidence of *Monte Cassino A* is, however, ambiguous; and it is not immediately clear from the rubrics how the Easter candle featured in the initial stages of the ceremony. Much of the difficulty revolves around the interpretation of *cereus* in the following passage from that document :

> Et accenso *cereo,* procedunt omnes de secretario cum ipso *cereo*
> in aeclesiam cum silentio et, posito in candelabro *cereo,* por-
> tante acolito, procedunt ad altare. Acolytus vero portat *cereum*
> ad ammonem et dicit tribus vicibus : Lumen Christi, plane.[2]

---

[1]Printed as §1 on p.292 of *PR XII* in M.Andrieu, *Le Pontifical Romain au Moyen Age.* The contemporary *Monte Cassino B* (p.293 §2) is to be identified with the twelfth-century Ordinary of Monte Cassino, known to Martène (= M 1139). The exact milieu of *Monte Cassino A* is unknown, but its comparison with *Monte Cassino B* by the compiler of the latter and the presence of the *Lumen Christi* would suggest a central Italian location not far from Monte Cassino.

[2]*PR XII* I p.229 §1. The writer's italics.

From the *Pontificale Romano-Germanicum* and *Monte Cassino B,* we know that *cereus* may refer (a) to the small candle used for bringing the new fire into church or (b) to the Easter candle or (c) to one of the two large candles of the Roman Vigil. In view of the mention of only one candle, we may at once discount the third possibility. However, because of the absence of any article in Latin, definite or indefinite, the first occurrence of *cereus* in the above passage could equally be (a) or (b). Likewise, the second occurrence of the word presents a choice of interpretation. The identification of *cereo,* which is the substantial element in the ablative absolute, depends on the interpretation of *posito.* This may be translated either (i) 'the acolyte who bears the candle places it in a candlestick' or (ii) 'an acolyte bears the candle (that is, the Easter candle) which has (previously) been placed in a candlestick', since it is not clear who is carrying the lighted candle (that is, the first *cereo*). Then again, the candle which the acolyte takes to the ambo may be a small lighted candle if the Easter candle, previously unmentioned, is already in position by the ambo. The situation becomes even more complex if a distinction is then made between the first and second occurrence of *cereo.* For the former would refer to the small candle used to bring in the new fire and the second to the Easter candle, especially as *ipso* seems to give some emphasis to the noun which it qualifies.

Most of the difficulties disappear, however, when we compare the rubrics of Ordo 28, supplemented by those of Ordo 31, with those contained in *Monte Cassino A. (Table 59).*

The similarities between Ordo 28 and *Monte Cassino A* leave us in little doubt that the latter perpetuates the ceremonial of Ordo 28 in its entirety and has added to the ritual only the cry of *Lumen Christi.* It is remarkable that so little change had occurred in the liturgy of this tradition over nearly four hundred years. Ordo 31 clearly belongs to the same tradition in spite of the smaller number of rubrics. Its importance, however, for our present argument lies in the fact that in enlarging on the identity of the candle in Rubrics 2 and 5, it enables

Ordo 28 (§§58–63)	Ordo 31 (§63–67)	Monte Cassino A
1. Robing at 9th hour		Robing at 9th hour
2. Candle is lit	Candle to be blessed is lit in the	Candle is lit
3. Procession from sacristy	sacristy	Procession from sacristy
4.	Silent procession	Silent procession
5. Candle in candlestick	Candle to be blessed in candlestick	Candle in candlestick
6. at altar	at altar	at altar
7.	(Lessons later read at ambo)	Candle is taken to ambo (Cry of Lumen Christi)
8. Deacon asks for blessing	(Archdeacon sings)	Deacon asks for blessing
9. Exultet	Exultet	Exultet
10. Two candles lit	Two large candles lit	Two candles lit
11. New fire taken to every home		New fire taken to every home

Table 59

us to interpret *cereus* correctly in the above-quoted passage from *Monte Cassino A* and to show conclusively that the Easter candle was lit in the sacristy and borne in procession into church, first to the altar and then to the ambo. The passage may now be translated :

> After the Easter candle has been lit, they all proceed from the sacristy with the Candle into church in silence. The acolyte who bears the Candle places it in a candlestick, and they move to the altar. Then the acolyte takes the Candle to the ambo and proclaims three times : *Lumen Christi.*

APPENDIX 11

The *Inventor Rutili* of Prudentius

In view of the relatively late attestation (tenth century) for its earliest use on Holy Saturday, it would seem that this hymn, which was originally composed for use at the *Lucernarium,* was recommissioned for use at the new fire ceremony when that ritual was incorporated into the paschal liturgy of the Gallican Church, probably in the eighth century;[1] and it is not difficult to see why the hymn came to be sung on Holy Saturday, assuming that its use had generally fallen into desuetude with the disappearance of the daily office of the *Lucernarium.* [2]

The principal themes of the hymn are God's provision of light which brings salvation, and deliverance from the darkness of this world's evil. The tone of the hymn is both eschatological and full of expectation, with references to the Deliverance in Exodus being reminiscent of the themes of the Romano-Gallican Paschal Preface. After an initial invocation to God as the source of light (1.1), the petition for the provi-

[1]Ordo 26 is our earliest evidence for that ceremony.

[2]Although the hymn was written by Prudentius, who was himself a Spaniard, there is no evidence for its use on Holy Saturday in the Mozarabic rite. We have already shown that its use was confined almost exclusively to the regions east and north of the Alps.

sion of light for the faithful, which looks forward to the return of that light after its disappearance, suggests an approaching conclusion to a commemoration of the Crucifixion (1.4). References to the Passover (ll.37–38), Christ's descent to the underworld (1.127), the keeping of a watch (1.137), and the Resurrection (1.132) strongly suggest the paschal vigil of Holy Saturday. This is reinforced by a reference to the production of fire from a flint (1.7). It is not difficult to understand why the hymn was once thought to have been composed for the Vigil of Holy Saturday.[3]

We have referred elsewhere to the highly poetic language of Prudentius. This being taken into account, it would seem that the content of the *Inventor rutili* relates to the primitive vigil of Saturday which was held in preparation for the weekly commemoration of the Resurrection every Sunday. It is possible that the *Lucernarium*, having been originally a daily service, had developed into a weekly office held every Saturday evening and that Prudentius' hymn was written for this weekly celebration.[4]

[3]Mabillon II p.141.

[4]A weekly performance of the *Lucernarium* is favoured by Capelle, *Le rite des cinq grains* p.3.

APPENDIX 12

The Mozarabic and Milanese Rites

(A) THE MOZARABIC RITE.[1] In a comparative study of the liturgies of Holy Saturday, the development of the ceremony of light from the *Lucernarium* is more apparent in the Mozarabic rite than in any other western rite. For in addition to the lighting and bearing in procession of the Easter candle, the lamp, which had formerly been the principal source of light at the *Lucernarium,* continued to be accorded similar veneration. The influence of the Jerusalem liturgy of Holy Saturday was also obvious in the Spanish ritual. There is general agreement amongst scholars that the production of fire by the bishop in a sacristy from which all light had been excluded and the procession of light into the church, to be followed by the Vigil, was derived directly from Jerusalem.

Not all the precursors of the Mozarabic rite, however, are to be found in the East, as Capelle was forced to admit.[2] In Part Four, we have attempted to account for what Dendy sees as a superfluous second blessing of both the lamp and the Easter candle. The presence, however, of both the lamp and the Easter candle, and the blessing of both, are clear indications of the composite character of the Spanish rite. The writer

[1]Léon Antiphonary pp.280–83; Férotin pp. 210–15.
[2]*La Procession* p.109.

487

believes that the three principal features of the ritual which
do not have their provenance in Jerusalem, namely, the Easter
candle, the striking of the fire, and the triple *Deo gratias,* were
elements imported into Spain from Gaul, possibly as early
as the sixth century. Elsewhere, we have discussed the likely
Northern Italian origin of the Easter candle, the markings on
the Candle in Rome, and the kindling of fire in Northern Europe. The threefold cry of *Deo gratias* is almost certainly derived from the triple *Lumen Christi,* which, we have argued,
had its origin in Central or Southern Italy.

The influence of Jerusalem occurred in the three centuries
or so which separate the visit of Egeria to Jerusalem from the
Moorish conquest of Spain at the beginning of the eighth century. A date nearer the former event seems more likely. The
Gallican influence may be assigned to a later date; and we
have suggested the sixth century, in view of the evidence of
Canon 9 of the Fourth Council of Toledo, which was held
in 633[3] :

> The Lamp and the Candle are not blessed in some churches
> on Easter Eve . . . It is fitting for unity and peace that the
> [same] rite be observed in the churches of Galicia.[4]

The fact that the lamp and the Easter candle did not feature
in the same ceremony in all parts of Spain by 633 would suggest that the combination of both these liturgical light-sources
within the same ceremony was not of great antiquity in that
country.

The changes resulting from the introduction in 1500 of the
Missale Mixtum as the official Mass-book of the Mozarabic rite
hardly affected the ceremonies involving the new fire and the
blessing of the paschal light. The insertion of the five grains
of incense into the Easter candle and the introduction of the
two additional candles, which were lit from the Easter candle,
hardly affected the character of the ceremonial.[5]

[3]PL 84.369B.
[4]Dendy wrongly translates 'the churches of Gaul' (p.130).
[5]PL 85.442C.

(B) THE MILANESE RITE. Like the Holy Saturday liturgy of the Mozarabic rite, the corresponding Ambrosian ceremonial of Milan had ritual elements inherited both from the *Lucernarium* and from the liturgy of Jerusalem. Prominent amongst the former was the lighting of a lamp from the new fire and the carrying of that lamp for the lighting of the Easter candle. This lamp was also used to light the two large candles which burned during the blessing of the font.[6]

It is very likely that the use in the twelfth century of two churches for the new fire ceremony derived from the practice at Jerusalem. For it is significant that the new fire was kindled and blessed in the Church of the Holy Sepulchre in Milan and subsequently taken to the 'summer' church, wherein the paschal vigil took place.[7] These buildings corresponded to the Anastasis and the Martyrium in Jerusalem.[8] In later centuries, the new fire was kindled in the sacristy of the cathedral, as in the Mozarabic rite, the former arrangement being preserved to a point. The use of the sacristy is perpetuated in the rite revised after Vatican II, although a location outside the church is now permitted.[9]

[6]Beroldus pp.110–11; 1768 Missal p.125.
[7]Beroldus pp.109–10.
[8]For the paschal vigil at Jerusalem, see Bertonière pp.121ff.
[9]1981 Missal p.242.

APPENDIX 13

The *Chartae*

The *Charta* at Reims Cathedral in 1585

Benedictus est hic Cereus in honorem & laudem Domini nostri
JESU-CHRISTI, qui cum Patre & Spiritu-sancto vivit
& regnat Deus in saecula saeculorum   Amen

Annus ab origine mundi juxta Hebraeorum	V.M.V.C.LIX
supputationem est	
Annus ab Incarnatione Domini	M.V.C.LXXXV
Annus a passione eiusdem	M.V.C.LII
Annus a Nativitatis B.Virginis Mariae	M.V.C.LXXXXIX
Annus ab Assumptione ejusdem	M.V.C.XXXVI
Annus Calendarii Gregoriani reformati	IV

Littera Dominicalis usque ad Circumcisionem est
F. & deinceps toto sequente anno erit E.
Aureus numerus est 9. anni vero sequentis est 10.
Epacta eo ipso die cui respondet in Calendario,
novam lunam in singulis mensibus indicat
Epacta lunae Paschalis semper quaerenda est inter
Octavum diem Martii & quintum Aprilis
Dies Paschae hoc anno incidebat in 14.Aprilis, sed
ne Judaeos sequi videamur, differtur in 21.
diem. Anno sequenti erit 6.Aprilis.

Annus Cycli solaris	XXVI
Annus Indictionis	XIII
Annus pontificatus Sanctissimi	XIII
D.D.N.Papae Gregorii	

Annus a conversione & baptismo Clodovei primi	M.LXXXVI
ex Francorum regibus Christianam fidem	
complexi	
Annus aetatis Christianissimi nostri regis Henrici	XXXIV
tertii	
Annus regni ejusdem	XI
Annus Archiepiscopatus Reverendissimi D.D.	XI
Ludovici a Guisia	

The *Charta* at Chalons Cathedral in 1708

Benedictus est hic Cereus in honorem Agni immaculati
Domini nostri Jesu-Christi. BB.Virginis Mariae,
BB.Protomartiris Stephani,
omniumque Sanctorum & Sanctarum.

Anno Periodi Julianae	VI.M.CD.XXI.
Anno Aerae Christianae	M.VII.VIII.
Anno reparatae salutis	M.VI.LXXV.
Anno post missos in Galliam viros Apostolicos &	
praesertim B.Memmium hujus Ecclesiae	
Cathalaunensis conditorem	
Anno post Attilam Hunnorum Regem a Meroveo	M.II.LVI.
Francorum Rege & Aetio Romanorum duce	
profligatum in Campis Cathalaunicis.	
Anno a Francorum Regno condito	M.CC.LXXXVIII.
Anno a translatione Regni Francorum a Caroli	V.CC.XX.
Magni stirpe ad Capetanos	
Anno a baptizato Clodoveo Franciae Rege die	M.CC.XIV.
Natali Domini 496	
Anno a vastatis prima vice fortuito incendio hisce	V.LXX.
sacris aedibus	
Anno Dedicationis hujus Templi ab	V.LXI.
Eugenio Pontifice Maximo 26 Octobris	
Anno Expugnationis Jerosolymorum a Saladino	V.XX.
Anno ab extinctione Ordinis Templariorum in	CCC.LXXXXVII.
Concilio generali Viennensi 6.nonas Maji	
Anno ab Elephantiacorum crimine & nece	IV.XCVII.
Anno ab Urbe per Armeniacos liberata	CC.LXXIX.
Anno a Constantinopoli per Turcos expugnata	CC.LIV.
Anno ab Henrici magni Carnuti inauguratione	C.XV.
tertio Calendas Martii	

Anno Pontificatus SS.Domini Clementis Papae Undecimi	VIII.
Anno Regni Christianissimi Regis Nostri Ludovici Magni	LXV.
Anno Ordinationis Illustrissimi Domini D.Gastonis Joannis Baptistae Ludovici de Noailles Episcopi & Comitis Cathalaunensis Franciae Paris	XII.
Anno ab extructo hujus Templi propilaeo	LXXIV.
Anno a secundo hujus Templi incendio	XLI.
Anno Cycli Solaris currente	VIIII.
Anno Cycli decennovennalis seu numeri aurei	XVIII.
Anno Cycli Indictionis	I.
Anno Cycli Epactarum	VII.
Littera Dominicalis	G.
Littera Martyrologii	G.
Concurrens	VII.
Pascha	VIII.Aprilis.
Rogationes	XIIII.Maji.
Pentecostes	XXVII.Maji.
Dies Adventus	II.Decembris.
Dominica Septuagesimae	XXVII.Januarii.
Feria Cinerum	XIII.Februarii.
Dominicae Post Pentecosten	XXVI.

The *Charta* at Rouen Cathedral in 1678

Annus ab origine mundi	5678
Annus ab universali diluvio	4033
Annus ab Incarnatione Domini	1678
Annus a passione ejusdem	1645
Annus a Nativitate B.Mariae	1692
Annus ab assumptione ejusdem	1628
Annus indictionis	1
Annus cycli solaris	7
Annus cycli lunaris	7
Annus praesens a Pascha praecedente usque ad pascha sequens est communis adund. Epacta.	7
Aureus numerus	7
Littera Dominicalis	B
Littera Martyrologii	g
Terminus Paschae	17 Aprilis
Dies Paschae	10 Aprilis
Luna ipsius	5 Aprilis
Annotinum Paschale	18 Aprilis

Dies rogationum	16 Maji
Dies Ascensionis	19 Maji
Dies Pentecostes	29 Maji
Dies Eucharistiae	9 Junii
Dominicae a Pentecoste usque ad adventum	25
Dominica prima adventus	27 November
Littera dominicalis anni sequentis	A
Annus sequens est	1679 Comm.Ord.
Littera Martyrologii anni sequentis	T
Dominicae a Nativitate Domini usque ad septuagesimam anni sequentis	4
Terminus septuagesimae anni sequentis	11 Februarii
Dominica septuagesimae anni sequentis	29 Januarii
Dominica I. quadragesimae anni sequentis	19 Februarii
Dies Paschae anni sequentis	2 Aprilis
Annus ab institutione Sancti Melloni	1419
Annus a transitu ejusdem	1368
Annus ab institutione S.Romani	1032
Annus a transitu ejusdem	989
Annus ab institutione S.Audoeni	1046
Annus a transitu ejusdem	1033
Annus a dedicatione hujus Ecclesiae Metropolitanae	614
Annus ab institutione Rollonis primi ducis Normanniae	766
Annus a transitu ejusdem	760
Annus a coronatione Guillelmi primi ducis Normanniae in regno Angliae	604
Annus ab obitu ejusdem	590
Annus a reductione ducatus Normanniae ad Philippum II. Franciae regem	474
Annus ab alia reductione ducatus Normanniae ad Carolum VII. Franciae regem	228
Annus Pontificatus SS.Patris & D.D.Innocentii Papae XI.	2
Annus ab institutione R.Patris & D.D.Francisci IV. Archiepiscopi Rotomagensis & Normanniae primatis	7
Annus a nativitate Christianissimi principis Ludovici XIV. Franciae & Navarrae regis	40
Annus regni ipsius	35

Consecratus est iste cereus in honore Agni immaculati, & in honore gloriosae virginis ejus genetricis Mariae.

APPENDIX 14

The Suburbicarian Dioceses

Much of the uncertainty over the interpretation of the term 'suburbicarian' *vis-à-vis* the blessing of the Easter candle arises from Duchesne's statement that 'the ceremony [of the Easter candle] was so popular that the Popes, although they did not adopt it in their own church, were obliged to permit its use in the "suburbicarian" diocese'.[1] He was commenting on the authorization granted by Pope Zosimus (417–418) to churches subject to papal jurisdiction permitting them to introduce the ceremony of the Easter candle :

> per parrocia [*paroccias*] concessa licentia cereum benedici.[2]

According to Duchesne, *parocciae* referred to the suburban parish churches of the Diocese of Rome. Since, however, there is no documentary evidence before the tenth century for the existence of the Easter candle in the papal rite,[3] it seems most unlikely that for over five hundred years the rite as observed in the Cathedral of St John Lateran resisted the introduction of the Easter candle, which was blessed in other churches

---

[1]*Christian Worship* p.252.

[2]'Permission was granted throughout the *parishes* for the Easter candle to be blessed.' Duchesne, *Liber Pontificalis* I p.225.

[3]It is first attested in the Roman rite in *PRG c.*950.

494

within the City and Diocese of Rome. It would appear that Duchesne overlooks the fact that *paroccia* at this period in the Church's history indicated 'diocese' rather than 'parish'. It is possible that the seven ancient Suburbicarian Dioceses within the immediate vicinity of Rome are here intended, but our observation regarding the parish churches of the Diocese of Rome is almost equally applicable in this instance. It is the writer's belief that *parocciae* refers either to those dioceses beyond the immediate vicinity of Rome, which were subject to papal influence, or to those regions which had been converted to Christianity by missionaries who owed their allegiance to Rome or, most likely, to both.

This view is based partly on the evidence of Ordo 25, which states that the blessing of the Easter candle took place in *suburbanis civitatibus*.[4] Moreover, Amalarius observes :

> Romanis ita agentibus, nobis praeceptum est a papa Zosimo benedicere cereum.[5]

It is clear from Amalarius' statement that Zosimus' decree had been binding in regions beyond the confines of Italy. The phrase *'ordo* suburbicaire' is applied somewhat loosely by Capelle (and accepted by Andrieu) to Ordo 26, a Roman *ordo* with Gallican influences.[6] Chavasse argues in favour of an intermediate zone between the Lateran Church and the neighbouring dioceses of Italy, corresponding to the seven Suburbicarian Dioceses, for the provenance of Ordo 26.[7] His theory, however, is based on a questionable understanding of the relationship of the compiler of the ordo *vis-à-vis* the grammatical subject of *faciunt* in §8.

---

[4]OR 25.2, dated *c*.800. The phrase relates to cities and states outside Rome as far as Gaul.

[5]'This is the practice at Rome [the making of the wax *Agnus Dei*'s]; we were permitted to bless the Easter candle.' *Liber Officialis* I.18.1.

[6]Andrieu, *Les* Ordines Romani III p.322.

[7]*Le Sacramentaire* pp.103–04.

KEY TO BIBLIOGRAPHY

The key provides a rapid reference to the primary sources listed in Sections (b) and (c) of the bibliography. The vast majority of the documents which the writer has consulted relate to or are associated with specific locations. Reference should therefore be made in the first instance to the left-hand column. The figure in the right-hand column relates to the corresponding entry in either Section (b) or Section (c) of the bibliography. A number of primary sources, mainly those not associated with a specific place, are listed in Section (a) of the bibliography.

Figures in italics and preceded by the letter *M* refer to the documents cited by Edmond Martène in *De Antiquis Ecclesiae Ritibus,* and identified and classified with corresponding numeration by A.-G.Martimort in *La documentation liturgique de Dom Edmond Martène.*

Abo	Manual	*c.*1522	269
Ainay, St-Martin	Missal	1531	*M 175*
Alès	Breviary	1758	143
Amiens	Missal	1555	94
Amiens	Missal	1752	140
Amiens	Pontifical	11 C	214
Anderlecht	Ordinary	14 C	252
Angers	Missal	1489	18
Angers	Ceremonial	1731	127

Angers	Ceremonial	1734	128
Angers, St-Aubin	Pontifical	14 C	*M 348*
Angoulême	Sacramentary	8 C	206
Apamea	Pontifical	1214	*M 25*
Aquileia	Missal	1519	72
Arbuthnott	Missal	*c.* 1480	225
Arles	Pontifical	14 C	*M 30*
Arras	Missal	1508	54
Arras, St-Vedast	Ordinal	*c.* 1300	204
Auch	Missal	1836	176
Auch	Ritual	1838	178
Auch	Sacramentary	*c.* 1000	220
Augsburg	Missal	1555	97
Austin Friars	Missal	1491	20
Austin Friars	Ceremonial	1714	124
Autun	Sacramentary	8 C	242
Autun	Missal	1555	95
Autun	*Supplement*	1700	96
Autun	Missal	1845	181
Auxerre	Breviary	1736	129
Auxerre	Missal	1537	*M 39*
Avranches	Pontifical	12 C	*M 339*
Bamberg	Missal	1499	31
Bangor	Antiphonary	7 C	288
Barking	Ordinal	1404	284
Basel	Missal	1488	17
Bayeux	Ceremonial	1677	120
Bayeux	*Sem. Ste.*	1730	126
Bayeux	*Sem. Ste.*	1780	155
Bayeux	Missal	1790	163
Bayeux	Ordinary	13 C	208
Bayonne	Missal	1543	219
Bazas	Missal	1503	42
Beauvais	Ritual	1783	160
Beauvais	Pontifical	15 C	*M 212*
Bec	Missal	*c.* 1270	246
Benedictines	Missal	1481	6
Benedictines	Missal	1518	71
Beneventum	Missal	11 C	234

Beneventum	Ritual	11 C	265
Bergamo	Sacramentary	c. 900	268
Besançon	Ceremonial	1682	121
Besançon	Ceremonial	1707	123
Besançon	Missal	1766	146
Biasca	Sacramentary	c. 1000	241
Boulogne	Ritual	1780	156
Bourges	Missal	1741	132
Braga	Missal	1512	61
Braga	Missal	1558	99
Bremen	Missal	1511	59
Breslau	Missal	1483	10
Breslau	Missal	1519	73
Bressanone	Missal	1511	60
Burgos	Missal	1546	90
Bursfeld	Missal	1498	29
Bury St Edmunds	Customary	c. 1234	236
Bystorp	Manual	c. 1505	279
Cahors	Missal	1760	144
Cahors	Sacramentary	12 C	*M 97*
Camaldolese	Missal	1503	38
Camaldolese	Ceremonial	1634	114
Cambrai	Missal	1507	49
Canterbury	Customary	13 C	281
Canterbury, St Augustine	Missal	13 C	273
Capuchins	Ceremonial	1775	153
Carcassonne	Missal	1749	139
Carcassonne	Sacramentary	13 C	*M 98*
Carmelites	Missal	1504	43
Carmelites	Missal	1664	117
Carmelites	Ordinary	c. 1312	298
Cassino	Missal	1507	50
Cassino	*ordo*	12 C	256
Cassino	Ordinary	c. 1100	*M 1139*
Châlons-s.-M.	Missal	1748	138
Châlons-s.-M.	Missal	1543	*M 84*
Chalon-s.-S.	Ordinary	13 C	*M 67*
Chartres	Missal	1782	157

Chartres	Ordinal	13 C	215
Chartres, St-Pierre	Sacramentary	10 C	*M 75*
Chartres, St-Jean	Ordinary	12 C	*M 76*
Chester	Customary	11 C	198
Chezal-Ben.	Ceremonial	1531	*M 1180*
Chezal-Ben.	Breviary	1586	*M 1181*
Cistercians	Missal	1487	14
Cistercians	Missal	1669	119
Cistercians	Ritual	1689	122
Cluny	Missal	1510	57
Cluny	Customary	11 C	198
Coimbra	Ordinary	1579	107
Coire	Missal	1589	109
Cologne	Missal	1494	24
Cologne	Missal	1514	66
Cologne	Missal	1525	81
Cologne	Missal	1626	113
Cologne	Ritual	12 C	Gg 15*
Copenhagen	Missal	1510	279
Corbie	*ordo*	10 C	*M 1145*
Corbie	Ordinary	12 C	*M 1146*
Corbie	Customary	13 C	*M 1147*
Cordoba	Missal	1561	103
Cosenza	Missal	1549	91
Cosenza	Ordinary	*c.*1220	*M 107*
Coutances	Missal	1557	98
Coutances	Ceremonial	1825	167
Dijon, St-Bénigne	Customary	11 C	*M 1150*
Dominicans	Missal	1482	9
Dominicans	Missal	1504	44
Dominicans	Missal	1908	189
Dominicans	H.W.Offices	1927	190
Durham	Missal	14 C	226
Durham	Ritual		278
Eichstadt	Missal	1517	68
Essen	Ordinary	14 C	202
Esztergom	Missal	1501	36

*For this document cited by Martène (*DAER* 4.24.3 p.145), see Martimort.

Esztergom	Missal	1512	62
Evesham	Ritual	*c.*1250	296
Evreux	Missal	1740	131
Exeter	Ordinal	1337	212
Farfa	Customary	11 C	198
Fleury	Customary	11 C	198
Fontevrault	Missal	1534	84
Freising	Missal	1487	15
Freising	Missal	1579	108
Fruttuaria	Customary	11 C	198
Fulda	Sacramentary	10 C	271
Gastine	Ordinary	12 C	*M 126*
Gellone	Sacramentary	8 C	221
Gilbertines	Ordinal	12 C	297
Glandèves	Missal	*c.*1420	*M 144*
Grandmont	Customary	11 C	*M 1184*
Halberstadt	Missal	*c.*1505	47
Hamburg	Missal	1509	55
Hereford	Breviary	13 C	232
Hereford	Missal	1502	243
Hildesheim	Missal	1499	32
Hungary	Ritual	1815	164
Ireland	Missal	*c.*1200	290
La Rochelle	Missal	1835	174
Langres	Missal	1492	22
Langres	Missal	1517	69
Langres	Directory	1844	180
Langres	Ordinary	13 C	*M 168*
Laon	Rite	(1662)	203
Laon	Customary	14 C	*M 1164*
Laon	Ordinary	13 C	*M 156*
Le Mans	Ceremonial	1789	162
Le Mans	Ordinary	13 C	*M 89*
Le Puy	Missal	1783	159
Le Puy	Ceremonial	1836	175
Léon	Antiphonary	10 C	205
Lesnes	Missal	13 C	248

Liège	Directory	1492	23
Liège	Missal	1540	85
Liège, St James	Ordinary	13 C	287
Limoges	Missal	1830	170
Limoges	Ordinary	1630	*M 158*
Limoges	Missal	1483	*M 159*
Limoges	Breviary	1495	*M 160*
Linköping	Ritual	*c.* 1525	228
Lisieux	Ritual	*c.* 1530	83
Lisieux	Ritual	1744	136
Lisieux	Missal	1752	141
Lübeck	Missal	1505	46
Luçon	Missal	1828	168
Lund	Missal	1514	67
Lyon	Missal	1510	58
Lyon	Missal	1771	151
Lyon	Ceremonial	1838	179
Lyon	Missal	1846	183
Lyon	Missal	1904	188
Lyon	Ordinary	*c.* 1200	*M 173*
Lyre	Customary	*c.* 1400	*M 1154–5*
Magdeburg	Missal	1480	5
Magdeburg	Missal	1503	40
Mainz	Missal	1507	52
Mainz	Pontifical	14 C	*M 190*
Marseille	Manual	13 C	207
Meaux	Missal	1845	182
Meissen	Breviary	1520	76
Melk	Missal	1495	26
Melun	Missal	1489	*M 185*
Mende	Missal	1776	147
Mende	Pontifical	14 C	*M 187*
Metz	Missal	1829	169
Milan	Manual	11 C	260
Milan	Missal	1475	1
Milan	Missal	1560	100
Milan	Missal	1594	110
Milan	Missal	1768	149
Milan	Missal	1902	187

Milan	Missal	1981	196
Milan	Missal	1986	197
Minden	Missal	1513	64
Nantes	Missal	1837	177
Narbonne	Missal	1528	82
Narbonne	Ordinary	14 C	*M 202*
Nevers	Sacramentary	*c.*1050	274
Nidaros	Breviary	1519	74
Nidaros	Manual	13 C	222
Nidaros	Ordinary	13 C	235
Norbertine	Sacramentary	12 C	292
Norbertine	Breviary	1930	192
Norway	Missal	1519	75
Norwich	Customary	*c.*1265	283
Notmark	Manual	15 C	279
Noyon	Missal	1541	88
Noyon	Sacramentary	9 C	*M 202*
Odense	Missal	1483	279
Osma	Missal	1561	104
Palencia	Missal	1568	105
Palermo	Missal	1130	280
Paris	Missal	1543	89
Paris	Ceremonial	1662	116
Paris	Missal	1666	118
Paris	Missal	1762	145
Paris	Breviary	1778	154
Paris	Pontifical	15 C	*M 212*
Paris, Royal Chapel	*Sem. Ste.*	1741	133
Passau	Missal	1503	41
Périgueux	Missal	1782	158
Poitiers	Missal	1524	80
Poitiers	Missal	1767	148
Poitiers	Missal	1498	*M 222*
Poland	Manual	1819	165
Prague	Missal	1498	30
Prague	Sacramentary	8 C	218
Ratisbon	Missal	1518	70
Ratisbon	Ritual	1570	106

Regensburg	Pontifical	10 C	233
Reims	Missal	1770	150
Reims	Ordinary	c.1200	209
Reims, Abbey of			
St Remigius	Sacramentary	c.800	209
Reims	Ordinary	c.1300	M 251
Reims	Ritual	1585	M 252
Reims	Missal	1491	M 254
Reims	Ritual	14 C	M 261
Rennes	Missal	1523	79
Rennes, St-Melan	Missal	12 C	M 239
Rhenau	Sacramentary	8 C	238
Rheinau	Ritual	1114	247
Ripoll	Sacramentary	1038	267
Rome	Missal	1477	2
Rome	Missal	1484	11
Rome	Missal	1491	21
Rome	Missal	1500	33
Rome	Missal	1501	35
Rome	Missal	1506	48
Rome	Missal	1520	77
Rome	Ceremonial	1600	111
Rome	Ritual	1848	184
Rome	H.W.Offices	1897	186
Rome	Missal	1950	193
Rome	Missal	1970	194
Rome	Missal	1754	213
Rome	Missal	1474	257
Rome	Missal	1574	257
Rome	Breviary	1879	261
Rome	Missal	1558	101
Rome	Missal	1560	102
Rome	Missal	1928	191
Roskilde	Manual	1513	229
Rouen	Breviary	1480	4
Rouen	Missal	1497	27
Rouen	Ritual	1640	115
Saintes	Missal	c.1500	34
Salisbury	Missal	c.1486	13

504 *Key to Bibliography*

Salisbury	Ritual	13 C	210
Salisbury	Missal	13 C	217
Salisbury	Ordinal	c.1210	231
Salisbury	Customary	13 C	231
Salisbury	Processional	1517	245
Salisbury	Missal	c.1300	255
Salisbury	Breviary	1531	270
Salisbury	Missal	13 C	291
Salzburg	Missal	1507	53
Saragossa	Missal	1552	93
Sées	Missal	1742	134
Sées	Ritual	1834	173
Senlis	Ordinary	14 C	M 301
Sens	Missal	1520	78
Sens	Missal	1715	125
Sens	Ritual	1555	M 299
Seville	Missal	1507	51
Slesvig	*Agenda*	1512	230
Soissons	Missal	1745	137
Soissons	Ritual	1753	142
Soissons	Ritual	1856	185
Soissons	Ritual	c.1185	M 305
Spires	*Agenda*	1512	63
St-Bertrand	Missal	1773	152
St-Denys	Customary	c.1273	M 1158
St-Germain-des-Prés	Customary	1394	M 1165
St-Germain-des-Prés	Pontifical	12 C	M 230
St-Florian	Ritual	12 C	227
St-Malo	Missal	1503	39
Strasbourg	Ritual	1742	135
Strasbourg	Ordinal	1364	M 35
Tongres	Ordinary	15 C	253
Toul	Missal	1551	92
Toul	Ordinary	14 C	M 1160
Toulon	Missal	14 C	M 310
Toulouse	Missal	1832	171
Toulouse	Missal	1490	M 311
Tournai	Missal	1540	86
Tours	Missal	1784	161

Tours	Sacramentary	9 C	*M 320*
Tours	Missal	13 C	*M 324*
Tours, St-Martin	Ritual	13 C	272
Trier	Missal	*c.*1487	16
Trier	Ordinary	*c.*1300	249
Troyes	Missal	1736	130
Upsala	Missal	1513	65
Utrecht	Missal	1497	28
Utrecht	Missal	1540	87
Uzès	Missal	1495	25
Uzès	Ordinary	14 C	*M 346*
Valence	Missal	1504	45
Vallombrosa	Missal	1503	37
Verdun	Missal	1486	12
Verdun	Missal	1481	7
Verdun, St Vito	Customary	11 C	198
Verdun	Ceremonial	1832	172
Verona	Ritual	1609	112
Viborg	Missal	1500	279
Vich	Sacramentary	1038	266
Vienna	Missal	1782	166
Westminster	Missal	*c.*1370	254
Westminster, St Peter	Customary	13 C	282
Worcester	Antiphonary	13 C	263
Worms	Missal	1490	19
Würzburg	Directory	1477	3
Würzburg	Missal	1481	8
Würzburg	Missal	1509	56
York	Missal	14 C	244
York	Breviary	*c.*1050	250
York, St Mary	Ordinal	*c.*1400	277

BIBLIOGRAPHY

(i) Medieval Writers and Documents

The figure-references (No.) following the sources below relate to the corresponding numbered entries in Sections (ii) and (iii) of the Bibliography. Most of the rest of the works are to be found in the volumes of J.-P.Migne's *Patrologia Latina* (PL).

Peter Abelard : in PL 178.
Acta Vetera of Rouen Cathedral (11 C) : in PL 147.
Alcuin : Liber de divinis officiis in PL 101.
Amalarius (*c.*830) : *Liber Officialis* in Vol.2, and *Liber de Ordine Antiphonarii* in Vol.3 of No.239.
Bede : in PL 90–95, except *A History of the English Church and People*, [ET L.Sherley-Price] (Penguin Books, Harmondsworth, 1955).
Beroldus : No.259.
Bindo Fesulani (1377) : in No.275.
The Bobbio Missal : in No.258.
Codex Avignon 1706 (*c.*1350) : in No.275.
Drepanius Florus : in PL 61.
Durandus : (see Bibliography, Section (d)).
The Pontifical of Egbert : No.237.
Flodoardus : in PL 135.
The Gelasian Sacramentary : No.264.

The Gradual of Beneventum : in Hesbert.

The Gregorian Sacramentary : No.293.

Gregory of Tours : *Historia Francorum* in PL 71.

Haymo's *Ordines* : Nos.240 and 285.

Honorius of Autun : *Gemma Animae, Sacramentarium, Speculum* in PL 172.

Hugh of St Victor : in PL 177.

John Beleth : *Rationale* in PL 202.

John of Avranches : *Liber de officiis ecclesiasticis* in PL 147.

Lanfranc : *Decreta Pro Ordine Sancti Benedicti* in PL 150.

The Lateran Missal : in Schmidt Vol.II.

The Lateran Ordo : No.224.

The Leofric Collectar : No.216.

The Leofric Missal : No.289.

Liber Ordinum (Mozarabic) : No.223.

Magdelen College Pontifical : No.294.

Micrologus : in PL 151.

The Missal of Robert of Jumièges : No.295.

Missale Antiquum (Beneventum) : in Hesbert.

Missale Mixtum : in PL 85.

Monte Cassino A and *B* : in No.199.

Nomasticon Cisterciense : No.276.

Ordines Romani 11-30B : in No.200.

Ordines Romani X-XV : in PL 78.

Ordo Albini : in Fabre Vol.2.

Ordo Romanus I : in No.201.

The Constitutions of John Orsini : in Mallardo.

The Pontifical of Poitiers : No.262.

Pontificale Gulielmi Durandi (13 C) : No.199 (III).

Pontificale Romanae Curiae (13 C) : No.199 (II).

Pontificale Romano-Germanicum : No.286.

Pontificale Romanum (12 C) : No.199 (I).

Prudentius : *Carmina* in No.211.

Rabanus Maurus : in PL 107.

Regularis Concordia : in PL 137.

Robert Paululus : in PL 177.

The Rosslyn Missal : No.251.

Rupert of Deutz (*c*.1110) : *De Divinis Officiis* in PL 170.

Sacramentarium Vetus (11 C) : in PL 151.

Sicardus : *Mitrale* in PL 213.

(ii) Original Primary Sources

1. Missale Ambrosianum (tpm), Milan, 1475.
2. Missale Romanum (tpm), Venice, 1477.
3. Ordinarius Herbipolensis (tpm), Spires, 1477.
4. Breviarium Rothomagense (tpm), Rouen, 1480.
5. *Missale ad usum ecclesiae Magdeburgensis,* Magdeburg, 1480.
6. Missale Benedictinum (tpm), Bamberg, 1481.
7. *Missale . . . Virdunensis Ecclesiae,* Paris, 1481.
8. Missale Herbipolense (tpm), Würzburg, 1481.
9. Missale ad usum Ordinis Praedicatorum (tpm), Venice, 1482.
10. Missale Vratislavense (tpm), Mainz, 1483.
11. Missale Romanum (tpm), Nürnberg, 1484.
12. Missale Virdunense (tpm), Magdeburg, 1486.
13. Missale ad usum ecclesiae Sarum (tpm), Basel, *c.*1486.
14. Missale Cisterciense (tpm), Strasbourg, 1487.
15. Missale Frisingense, Bamberg, 1487.
16. Missale Treverense (tpm), Basel, *c.*1487.
17. Missale Basiliense (tpm), Basel, 1488.
18. *Missale Andegavense,* Paris, 1489.
19. Missale Wormatiense (tpm), Basel, 1490.
20. Missal of the Augustinian Friars (tpm), Nürnberg, 1491.
21. Missale Romanum (tpm), Papie, 1491.
22. *Missale ad usum ecclesiae Lingonensis,* Paris, 1492.
23. *Ordinarius ecclesiae maioris Leodiensis,* Cologne, 1492.
24. Missale Coloniense (tpm), Cologne, 1494.
25. Missale Uceciense (tpm), Mainz and Lyon, 1495.
26. *Missale Benedictinae religionis Monachorum cenobii Mellicensis,* Nürnberg, 1495.
27. *Missale secundum usum insignis ecclesiae Rothomagensis,* Rouen, 1497.
28. *Missale insignis ecclesiae Traiectensis,* Paris, 1497.
29. *Missale ordinis Sancti Benedicti burszfeldensis ordinis,* Spires, 1498.
30. *Missale emendatum iuxta rubricas Pragensis ecclesiae,* Leipzig, 1498.
31. *Liber missalis secundum ordinem ecclesiae Bambergensis,* Bamberg, 1499.
32. *Missale Hildersemense,* Nürnberg, 1499.
33. *Missale secundum usum romanae ecclesiae,* Lyon, 1500.
34. Missale Santonense (tpm), Paris, *c.*1500.
35. *Missale Romanum,* Venice, 1501.
36. Missale Strigoniense (tpm), Lyon, 1501.

37. *Missale monasticum secundum consuetudinem ordinis Vallisumbrosae,* (Venice, 1503), reprinted in London, nd.

38. *Missale monasticum secundum ordinem Camaldulensem,* Venice, 1503.

39. *Missale ad usum insignis ecclesiae maclonensis,* Rouen, 1503.

40. Missale Magdeburgense (tpm), Nürnberg, 1503.

41. *Missale Pataviense,* Vienna, 1503.

42. *Missale . . . ad usum ecclesiae vasatensis,* Roelle, 1503.

43. *Missale secundum usum Carmelitarum,* (1504), reprinted in London, 1936.

44. *Missale Praedicatorum,* Venice, 1504.

45. *Missale ad usum ecclesiae valentinensis,* Valence, 1504.

46. Missale Lubicense (tpm), Speyer, 1505.

47. Missale Halberstatense (tpm), Mainz, *c.*1505.

48. *Missale Romanum,* Venice, 1506.

49. *Missale secundum usum venerabilis ecclesiae Cameracensis,* Paris, 1507.

50. *Missale . . . secundum morem et ritum Casinensis congregationis,* Venice, 1507.

51. *Missale secundum usum almae ecclesiae hyspalensis,* Seville, 1507.

52. *Missale Maguntinum,* Mainz, 1507.

53. *Missale Saltzburgense,* Venice, 1507.

54. *Missale ad usum insignis ecclesiae Atrebatensis,* Arras, 1508.

55. *Ordo missalis secundum ritum laudabilis ecclesiae Hamburgensis,* Strasbourg, 1509.

56. *Missale secundum usum ecclesiae Herbipolensis,* Lyon, 1509.

57. *Missale Ordinis Cluniacensis,* Paris, 1510.

58. *Missale ad usum lugdunensis ecclesiae,* Lyon, 1510.

59. *Missale secundum ritum ecclesiae Bremensis,* Strasbourg, 1511.

60. *Missale secundum ritum ecclesiae Brixinensis,* Basel, 1511.

61. *Missale secundum ritum et consuetudinem almae Bracharensis ecclesiae,* Salmantice, 1512.

62. *Missale secundum chorum ecclesiae Strigoniensis,* Venice, 1512.

63. *Agenda Spirensia,* Spires, 1512.

64. Missale Mindense (tpm), Nürnberg, 1513.

65. Missale Upsalense (tpm), Basel, 1513.

66. *Missale Diocesis Coloniensis,* Paris, 1514.

67. *Missale Lundense av år 1514,* Faksimiledition, Malmo, 1946.

68. *Missale secundum chorum et ritum Eystetensis Ecclesiae,* Nürnberg, 1517.

69. *Missale diocesis Lingonensis,* Paris, 1517.

70. *Missale secundum usum ecclesiae ratisponensis,* Bamberg, 1518.
71. *Missale . . . Ordinis Sancti Benedicti,* Hagen, 1518.
72. *Missale Aquileyensis Ecclesiae,* (Venice, 1519), reprinted in Brussels, 1963.
73. *Missale secundum Rubricas Vratislavensis diocesis,* Basel, 1519.
74. *Breviaria ad usum ritumque sacrosanctae Nidrosiensis Ecclesiae,* Oslo, 1519.
75. *Missale pro usu totius regni Norvegiae,* (1519), reprinted in Oslo, 1959.
76. *Breviarius . . . Misnensis Ecclesiae,* Meissen, 1520.
77. *Missale ad Romanae ecclesiae usum,* Paris, 1520.
78. *Missale Senonense,* Paris, 1520.
79. Missale Redonense (tpm), Paris, 1523.
80. Missale Pictaviense (tpm), Limoges, 1524.
81. *Missale Diocesis Coloniensis,* Paris, 1525.
82. *Missale ad usum sanctae Narbonensis ecclesiae,* Lyon, 1528.
83. *Manuale sacerdotum continens ecclesiae sacramenta et modum administrandi,* Pestaudemer, *c.*1530.
84. Missal of Fontevrault, Paris, 1534.
85. *Missale ad usum insignis ecclesiae Leodiensis,* Paris, 1540.
86. *Missale ad usum insignis ecclesiae Tornacensis,* Antwerp, 1540.
87. *Missale ad verum cathedralis ecclesiae Traiectensis ritum,* Antwerp, 1540.
88. *Missale ad usum insignis ecclesiae Noviomensis,* Paris, 1541.
89. *Missale ad usum ecclesiae Parisiensis,* Paris, 1543.
90. *Missale secundum consuetudinem Burgensis ecclesiae,* Burgos, 1546.
91. *Missale secundum consuetudinem Ecclesiae Cosentinae,* Venice, 1549.
92. Missale Tullense (tpm), Toul, 1551.
93. *Missale Cesaraugustanum,* Saragossa, 1552.
94. *Missale Ambianense,* Paris and Amiens, 1555.
95. *Sacrorum Codex iuxta ritum Ecclesiae Heduensis,* Lyon, 1555.
96. *Supplementum Missalis Aeduensis, c.*1700.
97. *Missale secundum ritum Augustensis ecclesiae,* Dillingen, 1555.
98. *Missale . . . Constanciensis Ecclesiae,* Rouen, 1557.
99. *Missale iuxta usum et ordinem Almae Bracarensis Ecclesiae,* Lyon, 1558.
100. *Missale Ambrosianum,* Milan, 1560.
101. *Missale Romanum,* Venice, 1558.
102. *Missale Romanum,* Venice, 1560.
103. *Missale Cordubensis Ecclesiae,* Cordova, 1561.

104. *Missale secundum usum . . . sanctae ecclesiae Oxomensis,* Cordova, 1561.
105. *Missale Pallantinum,* (C.Fernandez à Valtodano), Palencia, 1568.
106. *Obsequiale . . . secundum antiquum usum . . . Ecclesiae Ratisbonensis,* Ingolstadt, 1570.
107. *Ordinario dos Canonicos Regulares de Ordem do . . . S.Augustinho de congregaçao de sancta Cruz de Coimbra,* Lisbon, 1579.
108. *Missale Frisingense,* Munich, 1579.
109. *Missale secundum ritum Curiensis ecclesiae,* Constance, 1589.
110. *Missale Ambrosianum,* Milan, 1594.
111. *Caeremoniale Episcoporum,* 1st edition, Rome, 1600.
112. *Rituale Ecclesiae Veronensis,* (Alberto Valerio), Verona, 1609.
113. *Missale Coloniense,* Cologne, 1626.
114. *Ceremoniale Eremitarum Camaldulensium S.Romualdi,* Florence, 1634.
115. *Sacerdotale seu Manuale Ecclesiae Rothomagensis,* Rouen, 1640.
116. *Caeremoniale Parisiense ad usum Urbis et Diocesis Parisii,* Paris, 1662.
117. *Missale Fratrum Beatae Dei Genetricis Virginis Mariae de Monte Carmelo,* Paris, 1664.
118. *Missale Parisiense,* (Harduin de Péréfixe), Paris, 1666.
119. *Missale Cisterciense,* Paris, 1669.
120. *Cérémonial pour l'Eglise et le Diocèse de Bayeux,* Caen, 1677.
121. *Cérémonial du diocèse de Besançon,* (A.P. de Grammont), Besançon, 1682.
122. *Rituale Cisterciense,* Paris, 1689.
123. *Cérémonial du Diocèse de Besançon,* Besançon, 1707.
124. *Sacrae Caeremoniae . . . iuxta ritum . . . Fratrum Eremitarum S.Augustini,* Rome, 1714.
125. *Missale Senonense,* (H.F. de la Hoguette), Sens, 1715.
126. *Semaine Sainte à l'usage du Diocèse de Bayeux,* (J.-D. de Cheylus), Bayeux, 1730.
127. *Cérémonial de l'Eglise d'Angers,* Chateaugontier, 1731.
128. *Diurnale Andegavense,* Angers, 1734.
129. *Breviarium Autissiodorense,* Paris, 1736.
130. *Missale sanctae ecclesiae Trecensis,* (J.B.Bossuet), Troyes, 1736.
131. *Missale Ebroicense,* (P.-J.-C. de Rochechouart), Paris, 1740.
132. *Missale Bituricense,* (F.H. de Roye de la Rochefoucauld), Bourges, 1741.

133. *L'Office de la Semaine-Sainte à l'usage de la Maison du Roy*, (L'Abbé de Bellegarde), Paris, 1741.

134. *Missale Sagiense*, (L.-F. Néel de Christot), Paris, 1742.

135. *Rituale Argentinense*, (Armand, Cardinal de Rohan), Strasbourg, 1742.

136. *Rituale Lexoviense*, (H.-I. de Brancas), Paris, 1744.

137. *Missale Suessionense*, (F. Duc de Fitz-James), Paris, 1745.

138. *Missale . . . Ecclesiae Cathalaunensis*, (Choiseul-Beaupré), Châlons-sur-Marne, 1748.

139. *Missale Carcassonense*, (A.Bazin de Besons), Paris, 1749.

140. *Missale sanctae Ambianensis ecclesiae*, (D'Orléans de la Motte), Amiens, 1752.

141. *Missale Lexovicense*, (H.-I. de Brancas), Lisieux, 1752.

142. *Rituel du Diocèse de Soissons*, (F. Duc de Fitz-James), Paris, 1753.

143. *Breviarium Alesiense*, Paris, 1758.

144. *Missale Cadurcense*, (B.-D.-R. du Guesclin), Paris, 1760.

145. *Missale Parisiense*, (C.-G.-G. de Vintimille), Paris, 1762.

146. *Missale Bisuntinum*, (A.-C. de Choiseul-Beaupré), Besançon, 1766.

147. *Missale Mimatense*, (G.-F. de Choiseul-Beaupré), Paris and Mende, 1766.

148. *Missale Pictaviense*, (M.-L. de Beaupoil de St-Aulaire), Poitiers, 1767.

149. *Missale Ambrosianum*, Milan, 1768.

150. *Missale sanctae ecclesiae metropolitanae Remensis*, (C.-A. de la Roche-Aymon), Paris, 1770.

151. *Missale Sanctae Lugdunensis Ecclesiae*, Lyon, 1771.

152. *Missale Convenarum*, (C.-A.-G. Osmond), Toulouse, 1773.

153. *Memoriale Rituum sive Caeremoniale in Ordine FF Minorum S.Francisci Cappucinorum*, Rome, 1775.

154. *Breviarium Parisiense*, Pars Verna, Paris, 1778.

155. *Semaine Sainte à l'usage du Diocèse de Bayeux*, Bayeux, 1780.

156. *Rituel de diocèse de Boulogne*, (F.-J. de Portz de Pressy), Boulogne, 1780.

157. *Missale Carnotense*, (J.-B.-J. de Lubersac), Chartres, 1782.

158. *Missale Petrocorense*, (E.-L. de Grossolles de Flamarens), Paris, 1782.

159. *Missale ecclesiae Aniciensis*, (M.-J. de Galard de Terraube), Paris, 1783.

160. *Rituale Bellovacense*, (F.-J. de le Rochefoucauld), Beauvais, 1783.

Bibliography 513

161. *Missale Turonense,* (J.-M.-F. de Conzié), Paris, 1784.

162. *Cérémonial de l'Eglise Cathédrale de St-Juliane du Mans,* Le Mans, 1789.

163. *Missale Bajocense,* (J.D. de Cheylus), Lyon, 1790.

164. *Rituale Agriense,* (S.Fischer de Nagy-Szalatnya), Budapest, 1815.

165. *Manuale Caeremoniarum Romanarum . . . ad usum Ecclesiarum Poloniae,* Part II, Warsaw, 1819.

166. *Missale ad usum provinciae Viennensis,* (1782 Missal), Graz, 1822.

167. *Cérémonial du Diocèse de Coutances,* (P.Dupont-Poursat), Coutances, 1825.

168. *Missale Lucionense,* (R.F.Soyer), Lyon, 1828.

169. *Missale Metense,* (J.-F. Besson), Metz, 1829.

170. *Missale Lemovicense,* Limoges, 1830.

171. *Missale Tolosanum,* Toulouse, 1832.

172. *Cérémonial à l'Usage de la Cathédrale et du Diocèse de Verdun,* (Mgr de Villeneuve), Verdun, 1832.

173. *Rituale Sagiense,* (L.-F. Néel de Cristot), Sées, 1834.

174. *Missale Rupellense,* (D.J.Bernet), Paris, 1835.

175. *Cérémonial à l'usage de l'Eglise du Puy,* (L.-J.-M. de Bonald), Le Puy, 1836.

176. *Missale Auscitanum,* (J.-F. de Montillet), Auch, 1836.

177. *Missale Nannetense,* (J.M. Micolon de Guérines), Nantes, 1837.

178. *Rituel à l'usage du Diocèse d'Auch,* (Cardinal D'Isoard), Auch, 1838.

179. *Le Cérémonial de la sainte Eglise de Lyon,* Lyon, 1838.

180. *Pastorale Lingonense,* Langres, 1844.

181. *Missale Aeduense,* (B.-U.-J.-M. du Trousset D'Héricourt), Autun, 1845.

182. *Missale Meldense,* (R.-F. Gallard), Meaux, 1845.

183. *Missale Sanctae Lugdunensis Ecclesiae,* Lyon, 1846.

184. *Rituale Romanum,* (as revised and enlarged by Benedict XIV), Rome, 1848.

185. *Rituale seu Mandatum insignis ecclesiae Suessionensis,* Soissons, 1856.

186. *Officia Hebdomadae Sanctae,* (According to the Breviary), Tournai, 1897.

187. *Missale Ambrosianum,* t.e., (authorised 21 December 1901), Milan, 1902.

188. *Missale Romanum in quo antiqui ritus Lugdunenses servantur,* Lyon, 1904.

189. *Missale iuxta ritum Sacri Ordinis Praedicatorum,* Rome, Tournai, 1908.
190. *The Office of Holy Week according to the Dominican rite,* (Burns, Oates, Washbourne, London, 1927).
191. *Daily Missal,* edited by Dom G.Le Febvre, (Bruges and London, 1928).
192. *Breviarium Praemonstratense* (Burns, Oates, Washbourne, London, 1930).
193. *Missale Romanum (ex decreto sacrosancti Concilii Tridentini),* Rome, 1950.
194. *Missale Romanum* t.e. (Rome, 1970).
195. *Pope John Sunday Missal,* edited by Mgr M.Buckley, (Kevin Mayhew, Leigh-on-Sea, 1978).
196. *Missale Ambrosianum* t.e. (Casa Archivescovile, Milan, 1981).
197. *Messale Ambrosiano* t.e. (Casa Archivescovile, Milan, 1986).

(iii) Modern Editions of Primary Sources

198. Albers, B., *Consuetudines Monasticae,* 5 vols (Stuttgart, Vienna, Monte Cassino, 1900–1911).
199. Andrieu, M., *Le Pontifical Romain au Moyen-Age,* Vol.I : Le Pontifical Romain du XII siècle; Vol.II : Le Pontifical de la Curie Romaine au XIII siècle; Vol.III : Le Pontifical de Guillaume Durand, Studi e Testi Nos.86, 87, 88 (Vatican, 1938, 1940, 1940).
200. Andrieu, M., *Les "Ordines Romani" du Haut Moyen-Age,* 5 vols, Spicilegium Sacrum Lovaniense (Louvain, 1931–1961).
201. Atchley, E.G.C.F., *Ordo Romanus Primus,* Library of Liturgiology and Ecclesiology for English Readers, Vol.6 (London, 1905).
202. Arens, F., *Liber Ordinarius der Essener Stiftskirche* (Paderborn, 1908).
203. Bellotte, A., *Observationes ad ritus Ecclesiae Laudunensis Redivivos* (Paris, 1662).
204. Brou, L., *The Ordinal of St Vedast's Abbey, Arras,* Henry Bradshaw Society Publications, Vol.86 (London, 1957).
205. Brou, L. and Vives, J., *Antifonario Visigotico Mozarabe de la Catedral de León,* Monumenta Hispania Sacra [*Series Latina,* Vol.V.1] (Barcelona, Madrid, 1959).

206. Cagin, P., *Le Sacramentaire Gelasien d'Angoulême* (Macon, 1919).
207. Chevalier, U., *Institutions Liturgiques de l'Eglise de Marseille*, Bibliothèque Liturgique, XIV (Picard et Fils, Paris 1910).
208. Chevalier, U., *Ordinaire et Coutumier de l'Eglise Cathédrale de Bayeux*, Bibliothèque Liturgique, VIII (Picard et Fils, Paris, 1902).
209. Chevalier, U., *Sacramentarium Abbatiae S. Remigii Remensis*, Bibliothèque Liturgique, VII (A.Picard, Paris, 1900).
210. Collins, A.J., *Manuale Sarum*, Henry Bradshaw Society Publications, Vol.91 (London, 1960).
211. Cunningham, M.P., *Aurelii Prudentii Clementis Carmina*, Corpus Christianorum [*Series Latina*] (Turnholt, 1966).
212. Dalton, J.N., *Ordinale Exonense*, Henry Bradshaw Society Publications, Vol.37 (London, 1909).
213. De Azevedo, E., *Vetus Missale Romanum Monasticum* (Rome, 1754).
214. De Beauville, V. and Josse, H., *Le Pontifical d'Amiens (du XI⁰ siècle)* (T.Jeunet, Amiens, 1885).
215. Delaporte, Y., *L'Ordinaire chartrain du XIII⁰ siècle* (Société Archéologique d'Eure-et-Loire, Chartres, 1953).
216. Dewick, E.S. and Frere, W.H., *The Leofric Collectar*, Vol.2, Henry Bradshaw Society Publications, Vol.56 (London, 1921).
217. Dickinson, F.H., *Missale ad usum insignis et praeclarae ecclesiae Sarum* (Burntisland, 1861–1883).
218. Dold, A. and Eizenhöfer, L., *Das Prager Sakramentar* (Beuroner Kunstverlag, Beuron in Hohenzollern, 1949).
219. Dubarat, V., *Le Missel de Bayonne de 1543* (Pau, Paris, Toulouse, 1901).
220. Duffour, J., 'Fragments d'un Ancien Sacramentaire d'Auch', in *Archives Historiques de la Gascogne* (Léonce Cochareaux, Auch, 1912).
221. Dumas, A., *Liber Sacramentorum Gellonensis*, Corpus Christianorum [*Series Latina, CLIX*] (Turnholt, 1981).
222. Faehn, H., *Manuale Norvegicum* (Presta Handbôk), Libri Liturgici Provinciae Nidrosiensis Medii Aevii, Vol.1 (Oslo, 1962).
223. Férotin, D.M., *Le Liber Ordinum (en usage dans l'église wisigothique et mozarabe d'Espagne)*, originally published in Paris, 1909 (Gregg International Publishers, Farnborough, 1969).
224. Fischer, L., *Ordo Officiorum Ecclesiae Lateranensis* (Munich and Freising, 1916).

225. Forbes, A.P., *Liber Ecclesiae Beati Terrenani de Arbuthnott* (Burntisland, 1864).

226. Fowler, J.T., 'The Durham Missal', in *The Rites of Durham*, Surtees Society Publications, Vol.107 (Durham, 1903), pp.172–91.

227. Franz, A., *Das Rituale von St Florian aus dem zwölften Jahrhundert* (Freiburg (im Br.), 1904).

228. Freisen, J., *Manuale Lincopense, Breviarium Scarense, Manuale Aboense* (Paderborn, 1904).

229. Freisen, J., *Manuale curatorum secundum usum ecclesiae Roschildensis,* Copenhagen, 1513 (Paderborn, 1898).

230. Freisen, J., *Liber Agendarum ecclesiae et diocesis Sleszwicensis* (Paderborn, 1898).

231. Frere, W.H., *The Sarum Customary* (Cambridge U.P., 1898).

232. Frere, W.H. and Brown, L.E.G., *The Hereford Breviary,* Henry Bradshaw Society Publications, Vol.26 (London, 1904).

233. Gamber, K. and Rehle, S., *Das Sakramentar-Pontifikal des Bischops Wolfgang von Regensburg* (F.Pustet, Regensburg, 1985).

234. Gamber, K., *Missale Beneventum von Canosa* (F.Pustet, Regensburg, 1972).

235. Gjerldw, L., *Ordo Nidrosiensis Ecclesiae,* Libri Liturgici Provinciae Nidrosiensis Medii Aevi, Vol.2 (Oslo, 1968).

236. Gransden, A., *Consuetudines Burienses,* Henry Bradshaw Society Publications, Vol.99 (London, 1973).

237. Greenwell, W., *The Pontifical of Egbert,* Surtees Society Publications, Vol.27 (Newcastle, 1853).

238. Hänggi, A. and Schönherr, A., *Sacramentarium Rhenaugiense* (Freiburg (Sw.) 1970).

239. Hanssens, J.M., *Amalarii Episcopi Opera Liturgica Omnia,* 3 vols, Studi e Testi, Nos.138, 139, 140 (Vatican, 1948–1950).

240. (Haymo of Faversham), *The Ordines of Haymo of Faversham,* Henry Bradshaw Society Publications, Vol.85 (London, 1953).

241. Heiming, O., *Das Ambrosianische Sakramentar von Biasca,* Corpus Ambrosiano Liturgicum II (Munich (W.F.), 1969).

242. Heiming, O., *Liber Sacramentorum Augustodunensis,* Corpus Christianorum [*Series Latina CLIXB*] (Turnholt, 1984).

243. Henderson, W.G., *The Hereford Missal* (Leeds, 1874).

244. Henderson, W.G., *Missale ad usum insignis Ecclesiae Eboracensis,* Surtees Society Publications, Vol.59 (Newcastle, 1872).

245. Henderson, W.G., *Processionale ad usum insignis ac praeclarae Ecclesiae Sarum* (Leeds, 1882).

246. Hughes, A., *The Bec Missal,* Henry Bradshaw Society Publications, Vol.94 (London, 1963).

247. Hürlimann, G., *Das Rheinauer Rituale,* Spicilegium Friburgense, No.5 (Universitatsverlag, Freiburg (Sw.), 1959).

248. Jebb, P., *Missale de Lesnes,* Henry Bradshaw Society Publications, Vol.95 (Worcester, 1964).

249. Kurzeja, A., *Der Älteste Liber Ordinarius der Trierer Domkirche,* Liturgiewissenschaftliche Quellen und Forschungen, Vol.52 (Munich (W.F.), 1970).

250. Lawley, S.W., *The York Breviary,* Surtees Society Publications, Vol.71 (Newcastle, 1879).

251. Lawlor, H.J., *The Rosslyn Missal,* Henry Bradshaw Society Publications, Vol.15 (London, 1899).

252. Lefèvre, P.F., *Les Ordinaires des collégiales Saint-Pierre à Louvain et Saints-Pierre-et-Paul à Anderlecht* (Publications Universitaires de Louvain, Louvain, 1960).

253. Lefèvre, P.F., *L'Ordinaire de Tongres : I. Le Temporal,* Spicilegium Sacrum Lovaniense, Vol.34 (Louvain, 1967).

254. Legg, J.W., *Missale ad usum Ecclesiae Westmonasteriensis,* Vol.2, Henry Bradshaw Society Publications, Vol.5 (London, 1893).

255. Legg, J.W., *The Sarum Missal* (Oxford U.P., 1916).

256. Leutermann, T., *Ordo Cassinensis hebdomadae maioris,* Miscellanea Cassinese, 20 (Monte Cassino, 1941).

257. Lippe, R., *Missale Romanum Mediolani, 1474,* 2 vols, Henry Bradshaw Society Publications, Vols.17 and 33 (London, 1899 and 1907).

258. Lowe, E.A., *The Bobbio Missal,* Henry Bradshaw Society Publications, Vol.58 (London, 1920).

259. Magistretti, M., *Beroldus : Ecclesiae Ambrosianae Mediolanensis Kalendarium et Ordines Saec. XII* (J.Giovanola, Milan, 1894).

260. Magistretti, M., *Manuale Ambrosianum,* Monumenta Veteris Liturgiae Ambrosianae, Part II (Milan, 1904).

261. Marquess of Bute, *The Roman Breviary,* Vol.1 (Winter) (W.Blackwood & Sons, London and Edinburgh, 1879).

262. Martini, A., *Il Cosidetto Pontificale Di Poitiers* (Herder, Rome, 1979).

263. Mocquereau, A., *L'Antiphonaire Monastique de Worcester,* Paléographie Musicale XII (Berne, 1971).

264. Mohlberg, L.C., with L.Eizenhöfer and P.Siffrin, *Liber Sacramentorum Romanae Aeclesiae Ordinis Anni Circuli,* Rerum Ecclesiasticarum Documenta, Fontes IV (Herder, Rome, 1960).

265. Odermatt, A., *Ein Rituale in Beneventanischer Schrift,* Spicilegium Friburgense 26 (Universitatsverlag, Freiburg (Sw.), 1980).

266. Olivar, A., *El Sacramentario de Vich* (Madrid and Barcelona, 1953).

267. Olivar, A., *Sacramentarium Rivipullense* (Madrid and Barcelona, 1954).

268. Paredi, A., *Sacramentarium Bergamense* (Bergamo, 1962).

269. Parvio, M., *Manuale seu Exsequiale Aboense (c.1522)* (Societas Historiae Ecclesiasticae Fennica, Helsinki, 1980).

270. Procter, F. and Wordsworth, C., *Breviarium ad usum insignis ecclesiae Sarum* (Cambridge U.P., 1882).

271. Richter, G. and Schönfelder, A., *Sacramentarium Fuldense,* 1912 edition reprinted as Henry Bradshaw Society Publication, Vol.101 (London, 1977).

272. *Rituel de Saint-Martin de Tours—XIII siècle,* Documents et Manuscrits (Paris, 1899).

273. Rule, M., *The Missal of St Augustine's Abbey, Canterbury* (Cambridge U.P., 1896).

274. *Sacramentarium ad usum Aecclesiae Nivernensis,* (Gregg International Publishers, Farnborough, 1969).

275. Schimmelpfennig, B., *Die Zeremonienbücher der Römischen Kurie in Mittelalter* (Tubingen, 1973).

276. Séjalon, H., *Nomasticon Cisterciense* (Solesmes, 1892).

277. Stanbrook, Abbess of and Tolhurst, J.B.L., *The Ordinary and Customary of St Mary's, York,* Vol.2, Henry Bradshaw Society Publications, Vol.75 (London, 1937).

278. Stevenson, J., *Rituale Ecclesiae Dunelmensis,* Surtees Society Publications, Vol.10 (Newcastle, 1841).

279. Strömberg, B., *The Manual from Bystorp,* Biblioteca Liturgica Danica, Vol.II (Egtved, Danmark, 1982).

280. Terrizzi, F., *Missale Antiquum S.Panormitanae Ecclesiae,* Rerum Christianarum Documenta, Fontes XII (Herder, Rome, 1970).

281. Thompson, E.M., *The Customary of the Benedictine Monasteries of St Augustine, Canterbury, and St Peter, Westminster,* Henry Bradshaw Society Publications, Vol.23 (London, 1902).

282. Thompson, E.M., *The Customary of St Peter, Westminster,* Vol.2,

Henry Bradshaw Society Publications, Vol.28 (London, 1904).

283. Tolhurst, J.B.L., *The Customary of Norwich,* Henry Bradshaw Society Publications, Vol.82 (London, 1948).

284. Tolhurst, J.B.L., *The* Ordinale and Customary of Barking Abbey, Vol.1, Henry Bradshaw Society Publications, Vol.65 (London, 1927).

285. Van Dijk, S.J.P., *The Ordinals of Haymo of Haversham and related documents, 1243-1307,* Sources of the Modern Roman Liturgy, Vol.II (Leiden, 1963).

286. Vogel, C. and Elze, R., *Le Pontifical Romano-Germanique du dixième siècle,* 2 vols, Studi e Testi, Nos.226 and 227 (Biblioteca Apostolica Vaticana, Vatican, 1963).

287. Volk, P., *Der Liber Ordinarius Des Lutticher St Jakobs-Klosters* (Aschendorff Verlag, Munich (W.F.), 1923).

288. Warren, F.E., *The Antiphonary of Bangor.* 2 vols, Henry Bradshaw Society Publications, Vols.4 and 10 (London, 1894–1895).

289. Warren, F.E., *The Leofric Missal* (Oxford U.P., 1883).

290. Warren, F.E., *Missale Vetus Hibernicum* (London, 1979).

291. Warren, F.E., *The Sarum Missal,* Alcuin Club Collections, No.11 (London, 1911).

292. Weyns, N.I., *Sacramentarium Praemonstratense,* Biblioteca Analectorum Praemonstratensium (Averbode, Prémontré, 1968).

293. Wilson, H.A., *The Gregorian Sacramentary,* Henry Bradshaw Society Publications, Vol.49 (London, 1915). See also, Menard in general bibliograpy.

294. Wilson, H.A., *The Magdalen College Pontifical,* Henry Bradshaw Society Publications, Vol.39 (London, 1910).

295. Wilson, H.A., *The Missal of Robert of Jumièges,* Henry Bradshaw Society Publications, Vol.11 (London, 1896).

296. Wilson, H.A., *Officium Ecclesiasticum abbatum secundum usum Eveshamensis monasterii,* Henry Bradshaw Society Publications, Vol.6 (London, 1891).

297. Woolley, R.M., *Ordinale Gilbertinum,* Henry Bradshaw Society Publications, Vol.59 (London, 1921).

298. Zimmermann, B., *Ordinaire de l'Ordre de Notre Dame du Mont Carmel par Sibert de Beka (vers 1312),* (A.Picard et Fils, Paris, 1910).

(iv) General Bibliography (Modern Writers)

Ahearne, P. and Lane, M., *Pontifical Ceremonies* (Burnes, Oates, Dublin, 1942).

Albers, D.B., 'Die Ältesten Consuetudines von Vallumbros', *Revue Bénédictine*, 23 (1911), pp.432–36.

Alleau, R., *Guide de la France Mystérieuse* (Paris, 1964).

Andrieu, M., 'Le Pontifical d'Apamée', *Revue Bénédictine*, 48 (1936), pp.321–48.

Armellini, M., *Lezioni di Archeologia Cristiana* (F.Cuggiani, Rome, 1898).

Atchley, E.G.C.F., *A History of the Use of Incense in Divine Worship*, Alcuin Club Collections, No.13 (London, 1913).

Avery, M., *The Exultet Rolls of Southern Italy*, (Princeton, 1936).

Avery, M., 'Beneventan Lections', *Studi Gregoriani* 1 (1947), pp.433–58.

Babylonian Talmud, [ET I.Epstein], *Shabbath 1* (Socino Press, London, 1938).

Baggs, C.M., *The Ceremonies of Holy Week at the Vatican and St John's Lateran* (Rome, 1839).

Baldeschi, J., *The Ceremonial according to the Roman Rite*, [ET J.D.H.Dale] (Charles Dolman, London, 1873).

Baring-Gould, S., *The Lives of the Saints*, 3rd edition (J.Hodges, London, 1878–1882).

Baronius, C., *Annales Ecclesiastici*, [Ed. J.D.Mansi and D.Gregorius], 38 vols (Lucca, 1738–1759).

Bannister, H.M., 'Ordine "Ambrosiano" per la settimana santa', *Miscellanea Ceriani* (Ulrico Hoepli, Milan, 1910).

Barbier de Montault, X., 'Le Chandelier Pascal à Rome', *Messager des Fidèles*, I (1884–1885), pp.73–75.

Batiffol, P., *A History of the Roman Breviary*, [ET E.M.Y.Bayley] (Longmans, Green, London, 1912).

Bauldry, M., *Manuale Sacrorum Caeremoniarum* (Venice, 1762).

Baumstark, A., *Comparative Liturgy*, [ET F.L.Cross] (A.R.Mowbray & Co., London, 1958).

Beauduin, L., 'Le cierge pascal', *La Maison-Dieu*, 26 (1951), pp.23–27.

Beauduin, L., 'Liminaire', *La Maison-Dieu*, 45 (1956), pp.5–8.

Benoit-Castelli, G., 'Le *Praeconium Paschale*', *Ephemerides Liturgicae*, LXVII (1953), pp.309–94.

Berlière, U., 'Le cierge pascal', *Revue Bénédictine,* 5 (1888), pp.106-16.

Bernal, J., 'Vicisitudes literarias e históricas de la oración hispana "Exaudi nos, Lumen indeficiens"', *Miscellanea Liturgica in onore di Sua Eminenza il Cardinale Giacomo Lercaro II* (Rome, 1967).

Bertonière, G., *The Historical Development of the Easter Vigil and Related Services in the Greek Church,* Orientalia Christiana Analecta 193 (Rome, 1972).

Bishop, E., *Liturgica Historica* (Oxford U.P., 1918).

Bisso, B., *Hierurgia sive Rei Divini Peractio* (Genoa, 1686).

Bolton, C.A., 'The New Fire', *Irish Ecclesiastical Record,* 59 (1947), pp.215-20.

Bonnet, H.N., 'Les Réalisations', *La Maison-Dieu,* 26 (1956) pp.55-72.

Borella, P., *Il rito ambrosiano* (Morcelliana, Brescia, 1964).

Bouyer, L., 'The Mystery of Easter', *Downside Review,* 66 (1947-1948), pp.117-26.

Bouyer, L., *The Paschal Mystery* [ET Mary Benoit] (Allen and Unwin, London, 1951).

Bouyer, L., 'Saintes Vigiles', *La Maison-Dieu,* 26 (1951), pp.11-22.

Bradshaw, H. and Wordsworth C., *Statutes of Lincoln Cathedral* (Cambridge U.P., 1897).

Bradshaw, P.F., *Daily Prayer in the Early Church,* Alcuin Club Collections, No.63 (London, 1981).

Briggs, K.M., *The Folklore of the Cotswolds* (Batsford, London, 1974).

Bugnini, A., 'De Reformatione Liturgica Generali', *Ephemerides Liturgicae,* LXX (1956), pp.414-29.

Bugnini, O. and Braga C., 'Ordo Hebdomadae Sanctae Instauratus', *Ephemerides Liturgicae,* LXX (1956), pp.81-228.

Bumpus, T.F., *The Cathedrals and Churches of Belgium* (Werner Laurie, London, 1928).

Bumpus, T.F., *The Cathedrals and Churches of Northern Italy* (Werner Laurie, London, 1907).

Butler C., *Benedictine Monachism,* 2nd edition (Longmans & Co., London, 1924).

Cabrol, F., *Les Origines Liturgiques* (Paris, 1906).

Cabrol, F. and Leclercq, H., *Dictionnaire d'Archéologie Chrétienne et de Liturgie* (Paris, 1903-1953).

Cabrol, F. and Leclercq, H., *Monumenta Ecclesiae Liturgica* (Paris, 1900–1902),

Callewaert, C., 'De Paaschkandelaar', *Liturgisch Parochieblad S.Pietersabdiy,* 4 (1922), pp.140–42.

Cairncross, H., Lamburn, E.C.R., Whatton, G.A.C., *Ritual Notes,* 8th edition (W.Knott & Son, London, 1935).

Cameron, M.L., *Old Etruria and Modern Tuscany* (Methuen, London, 1909).

Canivez, J.M., 'Le Rite Cistercien', *Ephemerides Liturgicae,* LXIII (1949), pp.276–311.

Canziani, E., *Through the Apennines and the Lands of the Abruzzi* (Heffer, Cambridge, 1928).

Capelle, B., 'L' ''Exultet'' Pascal Oeuvre de Saint Ambroise', in *Miscellanea Giovanni Marcati,* Studi e Testi, No.121 (Biblioteca Apostolica Vatican, Vatican), pp.219–46.

Capelle, B., 'La procession de *Lumen Christi* au Samedi-Saint', *Revue Bénédictine,* 44 (1932), pp.105–19.

Capelle, B., 'Le rite des cinq grains d'encens', *Les Questions Liturgiques et Paroissiales,* 17 (1932), pp.3–11.

Casel, O., 'Zur Feuerweihe', *Jahrbuch fur Liturgiewissenschaft,* 2 (1922), pp.90–91.

Chavasse, A., *Le Sacramentaire Gélasien* (Tournai, 1958).

Colti, J.B., *Dictionarium sacrorum rituum* (Pistoria, 1772).

Cook, A.B., *Zeus,* 3 vols (Cambridge U.P., 1914–1940).

Corsetti, B., *Praxis Sacrorum Rituum ac Caeremoniarum* (Brussels, 1656).

Cox, J.C., 'The Lights of a Medieval Church', *Curious Church Gleanings,* edited by W.Andrews (W.Andrews & Co., Hull, 1896), pp.57–59.

Crawford, F.M., *Ave, Roma Immortalis* (Macmillan, London, 1903).

Crossley, F.H., *The English Abbey,* rev. B.Little (Batsford, London, 1962).

Cuming, G.J., *Hippolytus : A Text for Students,* Grove Liturgical Studies, 8 (Grove Books, Bramcote, Notts., 1979).

Dalmais, I.H., *Introduction to the Liturgy,* [ET R.Capel] (Chapman, London, 1961).

Davies, J.G., *Holy Week, A Short History* (Lutterworth Press, London, 1963).

De Bralion, N., *Caeremoniale Canonicorum* (Paris, 1657).

De Choin, Bishop Joly, *Instructions sur le rituel de Toulon* (Lyon, 1790).

De Conny, M., *Cérémonial Romain*, 3rd edition (Maison Méquiquoi, Paris, 1858).

De Grassis, P., *De Ceremoniis Cardinalium et Episcoporum in eorum diocesibus* (Rome, 1564).

De la Croix, J.F., *Dictionnaire historique des cultes religieuses*, 4 vols (Versailles, 1820).

De Moléon—see Des Marettes.

Dendy, D.R., *The Use of Lights in Christian Worship*, Alcuin Club Collections, No. 41 (London, 1959).

Dennis, G., *The Cities and Cemeteries of Etruria*, 2 vols (Dent, London / Dutton, New York, 1907).

De Rubeis, B.M., *De Vetustis Liturgicis Aliique Sacris Ritibus . . . in aliquibus Forojulensis Provinciae Ecclesiis* (Venice, 1754).

Deshusses, J., *Le Sacramentaire Grégorien* (Freiburg (Sw.), 1971).

Desideri, F., *Praxis Sacrorum Rituum* (Florence, 1739).

Des Marettes, J.B.Le B. (Le sieur de Moléon), *Voyages Liturgiques de France, ou Recherches faites en diverses villes du royaume* (Paris, 1718).

De Vaux, R., *Ancient Israel : Its Life and Institutions*, [ET J.McHugh], 2nd edition (Darton, Longman, Todd, London, 1980).

De Vert, C., *Explication simple, littérale, et historique des Cérémonies de l'Eglise,* 4 vols (Paris, 1709–1713).

Diekmann, G.L., *The Masses of Holy Week and the Easter Vigil* (Longmans, Green & Co., London, New York, Toronto, 1957).

Dix, G., *The Shape of the Liturgy*, 2nd edition (Dacre Press, Westminster, 1947).

Doblado, L., *Letter from Spain* (Henry Colburn, London, 1822).

Dolger, F.J., 'Sol Salutis. Gebetund Gesang im christ lichen Altertum', in *Liturgiegeschichtliche Forschungen*, Vol. 4–5 (Münster (W.F.), 1925), pp.364–65.

Dolger, F.J., 'Das Karsamstag Feuer aus der Kristal Linse', *Antike und Christentum*, 6 (1940), pp.286–96.

Du Cange, C. du F., *Glossiarium Mediae et Infimae Latinitatis,* new edition (Le Favre, Niort, 1886).

Duchesne, L., *Christian Worship : Its Origin and Evolution*, [ET M.L.McClure], 3rd English edition (S.P.C.K., London, 1910).

Duchesne, L., *Le Liber Pontificalis* (Paris, 1886).

Dudden, F.H., *The Life and Times of St Ambrose* (Oxford U.P., 1935).

Durandus, G., *Rationale Divinorum Officiorum* (Lyon, 1562).

Duval, P.-M., *Les Dieux de la Gaule,* Mythes et Religions, 33 (Paris, 1957).

Dykmans, M., *L'Œuvre de Patrizi Piccolomini,* Vol.2, Studi e Testi, 294 (Biblioteca Apostolica Vaticana, Vatican, 1982).

Dymond, R., 'The Parish of St Petrock', *Report and Transactions of the Devonshire Association,* XIV (1882), pp.410-13.

Eisenhöfer, L., *Handbuch der Katholischen Liturgik,* Vol.1 (Freiburg (im Br.), 1932).

Eisenhöfer, L. and Lechner, J., *The Liturgy of the Roman Rite,* [ET A.J. and J.F.Peeler] (Herder, Freiburg / Nelson, Edinburgh, London, 1961).

England, J., *The Ceremonies of Holy Week in the Chapels of the Vatican* (Rome, 1833).

Fabre, M.P., (editor), *Liber Censuum,* 2 vols (A.Fontemoign, Paris, 1905).

Farbridge, M.H., *Studies in Biblical and Semitic Symbolism* (New York, 1970).

Feasey, H.P., *Ancient Holy Week Ceremonial* (T.Baker, London, 1897).

Feasey, H.P., 'The Easter Sepulchre', *American Ecclesiastical Review,* 32 (1905), pp.337-55.

Feasey, H.P., 'The Paschal Candle', *American Ecclesiastical Review,* 34 (1906), pp.353-71.

Feasey, H.P., 'The Paschal *Preconium*', *American Ecclesiastical Review,* 36 (1907), pp.249-61.

Fermor, P.L., *Between the Woods and the Water* (Penguin Books, London, 1987).

Fletcher, B., *A History of Architecture,* 17th edition (The Athlone Press, London, 1961).

Forbes, S.R., *Rambles in Rome* (Thomas Nelson, London, 1892).

Forcadell, A., 'Ritus Carmelitarum Antiquae Observantiae', *Ephemerides Liturgicae,* LXIV (1950), pp.5-52.

Fortescue, A., *The Ceremonies of the Roman Rite Described,* 2nd edition (Burns and Oates, London, 1919).

Fortescue, A., *The Mass, a Study of the Roman Liturgy* (London, 1912).

Fortescue, A. and O'Connell, J.B., *The Ceremonies of the Roman Rite Described,* 4th edition (Burns, Oates, and Washbourne, London, 1932).

Fortescue, A. and O'Connell, J.B., *The Ceremonies of the Roman Rite Described*, 6th edition (Burns, Oates, and Washbourne, London, 1937).

Fortescue, A. and O'Connell, J.B., *The Ceremonies of the Roman Rite Described*, 11th edition (Burns, Oates, and Washbourne, London, 1960).

Fowler, J.T., *Memorials of the Church of SS Peter and Wilfred, Ripon*, Surtees Society Publications, Vol.81 (Newcastle, 1882).

Fowler, J.T., *Notes on the Rites of Durham*, Surtees Society Publications, Vol.107 (Durham, London, Edinburgh, 1903).

Franklin, J.W., *The Cathedrals of Italy* (Batsford, London, 1958).

Franz, A., *Die kirchlichen Benediktionen in Mittalalter*, Vol.1 (Freiburg (im Br.), 1909), reprinted by Akademische Druck-U. Verlagsanstalt, Graz, 1960.

Frazer, J.G., (editor), *Apollodorus*, Vol.2, Loeb Classical Library (Heinemann, 1921).

Frazer, J.G., *The Fasti of Ovid*, 5 vols (Macmillan, London, 1929).

Frazer, J.G., *The Golden Bough*, 13 vols (Macmillan, London, 1923).

Frazer, J.G., *Myths of the Origin of Fire* (Macmillan, London, 1930).

Freshfield, E., 'On the Parish Books of St Margaret-Lothbury, St Christopher-le-Stocks, and St Bartholemew-by-the Exchange', *Archaeologia*, 45 (1877), pp.57–126.

Fry, T., (editor), *The Rule of St Benedict* (The Liturgical Press, Collegeville, Minn., 1981).

Gaillard, J., 'Les antiennes de Matines et de Laudes de la Semaine Sainte', *Revue Grégorienne*, 28 (1949), pp.41–57.

Gaillard, J., 'Feu', *Catholicisme*, 4 (1956), cols.1231–32.

Gaillard, J., 'The Great Night', [ET W.Busch], *Worship*, 28 (1953–1954), pp.168–75.

Gaillard, J., *Holy Week and Easter*, [ET W.Busch] (The Liturgical Press, Collegeville, Minn., 1954).

Gasquet, F.A., *Parish Life in Medieval England* (Methuen, London, 1906).

Gattinari, T., *Sacrorum Caeremoniarum Enchiridion* (Parma, 1771).

Gavanti, B., *Thesaurus Sacrorum Rituum*, Vol.1 (Paris, 1652).

Gavanti, B., *Thesaurus Sacrorum Rituum*, revised by C.M.Merati (Venice, 1823).

Gerbert, M., *Vetus Liturgica Alemannica* (Saint Blaise, 1776).

Geyer, P., (editor), *Itinera Hierosolymitana saeculi IIII–VIII*, Corpus

Scriptorum Ecclesiasticorum Latinorum, Vol.39 (Vienna, 1898).

Goodrich-Freer, A., *Inner Jerusalem* (Constable & Co., London, 1904).

Gougard, L., 'De la veilleuse', *Ephemerides Liturgicae*, XLVI (1932), pp.435-38.

Gougard, L., *Christianity in Celtic Lands* [ET M.Joynt] (Sheed and Ward, London, 1932).

Grancolas, J., *Commentarius Historicus in Breviarium Romanum* (Venice, 1734).

Gray, D.C., (editor), *Holy Week Services,* 2nd edition (SPCK, London, 1983).

Grisar, H., *Das Missale im Lichte römischer stadtgeschichte* (Freiburg (im Br.), 1925).

Guéranger, P., *The Liturgical Year : Passion Time and Holy Week,* [ET L.Shepherd] (James Duffy, Dublin,1870).

Guignard, P., *Monuments primitifs de la Règle Cistercienne* (Dijon, 1864).

Guyet, C., *Heortologia sive de festis propriis locorum et ecclesiarum* (Venice, 1728).

Gy, P.-M., 'Semaine Sainte et triduum paschal', *La Maison-Dieu,* 41 (1955), pp.8-10.

Hale, J.R., (editor), *The Italian Journal of Samuel Rogers* (Faber, London, 1956).

Harbert, B., 'A Song at Twilight', *Liturgy,* Vol.7, No.6 (1983), pp.232-43.

Hare, A.J.C., *Days near Rome* (Kegan, Paul, London, 1907).

Hare, A.J.C., *Walks in Rome,* 2 vols, 5th edition (Daldy, Isbiter, London, 1876).

Hartel, G., *Magni Felicis Ennodi opera omnia,* C.S.E.L., 6 (Vienna, 1882).

Heintz, J., 'La célébration de la vigile pascale en France', *La Maison-Dieu,* 37 (1954), pp.120-22.

Herrera, M.L., 'Some Typical Spanish Traditions', in *Folklore Studies in the Twentieth Century,* edited by V.J.Newall (Woodbridge and Totowa, 1980).

Hesbert, R.-J., 'L'*Antiphonale Missarum* de l'ancien rit bénéventan', *Ephemerides Liturgicae,* LXI (1947), pp.153-210.

Heuser, H.J., 'The Tenebrae and the New Fire', *American Ecclesiastical Review,* 36 (1907), pp.225-31.

Hillgarth, J.N., 'Visigothic Spain and Early Christian Ireland', *Proceedings of the Royal Irish Academy,* 62 (1962), No.6.

Houssaye, M., 'Les Cérémonies de la Semaine Sainte', *Revue des Questions Historiques,* 28 (1878), pp.447-87.

Huglo, M., 'L'auteur de l'Exultet pascal', *Vigiliae Christianae,* 7 (1953), pp.79-88.

Hutton, E., *Assisi and Umbria Revisited* (Methuen, London, 1953).

Hutton, E., *A Wayfarer in Unknown Tuscany* (Methuen, London, 1909).

James, A., *The Story of Downside Abbey Church* (Downside, 1961).

Jelmini, A., 'Die Feier der Osternacht in Der Schweiz', *Liturgisches Jahrbuch,* 3 (1953), pp.225-29.

Jones, C.P.M., *A Manual for Holy Week* (London, 1967).

Jones-Baker, D., *The Folklore of Hertfordshire* (Batsford, London, 1977).

Jounel, P., 'Les Missels Diocésains Français du 18e siècle', *La Maison-Dieu,* 141 (1980), pp.91-96.

Jounel, P., 'Le nouvel ordo de la semaine sainte', *La Maison-Dieu,* 45 (1956), pp.16-35.

Jounel, P., 'La Semaine Sainte en France aux XVIIe et XVIIIe siècles', *La Maison-Dieu,* 41 (1955), pp.132-52.

Juglar, J., 'A propos de la vigile pascale', *Ephemerides Liturgicae,* LXV (1951), pp.182-86.

Jungmann, J.A., *The Early Liturgy,* [ET F.A.Brunner] (Darton, Longman, Todd, London, 1960).

Keating, G., *The History of Ireland,* [ET J.O'Mahoney] (New York, 1857).

Kellner, K.A.H., *Heortology,* [ET anon.], International Catholic Library (London, 1908).

King, A.A., *Eucharistic Reservation in the Western Church* (Mowbray, London, 1962).

King, A.A., 'Holy Week in Ambrosian Switzerland', *Westminster Cathedral Chronicle* (1951), pp.96-99.

King, A.A., *Liturgies of the Past* (Longmans, Green, London, 1959).

King, A.A., *Liturgies of the Primatial Sees* (Longmans, Green, London, 1957).

King, A.A., *Liturgies of the Religious Orders* (Longmans, Green, London, 1956).

King, A.A., *The Liturgy of the Roman Church* (Longmans, Green, London, 1975).

Kirk, G.S., *The Nature of Greek Myths* (London, 1974).

Kirk, R.E.G., *The Accounts of the Obedientiars of Abingdon Abbey*, Camden Society Publications, Vol.51 (new series), 1892.

Kirschbaum, E., *The Tombs of St Peter and St Paul*, [ET J.Murray] (Secker and Warburg, London, 1959).

Kitzinger, E., *Early Medieval Art*, 3rd edition (British Museum Publications, London, 1983).

Klauser, T., *A Short History of the Western Liturgy*, [ET J.Halliburton] (Oxford U.P., London, 1969).

Krautheimer, R., Corbett, S., Frank, W., *Corpus Basilicarum Christianarum Romae* (Vatican, 1967).

Latis, A., 'De Praeconio Paschali', *Ephemerides Liturgicae*, XVI (1902), pp.123-32.

Le Braz, A., *The Land of Pardons*, 5th edition (Methuen, London, 1924).

Lees, D.N., *Tuscan Feasts and Tuscan Friends* (Chatto and Windus, London, 1907).

Le Febvre, G., (editor), *Daily Missal* (Liturgical Apostolate, Bruges & London, 1928).

Lefèvre, P.F., 'La Liturgie de Prémontre', *Ephemerides Liturgicae*, LXII (1948), pp.195-229.

Lesage, R., *Vestments and Church Furniture*, [ET F.Murphy] (Burns, Oates, London, 1960).

Le Vavasseur, L., *Cérémonial selon le rit romain (d'après J.Baldeschi)* (Paris, 1859).

Lévi-Strauss, C., *From Honey to Ashes*, [ET J. & D.Weightman] (London, 1973).

The Liturgical Commission of the Church of England, *Lent, Holy Week, Easter* (Church House Publishing, Cambridge U.P., S.P.C.K., 1986).

D.G.M., 'La liturgie de Naples au temps de St.Grégoire', *Revue Bénédictine*, 8 (1891), pp.481-93 and 529-37.

Mabillon, J., *De Liturgia Gallicana* (Paris, 1685).

McArthur, J.A., *The Evolution of the Christian Year* (London, 1953).

Macdonald, A.B., *Christian Worship in the Primitive Church* (T. & T.Clark, Edinburgh, 1934).

Mackinnon, A.G., *Rome* (Seeley, London, nd).

Macri, D., *Hierolexicon sive Sacrum Dictionarium* (Rome, 1677).

Maigne D'Arnis, W.H., *Lexicon Manuale ad scriptores mediae et infimae latinitatis* (J.-P.Migne, Paris, 1866).

Mâle, E., *The Early Churches of Rome,* [ET D.Buxton] (E.Benn, London, 1960).

Mallardo, D., 'La Pasqua e la settimana maggiore a Napoli', *Ephemerides Liturgicae,* LXVI (1952), pp.3–36.

Mannix, D.P., *Those About To Die* (Hamilton & Co., London, 1958).

Marcora, C., *La Vigilia Nella Liturgia,* Archivio Ambrosiano, VI (Milan, 1954).

Martène, E., *De Antiquis Ecclesiae Ritibus,* 4 vols (Venice, 1764).

Martimort, A.G., *La documentation liturgique de Dom Edmond Martène,* Studi e Testi, 279 (Biblioteca Apostolica Vaticana, Vatican, 1978).

Marwick, E.W., *The Folklore of Orkney and Shetland* (Batsford, London, 1975).

Masson, G., *The Companion Guide to Rome* (Collins, London, 1965).

Menard, H., *Liber sacramentorum . . . editus ex missali Ms Sancti Eligii,* (Paris, 1642).

Merati, C.M., *Ceremonies of the Church (Selections)* (London, 1837).

Mercenier, E., *La Prière des Eglises de Rite Byzantin,* 2 vols, 2nd edition, edited by G.Bainbridge (Editions de Chevetogne, Chevetogne, 1953).

Mohrmann, C., 'Exultent divina mysteria', *Ephemerides Liturgicae,* LXVI (1952), pp.274–81.

Moreton, B., *The Eighth-Century Gelasian Sacramentary* (Oxford U.P., 1976).

Morlot, F., 'La Nuit Pascale : Enquête', *La Maison-Dieu,* 67 (1961), pp.110–58.

Nicholls, J.G., *The Diary of Henry Machin,* Camden Society Publications, Vol. 42 (old series), 1848.

Novarinus, A., *Sacro-prophana* (Lyon, 1635).

O'Connell, J.B., 'The New Order of Holy Week II', *Clergy Review,* 41 (1956), p.131.

O'Dea, W.T., 'Artificial lighting prior to 1800', *Folk-Lore,* LXII (June 1951) pp.314–17.

Oeconomia domus domini seu Liber de Sacramentorum administratione . . . in urbe Tholosa (Paris, 1553).

O'Kane, J., *Notes on the Rubrics of the Roman Ritual,* 4th edition (J.Duffy & Sons, Dublin, 1868).

O'Loan, D., *The Ceremonies of some Ecclesiastical Functions* (Dublin, nd).

O'Shea, W.J., *The Meaning of Holy Week* (The Liturgical Press, Collegeville, Minn., 1958).

Pamelius, J., *Liturgica Latinorum* (Cologne, 1571).

Paschal, J.-B.-E., *La Liturgie Catholique* (J.-P.Migne, Paris, 1844).

Pascher, J., 'Die Osterkerze', *Liturgisches Jahrbuch,* 2 (1952), pp.132–34.

Passmore, T.H., *In Further Ardenne* (J.M.Dent, London, 1905).

Peacock, E., *English Church Furniture* (John C.Hotten, London, 1866).

Peacock, E., 'Hearse : how a word has changed its meaning', in *Curious Church Gleanings,* edited by W.Andrews (W.Andrews & Co., Hull, 1896), pp.214–17.

Pellicia, A.A., *Polity of the Christian Church* [ET J.C.Bellett] (Masters & Co., London, 1883).

Philippeau, H.-R., 'Note sur l'utilisation liturgique du cierge pascal', *La Maison-Dieu,* 31 (1952), pp.145–49.

Pinell, J., 'La Benedicció Del Ciri Pasqual i Els Seus Textos', *Liturgia,* II (Montserrat, 1958), pp.85–100.

Pinell, J., 'Vestigis Del Lucernari a Occident', *Liturgia,* I (Montserrat, 1956), pp.91–149.

Podhradsky, G., *A New Dictionary of the Liturgy,* edited by L.Sheppard (Geoffrey Chapman, London, 1967).

Powicke, F.M. and Cheney, C.R., *Councils and Synods relating to the English Church,* 2 vols (Oxford U.P., 1964).

Pugin, A.W., *A Glossary of Ecclesiastical Ornament and Costume* (C.Tilt, London, 1844).

Rabotin, H., 'Les Grains d'Encens du Cierge Pascal', *La Vie et Les Arts Liturgiques,* 7 (1920–1921), pp.221–25.

Rahner, H., *Greek Myths and Christian Ritual,* [ET M.Benoit] (Burns, Oates, London, 1963).

Raine, J., *The Rites of Durham,* Surtees Society Publications, No.15 (London and Edinburgh, 1842).

Rees, A.D. and Rees, B.R., *Celtic Heritage* (Thames and Hudson, London, 1961).

Rees, U., *The Cartulary of Haughmond Abbey* (Shropshire Archaeological Society and University of Wales Press, Cardiff, 1985).

Reinhold, H., 'Lugano and Holy Week', *Worship*, 28 (1953-1954), pp.426-32.

Righetti, M., *Manuale di Storia Liturgia*, 2 vols, 2nd edition (Ancora/Milan, 1955).

Rock, D., *The Church of Our Fathers*, 4 vols (John Murray, London, 1905).

Rock, D., *Hierurgia*, 2nd edition (London, 1851).

Rosenwein, B.H., *Rhinoceros Bound : Cluny in the Tenth Century* (Philadelphia, 1982).

Ross, A., *The Folklore of the Scottish Islands* (Batsford, London, 1974).

Sacrarum caeremoniarum sive rituum ecclesiasticorum sanctae Romanae ecclesiae libri tres (Venice, 1582).

Schelstrate, E., *Antiquitas Ecclesiae* (Rome, 1697).

Schmidt, H.A.P., *Hebdomada Sancta*, 2 vols (Herder, Rome, Freiburg (im Br.), Barcelona, 1956-1957).

Schmitz, P., *L'Histoire de l'Ordre de Saint-Benoit*, 7 vols (Les Editions de Maredsous, Maredsous, 1942-1956).

Schoenbechler, R., 'The New Insignia on the Easter Candle', *American Ecclesiastical Review*, 128 (1953), pp.273-80.

Scullard, H.H., *Festivals and Ceremonies of the Roman Republic* (London, 1981).

Seasoltz, R.K., *New Liturgy, New Laws* (The Liturgical Press, Collegeville, Minn., 1980).

Seeck, O., (editor), *Notitia Dignitatum* (Berlin, 1876).

Shepherd, M.H., *The Paschal Liturgy and the Apocalypse* (Lutterworth Press, London, 1960).

Shutt, F.J., 'Triduum Sacrum', *Clergy Review*, 36 (1951), pp.20-27.

Sladden, D. and Lorimer, N., *Queer Things about Sicily* (Treherne, London, 1905).

Smith, L.M., *Cluny in the Eleventh and Twelfth Centuries* (P.Allan, London, 1930).

Stevenson, K., 'The Ceremonies of Light : Their Shape and Function in the Paschal Vigil Liturgy', *Ephemerides Liturgicae*, XCIX (Mar/Apr. 1985), pp.170-85.

Stokes, W., *Lives of the Saints from the Book of Lismore* (Oxford, 1890).

Sullivan, J., 'Setting the Theme : Subliminal Influence of Liturgy "A School of Prayer" ', *Spiritual Life*, Vol.27, No.1 (1981), pp.14-23.

Thibaut, J.B., *Ordres des offices de la semaine sainte à Jérusalem du ive au xe siècle* (Paris, 1929).

Thomassin, L., *De Dierum Festorum Celebratione* (Venice, 1729).

Thompson, S., *A Motif-Index of Folk-Literature,* 6 vols (Copenhagen, 1955-1957).

Thomson, P.D., *Parish and Parish Church* (T.Nelson, London, 1948).

Thurston, H., 'The Early Cultus of the Blessed Sacrament', *The Month* (April 1907), pp.382–88.

Thurston, H., 'The Easter Sepulchre', *The Month* (April 1903), pp.404–14.

Thurston, H., 'The *Exultet* and the Paschal Candle', *The Month* (April 1896), pp.502–18.

Thurston, H., *Holy Saturday* (Catholic Truth Society, London, 1937).

Thurston, H., *Lent and Holy Week* (Longmans, London, 1904).

Thurston, H., 'The Sign of the Cross', *The Month* (December 1911), pp.586–602.

Thurston, H., *Tenebrae* (Catholic Truth Society, London, 1931).

Thurston, H., 'Votive Candles', *The Month* (August 1932), pp.141–51.

Tyrer, J.W., *A Historical Survey of Holy Week,* Alcuin Club Collections, No.29 (SPCK, London, 1932).

Ughelli, F., *Italia Sacra,* 10 vols (Venice, 1717-1722).

Van Der Stappen, J.F., *Sacra Liturgia* (Mechlin, 1906).

Van Dijk, S.J.P., *Sources of the Modern Roman Liturgy,* 2 vols (Leiden, 1963).

Van Doren, R., 'La cérémonie du feu nouveau au Samedi-Saint', *Les Questions Liturgiques et Paroissiales,* 13 (1928), pp.74–78.

Van Doren, R., 'Le cierge pascal', *Les Questions Liturgiques et Paroissiales,* 14 (1929), pp.65–77.

Van Gennep, A., *Manuel de Folklore français contemporain* (Paris, 1946-1958).

Varley, D., *Seven—The Number of Creation* (London, 1976).

Viale, E., 'La bénédiction du feu nouveau', *La Maison-Dieu,* 26 (1951), pp.41–52.

Vinitor, G., *Compendium Sacrorum Rituum et Caeremoniarum* (Cologne, 1685).

Vogel, C., *Introduction aux sources de l'histoire du culte chrétien au moyen âge* (Centro Italiano di Studi sull' Alto Medioevo, Spoleto, 1966).

Wade-Evans, A.W., *Life of St.David, (Rhygyfarch),* Translations of Christian Literature, Series 5 (London, 1923).

Walsh, M.J., 'Notes on Fire-Lighting Ceremonies', *Folk-Lore,* LVIII (June 1947), pp.282–84.

Warren, F.E., *The Liturgy and Ritual of the Celtic Church* (Oxford, 1881).

Warren, F.E., *The Sarum Missal, Part 1,* Library of Liturgiology and Ecclesiology, Vol.8 (London, 1911).

Weiser, F.X., *A Handbook of Christian Feasts and Customs* (New York, 1958).

Wilkins, D., *Concilia Magna Britanniae et Hiberniae,* 4 vols (London, 1737).

Wilkinson, J., *Egeria's Travels* (SPCK, London, 1971).

Wiseman, N., *Four Lectures on the Offices and Ceremonies of Holy Week* (London, 1839).

Wordsworth, C., *Ceremonies and Processions of the Cathedral Church of Salisbury* (Cambridge U.P., 1901).

Wordsworth, C., *Medieval Services in England* (T.Baker, London, 1898).

Wright, T., *Early Travels in Palestine* (Bohn's Antiquarian Library, London, 1848).

Wuest, J., *Matters Liturgical,* [ET of *Collectio Rerum Liturgicarum* by T.W.Mullaney, 10th edition] (New York and Cincinnati, 1959).

Yarnold, E., *The Awe-Inspiring Rites of Initiation* (St Paul Publications, Slough, 1972).

Zarnecki, D., *The Monastic Achievement* (London, 1972).

Zazzera, P., *SS.Ecclesiae Rituum Divinorumque Officiorum Explicatio* (Rome, 1784).

INDEX